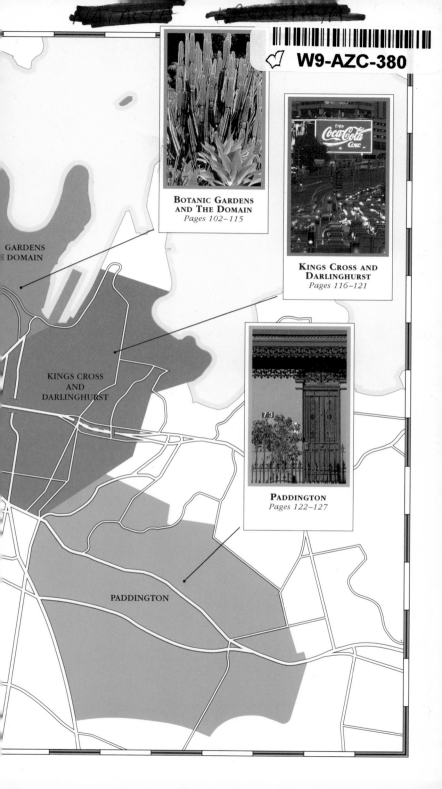

**BOTANIC GARDENS
AND THE DOMAIN**
Pages 102–115

**KINGS CROSS AND
DARLINGHURST**
Pages 116–121

PADDINGTON
Pages 122–127

GARDENS
E DOMAIN

KINGS CROSS
AND
DARLINGHURST

PADDINGTON

EYEWITNESS *TRAVEL GUIDES*

SYDNEY

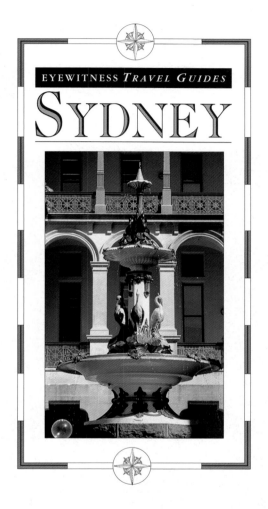

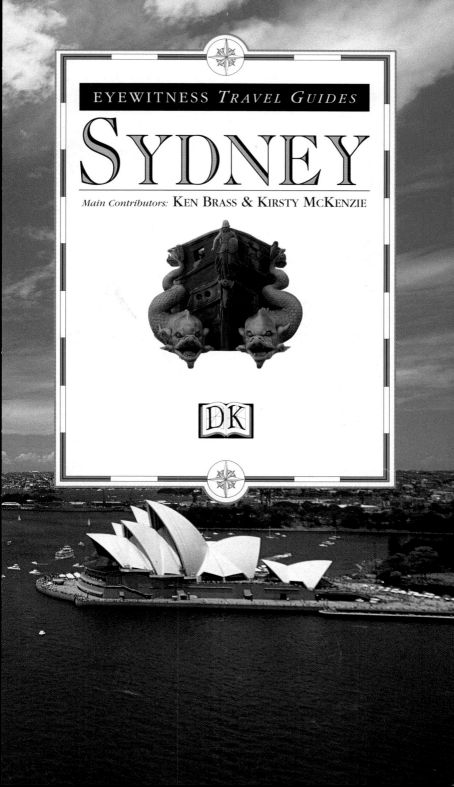

EYEWITNESS *TRAVEL GUIDES*

SYDNEY

Main Contributors: KEN BRASS & KIRSTY MCKENZIE

DK

A DK PUBLISHING BOOK

Produced by The Watermark Press
Sydney, Australia
PROJECT EDITOR Siobhán O'Connor
ART EDITOR Claire Edwards
EDITORS Robert Coupe, Leith Hillard, Jane Sheard
DESIGNERS Katie Peacock, Claire Ricketts, Noel Wendtman
PICTURE RESEARCH Wendy Canning
DTP DESIGNER Leanne Hogbin

Dorling Kindersley Limited
SENIOR EDITOR Fay Franklin
SENIOR ART EDITOR Jane Ewart
DEPUTY EDITORIAL DIRECTOR Douglas Amrine
US EDITORS Mary Sutherland, Michael Wise
DEPUTY ART DIRECTORS Gillian Allan, Gaye Allen
MAP CO-ORDINATORS Michael Ellis, David Pugh
PRODUCTION David Proffit

CONTRIBUTORS
Anna Breuchert, John Dengate, Carrie Hutchinson,
Graham Jahn, Susan Skelly

MAPS
Gary Bowes, Fiona Casey, Anna Nilsson, Christine Purcell,
Richard Toomey (Era-Maptec Ltd)

PHOTOGRAPHERS
Max Alexander, Michael Nicholson,
Rob Reichenfeld, Alan Williams

ILLUSTRATORS
Richard Draper, Stephen Gyapay, Alex Lavroff Associates,
The Overall Picture, Robbie Polley

Film outputting by Cooling Brown (London)
Reproduced by Colourscan (Singapore)
Printed and bound by G. Canale (Italy)

First American Edition, 1996
2 4 6 8 10 9 7 5 3 1
Published in the United States by
DK Publishing, Inc., 95 Madison Avenue,
New York, New York 10016
http://www.dk.com

Copyright 1996 © Dorling Kindersley Limited, London

Library of Congress Cataloging-in-Publication Data

Sydney. -- 1st American ed.
    p.   cm. -- (Eyewitness travel guides)
    ISBN 0-7894-1069-9
    1. Sydney (N.S.W.)--Guidebooks. I. Series.
DU178.S926 1996
919.44'10463--dc20   94-14187 CIP

Every effort has been made to ensure that the information in this book is as
up-to-date as possible at the time of going to press. However, details such as
telephone numbers, opening hours, prices, gallery hanging arrangements, and
travel information are liable to change. The publishers cannot accept
responsibility for any consequences arising from the use of this book.

We would be delighted to receive any corrections and
suggestions for incorporation in the next edition. Please write to:
Deputy Editorial Director, Eyewitness Travel Guides,
Dorling Kindersley, 9 Henrietta Street, London WC2E 8PS.

THROUGHOUT THIS BOOK, FLOORS ARE REFERRED TO IN ACCORDANCE WITH AUSTRALIAN
USAGE, I.E."FIRST FLOOR" IS ONE FLOOR UP.

CONTENTS

HOW TO USE THIS
GUIDE 6

INTRODUCING SYDNEY

**A view of the Royal Botanic
Gardens and city skyline**

PUTTING SYDNEY ON
THE MAP 10

THE HISTORY OF
SYDNEY 16

SYDNEY AT A
GLANCE 30

SYDNEY THROUGH
THE YEAR 48

SPORTS IN SYDNEY 52

Tamarama beach and surf club

BEYOND SYDNEY

EXPLORING BEYOND
SYDNEY *152*

PITTWATER AND
KU-RING-GAI CHASE *154*

HAWKESBURY TOUR *156*

HUNTER VALLEY *158*

BLUE MOUNTAINS *160*

SOUTHERN HIGHLANDS
TOUR *162*

Façade of Sydney Town Hall

ROYAL NATIONAL
PARK *164*

TRAVELERS'
NEEDS

WHERE TO STAY *168*

RESTAURANTS, CAFÉS,
AND PUBS *178*

**Kangaroo loin fillet served
on a bed of wilted greens**

SHOPS AND
MARKETS *198*

ENTERTAINMENT IN
SYDNEY *208*

SURVIVAL GUIDE

PRACTICAL
INFORMATION *218*

TRAVEL
INFORMATION *228*

SYDNEY
STREET FINDER *238*

GENERAL INDEX *250*

ACKNOWLEDGMENTS
263

TRANSPORTATION MAP
Inside back cover

THE CITY SHORELINE *56*

SYDNEY
AREA BY AREA

THE ROCKS AND
CIRCULAR QUAY *62*

CITY CENTER *78*

DARLING HARBOUR *90*

BOTANIC GARDENS
AND THE
DOMAIN *102*

KINGS CROSS AND
DARLINGHURST *116*

PADDINGTON *122*

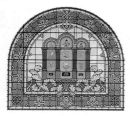

**Stained-glass window,
Queen Victoria Building**

FARTHER AFIELD *128*

FOUR GUIDED
WALKS *140*

**Sydney
Opera House**

How to Use this Guide

THIS GUIDE helps you to get the most from your visit to Sydney. It provides both expert recommendations and detailed practical information. *Introducing Sydney* locates the city geographically, sets modern Sydney in its historical and cultural context, and describes events through the entire year. *Sydney at a Glance* is an overview of the city's main attractions, including a feature on the city shoreline and Sydney's best beaches. *Sydney Area*

Strolling at the Royal Easter Show

by Area is the main sightseeing section, covering all the sights, with photographs, maps, and drawings. *Farther Afield* looks at sights just outside the city center while *Beyond Sydney* explores other places close to Sydney. Carefully researched tips on hotels, restaurants, pubs, and entertainment spots are found in *Travelers' Needs*. The *Survival Guide* contains useful practical advice on everything from the Australian telephone system to public transportation.

FINDING YOUR WAY AROUND THE SIGHTSEEING SECTION

The center of Sydney has been divided into six sightseeing areas. Each area has its own chapter and is color-coded for easy reference. Every chapter opens with a list of the sights described. All sights are numbered and plotted on an *Area Map*. Detailed information for each sight is presented in numerical order, making it easy to locate within the chapter.

Each area has color-coded thumb tabs.

A suggested route takes in the most interesting and attractive streets in the area.

A locator map shows where you are in relation to other areas in the city center.

Locator map

1 Introduction to the area
For easy reference, the sights are numbered and located on an area map. This map also shows bus terminals, ferry boarding points, JetCat or RiverCat boarding points, CityRail stations, and parking lots. The sights are also shown on the Sydney Street Finder *on pages 240–45.*

The area shaded pink is shown in greater detail on the Street-by-Street map on the following pages.

2 Street-by-Street map
This gives a bird's eye view of the most important parts of each sightseeing area. The numbering of the sights ties in with the area map and the fuller descriptions on the pages that follow.

The list of star sights recommends the places that no visitor should miss.

SYDNEY AREA MAP

THE COLORED areas shown on this map *(see pp14–15)* are the six main sightseeing areas – each covered by a full chapter in *Sydney Area by Area (pp60–149)*. The six areas are highlighted on other maps throughout the book. In *Sydney at a Glance (pp30–47)*, for example, they help locate the top sights, including art galleries and museums and parks and preserves. They are also used to show some of the top restaurants, cafés, and pubs *(pp184–5)* and shopping areas *(pp200–201)*.

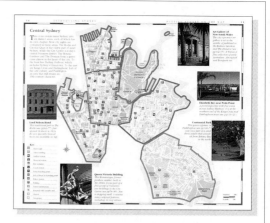

Façades of important buildings are often shown to help you recognize them quickly.

Practical information lists all the information you need to visit every sight, including a map reference to the *Street Finder (pp240–45)*.

Numbers refer to each sight's position on the area map and its place in the chapter.

The visitors' checklist provides all the practical information needed to plan your visit.

3 Detailed information on each sight

All the important sights in Sydney are described individually. They are listed in order, following the numbering on the area map. Addresses and practical information are provided. The key to the symbols used in the information block is on the back flap.

Stars indicate the features no visitor should miss.

4 Sydney's top sights

Museums and galleries have color-coded floor plans to help you locate the most interesting exhibits; historic buildings are dissected to reveal their interiors.

INTRODUCING
SYDNEY

PUTTING SYDNEY ON THE MAP 10-15

THE HISTORY OF SYDNEY 16-29

SYDNEY AT A GLANCE 30-47

SYDNEY THROUGH THE YEAR 48-51

SPORTING SYDNEY 52-55

THE CITY SHORELINE 56-59

Putting Sydney on the Map

Situated on Australia's eastern coastline within the state of New South Wales, Sydney spreads with the rare luxury of space – 3,700 sq km (1,430 sq miles) in all – around what is often described as one of the finest harbors in the world. Greater Sydney is home to over 4 million people and, while it is not the nation's capital, it is Australia's oldest and largest city, as well as its media and financial center. Sydney is also the main gateway to Australia, and it enjoys good air, road, and rail links to other major centers.

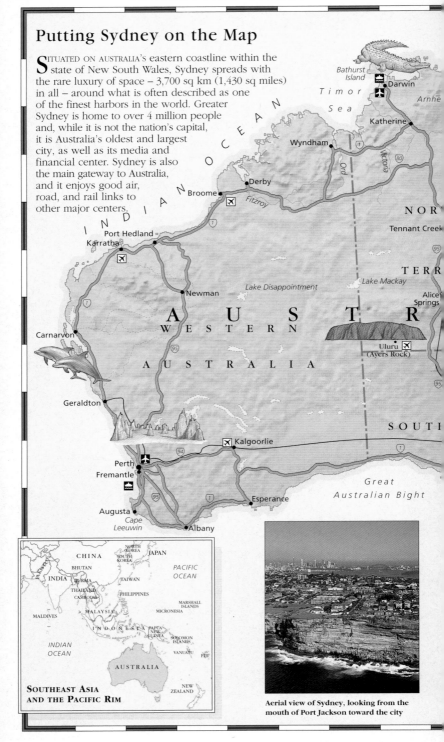

INDIAN OCEAN

Timor Sea

Bathurst Island

Darwin

Arnhe

Katherine

Wyndham

Ord

Victoria

Derby

Broome

Fitzroy

Port Hedland

Karratha

Newman

Lake Disappointment

Lake Mackay

NOR

Tennant Creek

TERR

Alice Springs

A U S T R A

W E S T E R N

A U S T R A L I A

Carnarvon

Geraldton

Uluru
(Ayers Rock)

Kalgoorlie

Perth

Fremantle

Augusta

Cape Leeuwin

Albany

Esperance

Great Australian Bight

SOUTH

CHINA

NORTH KOREA

SOUTH KOREA

JAPAN

BHUTAN

INDIA

BURMA

TAIWAN

PACIFIC OCEAN

THAILAND

CAMBODIA

PHILIPPINES

MALDIVES

MALAYSIA

MARSHALL ISLANDS

MICRONESIA

I N D O N E S I A

PAPUA NEW GUINEA

SOLOMON ISLANDS

INDIAN OCEAN

VANUATU

FIJI

AUSTRALIA

SOUTHEAST ASIA AND THE PACIFIC RIM

NEW ZEALAND

Aerial view of Sydney, looking from the mouth of Port Jackson toward the city

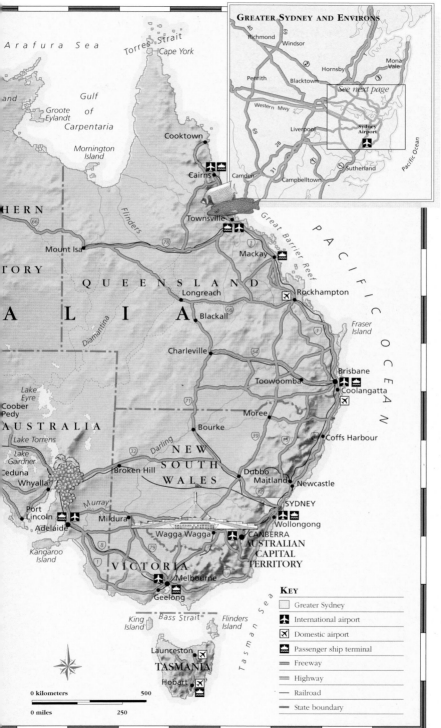

GREATER SYDNEY AND ENVIRONS

Richmond
Windsor
Hornsby
Mona Vale
Penrith
Blacktown
See next page
Western Mwy
Liverpool
Sydney Airport
Camden
Campbelltown
Sutherland
Pacific Ocean

Arafura Sea

Torres Strait
Cape York

Gulf
of
Carpentaria

Groote
Eylandt

Mornington
Island

Cooktown

Cairns

Camden

Townsville

Mount Isa

Mackay

QUEENSLAND

Longreach

Rockhampton

Blackall

*Fraser
Island*

Charleville

Diamantina

Toowoomba

Brisbane
Coolangatta

Flinders

Moree

PACIFIC OCEAN

*Lake
Eyre*

Coober
Pedy

AUSTRALIA

Lake Torrens

Bourke

NEW

Darling

SOUTH

Coffs Harbour

Ceduna

*Lake
Gairdner*

Broken Hill

WALES

Whyalla

Dubbo
Maitland

Newcastle

Port
Lincoln

Murray

Mildura

SYDNEY

Adelaide

Wagga Wagga

Wollongong

*Kangaroo
Island*

VICTORIA

CANBERRA
AUSTRALIAN
CAPITAL
TERRITORY

Melbourne

Geelong

*King
Island*

Bass Strait

*Flinders
Island*

Tasman Sea

Launceston

TASMANIA

Hobart

0 kilometers   500

0 miles   250

KEY

☐ Greater Sydney

✈ International airport

☒ Domestic airport

⛴ Passenger ship terminal

▬ Freeway

▬ Highway

· Railroad

▬ State boundary

Central Sydney and Suburbs

Sydney has gradually expanded to fill both sides of the harbor. Parramatta to the west was once a separate settlement, but is now very much a part of the city. To the east are the beaches and seaside suburbs that have come to typify Sydney living. The area as a whole is served by CityRail lines and roads.

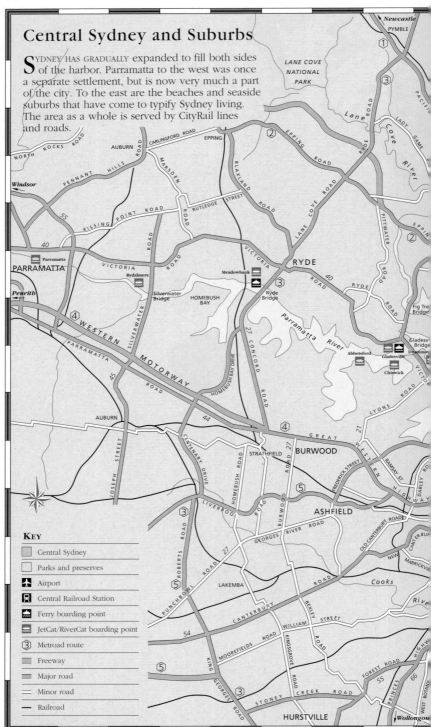

KEY

▢	Central Sydney
▢	Parks and preserves
✈	Airport
🚉	Central Railroad Station
⛴	Ferry boarding point
⛴	JetCat/RiverCat boarding point
③	Metroad route
▬	Freeway
▬	Major road
—	Minor road
—	Railroad

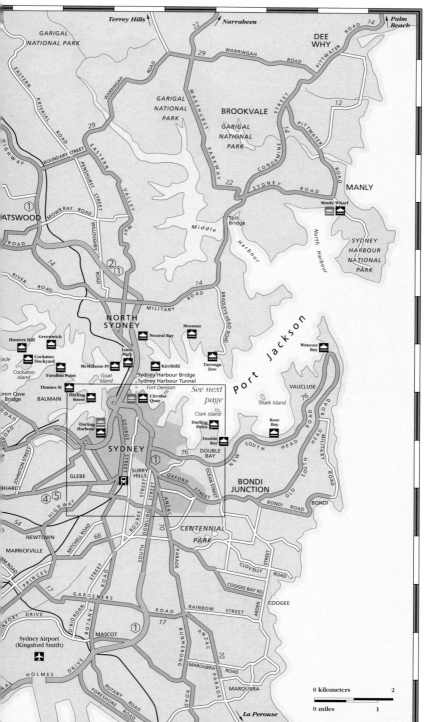

Central Sydney

THIS GUIDE DIVIDES inner Sydney into six distinct areas, each of which has its own chapter. Most city sights are contained in these areas. The Rocks and Circular Quay is the oldest part of inner Sydney, while the City Center is today's central business district. The Botanic Gardens and The Domain form a green oasis almost in the heart of the city. To the west lies Darling Harbour, which includes Sydney's Chinatown. To the east are Kings Cross and Darlinghurst, hub of the café culture, and Paddington, an area that still retains its 19th-century character.

Lord Nelson Hotel
This traditional pub in The Rocks (see pp62–77) first opened its doors in 1834. Its own specially brewed beers are available on tap.

KEY

	Major sight
	Other building
🚆	CityRail station
🚝	Monorail station
🚌	Bus terminal
🚍	Bus station
⛴	Ferry boarding point
🚢	JetCat/RiverCat boarding point
👮	Police station
P	Parking
ℹ	Tourist information
✚	Hospital with emergency room
✝	Church
✡	Synagogue

Queen Victoria Building
This Romanesque former produce market, built in the 1890s, forms part of a fine group of Victorian-era buildings in the City Center (see pp78–89). Now a shopping mall, it retains many original features, including its roof statues.

Fort
Denison

BOTANIC
~~ARDEN AND~~
~~THE DOMAIN~~

Farm
Cove

OYAL
TANIC
RDENS

Art Gallery of
New South
Wales

**Art Gallery of
New South Wales**
*The city's premier art
gallery is set in the
middle of parkland in
the Botanic Gardens
and The Domain (see
pp102–15). It houses a
fine collection of early
Australian, Aboriginal,
and European art.*

Elizabeth Bay near Potts Point
*A picturesque bay with fine views
across Sydney Harbour, it is at the
northern end of the Kings Cross and
Darlinghurst area (see pp116–21).*

Centennial Park
*This green expanse in
Paddington (see pp122–7)
was once part of a sand
dune system that extend-
ed from Botany Bay
in the south.*

KINGS CROSS
AND
DARLINGHURST

PADDINGTON

MOORE
PARK

Kippax
Lake

SYDNEY
FOOTBALL
STADIUM

SYDNEY
CRICKET
GROUND

ROYAL AGRICULTURAL
SOCIETY SHOWGROUND
(MAIN ARENA)

CENTENNIAL
PARK

| 0 meters | | 250 |
| 0 yards | | 250 |

THE HISTORY OF SYDNEY

THE FIRST inhabitants of Australia were the Aboriginal peoples. Their history began in a time called the Dreaming when the Ancestor Spirits emerged from the earth and gave form to the landscape. Anthropologists believe the Aboriginal peoples arrived

Sydney's coat of arms, Sydney Town Hall

from Asia more than 50,000 years ago. Clans lived in the area now known as Sydney until the Europeans caused violent disruption to this world.

In 1768, Captain James Cook began a search for the fabled "great south land." Traveling in the wake of other European explorers, he was the first to set foot on the east coast of the land the Dutch had named New Holland, and claimed it for King and country. He landed at Botany Bay in 1770, naming the coast New South Wales.

At the suggestion of Sir Joseph Banks, Cook's botanist on the *Endeavour*, a penal colony was established here to relieve Britain's overflowing prisons. The First Fleet of 11 ships reached Botany Bay in 1788, commanded by Captain Arthur Phillip. He felt the land there was swampy and the bay windswept. Just to the north, however, he found "one of the finest harbours in the world," naming it Sydney Cove, after the Home Department's Secretary of State. Here, 1,485 convicts, guards, officers, officials, wives, and children landed. This marked the beginning of the rapid decimation of the Aboriginal peoples, as they fell to introduced diseases and battled an undeclared war against the settlers. It is only in recent years that they have been granted full citizenship rights and their traditions accorded respect.

In stark contrast, the city of Sydney flourished, with the construction of impressive public buildings befitting an emerging maritime power. In 1901, amid a burgeoning nationalism, the federation drew the country's six colonies together and New South Wales became a state of Australia.

In its two centuries of European settlement, Sydney has experienced alternating periods of growth and decline. It has weathered the effects of gold rush and trade booms, depressions and world wars, to establish a distinctive city marked by a vibrant eclecticism. The underlying British culture, married with Aboriginal influences and successive waves of Asian and European migration, has produced today's modern cosmopolitan city.

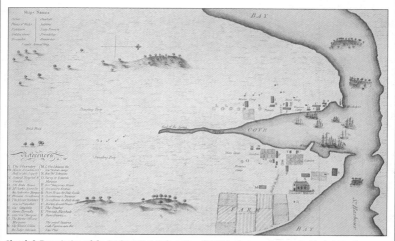

Sketch & Description of the Settlement at Sydney Cove (1788) by transported convict Francis Fowkes

◁ *Desmond, a New South Wales Chief* (about 1825) by Augustus Earle

Sydney's Original Inhabitants

ANTHROPOLOGISTS BELIEVE that Aboriginal peoples reached Sydney Harbour at least 40,000 years ago. One of the clans of coastal Sydney was the Eora. Their campsites were usually close to the shore, particularly in the summer when fish were plentiful. Plant and animal foods supplemented their seafood diet. Artistic expression was a way of life, with their shields decorated with ocher, designs carved on their implements, and their bodies adorned with scars, animal teeth and feathers. Sacred and social ceremonies are still important today. Oral traditions recount stories of the Dreaming *(see p17)* and describe the Eora's strong attachment to the land.

Hafted stone ax

Aborigines Fishing *(1819)*
Sixty-seven Eora canoes were counted in the harbor on a single day. Spears were used as tools and weapons.

Berowra Waters

This Berowra Waters carving is hard to inter-pret; experts believe that it may represent a koala.

Glenbrook Crossing
The Red Hand Caves near Glenbrook in the lower Blue Mountains contain stencils where ocher was blown over outstretched hands.

The name Parramatta means place where eels lie down or sleep, or the head of the river.

Glenbrook •

Parramatta •

Glenbrook Caves ocher hand stencils

Cabramatta •

Cabramatta means land where the *cobra* grub is found.

Red Ocher and Shell Paint Holder
Ocher was a common-ly used material in rock painting. Finely ground, then mixed with water and a binding agent, it would be applied by brush or hand.

ABORIGINAL ROCK ART

There are approximately 5,500 known rock art sites in the Sydney basin alone. Early colonists such as Watkin Tench said that paintings and engravings were on every kind of surface. The history of col-onization was also recorded in rock engravings, with depictions of the arrival of ships and fighting.

TIMELINE

50,000 BC		20,000 BC	
43,000–38,000BC Tools found in a gravel pit beside Nepean River are among the oldest firmly dated signs of human occupation in Australia	*Diprotodon*	**20,000** Humans lived in the Blue Mountains despite extreme conditions. Remains found of the largest mammal, *Diprotodon*, date back to this period	**11,000** Burial site excavated in Victoria of more than 40 individuals of this period
28,000 Funerary rites at Lake Mungo, NSW. Complete skeleton has been found of man buried at this time		**18,000** People now inhabit the entire continent, from the deserts to the mountains	
23,000 One of the world's earliest known cremations carried out in Western NSW			**13,000** Final stages of Ice Age, with small glaciers in the Snowy Mountains

Ku-ring-gai is named after clans who lived in this coastal district. It is rich in rock engravings.

Hunting and Fishing Implements
Multipronged Eora spears were used for fishing, while canoes were shaped from a single piece of bark. Boomerangs are still used today for hunting and music making.

WHERE TO SEE ABORIGINAL ROCK ART AND ARTIFACTS

The soft sandstone of Sydney was a natural canvas. Much of the rock art of the original inhabitants remains and can be found on walking trails in Ku-ring-gai Chase National Park *(see pp154–5)* and the Royal National Park *(p165)*. The National Parks & Wildlife shop at Cadman's Cottage *(p68)* has a range of pamphlets about Aboriginal sites.

Fish Carving at West Head
This area in Ku-ring-gai Chase has 51 figures and is acknowledged as one of the richest sites in the greater Sydney region.

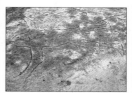

Gumbooya Reserve *in suburban Allambie Heights has a collection of 68 rock carvings. This human figure appears to be inside or on top of a whale.*

Allambie Heights

Bondi is from *boondi*, the sound of water crashing. This carving is of a shark and fish.

Bondi

Coogee means bad smell of rotten seaweed washed ashore.

Coogee

Maroubra

Shell Fishhooks
Introduced from the Torres Strait, these hooks were ground-down mollusk shells.

This python skeleton *is on view at the Australian Museum (see pp88–9), along with a large collection of Aboriginal artifacts.*

Maroubra comes either from the *merooberah* tribe, or means place where shells are found.

Water Carrier
These bags were usually made of kangaroo skin. The skin was removed in one piece and either turned inside out or tanned with the sap from a gum tree.

This carving of a leaping kangaroo is found in the Royal National Park.

Bundeena

8,000 BC The oldest returning boomerangs are in use in South Australia	**2,000 BC** Dingo reaches Australia, thought to have been brought by seafarers		*Captain James Cook*
		AD 1606 Dutch ship, *Duyfken*, records first European sighting of the continent. Lands on the eastern coast of Gulf of Carpentaria	
10,000 BC		**AD 1**	
10,000–8,500 BC Tasmania is separated from mainland Australia by rising seas	*Copperplate print of a dingo*	**AD 1700** Macassans search for trepang or sea slugs off Australia's north coast	
		AD 1770 James Cook lands at Botany Bay	

The Early Colony

Hat made from cabbage palm

THE COLONY'S BEGINNINGS were rugged and hungry, imbued with a spirit that would give Sydney its unique character. Convicts were put to work establishing roads and constructing buildings out of mud, reeds, unseasoned wood, and mortar made from a crushed shell mixture. From these simple beginnings, a town grew. Officers of the New South Wales Corps became farmers, encouraged to work their land alongside convict labor. Because the soldiers paid for work and goods in rum, they soon became known as the Rum Corps, in 1808 overthrowing Governor Bligh (of *Bounty* fame) when he threatened their privileges. By the early 1800s farms were producing crops, with supplies arriving more regularly – as were convicts and settlers with more appropriate skills and trades.

GROWTH OF THE CITY

☐ *1810*	▨ *Today*

Boat building at the Government dockyard

Pitts Row

First Fleet Ship (*c.1787*)
This painting by Francis Holman shows three angles of the Borrowdale, *one of the fleet's three commercial storeships.*

Government House

Scrimshaw
Engraving whale ivory was a skillful way to pass time during long months spent at sea.

A VIEW OF SYDNEY COVE

This idyllic image, drawn by Edward Dayes and engraved by F Jukes in 1804, shows the Aboriginal peoples living peacefully within the infant colony alongside the flourishing maritime and agricultural industries. In fact, they had been entirely ostracized from the life and prosperity of the town by this time.

TIMELINE

1787 The First Fleet leaves Portsmouth, bound for Botany Bay

1788 First white child born in the colony – and the first man hanged

Barrington, the convict and thespian star of The Revenge

1796 *The Revenge* opens Sydney's first, but short-lived, playhouse, simply named The Theatre

1785	1790	1795

Bennelong pictured in European finery

1789 The Aborigine Bennelong is held captive and ordered to act as an inter-mediary between the whites and blacks

1790 First detachment of the New South Wales Corps arrives in the colony. Fears of starvation are less-ened with the arrival of the supply ship *Lady Juliana*

1793 Arrival of the first free settlers

1797 Merino sheep arrive from Cape of Good Hope

The Arrest of Bligh
This shameful, and invented, scene shows the hated Governor William Bligh, in full regalia, hiding under a servant's bed to avoid arrest by the NSW Rum Corps in 1808.

WHERE TO SEE EARLY COLONIAL SYDNEY

The Rocks was the hub of early Sydney. Wharves, ware-houses, hotels, rough houses and even rougher characters gave it its color. Dramatic cuts were made in the rocky point to provide building materials and filling for the construction of Circular Quay, and allow for streets. The houses are gone, except for Cadman's Cottage *(see p68)*, but the irregular, labyrinthine lanes are still rich in the flavor of convict history.

The buildings may look impressive, but most were poorly built with inferior materials.

Male and female convicts housed separately

Waratah *(1803)*
John Lewin, naturalist and engraver, drew delicate and faithful representations of the local flora and fauna.

Barracks housing NSW Rum Corps

Elizabeth Farm *(pp138–9) at Parramatta is the oldest sur-viving building in Australia. It was built by convicts using lime mortar from the penal colony of Norfolk Island.*

Experiment Farm Cottage*, an early dwelling (see p139), displays marked, convict-made bricks. Masons also marked each brick, as they were paid according to the number laid.*

Kangaroo *(1813)*
Naturalists were amazed at Sydney's vast array of strange plant and animal species. The first pictures sent back to England caused a sensation.

1799 Explorers Bass and Flinders complete their circum-navigation of Van Diemen's Land (now Tasmania), before returning to Port Jackson

1803 The first issue of the weekly *Sydney Gazette*, Australia's first newspaper, is published

1808 Rum Rebellion brings social upheaval. Estimated population of New South Wales stands at 9,100

1800	**1805**	**1810**

1801 Ticket-of-leave system introduced, enabling the convicts to work for wages and to choose their own master

1802 Aboriginal leader Pemulwy is shot and killed following the killing of four white men by Aboriginal men

1804 Irish convict uprising at Castle Hill

Love token

1810 Recently arrived convicts craft such items as love tokens

The Georgian Era

Merino sheep for export wool

Sydney's early decades were times of turbulence and growth. One of the most significant figures was Lachlan Macquarie, governor from 1810 to 1821. He took over a town-with-a-jail and left behind a fully fledged city with a sense of civic pride. Noted for his sympathetic attitude to convicts and freed women and men, he commissioned many fine buildings, including work by convict Francis Greenway *(see p114)*. When Macquarie left in 1822, Sydney had main roads, streets, and an organized police system. By the 1830s, trade had expanded and labor and land were plentiful. In 1840, transport of convicts was abolished. A decade of lively debate followed: on immigration, religion, and education.

Growth of the City

☐ *1825*   ▨ *Today*

The domed saloon is elliptical, and has a cantilevered staircase.

Bedroom

The breakfast room was used for informal dining.

View from the Summit
Blaxland, Lawson, and Wentworth were the first Europeans to cross the Blue Mountains in 1813. Augustus Earle's painting shows convicts working on a road into this fertile area.

The kitchen was originally in a separate building to avoid the danger of fire.

The Macquaries
Governor Macquarie and his wife Elizabeth arrived in the city with a brief to "improve the morals of the Colonists."

Elizabeth Bay House

This extravagant Regency villa was built from 1835–9 for Colonial Secretary Alexander Macleay *(see p120)*. After only six years' occupancy, lavish building and household expenses forced him into bankruptcy.

Timeline

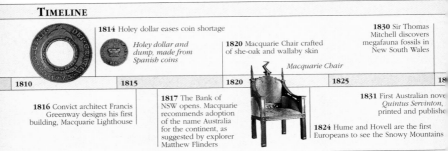

1814 Holey dollar eases coin shortage

Holey dollar and dump, made from Spanish coins

1820 Macquarie Chair crafted of she-oak and wallaby skin

Macquarie Chair

1830 Sir Thomas Mitchell discovers megafauna fossils in New South Wales

| 1810 | 1815 | 1820 | 1825 | 18 |

1816 Convict architect Francis Greenway designs his first building, Macquarie Lighthouse

1817 The Bank of NSW opens. Macquarie recommends adoption of the name Australia for the continent, as suggested by explorer Matthew Flinders

1824 Hume and Hovell are the first Europeans to see the Snowy Mountains

1831 First Australian novel *Quintus Servinton* printed and publishe

Lyrebird *(1813)*
As the colony continued to expand, more exotic birds and animals were found. The male of this species has an impressive tail that spreads into the shape of a lyre.

Aboriginal Explorer
Bungaree took part in the first circumnavigation of the continent, sailing with Matthew Flinders.

Servants' quarters

Drawing room

The Classical design was to be complemented by a colonnade, but money ran out.

The dining room was furnished in a florid style out of keeping with the Neo-Classical architecture.

WHERE TO SEE GEORGIAN SYDNEY

Governor Macquarie designated the street now bearing his name *(see pp112–15)* as the ceremonial center of the city. It has an elegant collection of buildings: the Hyde Park Barracks, St. James' Church, the Mint Museum, Parliament House and Sydney Hospital. Other fine examples are the Victoria Barracks *(p127)*, Vaucluse House *(p136)* and Macquarie Lighthouse *(p137)*.

Old Government House, *the oldest surviving public building in Australia (see p139), was erected in 1799. Additions ordered by Governor Macquarie were completed in 1816.*

High Fashion, 1838
Stylish ladies would promenade through Hyde Park (see pp86–7) in the very latest London fashions, now available from the recently opened David Jones department store.

	Naturalist and author, Charles Darwin	**1842** Sydney town becomes a city		**1848** Parramatta's Female Factory, a notorious women's prison, closes down
	1837 Victoria is crowned Queen of England		**1844** Edward Geoghegan's Australian musical comedy, *The Currency Lass*, first performed	
1835	**1840**		**1845**	**1850**
1836 Charles Darwin visits Sydney on HMS *Beagle*	**1841** Female Immigrants' Home established in Sydney by Caroline Chisholm. Gas lights illuminate Sydney			**1850** Work begins on NSW's first railroad line, from Sydney to Parramatta
1838 Myall Creek massacre of Aboriginal peoples	**1840** Transportation of convicts to NSW is abolished		*Caroline Chisholm, philanthropist*	

Victorian Sydney

Gold rush memorabilia

IN THE 1850s, gold was discovered in New South Wales, and Sydney came alive with gold seekers, big spenders, and a new wave of settlers. It was the start of a peaceful period of solid growth. Education became compulsory, an art gallery was opened, and the Australian Academy of Arts held its first exhibition. The city skyline became more complex, with spires and "tall" buildings. Terrace houses proliferated. Victorian decorum and social behavior borrowed from the mother country flourished, with much social visiting and enthusiasm for sports. It was an age of pleasure gardens and regattas, but also a time of unruliness and political agitation. In the 1890s, as the country moved toward Federation, fervent nationalism and an Australian identity began to take shape.

GROWTH OF THE CITY

☐ *1881*   ▨ *Today*

The structure was built of hollow pine.

The dome was 30 m (98 ft) in diameter.

Mrs. Macquaries Chair *(1855)*
This prime harbor viewing spot (see p106), *with the seat carved from rock for the governor's wife, was "the daily resort of all the fashionable people in Sydney."*

Boer War
The 1st Australian Horse division was praised for its bushcraft, horsemanship, and accurate shooting.

THE GARDEN PALACE
Built in the Botanic Gardens especially for the occasion, in 1879–80, the Garden Palace hosted the first international exhibition held in the southern hemisphere. Twenty nations took part. Sadly, the building and most of its contents were destroyed by fire in 1882.

TIMELINE

1851 The discovery of gold near Bathurst, west of the Blue Mountains, sparks a gold rush

Henry Parkes

1868 The Duke of Edinburgh visits and survives an assassination attempt. The Prince Alfred Hospital is later named in his honor

1872 Henry Parkes elected NSW Premier

1850

1860

1870

1857 *Dunbar* wrecked at The Gap with the loss of 121 lives and only one survivor

Henry Lawson, notable poet and author of short stories

1867 Henry Lawson born

1869 Trend in the colony toward the segregation of Aboriginal peoples on reserves and settlements

1870 The last British troops withdraw from the colony

The Waverly
This clipper ship, with its extra sails and tall masts, enabled the fast transport of wool exports and fortune seekers hastening to newly discovered colonial gold fields.

The "Strasburg" Clock
In 1887, Sydney clockmaker Richard Smith began work on this astronomical model now in the Powerhouse Museum (see pp100–101).

Some of the exhibits held in the Powerhouse Museum *(see pp100–101)* were rescued from this burning building.

The exhibition attracted over one million people.

Arthur Streeton
In 1891, Streeton and Tom Roberts, both Australian Impressionist painters, set up an artists' camp overlooking Sydney Harbour in Mosman.

WHERE TO SEE VICTORIAN SYDNEY

Sydney's buildings reflect the spirit of the age. The Queen Victoria Building *(see p82)*, Sydney Town Hall *(p87)*, and Martin Place *(p84)* mark grand civic spaces. In stark contrast, the Argyle Terraces and Susannah Place *(p67)* in The Rocks give some idea of the cramped living conditions endured by the working class.

St. Mary's Cathedral (see p86), *built in Gothic Revival style, is thought to be the largest Christian church in the former "Empire," outside Britain.*

Victorian terrace houses, *decorated with iron lace, began to fill the streets of Paddington (see pp122–7) and Glebe (p131) from the 1870s onward.*

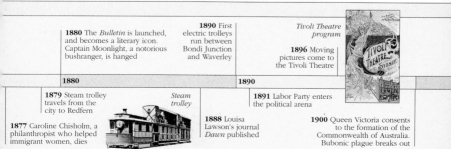

1880 The *Bulletin* is launched, and becomes a literary icon. Captain Moonlight, a notorious bushranger, is hanged

1890 First electric trolleys run between Bondi Junction and Waverley

Tivoli Theatre program

1896 Moving pictures come to the Tivoli Theatre

1880

1890

1879 Steam trolley travels from the city to Redfern

Steam trolley

1891 Labor Party enters the political arena

1877 Caroline Chisholm, a philanthropist who helped immigrant women, dies

1888 Louisa Lawson's journal *Dawn* published

1900 Queen Victoria consents to the formation of the Commonwealth of Australia. Bubonic plague breaks out

Sydney Between the Wars

Vegemite spread created in 1923

FEDERATION TOOK PLACE on January 1, 1901 and New South Wales became a state of the Australian nation. In Sydney, new wharves were built, roads widened, and slums cleared. The 1920s were colorful and gay in "the city of pleasure." The skyline bristled with cranes as modern, functional structures replaced their ornate predecessors. The country was hit hard by the Great Depression in 1931, but economic salvation came in the form of rising wool prices and growth in manufacturing. The opening of the Sydney Harbour Bridge in 1932 was a consolidation of all the changes brought by Federation and urbanization.

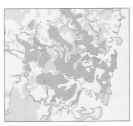

GROWTH OF THE CITY

☐ *1945*   ◼ *Today*

The poster depicts the youthful vigor of the nation.

Home in the Suburbs
The Federation bungalow became a unique architectural style (see p37). Verandas, gables, and chimneys featured amid much red brick.

Surf lifesaver

Bronzed Lifesavers
No surf beach was complete without these icons, forever looking to sea.

"Making Do"
This chair, made in 1910, used packing case lumber, thread spools, fencing wire, and the moldings of picture frames.

SYDNEY HARBOUR BRIDGE
After nine years of construction, the largest crowd ever seen in Sydney greeted the bridge's opening. Considered a wonder of engineering at the time, it linked the harbor's north and south shores.

TIMELINE

1901 Miles Franklin's *My Brilliant Career* is published

Miles Franklin

1912 High-rise era begins in Sydney with the erection of the 14-story Culwulla Chambers in Macquarie Street. First surfboard arrives in Sydney from Hawaii

1920 Prince Edward, the Prince of Wales, visits

1918 Sydneysiders greet the Armistice riotously

1900   **1910**   **1920**

1902 Women win the right to vote in New South Wales

1901 Proclamation of the Commonwealth of Australia. Edmund Barton elected as first prime minister

1907 Trunk line between Melbourne and Sydney opens

Poster for telephone trunk line

1919 The Archibald Prize for portraiture is first awarded. Influenza epidemic hits Sydney

1915 Anzacs land at Gallipoli

Luna Park

This harborside amuse-ment park opened in 1935 (see p132). A maniacally grinning face loomed at the entrance. Millions of Australians recall the terrifying thrill of running the gauntlet through the gaping mouth as children.

One million people crossed the bridge on its opening day.

Donald Bradman

The 1932 English team used "dirty" tactics to outsmart this brilliant cricketer, almost caus-ing a diplomatic rift with Great Britain.

Australian Women's Weekly

This magazine, first published in 1933, becomes a family institu-tion full of homespun wisdom, recipes, stories, and handy hints.

WHERE TO SEE EARLY 20TH-CENTURY SYDNEY

The years after Federation yielded stylish and sensible buildings like Central Railway Station, the Commonwealth Bank in Martin Place *(see pp38–9)* and the State Library of New South Wales. The suburbs of Haberfield and Strathfield best exemplify the Federation style of gentrified residential housing.

The Anzac Memorial *(1934) is in Hyde Park (see pp86–7). The Art Deco memorial, with its reflecting pool, commemorates all Australians killed in war.*

The radio *became a fixture in living rooms in the 1930s. This 1935 AWA Radiolette is held at the Powerhouse Museum (see pp100–101).*

1924 Sydney swimmer Andrew "Boy" Charlton wins a gold medal at the Paris Olympics

Painted glass pub sign

1937 Heyday of painted glass pub art depicting local heroes

1938 Sydney celebrates her 150th anniversary

1939 Australia declares war on Germany

1930

1940

1928 Kingsford Smith and Ulm make first flight across Pacific in the *Southern Cross*

Kingsford Smith, Ulm

1932 Sydney Harbour Bridge opens

1935 Luna Park opens

1941 Australia declares war on Japan

1942 Japanese midget sub-marines enter Sydney Harbour

1945 Street celebrations mark the end of World War II

Postwar Sydney

1950s Holden sedan

THE POSTWAR baby boom was accompanied by mass immigration and suburban sprawl. The hippie movement gave youth an extrovert voice that imbued the 1960s with an air of flamboyance. Australian involvement in the Vietnam War led to political unrest in the early 1970s, relieved for one seminal moment by the 1973 opening of the Sydney Opera House *(see pp74–7)*. In the 1980s, vast sums were spent on skyscrapers and glossy redevelopments like Darling Harbour, and on bicentennial celebrations. The city's potential was recognized in 1993 with the announcement that Sydney would host the year 2000 Olympics.

GROWTH OF THE CITY

☐ *1966*   ▨ *Today*

Drag queens pose in their Hollywood-style sequined finery or lampoon public figures of the day.

Sydney to Hobart Yacht Race
Australia's most prestigious and treacherous yacht race runs over 1,167 km (725 miles). Each Dec. 26 since 1945, spectators have watched yachts jostle at the starting line.

Elaborate floats and costumes can take a year to make, with prizes given to the best.

Bicentenary
The reenactment of the First Fleet's journey ended in Sydney Harbour on Australia Day, 1988. A chaotic flotilla greeted the "tall ships."

GAY AND LESBIAN MARDI GRAS

What began as a protest march involving 1,000 people in 1978 is now a multimillion dollar boost for Australian tourism. While the parade lasts for one rude and riotous night only *(see p49)*, the surrounding international festival offers a month of art, sports, and community events.

TIMELINE

1950 Gas, butter, and tea rationing ends	**1958** Qantas Airlines embarks on its first round-the-world flights	**1965** Conscription reintroduced; first regular army battalion sent to Vietnam	**1973** Official opening of the Sydney Opera House

Johnny O'Keefe

1950	1960	1970

1954 Elizabeth II is the first reigning monarch to visit Australia	**1959** Population of Australia reaches 10 million	*Patrick White*	**1973** Patrick White wins the Nobel Prize for Literature
1956 TV launched in Sydney. By the 1960s, the most popular show is *The Mickey Mouse Club*		**1964** Rocker Johnny O'Keefe, "The Wild One," continues to top the music charts	

Environmental Bans

In the 1970s, bans were placed on developments in the inner city considered harmful to the environment or cultural heritage.

The parade of ornate floats and showy dance troupes stretches for over 2 km (1¼ miles).

Dame Mary Gilmore
This 1957 portrait is by William Dobell, one of the most influential postwar artists. He won the coveted Archibald Prize three times.

Floats are marshaled in Elizabeth Street, before traveling along Oxford and Flinders Streets.

MR. ETERNITY

Arthur Stace (1885–1967), a recovered alcoholic, was inspired by an evangelist who said that he wanted to "shout eternity through the streets of Sydney." "I felt a powerful call from the Lord to write 'Eternity.'" At least 50 times a day, for over 30 years, he chalked this word in perfect handwriting on the footpaths and walls of the city. A plaque in Sydney Square pays tribute to Mr. Eternity's endeavors.

Arthur Stace and "Eternity," 1963

Oz Magazine, 1963–73

This satirical magazine, which had a major international influence, was the mouthpiece of an irreverent generation. It was declared obscene in 1964.

Aboriginal Land Rights

In 1975, the first handover of land was made to Vincent Lingiari, representative of the Gurindji people, by Prime Minister Gough Whitlam.

1977 Kerry Packer launches World Series Cricket

1978 Sydney artist Brett Whiteley wins Archibald Prize, Wynne Prize, and Sulman Prize for three different works of art

Façade detail of the Brett Whiteley Studio (see p130)

1993 Sydney wins the bid to host the year 2000 Olympic Games

1980

1990

1976 Nude sunbathing allowed on two Sydney beaches

1979 Sydney's Eastern Suburbs Railway opens

1988 Monorail begins operation

1989 Earthquake strikes Newcastle causing extensive damage

1992 Sydney Harbour Tunnel opens

1990 Population of Australia reaches 17 million

SYDNEY AT A GLANCE

THERE ARE MORE THAN 100 places of interest described in the *Area by Area* section of this book. A broad range of sights is covered: from the colonial simplicity of Hyde Park Barracks *(see p114)* to the ornate Victorian terraces of Paddington; from the tranquility of Centennial Park *(see p127)* to the bustle of the cafés and shops of Oxford Street. To help you make the most of your stay, the following 16 pages are a time-saving guide to the best Sydney has to offer. Museums and galleries, architecture and parks, and preserves all have sections of their own. There is also a guide to the diverse cultures that have helped to shape the city into what it is today. Below is a selection of attractions that no visitor should miss.

SYDNEY'S TOP TEN ATTRACTIONS

The Rocks
See pp62–77

Sydney Opera House
See pp74–7

Art Gallery of New South Wales
See pp108–11

Royal Botanic Gardens
See pp104–5

Sydney Tower
See p83

Oxford Street and Paddington
See pp116–27

Darling Harbour and Chinatown
See pp90–101

Taronga Zoo
See pp134–5

Harbor ferries
See pp234–5

Sydney's beaches
See pp54–5

◁ Sydney Harbour Bridge, opened in 1932 *(see pp70–71)*

Sydney's Best: Museums and Galleries

SYDNEY IS WELL ENDOWED with museums and galleries, and, following the current appreciation of social history, much emphasis is placed on the lifestyles of past and present Sydneysiders. Small museums are also a feature of the Sydney scene, with a number of historic houses recalling the colonial days. These are covered in greater depth on pages 34–5. Most of the major collections are housed in architecturally signif-icant buildings – the Classical

Bima figure, Powerhouse Museum

façade of the Art Gallery of NSW makes it a city landmark, while the MCA or Museum of Contemporary Art has given new life to a 1950s Art Deco-style building at Circular Quay.

Museum of Sydney
The Edge of the Trees is an interactive instal-lation by the entrance.

THE ROCKS AND
CIRCULAR QUAY

Merchants' House
A Harbour Bridge toy is just one of the idiosyn-cratic mementos in the National Trust's fine Childhood Collection.

CITY CENTRE

Museum of Contemporary Art
The Rouge Series No. 21 *by Li Shan was recently displayed during the* MCA exhibition Mao Goes Pop.

DARLING
HARBOUR

National Maritime Museum
The museum is the home port for HMB Endeavour, *a replica of the vessel that charted Australia's east coast in 1770, with Cap-tain Cook in command.*

Powerhouse Museum
The sun and moon design in the terrazzo floor of the foyer of the King's Cinema is a 1980s tribute to 1930s style, with tiles laid using techniques of the period. Movies are shown daily.

0 meters	500
0 yards	500

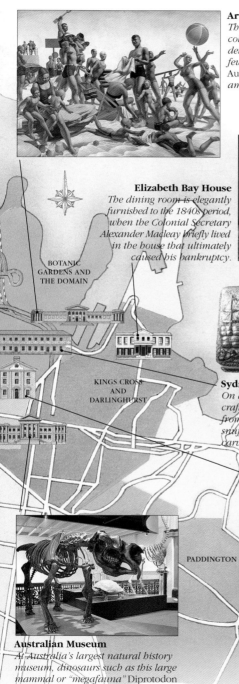

Art Gallery of New South Wales
The Australian collection includes colonial watercolors that, to avoid deterioration, are only shown for a few weeks each year. Charles Meere's Australian Beach Pattern *(1940) is among more recent works.*

Elizabeth Bay House
The dining room is elegantly furnished to the 1840s period, when the Colonial Secretary Alexander Macleay briefly lived in the house that ultimately caused his bankruptcy.

BOTANIC
GARDENS AND
THE DOMAIN

KINGS CROSS
AND
DARLINGHURST

Sydney Mint Museum
On display here are exquisitely crafted presentation pieces made from gold and silver. This lavish snuff box with gilt interior was carved around 1835.

PADDINGTON

Hyde Park Barracks
Originally built by convicts for their own incarceration, these barracks were later home to poor female immigrants. Exhibits recall the daily life of these occupants.

Australian Museum
At Australia's largest natural history museum, dinosaurs such as this large mammal or "megafauna" Diprotodon skeleton are a major attraction.

Exploring Museums and Galleries

Nautilus scrimshaw, National Maritime Museum

SYDNEY BOASTS A RICH VARIETY of museums and galleries that reflects the cultural, artistic, and historical heritage of this, the country's oldest city – and of Australia as a whole. The growth of such institutions in recent years parallels a corresponding growth in public interest in all things cultural, a phenomenon that seems at odds with Sydney's predominantly hedonistic image. In fact, Sydney has a long-standing cultural tradition, one that has not always been widely recognized. It may even surprise some people that museums and galleries attract more people than do high-profile soccer games.

Detail from *Window of Dreams* at the National Maritime Museum

Collage on one of the internal doors of the Brett Whiteley Studio

VISUAL ARTS

THE TRADITIONALLY conservative curatorial policy of the **Art Gallery of NSW** has been abandoned in recent times, and it now has one of the finest existing collections of modern Australian and Aboriginal art. Thanks to its former policy,

however, it also possesses an outstanding collection of late 19th- and early 20th-century English and Australian works. Thematic temporary exhibitions are also a regular feature.

The far newer **Museum of Contemporary Art** (MCA) is best known for blockbuster exhibitions. Many of these take advantage of its prime harbor site to create a fine sense of spectacle. It also has a considerable permanent collection, and hosts mini film festivals, literary readings, and talks.

The **Brett Whiteley Studio** opened even more recently. Housed in the studio of the late artist, it commemorates the life and works of perhaps the most celebrated and controversial Sydney painter of the late 20th century.

The substantial collection of Australian painting and sculpture held by the **SH Ervin Gallery** is supplemented by frequent thematic and other specialized exhibitions.

TECHNOLOGY AND NATURAL HISTORY

THE UNDISPUTED leader in this area is the **Powerhouse**, with traditional and interactive displays covering fields as diverse as space travel, silent films, and solar energy. The **National Maritime Museum** has the world's fastest boat, *Spirit of Australia*, as part of its extensive indoor and outdoor displays. The **Harris Street Motor Museum** has regularly changing exhibitions of classic vehicles, from vintage cars to contemporary designs.

The **Australian Museum**, in contrast, emphasizes natural history with its displays of the exotic and extinct: from birds, insects, and rock samples to giant Australian megafauna.

ABORIGINAL CULTURE

WITH MORE THAN 200 works, both traditional and contemporary, on display, the **Art Gallery of NSW**'s Yiribana Gallery has the best and most

Jabarrgwa Wurrabadalumba's *Dugong Hunt* (1948), Art Gallery of NSW

comprehensive collection of Aboriginal art in the country. The **Australian Museum**, Australia's oldest museum, has a fascinating archaeological exhibit ranging from the pre-historic era right up to the start of European settlement.

The First Australians exhibit at the **National Maritime Museum** includes audio and video material, with traditional tools, boats, and fishing nets made by present-day Aboriginal communities in northern Australia also on display.

The **Museum of Sydney** uses images, artifacts, and oral histories to evoke the life of the Eora, the indigenous people of the Sydney region, up to the years of first contact with the European colonists.

The Georgian-style front bedroom in the cottage at Elizabeth Farm

COLONIAL HISTORY

THE SUPERB interior of **Elizabeth Bay House** has been furnished to show early colonial life at its most elegant, but while at first the house may appear to celebrate a success story, the enormous cost of its construction brought bankruptcy to its owner. Also built in grand style, **Vaucluse House** celebrates the life and times of WC Wentworth, explorer and politician. The **Merchants' House** replicates a typical city residence of the 1850s and contains a special childhood collection.

Experiment Farm Cottage, **Hambledon Cottage**, and **Elizabeth Farm** in and around Parramatta are testament to the crucial role of agriculture in the survival of a colony that was brought to the brink of starvation. The first has been restored as a gentleman's cottage of the mid-19th century, while the last two have been furnished to the period of 1820–50. Parramatta's **Old Government House** was once the vice-regal "inland" residence when Parramatta had more people than Sydney. The colonial furniture on display predates 1855. The **Museum of Sydney** is on the site of the

Water dip at Experiment Farm Cottage

first Government House, close to Sydney Cove. On display are recently unearthed relics of that building, some of which are visible under windows at the entrance to the museum.

Susannah Place provides an insight into working-class life in the 19th century. **Cadman's Cottage**, also in The Rocks, is a simple stone dwelling dating from 1816 and the city's oldest extant building. Adjacent is the **Sailors' Home**, built in 1864 and now The Rocks Visitors Centre. It also has permanent exhibitions detailing the area's architectural, archaeological and social heritage. The important role of gold in Australia's history and how it has determined patterns of migration and development is shown at the **Sydney Mint Museum**. **Hyde Park Barracks** evokes the often brutal lives and times of the convicts housed there in the early 19th century, while not neglecting its history as an immigration depot.

Side view of the veranda at Elizabeth Farm, near Parramatta

SPECIALTY MUSEUMS

AUTHOR MAY GIBBS' home on the harbor, **Nutcote**, has been refurbished in the style of the 1930s. The **Justice and Police Museum** examines a far less comfortable history, investigating Australian crime and punishment, and the **Westpac Museum** traces local financial transactions from first coins through to credit cards. Experiences of Jewish migrants to Australia and the story of the Holocaust are examined at the **Sydney Jewish Museum**.

FINDING THE MUSEUMS AND GALLERIES

Art Gallery of NSW pp108–11
Australian Museum pp88–9
Brett Whiteley Studio p130
Cadman's Cottage p68
Elizabeth Bay House p120
Elizabeth Farm pp138–9
Experiment Farm Cottage p139
Hambledon Cottage p139
Harris Street Motor Museum p98
Hyde Park Barracks pp114–15
Justice and Police Museum p72
Merchants' House pp66–7
Museum of Contemporary Art p73
Museum of Sydney p85
National Maritime Museum pp94–5
Nutcote pp132–3
Old Government House p139
Powerhouse Museum pp100–101
Sailors' Home p67
SH Ervin Gallery, National Trust Centre p73
Susannah Place p67
Sydney Jewish Museum p121
Sydney Mint Museum p114
Vaucluse House p136
Westpac Museum p68

Sydney's Best: Architecture

For such a young city, Sydney possesses a remarkable diversity of architectural styles. They range from the simplicity of Francis Greenway's Georgian buildings *(see p114)* to Jørn Utzon's Expressionist Sydney Opera House *(see pp74–7)*. Practical Colonial structures gave way to elaborate Victorian edifices such as Sydney Town Hall, and the same passion for detail is seen on a smaller scale in Paddington's terraces. Later, Federation warehouses and bungalows brought in a particularly Australian style.

Contemporary
Governor Phillip Tower is a modern commercial building incorporating a historical site (see p85).

Colonial Convict
The first structures were very simple yet formal English-style cottages with shingled roofs and no verandas. Cadman's Cottage is a fine representative of this style.

THE ROCKS AND CIRCULAR QUAY

Colonial Georgian
Francis Greenway's courthouse design was ordered to be adapted to suit the purposes of a church. St. James Church is the result.

CITY CENTRE

American Revivalism
Shopping arcades connecting streets, such as the Queen Victoria Building, were 1890s vogue.

Victorian
The Town Hall interior includes Australia's first pressed metal ceiling, installed for fear that the organ might loosen a plaster ceiling.

DARLING HARBOUR

Contemporary Expressionism
Innovations in sports stadiums, and museum architecture, such as the National Maritime Museum, emphasize roof design and the silhouette.

Interwar Architecture
Bruce Dellit's Anzac Memorial in Hyde Park, with sculptures by Rayner Hoff, encapsulates the spirit, form, and detail of Art Deco.

0 meters   500

0 yards   500

Modern Expressionism
One of the world's greatest examples of 20th-century architecture, Jørn Utzon's Sydney Opera House beat 234 entries in a design competition. Work began in 1958 and, despite the architect's resignation in 1966, it was opened in 1973.

Early Colonial
The first buildings of character and quality, such as Hyde Park Barracks, were for governmental uses.

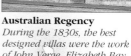

BOTANIC
GARDENS AND
THE DOMAIN

KINGS CROSS AND
DARLINGHURST

Australian Regency
During the 1830s, the best designed villas were the work of John Verge. Elizabeth Bay House was his masterpiece.

Colonial Military
Victoria Barracks, designed by engineers, is an impressive example of a well-preserved Georgian military compound.

PADDINGTON

Colonial Grecian
Greek Revival was the major style for public buildings, such as the Darlinghurst Court House, designed by the Colonial Architect in the 1820–50 period.

Victorian Iron Lace
Festooned with a filigree of cast-iron lace in a wide range of prefabricated patterns, Paddington verandas demonstrate 1880s workmanship.

Exploring Sydney's Architecture

Federation era stained glass

WHILE EUROPEAN SETTLEMENT in Sydney has a relatively short history, architectural styles have rapidly evolved from provincial British buildings and simple convict structures. From the mid-19th century until the present day, architectural innovations have borrowed from a range of international trends to create vernacular styles more suited to local materials and conditions. The signs of affluence and austerity, from gold rush to depression, are also manifested in bricks and mortar.

Façade of the Colonial Susannah Place, with corner shop window

COLONIAL ARCHITECTURE

LITTLE REMAINS of the Colonial buildings from 1790–1830. The few structures still standing have a simple robustness and unassuming dignity. They rely more on form, proportion, and mass than on detail.

The Rocks area has one of the best collections of early Colonial buildings: **Cadman's Cottage** (1816), the **Argyle Centre** (1826), and **Susannah Place** (1844). The Georgian **Hyde Park Barracks** (1819) and **St. James' Church** (1820), by Francis Greenway *(see p114)*, as well as the Greek Revival **Darlinghurst Court House** (1835) and **Victoria Barracks** (1841–8) are excellent examples of this period.

AUSTRALIAN REGENCY

JUST AS THE Colonial style was reaching its zenith, the city's increasingly moneyed society abandoned it as undignified and unfashionable. London's residential architecture, exemplified by John Soane under the Prince Regent's patronage, was in favor from the 1830s to the 1850s. Fine examples of this shift towards Regency are John Verge's stylish town houses at **39–41 Lower Fort Street** (1834–6), The Rocks, and the adjoining **Bligh House**, built for a wealthy merchant in 1833 in High Colonial style, complete with Greek Classical Doric veranda columns.

Regency-style homes often had Grecian, French, and Italian details. **Elizabeth Bay House** (1835–8), internally the finest of all John Verge's works, is particularly noted for its cantilevered staircase rising to the arcaded gallery. The cast-iron Ionic-columned **Tusculum Villa** (1831) by the same architect at Potts Point *(see p118)* is unusual in that it is encircled by a two-level veranda, now partially enclosed.

Entrance detail from the Victorian St. Patrick's Seminary in Manly

VICTORIAN

THIS PROSPEROUS ERA featured confident business people and merchants who designed their own premises. Tracts of the city west of York Street and south of Bathurst Street are testimony to these self-assured projects. The cast-iron and glass **Strand Arcade** (1891) by JB Spencer originally included a gas and electricity system, and hydraulic elevators.

Government architect James Barnet's best work includes the "Venetian Renaissance" style **General Post Office**, Martin Place (1864–87), and the extravagant **Lands Department Building** (1877–90) with its four iron staircases and, originally, elevators operated by water power. The **Great Synagogue** (1878), **St. Mary's Cathedral** (1882), **St. Patrick's Seminary** (1885), **Sydney Town Hall**, and **Paddington Street** are also of this period.

AMERICAN REVIVALISM

AFTER FEDERATION in 1901, architects looked to styles such as Edwardian, American Romanesque, and Beaux Arts from overseas for commercial buildings. The former **National Mutual Building** (1892) by Edward Raht set the change of direction, followed by warehouse buildings in Sussex and Kent Streets. The Romanesque **Queen Victoria Building**

The Australian Regency-style Bligh House in Dawes Point

(1893–98) was a grand council project by George McRae. The Beaux Arts **Commonwealth Savings Bank** (1928) features an elaborate chamber in Neo-Classical style.

INTERWAR ARCHITECTURE

ARCHITECTURE BETWEEN World Wars I and II produced skyscrapers such as the **City Mutual Life Assurance Building** (1936), by Emil Sodersten. This building exhibits German Expressionist influences such as pleated or zigzag windows.

Two important structures are the **ANZAC Memorial** (1929–34) in Hyde Park and **Delfin House** (1938–40), by the Art Deco architect Bruce Dellit. The latter, a skyscraper, features a vaulted ceiling and a granite arch decorated with an allegory of modern life.

MODERN ARCHITECTURE

Modern MLC Centre, Martin Place

FROM THE mid-1950s, modern architecture was introduced to the city through glass-clad curtain-walled office buildings, proportioned like matchboxes on their ends. The contrasting expressed frame approach of **Australia Square** (1961–7) gives structural stability to one of the world's tallest lightweight concrete office towers. This city block was formed by amalgamating 30 properties. Harry Seidler's **MLC Centre** (1975–8) is a 65-story office

FEDERATION ARCHITECTURE

This distinctly urban style of architecture was developed to meet the demands of the prosperous and newly emerging middle classes at the time of Federation in 1901. Particular features are the high-pitched roofs, which form a picturesque composition or architectural tableau, incorporating intricate gables, wide verandas and chimneys. The decorative timber fretwork of the verandas and archways and the leadlight windows reveal the influence of the Art Nouveau period, as do the vibrant red roof tiles. Patriotic references are seen throughout, and Australian flora and fauna are recurring decorative motifs.

"Verona" in The Appian Way, Burwood

tower comprising a reinforced concrete tube structure with column-free floors.

Jørn Utzon's **Sydney Opera House** (1959–73) is widely regarded as one of the architectural wonders of the world.

CONTEMPORARY ARCHITECTURE

DRAMATIC DESIGNS in recent sports and recreation buildings, such as the elliptical **Sydney Football Stadium** (1985–8) by Philip Cox, use advanced steel engineering systems. Beneath the vast roof of the **National Maritime Museum** (1986–9), also by Cox, there is ample space for a wide range of exhibitions.

Detailed masonry has made a return to commercial buildings such as the highly regarded **Governor Phillip Tower** (1989–94). The dictates of office design do not detract from the historical Museum of Sydney, ingeniously sited on the lower floors.

Masonry detail from the contemporary Governor Phillip Tower

WHERE TO FIND THE BUILDINGS

Anzac Memorial *p86*
Argyle Centre *p68*
Australia Square, Cnr George & Bond Sts. **Map** 1 B3.
Bligh House, 43 Lower Fort St, Dawes Point. **Map** 1 B2.
Cadman's Cottage *p68*
City Mutual Life Assurance Building, Cnr Hunter & Bligh Sts. **Map** 1 B4.
Commonwealth Savings Bank of Australia, Martin Place *p84*
Darlinghurst Court House *p121*
Delfin House, 16–18 O'Connell St. **Map** 1 B4.
Elizabeth Bay House *p120*
General Post Office, Martin Place *p84*
Governor Phillip Tower *p85*
Great Synagogue *p86*
Hyde Park Barracks *pp114–15*
Lands Department Building *p84*
39–41 Lower Fort Street, Dawes Point. **Map** 1 A2.
MLC Centre, Martin Place *p84*
National Maritime Museum *pp94–5*
National Mutual Building, 350 George St. **Map** 1 B4.
Paddington Street *p126*
Queen Victoria Building *p82*
St. James' Church *p115*
St. Mary's Cathedral *p86*
St. Patrick's Seminary *p147*
Strand Arcade *p84*
Susannah Place *p67*
Sydney Football Stadium, Moore Park. **Map** 5 C4.
Sydney Opera House *pp74–7*
Sydney Town Hall *p87*
Tusculum Villa *p118*
Victoria Barracks *p127*

Sydney's Many Cultures

SYDNEY HAS ONE of the world's most cosmopolitan societies, reflected in the extraordinary variety of restaurants, religions, community centers and cultural activities to be found throughout the city and its environs. Over 235 birthplaces outside Australia were named in the last census. Indeed, the Sydney telephone directory lists interpreting services for 22 languages, including Greek, Italian, Spanish, Chinese, Vietnamese, Turkish, Korean, and Arabic, and many of these groups have their own newspapers. While immigrants have settled all over the city, there are still pockets of Sydney that retain a distinctive ethnic flavor.

Thai Community
Thai culinary traditions have caused a revolution in Sydney eating houses. The Loy Krathong Festival in Parramatta celebrates the transplanted Thai culture.

Auburn Mosque
This lavish mosque rises above the thriving Turkish businesses nearby. Halal meat markets and candy shops are proof of their influence.

Indonesian
The Indonesian restaurants in Randwick are popular with students at the University of New South Wales nearby.

Thailand

Turkey

Indonesia

Vietnam

Filipinos
Over 60 percent of this rapidly expanding migrant group arrive as the brides of Australian men.

Philippines

Lebanon

Vietnamese
This sculpture of a cow stands in Cabramatta's Freedom Plaza, an area offering all the sights, smells, and street life of Southeast Asia.

Lakemba
A living monument to Islam, the fastest growing religion in Australia, this center is a meeting place for local Lebanese people.

0 kilometers   4

0 miles   2

Irish Parade
Sydney's first settlers, many of them Irish, made their home in The Rocks. With its proliferation of pubs, it is the focal point for jubilant St. Patrick's Day celebrations on March 17 each year.

Little Italy
Long home to the Italian community, Leichhardt evokes the flavor of Europe with its bars, cafés, restaurants, and a sprawling annual street fair.

Jewish Delicatessen
The sizable Jewish community in the city's eastern suburbs, about half of whom were born in Australia, is well served by kosher supermarkets and butcher shops.

Ireland

Italy China Israel

Greece

Chinese New Year
Each year, revelers pack Dixon Street, at the heart of Chinatown, to celebrate with fireworks and Chinese dragons.

Indigenous Australia

Aboriginal Peoples
Yarra Bay in La Perouse hosts the Survival concert every 26 January, the culmination of a week of cultural exchange.

St. Nicholas Church
Marrickville's Greek Orthodox church is the home of worship for the community, mostly based in the southern suburbs.

Exploring Sydney's Many Cultures

Poster to tempt migrants

IN THE MID-20TH CENTURY, most Australians could trace their ancestry back to the British Isles. The building of postwar Australia, dependent as it was on skilled migrant labor, changed all that. Between 1947 and 1972, there were more than two million arrivals, and soon communities of Italians, Greeks, Croatians, Macedonians, and Turks had been established. As the country looked to its close neighbors for trade in the 1970s and 1980s, and wars wreaked havoc in Asian countries, priorities changed. Today, more than 8 percent of New South Wales's population is Asian-born, and a large proportion have settled in Sydney.

The Aboriginal Bangarra Dance Theatre, based in Sydney

ABORIGINAL PEOPLES

SYDNEY CONTAINS the largest urban Aboriginal population in Australia. The largest communities are at La Perouse and Redfern. The richness of the Aboriginal culture in a variety of fields is, however, far more pervasive. Indigenous artwork is now much sought after and there are several specialty Aboriginal art shops in the city *(see pp206–7).* The Yiribana Gallery is a permanent exhibition space at the Art Gallery of New South Wales *(p111).* The Bangarra Dance Theatre *(p213)* and Aboriginal Islander Dance Theatre, both based in Sydney, are noted for their innovative blends of traditional and contemporary dance.

In 1988, indigenous peoples around Australia replaced the term "Aborigines" with names from their own languages. "Koori," defined as "people," is now in common usage in New South Wales.

THE BRITISH

FOR MORE THAN 150 years, Sydney lifestyle was influenced by Great Britain. From the "mother country" came art, literature, fashion, morals, administration, and manners – not to mention breakfast sausages, meat pies, stewed fruit, and steamed plum pudding. Many rituals and celebrations have their roots in British tradition, which may explain why a lot of Sydneysiders persist with hot Christmas dinners in the midst of summer, approach cricket with almost religious fervor, and take pride in the brewing of many fine local beers.

THE CHINESE

THE FIRST CHINESE arrivals were almost all men who came to seek their fortune when gold was discovered in the 1850s. At the end of the gold rushes, many settled in tight-knit communities with undeservedly dubious reputations. In the cities and towns where they settled, there were many cultural conflicts with the predominantly Anglo-Celtic settlers. Eventually, the Chinese were deterred by taxes and then excluded from settlement after the introduction of the Immigration Restriction Act in 1901. Entry restrictions for non-European migrants were only relaxed in the 1960s.

Many Chinese students were allowed to remain in Australia after the Tiananmen Square massacre in 1989. Today, the

The Chinese Garden *(see p98)*

Chinese are the fastest growing community in Sydney, with most new arrivals from China, Hong Kong, and Taiwan. It is not only Chinese Australians who throng to Chinatown. All locals browse, sample the delicacies, and treat themselves to lunchtime *yum cha (see p180).*

THE GREEKS

SEVEN CONVICTS transported for piracy in 1829, two of whom stayed on, were probably the first Greek arrivals. Although the early pioneers in the 19th century were mainly from islands such as Kythera, many Greeks also arrived from Cyprus and North Africa.

In the 1940s, new migrants began to set up small businesses such as cafés, fish-and-chip shops, and fruit and vegetable shops. The Greek community gradually grew and has maintained its strong networks through the church, social and sports organizations. Every year, on the Sunday following January 6, the Greek Orthodox

Dancers in traditional Greek costume at the Opera House

Church celebrates the Epiphany with the Blessing of the Waters at Yarra Bay in Sydney's south. The nearby suburb of Sutherland is becoming the city's "Little Athens."

THE IRISH

THE IRISH HAVE HAD a profound impact on politics, literature, music, religion, and law in Australia. About one-third of the convicts transported here were Irish, and many more migrated later. In 1831, Cork's Foundling Hospital sent 50 girls, the first government-assisted migrants. The idea was that "in consequence of the very great disproportion of males to females in New South Wales it would be extremely beneficial to . . . have introduced there some females properly educated and of virtuous habits."

While the Irish are much dispersed today, a St. Patrick's Day parade runs through the city streets each year *(see p50)*. Many pubs, particularly those in The Rocks, draw boisterous crowds to mark the occasion.

"St. Patrick" in St. Patrick's Day Parade

THE ITALIANS

ITALIAN IMMIGRATION peaked in the 1950s and 1960s, but the strong Italian community has been established since the gold rushes of the 1850s. The Italians brought with them much-needed industrial labor, as well as cheese-making skills and wine-growing expertise.

Although Italians now live all over Sydney, Leichhardt's Norton Street, with its restaurants, cafés, and nightspots, is still the Italian heartland. East Sydney's Stanley Street is the "Little Italy" of the inner city, and pasta and cappuccino are as much a part of Sydney life as meat pies and beer.

One of the most important Italian festivals is the Blessing of the Fleet in October *(p48)*. The community also makes its presence felt whenever Italy advances through to the finals of the soccer World Cup.

THE LEBANESE

LEBANESE MIGRANTS first began arriving in the 1840s with the majority being Orthodox Christians or Catholics. It was not until 1976, as a result of Lebanon's civil war, that Muslims began to migrate in large numbers. While early settlers largely comprised shopkeepers living in rural areas, later migrants, being the largest group of Arabic-speaking citizens in the city, established it as the Lebanese center. In the southwest of Sydney, Punchbowl and Lakemba have a high Lebanese profile. They have places of worship for all Lebanese Australians wishing to maintain their religious and cultural traditions. The city's Arabic-language newspapers are also based there.

THE VIETNAMESE

FROM 1976 TO 1981, 54 boats laden with refugees from war-torn Vietnam reached Darwin in Australia's north. Tens of thousands of "boat people" and other refugees risked rough seas, pirates, starvation, and imprisonment to escape.

A number of suburbs have large Vietnamese communities, notably Cabramatta in Sydney's southwest, where they are the most numerous of 109 nationalities. Along with Cambodians, they have made Cabramatta a dynamic commercial center.

New Zealand Maori dancers taking part in the Te Aroha Festival

THE MELTING POT

AFTER THE CHINESE community, the fastest-growing migrant group in New South Wales is the Filipinos, living predominantly in the western suburbs of Fairfield and Blacktown.

Fairfield also has a booming South American, particularly Chilean, community, as well as a significant group of East Timorese living in exile.

Don Moon, a highly successful Korean businessman, saw huge potential in the rundown suburb of Campsie not far from the city. He encouraged other Korean immigrants to invest in the area, which now has a popular shopping district.

The restaurants and cafés in Randwick show the presence of an Indonesian and Malay community. As a cosmopolitan South Pacific city, Sydney has migrants from Tonga, Western Samoa, and Fiji, as well as New Zealanders, including Maoris, dispersed throughout the city.

Pailau Gate at the entrance to Freedom Plaza in Cabramatta

Sydney's Best: Parks and Preserves

Flannel flower

SYDNEY IS ALMOST completely surrounded by national parks and intact bushland. There are also a number of national parks and preserves within Greater Sydney itself. Here, the visitor can gain some idea of how the landscape looked before the arrival of European settlers. The city parks, too, are filled with plant and animal life. The more formal plantings of both native and exotic species are countered by the indigenous birds and animals that have adapted and made the urban environment their home. One of the highlights of a trip to Sydney is the huge variety of birds to be seen, from large birds of prey such as sea eagles and kites, to the shyer species such as wrens and tiny finches.

Garigal National Park
Rain forest and moist gullies provide shelter for superb lyrebirds and sugar gliders.

North Arm Walk
In spring, grevilleas and flannel flowers bloom profusely on this seaside walk.

Lane Cove National Park
The open eucalyptus forest is dotted with grass trees, as well as fine stands of red and blue gums. The rosella, a type of parrot, is common.

Bicentennial Park
Situated at Homebush Bay on the Parramatta River, the park features a mangrove habitat. It attracts many water birds, including pelicans.

Hyde Park
Situated on the edge of the city center, the park provides a peaceful respite from the hectic streets. The native iris is just one of the plants found in the lush gardens. The sacred ibis, a water bird, is often seen.

Middle Head and Obelisk Bay

Gun emplacements, tunnels, and bunkers built in the 1870s to protect Sydney from invasion by sea dot the area. The superb fairy wren lives here, and water dragons can at times be seen basking on rocks.

North Head

Coastal heathland, with banksias, tea trees, and casuarinas, dominates the cliff tops. On the leeward side, moist forest surrounds tiny harbor beaches.

Grotto Point

Bottlebrushes, grevilleas, and flannel flowers line paths winding through the bush to the lighthouse.

Bradleys Head

The headland is a nesting place for the ringtail possum. Noisy flocks of rainbow lorikeets are also often in residence.

South Head

Unique plant species such as the sundew cover this heathland.

Neilsen Park

The kookaburra is easily identified by its call, which sounds like laughter.

The Domain

Palms and Moreton Bay figs are a feature of this former common. The Australian magpie, with its black and white plumage, is a frequent visitor.

Moore Park

Huge Moreton Bay figs provide an urban habitat for the flying fox.

Centennial Park

Open expanses and groves of paperbark and eucalyptus trees bring sulfur-crested cockatoos en masse. The brushtail possum is a shy creature that comes out at night.

0 kilometers 4

0 miles 2

Exploring the Parks and Preserves

DESPITE 200 YEARS of European settlement, Sydney's parks and preserves contain a surprising variety of native wildlife. Approximately 2,000 species of native plants, 1,000 cultivated and weed species and 300 bird species have managed to adapt favorably to the changes.

Several quite distinct vegetation types are protected in the bushland around Sydney, and these in turn provide shelter for a wide range of birds and animals. Even the more formal parks such as Hyde Park and the Royal Botanic Gardens are home to many indigenous species, allowing the visitor a glimpse of the city's diverse wildlife.

Colorful and noisy rainbow lorikeets at Manly's Collins Beach

COASTAL HINTERLAND

ONE REASON Sydney has so many heathland parks, such as those found at South Head and North Head, is that the soil along the city's coastline is deficient in almost every known nutrient. What these areas lack in fertility, they make up for in species diversity.

Heathland contains literally hundreds of species of plants, including some unique flora that have adapted to the poor soil. The most surprising ones are the carnivorous plants, which rely on passing insects for their food. The tiny sundew (*Drosera spathulata*), so called because of its sparkling foliage, is the most common of the carnivorous species. This low-growing plant snares insects on its sticky, reddish leaves, which lie flat on the ground. You will often stumble across them on walking trails in swampy ground, waiting patiently for a victim. Two

Red bottlebrush (Callistemon sp.)

other distinctive plants are casuarinas (*Allocasuarina* species) and banksias (*Banksia* species), both of which attract smaller birds such as honey-eaters and blue wrens.

RAIN FOREST AND MOIST FOREST

RAIN FOREST REMNANTS do exist in a few parts of Sydney, especially in the Royal National Park to the south of the city (*see pp164–5*). Small pockets can also be found in Garigal National Park, Ku-ring-gai Chase (*see pp154–5*) and some gullies running down to Middle Harbour. The superb lyrebird (*Menura novaehollandiae*) is a feature of these forest areas. The sugar glider (*Petaurus breviceps*), a small species of possum, can sometimes be heard calling to its mate during the night.

The deadliest spider in the world, the funnel-web (*Atrax robustus, see p89*), also lives here, but you are unlikely to see one unless you go poking

under rocks and logs. A common plant in this habitat is the cabbage tree palm (*Livistona australis*). The heart of this palm was used as a vegetable by the early European settlers.

The soft tree fern (*Dicksonia antartctica*) decorates the gullies and creeks of moist forest. You may see a ringtail possum (*Pseudocheirus peregrinus*) nest at the top of one of these ferns at Bradleys Head. The nest looks rather like a hairy ball and is found in hollow trees or ferns and shrubs.

Rainbow lorikeets (*Trichoglossus haematodus*) also inhabit Bradleys Head, as well as Clifton Gardens and Collins Beach. Early in the morning, they shoot through the forest canopy like iridescent bullets.

OPEN EUCALYPT FOREST

SOME OF the finest Sydney red gums (*Angophora costata*) can be seen in the Lane Cove National Park. The centuries-old trees, with their gnarled pinkish trunks, give the area an almost "lost world" feeling.

Tall and straight blue gums (*Eucalyptus saligna*) stand in the lower reaches of the park, where the soil is better, while the smaller yellowish scribbly gum (*Eucalyptus racemosa*), with its distinctive gum veins, lives on higher slopes. If you examine the markings on a scribbly gum closely, you will see they start out thin, gradually become thicker, then take a U-turn and stop. This is the track made by an *ogmograptis* caterpillar the previous year. The grubs that made the track

Coastal heathland lining the cliff tops at Manly's North Head

become small, brownish-gray moths and are commonly seen in eucalypt or gum forests.

Grass trees (*Xanthorrhoea* species), also common in open eucalypt forest, are an ancient plant species with a tall spike that bears white flowers in spring. Lyrebirds, echidnas, currawongs, and black snakes are predominant wildlife. The snakes, although beautiful, should be treated with caution.

A Sydney red gum, with gnarled limbs, in Lane Cove National Park

WETLANDS

More than 60 percent of New South Wales' coastal wetlands have been lost. This makes the remaining areas of wetland especially important. Most of Sydney's wetlands are mangrove swamps, with some of the best-preserved examples at Bicentennial Park and the North Arm Walking Track.

Mangrove swamps are one of the most hostile places for a plant or animal to live. There

A gray mangrove swamp near the Lane Cove National Park

is no fresh water and, unlike soil, the mud has no oxygen whatsoever below the very surface level. Mangroves have developed some fascinating ways around these problems.

First, excess salt is excreted from their leaves. Secondly, they get oxygen to the roots by pushing special peglike roots, called pneumatophores, into the air. At low tide, these can be clearly seen around the base of most mangroves. They allow air to diffuse down into the roots so that they can survive the stifling conditions under the mud. The Sydney rock oyster (*Faccoftrea commercialis*), a popular local delicacy, is found in mangrove areas, particularly around the Hawkesbury and Botany Bay.

CITY PARKS

An amazing number of birds and animals make the city parks their home. Silver gulls (*Larus novaehollandiae*) and sulfur-crested cockatoos (*Cacatua galerita*) are frequent daytime visitors to Hyde Park, Centennial Park, The Domain, and the Botanic Gardens.

After dark, brushtail possums (*Trichosurus vulpecula*) come out in search of food and may be seen scavenging in garbage cans. Also a night creature, the fruit-eating gray-headed flying fox (*Pteropus poliocephalus*) can be seen swooping through the trees. There is sometimes

The nocturnal gray-headed flying fox, at rest during the daytime

a temporary colony of these marsupials in the Botanic Gardens, where they hang upside down from trees in the park. Most of Sydney's flying foxes come from a large colony in Gordon, in the city's north.

Moore Park and The Domain are good places to spot flying foxes, and they also have wonderful specimens of Moreton Bay and other fig species.

While paperbarks (*Melaleuca* species) are a feature of Centennial Park, a range of palms can be seen in the Botanic Gardens. The exquisite superb fairy wren (*Malurus cyaneus*) can also be seen here, flitting between shrubs, while overhead honeyeaters dart after each other in the tree canopy.

STRANGLER FIGS

The majestic figs in the city parks hide a dark secret. While most of the Moreton Bay figs (*Ficus macrophylla*) you see have been grown by gardeners long past, in the wild these trees have a different approach. They start as a tiny seedling, sprouted from a seed dropped by a bird in the fork of a tree. Over decades, the pencil-thin roots grow downward. Once they reach the ground, new roots are sent down, forming a lacy network around the trunk of the host tree. They eventually become an iron-hard cage around the host tree's trunk so that it dies and rots away, leaving the fig with a hollow trunk.

The Moreton Bay fig, with its massive spreading canopy

SYDNEY THROUGH THE YEAR

S YDNEY'S TEMPERATE CLIMATE allows for the enjoyment of outdoor activities throughout the year. Seasons in Sydney are the opposite of those in the northern hemisphere. September ushers in the three months of spring; summer stretches from December to February; March, April, and May are the autumn months; and the shorter days and falling temperatures of June announce the onset of winter. In reality, however, Sydney seasons often merge

Reveler at the Mardi Gras

into one another with little to mark their changeover. Balmy nights, the sweet, pervasive scent of jasmine blossom, and the colorful blooming of shrubs and flowers are typical of spring. Summer caters to sun- and surf-lovers as well as being Sydney's festival season. Autumn, with its warm days and cooler nights, is often perfect for bushwalks and picnics. And the crisp days of winter are ideal for going on historic walks and exploring art galleries and museums.

SPRING

W ITH THE WARMER weather, the profusion of spring flowers brings the city's parks and gardens excitingly to life. Food, art, and music festivals abound. Sports teams finish their seasons with action-packed grand finals, professional and backyard cricketers warm up for their summer competitions, and the horse-racing fraternity gets ready to place its bets.

SEPTEMBER

David Jones Spring Flower Show *(first two weeks)*, Elizabeth Street department store. Breathtaking floral artwork fills the ground floor.
Festival of the Winds *(second Sun)*, Bondi Beach *(see p137)*. Multicultural kite-flying festival; music, dance.
Royal Botanic Gardens Spring Festival *(late Sep)*. Among glorious displays of spring blooms, enjoy the minstrels, brass bands, dance displays, sculpture exhibits,

Sacred ibis stilt-dancer at the Royal Botanic Gardens Festival

Traditional costumes at the Blessing of the Fleet, Darling Harbour

and food stands *(see pp104–5)*.
Spring Racing Carnival *(early Sep–early Oct)*. Horse races at Rosehill and Royal Randwick racecourses.
Australian Rugby League Grand Final, Sydney Football Stadium *(see p52)*.
New South Wales Rugby Union Grand Final, Waratah Rugby Stadium, Concord.
Aurora New World Festival *(late Sep–early Oct)*, Darling Harbour *(see pp92–3)*. Fiestas and parades, including music, dance, puppets, and fireworks.

OCTOBER

Manly Jazz Festival *(Australian Labour Day weekend)*. National and international musicians at a variety of venues *(see p133)*.
Aurora Blessing of the Fleet *(Labour Day weekend, Sun)*, Darling Harbour *(pp92–3)*. An Italian and Greek tradition: a fleet of gaily decorated fishing boats is officially blessed.

Leura Garden Festival *(from second to third weekends)*, Blue Mountains *(pp160–61)*. A village fair launches the festival, when magnificent private gardens may be viewed.
Teddy Bears' Picnic *(late Oct, Sun)*, Darling Harbour *(see pp92–3)*. Competitions, face painting, parades, and stalls; a popular fund-raiser for the city's children's hospital.

NOVEMBER

Melbourne Cup Day *(first Tue)*. The city almost grinds to a halt to tune in to Australia's most popular horse race. Restaurants and hotels offer special luncheons.
Kings Cross Carnival *(first Sun)*, Darlinghurst Road. Street fair: stalls, bargains, and food.
Sydney to the Gong Bicycle Ride *(first Sun)*. From Sydney's Moore Park to Flagstaff Point in Wollongong. Cyclists of all categories line up for this 92-km (57-mile) ride.

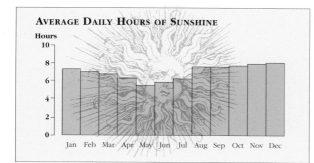

AVERAGE DAILY HOURS OF SUNSHINE

Hours

Jan Feb Mar Apr May Jun Jul Aug Sep Oct Nov Dec

Sunshine Hours
A sunny climate is one of Sydney's main attractions. There are very few days with no sunshine at all, even in the middle of winter. An up-to-date weather forecast is available by telephoning 1196. Coastal weather conditions can be obtained by dialing 11541.

SUMMER

SYDNEY TURNS FESTIVE in the summer months. Christmas pageants and open-air carol singing in The Domain mark the start of the season. Then there is the Sydney Festival, a month of cultural events and other popular entertainment, culminating in Australia Day celebrations on January 26. Summer, too, brings a feast for sport lovers, with surfing and lifesaving events, yacht races, and a host of local and international cricket matches.

"Santa Claus" at the surf: Christmas Day celebrations on Bondi Beach

DECEMBER

Carols in The Domain *(Sat before Christmas)*. Carols by candlelight in the parkland of the city's favorite outdoor gathering spot *(see p107)*.
Christmas at Bondi Beach *(Dec 25)*. Holidaymakers hold their own unofficial party on this famous beach *(see p137)*.
Sydney to Hobart Yacht Race *(Dec 26)*. The harbor teems with small craft as they escort racing yachts out to sea for the start of their journey.
New Year's Eve *(Dec 31)*. Street parties in The Rocks and Circular Quay and fireworks displays on Sydney Harbour.

JANUARY

Opera in the Park *(first or second Sat)*, The Domain *(see p107)*. A free performance of highlights from productions by the Australian Opera.
Cricket Test match, Sydney Cricket Ground *(see p52)*.
Symphony under the Stars *(second or third Sat)*, The Domain *(see p107)*. Free concert by the Sydney Symphony Orchestra.
Big Day Out *(26 Jan)*, Sydney Showground. Performances given by dozens of the best alternative and mainstream overseas and local rock bands, artists, and DJs.
Ferrython *(Jan 26)*, Sydney Harbour. Ferries compete fiercely for line honors, as do sailing vessels in the Tall Ships Race on the same day.
Australia Day Concert *(Jan 26)*, The Domain *(p107)*. Free evening concert featuring Australian popular entertainers.
Chinese New Year *(late Jan or early Feb)*. Lion dancing,

Chinese New Year lion

firecrackers, and other typical festivities in Chinatown *(see p99)*, Cabramatta *(p40)*, and the city's many Chinese restaurants.

FEBRUARY

Gay and Lesbian Mardi Gras Festival, various inner-city venues *(see pp28–9)*. A month of events which culminates in a flamboyant street parade, concentrated on Oxford Street, in early March.
Perspecta *(until late Mar, odd-numbered years)*, Art Gallery of NSW *(see pp108–11)*. A prestigious biennial exhibition of the very best contemporary art.
Coca-Cola World Sevens Tournament, Sydney Football Stadium *(see p52)*. International rugby league teams.
Bondi Beach Cole Classic *(first Sun)*, North Bondi *(see p137)*. A 2-km (1½-mile) race for any swimmer from age 13 to 70 game enough to enter.
Coogee Surf Carnival *(Sat in early Feb)*, Coogee *(see p55)*.

Australia Day Tall Ships race in Sydney Harbour

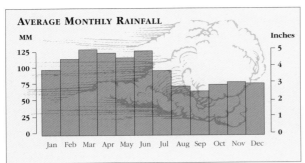

AVERAGE MONTHLY RAINFALL

MM | Inches
125 — 5
100 — 4
75 — 3
50 — 2
25 — 1
0 — 0

Jan Feb Mar Apr May Jun Jul Aug Sep Oct Nov Dec

Rainfall
Autumn is Sydney's rainiest season, with March being the wettest month, while spring is the driest time of year. Rainfall, however, can often be unpredictable. Long stretches of sunny weather are common, but so, too, are periods of unrelenting rain.

AUTUMN

A FTER THE HUMIDITY of the summer, autumn brings fresh mornings and cooler days that are tailor-made for outdoor pursuits. There are many sports and cultural events – some of them colorful and unusual – to tempt the visitor. The Royal Easter Show is the highlight of the season. Anzac Day (April 25) is a national holiday to commemorate the Australian war dead.

MARCH

St. Patrick's Day Parade *(Mar 17, or Sun before)*. Hyde Park *(see pp86–7)* to Prince Alfred Park. Pubs serve green beer on this day.
Kings Cross Bed Race *(Sun in mid-Mar)*, Darlinghurst Road, Potts Point. Fund raisers push their beds through a challenging but fun 100-m (110-yd) obstacle course.
Dragon Boat Races Festival

St. Patrick's Day beer

(second or third weekend before Easter), Darling Harbour *(see pp92–3)*. Brilliantly decorated Chinese dragon boats race across Cockle Bay.
Autumn Racing Carnival *(six weeks during Mar and Apr)*. Top-class races and big prize money, at Rosehill and Royal Randwick racetracks.

EASTER

Royal Easter Show *(starts one week before Good Friday)*, Sydney Showground. Country meets city. A parade through the city streets begins 12 days of ring events, livestock and produce judging, wood-chopping competitions, sheepdog trials, arts and crafts displays, and fairground attractions.
Hoopla! Circus and Street Theater Festival *(Easter school vacation)*, Darling Harbour *(see pp92–3)*. Street theater featuring magicians, acrobats, mimes, and performance artists.

Wood chopping at the Easter Show

APRIL

National Trust Heritage Week *(dates vary)*. Celebration of the natural, architectural, and cultural heritage of Sydney.
Archibald, Wynne, Sulman, and Dobell exhibitions *(six weeks mid-autumn)*, Art Gallery of NSW *(pp108–11)*. Annual exhibition of that year's entries in the portraiture, landscape, genre works, and drawing competitions.
Anzac Day *(Apr 25)*. Dawn memorial service held at the Cenotaph, Martin Place *(see p84)*, with a parade by war veterans along George Street.

MAY

Australian Antique Dealers Fair *(first weekend)*, Sydney Showground.
Bridge to Bridge Power Boat Race *(first weekend)*, Brooklyn Bridge to Upper Hawkesbury Power Boat Club, Windsor *(see pp156–7)*.
Sydney Morning Herald Half Marathon *(fourth Sun)*, from Pier One, The Rocks. An open 21-km (13-mile) run.

Traditional decorative dragon boats on Darling Harbour's Cockle Bay

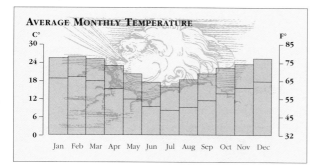

AVERAGE MONTHLY TEMPERATURE

Jan Feb Mar Apr May Jun Jul Aug Sep Oct Nov Dec

Temperature
This chart gives the average minimum and maximum temperatures for Sydney. Spring and autumn are generally free of extremes, but be prepared for sudden cold snaps in winter and occasional bursts of oppressive humid heat in summer.

WINTER

WINTER IN SYDNEY can be cold enough to require warm jackets; temperatures at night may drop dramatically away from the coast. The days are often clear and sometimes surprisingly mild. Arts are a major feature of winter. There are lots of exhibitions for those who want to stay indoors, and the Sydney Film Festival, which no film buff will want to miss.

JUNE

A Taste of Manly *(first weekend)*, Manly Beach *(see p133)*. Annual food and wine festival.
Home Computer Show *(fours days over the second weekend)*, Convention and Exhibition Centre, Darling Harbour *(see p98)*. The very latest in personal computer software, hardware, and entertainment.
Bandemonium *(mid-Jun to mid-Jul)*, Darling Harbour *(see pp92–3)*. Constantly changing lineup of jazz, blues, country, gospel, and world music bands.
Sydney Film Festival *(two weeks mid-Jun)*, State Theatre *(see p82)*. The latest short and feature films, as well as retrospectives and showcases.

JULY

Biennale of Sydney *(two months, mid-year)*, various venues. International festival, held in even-numbered years, encompassing many forms of visual art, from painting and

Australian soldiers or "Diggers" at an Anzac Day ceremony

The familiar logo of the Film Festival

sculpture to photography and performance art.
Yulefest *(throughout July)*, Blue Mountains *(see pp160–61)*. Hotels, guesthouses, and some restaurants celebrate a midwinter "Christmas" with log fires and all the yuletide trimmings.
Australian Book Fair *(mid-Jul)*, Convention and Exhibition Centre, Darling Harbour *(see p98)*. Australian book publishers' trade fair.
Open to the general public on the weekend, with plenty of attractions, including author appearances, book discussion panels, and lots of lively entertainment for children.
Sydney Boat Show *(late Jul)*, Convention and Exhibition Centre, Darling Harbour *(p98)*.
Needlework, Craft and Art Fair *(late Jul)*, Convention and Exhibition Centre, Darling Harbour *(see p98)*. A major exhibition of Australia's finest needlecraft, both traditional and modern, and including quilts and wearable art.

PUBLIC HOLIDAYS

New Year's Day (Jan 1)
Australia Day (Jan 26)
Good Friday (variable)
Easter Monday (variable)
Anzac Day (Apr 25)
Queen's Birthday (second Mon in Jun)
Bank Holiday (first Mon in Aug: only banks and some financial institutions are closed)
Labour Day (first Mon in Oct)
Christmas Day (Dec 25)
Boxing Day (Dec 26)

AUGUST

City to Surf Race *(second Sun)*. From the city to Bondi Beach *(see p137)*. A 14-km (9-mile) community event that attracts all types, from amateurs to leading marathon runners.
Great Sydney Showground Antiques Fair *(mid-month)*, Sydney Showground. Sale of antiques of every description.

Runners in the City to Surf Race, surging down William Street

SPORTS IN SYDNEY

THROUGHOUT AUSTRALIA sports is a way of life and Sydney is no exception. On any day you'll see the locals on golf courses at dawn, running along the streets keeping fit, or having a quick set of tennis after work. On the weekend, during both summer and winter, there is no end to the variety of sports you can watch. Thousands of people gather at the Sydney Football Stadium and Sydney Cricket Ground every weekend to catch their teams in action, and, for those who cannot make it to the ground, sports reign supreme on weekend television.

CRICKET

DURING THE SUMMER months Test cricket and one-day internationals are played at the Sydney Cricket Ground (SCG). Tickets for weekday sessions of the Tests can often be bought at the gate, although it is advisable to book well in advance (through **Ticketek**) for weekend sessions of Test matches and for all the one-day international matches.

RUGBY LEAGUE AND RUGBY UNION

THE POPULARITY of rugby league knows no bounds in Sydney. This is what people are referring to when they talk about "the footie." There are three major competition levels: local, State of Origin – which matches Queensland against New South Wales – and Tests. The "local" competition fields teams from all over Sydney, as well as Newcastle, Canberra, Brisbane, Perth, the Gold Coast, and Far North Queensland.

These matches are held all over Sydney, although the Sydney Football Stadium (SFS) is by far the biggest venue. Tickets for State of Origin and

Australia versus the All Blacks, SFS

Test matches often sell out as soon as they go on sale. Call **Ticketek** to check availability.

Rugby union is the second most popular football code. Again, matches at Test level sell out very quickly. For some premium trans-Tasman rivalry, catch a Test match between Australia's "Wallabies" and the New Zealand "All Blacks" at the Sydney Football Stadium. Phone Ticketeck for details.

GOLF AND TENNIS

GOLF ENTHUSIASTS need not do without their round of golf. There are many courses throughout Sydney where visitors are welcome at all times. These include **Moore Park**, St. Michael's, and **Warringah** golf courses. It is a good idea to phone ahead for a booking, especially on weekends.

Tennis is another favorite sport. Courts available for rent can be found all over Sydney. Many centers also have floodlit courts available for night play. Try **Cooper Park** or **Moore Park Tennis Courts**.

Playing golf at Moore Park, one of Sydney's public courses

AUSTRALIAN RULES FOOTBALL

ALTHOUGH NOT AS popular as in Melbourne, "Aussie Rules" has a strong following in Sydney. The local team, the Sydney Swans, plays its home games at the Sydney Cricket Ground about every second week during the season.

Rivalry between the Sydney supporters and their Melbourne counterparts is strong, with busloads of diehard fans from the south arriving to cheer on their teams. Tickets can usually be bought at the ground on the day of the game.

BASKETBALL

BASKETBALL HAS grown in popularity as both a spectator and recreational sport in recent years. Sydney has male and female teams competing in the National Basketball League. The games, held at the Sydney Entertainment Centre,

One-day cricket match between Australia and the West Indies, SCG

Aerial view of the Sydney Football Stadium at Moore Park

have much of the pizzazz, color, and excitement of American basketball. Tickets can be purchased from either Ticketek or at the box office at the Entertainment Centre.

CYCLING AND INLINE SKATING

SYDNEY BOASTS excellent, safe locations for the whole family to go cycling. One of the most frequented is Centennial Park *(see p127)*. You can rent bicycles and safety helmets from **Centennial Park Cycles**.

Another popular pastime, particularly on warm, summer evenings, is inline skating. **Bondi Boards & Blades**, near Centennial Park, rents inline skates, helmets, and protective gear by the hour. They have a shop at Bondi Beach if you prefer to skate near the ocean. **Inline Action** at Manly also rents skates and gear.

For those who like to keep both feet firmly on the ground, you can watch skateboarders and inline skaters practicing their moves at the ramps at Bondi Beach *(see p137)*.

Inline skaters enjoying a summer evening on the city's streets

HORSEBACK RIDING

FOR A LEISURELY ride, head to Centennial Park, where horses can be rented from the **Centennial Park Horse Hire and Riding School**. They also have guided rides around the park. **Samarai Park Riding School** conducts trail rides through Ku-ring-gai Chase National Park *(see pp154–5)*.

Farther afield, you can enjoy the magnificent scenery of the Blue Mountains *(see pp160–61)* on horseback. The **Megalong Valley Heritage Farm** has trail rides lasting from one hour to an overnight ride. All levels of experience are accommodated.

Riding in one of the parks surrounding the city center

ADVENTURE SPORTS

YOU CAN PARTICIPATE in guided bushwalking, mountain biking, canyoning, caving, rock climbing, and rappelling expeditions in the nearby Blue Mountains National Park. The **Blue Mountains Adventure Company** runs one-day or multi-day courses and trips for all levels of adventurer.

In the center of Sydney, the **City Crag Climbing Centre** has indoor classes and walls on which you can practice.

DIRECTORY

Blue Mountains Adventure Company
190 Katoomba St, Katoomba.
C *(047) 82 1271.*

Bondi Boards & Blades
230 Oxford St, Bondi Junction.
C *9369 2212.*
Also: Shop 2/148 Curlewis St,
Bondi Beach. **C** *9365 6555.*

Centennial Park Cycles
50 Clovelly Rd, Randwick.
C *9398 5027.*

Centennial Park Horse Hire and Riding School
RAS Showground, Moore Park.
Map 5 C5. C *9361 4513.*

City Crag Climbing Centre
499 Kent St. **Map 4 E3.**
C *9267 3822.*

Cooper Park Tennis Courts
Off Suttie Rd, Double Bay.
C *9389 9259.*

Inline Action
93–95 North Steyne, Manly.
C *9976 3831.*

Megalong Valley Heritage Farm
Megalong Road, Megalong
Valley. **C** *(047) 878 188.*

Moore Park Golf Club
Cnr Cleveland St & Anzac Parade,
Moore Park. **Map 5 B5.**
C *9663 3960.*

Moore Park Tennis Courts
Lang Rd, Moore Park.
C *9662 70333.*

St. Michael's Golf Club
Jennifer St, Little Bay.
C *9311 0621.*

Samarai Park Riding School
90 Booralie Road, Terrey Hills.
C *9450 1745.*

Ticketek
C *9266 4800.*

Warringah Golf Club
Condamine St, North Manly.
C *9905 4028.*

Sydney's Beaches

BEING A CITY BUILT AROUND THE WATER, it is no wonder that many of Sydney's recreational activities involve the sand, sea, and sun. There are many harbor and surf beaches throughout Sydney, most of them accessible by bus *(see p231)*. Even if you're not a swimmer, the beaches offer a chance to get away from it all for a day or weekend and enjoy the fresh air and relaxed way of life.

Scuba diving at Gordons Bay

SWIMMING

YOU CAN SWIM at either harbor or ocean beaches. Harbor beaches are generally smaller and are sheltered and calm. Popular harbor beaches include Camp Cove, Shark Bay, and Balmoral Beach.

One of the most distinctive features of the ocean beaches is the surf lifesavers in their red and yellow caps. Surf lifesaving carnivals are held throughout the summer. Call **Surf Life Saving NSW** for a calendar of events.

Well-patroled, safer surf beaches include Bondi, Manly, and Coogee. Bondi is a great place for "people watching," as is its neighbor Tamarama, although the surf can be rough with a strong rip *(see p223)*.

SURFING

SURFING IS MORE a way of life than a leisure activity for some Sydneysiders. If you're a beginner, try Bondi, Bronte, Palm Beach, or Collaroy.

Two of the best surf beaches are Maroubra and Narrabeen. Bear in mind that local surfers know one another well and do not take kindly to "intruders" who drop in on their waves

or leave litter on their beaches. If you'd like to learn, local surf shops should be able to help. To rent a surfboard, try **Bondi Surf Co.** or **Aloha Surf**.

If you'd like to catch some of the action but stay dry, there are plenty of vantage points on the walk from Bondi Beach to Tamarama *(see pp144–5)*.

WINDSURFING AND SAILING

THERE ARE LOCATIONS around Sydney suitable for every level of windsurfer. Boards can be rented from **Balmoral Sailboard School**. Lessons are also available here.

Good spots include Palm Beach, Narrabeen Lakes, La Perouse, Brighton-Le-Sands, and Kurnell Point (for beginner and intermediate boarders), and Long Reef Beach, Palm Beach, and Collaroy (for the more experienced boarder).

One of the best ways to see the harbor is while sailing. A sailing boat, including skipper, can be rented for the afternoon from the **Australian Sailing School and Club**. If you'd like to learn how to sail, the **Sirsi Newport Marina** has two-day courses and also rents sail- and motor boats to experienced sailors.

SCUBA DIVING

THE GREAT BARRIER REEF it may not be, but there are some excellent dive spots around Sydney, especially in winter when the water is clear, if a little cold. Favorite spots are Shelly Beach, Gordons Bay, and Camp Cove.

Pro Dive Coogee offers a complete range of courses, escorted dives, introductory dives for beginners, and rental equipment. **Dive Centre Manly** also runs courses, rents equipment, and conducts boat dives seven days a week.

DIRECTORY

Aloha Surf
44 Pittwater Rd, Manly.
(9977 3777.

Australian Sailing School and Club
The Spit, Mosman. (9960 3077.

Balmoral Sailboard School
The Esplanade, Balmoral Beach.
(9960 5344.

Beach Watch Info Line
(9901 7996.

Bondi Surf Co.
Shop 2, 72–76 Campbell Pde,
Bondi Beach. (9365 0870.

Dive Centre Manly
10 Belgrave St, Manly.
(9977 4355.

Pro Dive Coogee
27 Alfreda St, Coogee.
(9665 6333.

Sirsi Newport Marina
122 Crescent Rd, Newport.
(9979 6213.

Surf Life Saving NSW
(9663 4298.

Rock baths and surf lifesaving club at Coogee Beach

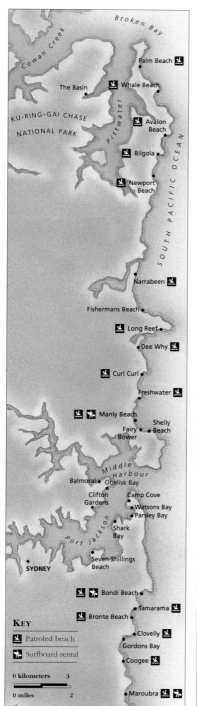

TOP 30 BEACHES

THE BEACHES shown here have been selected for their safe swimming, water sports, facilities available, or their picturesque setting.

	Swimming Pool	Surfing	Windsurfing	Fishing	Scuba Diving	Picnic/Barbecue	Restaurant/Café
Avalon	●			●		▦	
Balmoral	●		●	▦		▦	●
The Basin	●					▦	
Bilgola							
Bondi Beach	●	▦		▦	●	▦	●
Bronte		▦		▦	●	▦	●
Camp Cove					●		
Clifton Gardens	●		●	▦		▦	
Clovelly					●		
Coogee	●		●	▦	●	▦	●
Curl Curl	●	▦		▦			
Dee Why	●	▦		▦	●	▦	
Fairy Bower					●		
Fishermans Beach		▦	●	▦			
Freshwater	●	▦		▦			
Gordons Bay					●		
Long Reef		▦	●	▦	●		
Manly Beach	●	▦			●	▦	●
Maroubra		▦	●	▦		▦	
Narrabeen	●	▦		▦		▦	
Newport Beach	●	▦	●	▦		▦	
Obelisk Bay							
Palm Beach	●	▦	●	▦		▦	●
Parsley Bay							
Seven Shillings Beach	●						
Shark Bay	●					▦	
Shelly Beach					●	▦	●
Tamarama		▦	●	●		▦	●
Watsons Bay	●				●		●
Whale Beach	●	▦	●	▦		▦	

THE TYPES OF WAVES

Cresting waves can be identified by the foam that is created as they break from the top. These waves are ideal for board riding and body surfing.

Plunging waves curl into a tube before breaking close to the shore. Fondly known as "dumpers," these waves should be tackled only by experienced surfers.

Surging waves are those that don't appear to break. They often travel all the way into the beach before break-ing and can easily sweep a toddler or child off its feet.

Garden Island to Farm Cove

Waterlily in the Royal Botanic Gardens

SYDNEY'S VAST HARBOR, also named Port Jackson after a Secretary in the British Admiralty who promptly changed his name, is a drowned river valley that was transformed over millions of years. Its intricate coastal geography of headlands and secluded bays can sometimes confound even life-long residents. This waterway was the lifeblood of the early colony, with the maritime industry a vital source of wealth and supply. The legacies of alternate recessions and booms can be viewed along the shoreline: a representative story in a nation where an estimated 70 percent of the population cling to the coastal cities, especially along the eastern seaboard.

The city skyline is a result of random development. The 1960s indiscriminate destruction of architectural history was halted, and towers now stand amid Victorian buildings.

Two harbor beacons, known as "wedding cakes" because of their three tiers, are solar powered and equipped with a fail-safe back-up service. There are about 350 buoys and beacons now in operation.

The barracks for the naval garrison date from 1888.

Garden Island marks a 1940s construction project with nearly 30 acres reclaimed from the harbor.

Sailing on the harbor is a pastime not exclusively reserved for the rich and elite. Of the several hundred thousand pleasure boats registered, some are available to rent while others take out groups of inexperienced sailors.

Mrs. Macquaries Chair is a carved rock seat by Mrs. Macquaries Road (see p106). In the early days of the colony, this was the site of a fruit and vegetable garden that was farmed until 1805.

| 0 meters | 250 |
| 0 yards | 250 |

The Andrew (Boy) Charlton Pool
is a favorite swimming pool for inner-
city residents, and is named after the
Sydneysider who, at the age of 16, won
an Olympic gold medal in 1924. It was
erected in 1963 on the Domain Baths'
site, which had a grandstand for 1,700.

**Woolloomooloo Finger
Wharf** was a disembarka-
tion point when most
travelers arrived by sea.

LOCATOR MAP
See Street Finder, map 2

*Harry's Café de Wheels, a snack van,
has been a Sydney culinary institution
for more than 50 years. Photographs
of celebrity customers are pinned
to the van, attesting to its fame.*

The Royal Botanic Gardens
display a profusion of both
flowering and nonflowering
plants. Here the first trees were
planted by the newly arrived
European colonists; some of
these trees survive today.

Farm Cove has
long been a mooring
place for visiting naval
vessels. The land opposite,
now the Botanic Gardens,
has been continuously cultivated for over 200 years.

Sydney Cove to Walsh Bay

Conservatorium of Music

I**T IS ESTIMATED** that over 70 km (43 miles) of harbor shore have been lost as a result of the massive land reclamation projects carried out since the 1840s. That the 13 islands existing when the First Fleet arrived in 1788 have now been reduced to just eight is a startling indication of rapid and profound geographical transformation.

Detail from railing at Circular Quay

Redevelopments around the Circular Quay and Walsh Bay area from the 1980s have opened up the waterfront for public use and enjoyment, acknowledging that it is the city's greatest natural asset. Environmental and architectural aspirations for Sydney recognize the need to integrate city and harbor.

1857 Man O'War Steps

The Sydney Opera House *was designed to take advantage of its spectacular setting. The roofs shine during the day and seem to glow at night. The building can appear as a visionary landscape to the pedestrian onlooker.*

Government House, a Gothic Revival building, was home to the states' governors until 1996.

Harbor cruises *regularly depart from Circular Quay, taking visitors out and about both during the day and in the evening. They are an incomparable way to see the city and its waterways.*

The Sydney Harbour Bridge *was also known as the "Iron Lung" at the time of its construction. During the Great Depression it provided on-site work for approximately 1,400, while many more were employed in the special workshops.*

| 0 meters | 250 |
| 0 yards | 250 |

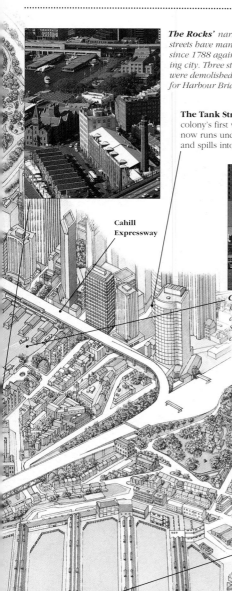

The Rocks' *narrow but stalwart streets have managed to hold out since 1788 against the encroaching city. Three streets, however, were demolished to make room for Harbour Bridge foundations.*

The Tank Stream, the colony's first water supply, now runs underground and spills into the quay.

LOCATOR MAP
See Street Finder, *maps 1 & 2*

Cahill Expressway

Circular Quay, *originally and more accurately known as Semi-Circular Quay, was the last and arguably greatest convict-built structure. Tank Stream mudflats were filled in to shape the quay, and sandstone from The Rocks formed the sea wall.*

The Wharf Theatre *resides on a pier that took six years to build, mostly due to the diversion of labor and materials during World War I. The theater was opened in 1984.*

The wharves were completed in 1922.

Imports and exports to and from the city were stored in these wharves until 1977.

The wharves' design *included a rat-proof sea wall around the port. This was an urgent response to the 1900 bubonic plague outbreak, attributed to rats on the wharves.*

SYDNEY AREA BY AREA

THE ROCKS AND CIRCULAR QUAY 62-77
CITY CENTER 78-89
DARLING HARBOUR 90-101
BOTANIC GARDENS
AND THE DOMAIN 102-115
KINGS CROSS AND DARLINGHURST 116-121
PADDINGTON 122-127
FARTHER AFIELD 128-139
FOUR GUIDED WALKS 140-149

THE ROCKS AND CIRCULAR QUAY

CIRCULAR QUAY, once known as Semi-Circular Quay, is often referred to as the "birthplace of Australia." It was here, in January 1788, that the First Fleet landed its human freight of convicts, soldiers, and officials, and the new British colony of New South Wales was declared. Sydney Cove became a rallying point whenever a ship arrived bringing much-needed supplies from "home." Crowds still gather here whenever there is something to celebrate. The Quay and The

Sculpture on the AMP Building, Circular Quay

Rocks are focal points for New Year's Eve revels, and Circular Quay drew huge crowds when, in 1994, Sydney was awarded the year 2000 Olympic Games. The Rocks area offers visitors a taste of Sydney's past, but it is a far cry from the time, less than 100 years ago, when most inhabitants lived in rat-infested slums and gangs ruled its streets. Now scrubbed and polished, The Rocks forms part of the colorful promenade from the Sydney Harbour Bridge to the spectacular Opera House.

SIGHTS AT A GLANCE

Historic Streets and Buildings
Campbell's Storehouses **1**
Cadman's Cottage **6**
Argyle Centre **8**
Sydney Observatory **10**
Hero of Waterloo **11**
Sydney Harbour Bridge pp70–71 **13**
Writers' Walk **15**
Customs House **17**
Macquarie Place **18**

Museums and Galleries
Centre for Contemporary Craft **2**
Merchants' House **3**
Susannah Place **4**
Sailors' Home **5**
Westpac Museum **7**
Justice and Police Museum **16**
Museum of Contemporary Art **19**
National Trust Centre **20**

Churches
Garrison Church **9**
St. Philip's Church **21**

Theatres and Concert Halls
Wharf Theatre **12**
Sydney Opera House pp74–7 **14**

GETTING THERE
Circular Quay is the best stop for ferries and trains. Sydney Explorer and bus routes 431, 432, 433, and 434 run regularly to The Rocks, while most buses through the city go to the Quay.

KEY

▦	Street-by-Street map *See pp64–5*
🚆	CityRail station
🚌	Bus terminal
⛴	Ferry boarding point
🚤	JetCat/RiverCat boarding point
P	Parking

◁ **The brilliant white walls of the Sailors' Home, close to the harbor waterfront in The Rocks**

Street-by-Street: The Rocks

Governor Arthur Phillip

NAMED FOR THE RUGGED CLIFFS that were once its dominant feature, this area has played a vital role in Sydney's development. In 1788, the First Fleeters under Governor Phillip's command erected makeshift buildings here, with the convicts' hard labor used to establish more permanent structures in the form of rough-hewn streets. The Argyle Cut, a road carved through solid rock using just hammer and chisel, took 18 years to build, beginning in 1843. By 1900, The Rocks was overrun with disease; the street now known as Suez Canal was once Sewer's Canal. Today, the area is still rich in colonial history and color.

Hero of Waterloo
Lying beneath this historic pub is a tunnel originally used for smuggling ⓫

★ Sydney Observatory
The first European structure on this prominent site was a windmill. The present museum holds some of the earliest astronomical instruments brought to Australia ❿

Garrison Church
Columns in this church are decorated with the insignia of British troops stationed here until 1870. Australia's first prime minister was educated next door ❾

Hero of Waterloo ↑

LOWER

WATSON ROAD

ARGYLE STREET

TRINITY AVENUE

UPPER FORT STREET

BRADFIELD HIGHWAY

CUMBERLAND STREET

GLOUCESTER

HARRINGTON STREET

ARGYLE STREET

PLACE

GEORGE STREET

Argyle Cut

Suez Canal

★ Museum of Contemporary Art
The stripped Classical façade belies the avant-garde nature of the Australian and international art displayed in an ever-changing program ⓳

Walkway along Circular Quay West waterfront

★ **Cadman's Cottage**
John Cadman, govern-
ment coxswain, resided
in what was known as
the Coxswain's Barracks
with his family. His wife
Elizabeth was also a sig-
nificant figure, believed
to be the first woman to
vote in New South Wales,
a right she insisted on ❻

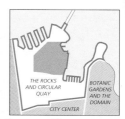

LOCATOR MAP
See Street Finder, *map 1*

Merchants' House
This Greek Revival building is the
only one of its kind left in The
Rocks. The rocking
kangaroo is housed in
its museum dedicated
to child-
hood ❸

The Rocks Market is a hive of
activity every weekend, offering
an eclectic range of craft items
and jewelry utilizing Australian
icons from gum leaves to koalas.

0 meters		100
0 yards		100

KEY

– – –   Suggested route

The Overseas
Passenger Terminal
is where some of the
world's luxury cruise
liners, including the
QEII, berth during
their stay in Sydney.

STAR SIGHTS

★ **Cadman's Cottage**

★ **Museum of**
Contemporary Art

★ **Sydney Observatory**

Campbell's Storehouses ❶

7–27 Circular Quay West, The Rocks.
Map 1 B2. 🚌 *Sydney Explorer, 431, 432, 433, 434.* 📷 ♿

IN 1839, the merchant Robert Campbell began constructing a private wharf and warehouses for the tea, sugar, spirits, and cloth he imported from India. Twelve sandstone bays had been built by 1861, and a brick upper story was added in about 1890. Part of the old sea wall and 11 of the original warehouses still remain.

Today the bond stores contain galleries and harborside restaurants catering to a range of tastes, from contemporary to Chinese and Italian. The pulleys that were used to raise cargo from the wharf can still be seen on the outside, near the top of the building.

Centre for Contemporary Craft ❷

Level 4, 88 George St, The Rocks.
Map 1 B2. 📞 9247 9126. 🚌 *431, 432, 433, 434.* 🕙 10am–5:30pm daily. ● *Dec 25–26.* 📷 ♿

THE HEADQUARTERS of the Centre for Contemporary Craft are housed in a fine late-Victorian Classical Revival

Exhibition poster from the Centre for Contemporary Craft

building from 1886. As well as administrative offices dealing with the more than 20,000 Centre for Contemporary Craft members, the building now contains a gallery called Craftspace and a retail outlet Designed and Made. Craftspace hosts regularly changing exhibitions of Australian professional crafts and design.

A broad spectrum of work is displayed, showing up-and-coming artisans, innovative forms, and techniques to the public. Many exhibitions offer work for sale. The shop Designed and Made sells superior craft and design objects that make unique gifts, as well as appealing to astute collectors.

Merchants' House ❸

43 George St, The Rocks. **Map** 1 B2. 📞 9241 5099. 🚌 *Sydney Explorer, 431, 432, 433, 434.* 🕙 10am–4pm Wed–Sun. ● *Dec 25.*

THE LAND on which this late-Georgian town house is built was originally owned by Robert Campbell of the nearby Campbell's Storehouses. He sold it to James Combes and John Martyn, painters, glaziers, and plumbers, in 1841.

In 1848, they commissioned architect John Bibb to design a Greek Revival sandstone, hardwood, and cedar house that would also be used as a warehouse. The building has been restored by the Sydney Cove Authority to the period of its original occupants (1850s). It is now run by the National Trust of Australia (NSW) as an historic house, children's museum, exhibition and function center, and shop. There are self-guided tours for adults and children – children simply follow a blue line linking relevant displays. The most popular exhibits with visitors of all ages, however, are the two rooms found on the entrance level. These contain the delightful Australian Childhood Collection of children's

Child's kangaroo teething ring, Merchants' House

Umbrellas shade the terrace restaurants overlooking the waterfront at Campbell's Storehouses

Old-style Australian products at the corner shop, Susannah Place

books, board games, toys, dolls, and more than 100 golliwogs. There is also a large folio of original artwork drawn from Australian children's literature.

Among the characters to be seen are the comic-strip street kid Ginger Meggs and some of his rascal friends, created in 1921 by Jimmy Bancks; Norman Lindsay's self-replenishing Magic Pudding; May Gibbs's cute gumnut babies Snugglepot and Cuddlepie, Bib and Bub, and the Banksia Men *(see pp132–3)*; and Felix the Cat, whose image has become the logo for the Merchants' House.

Billy Tea for sale at the Susannah Place shop

Susannah Place ❹

58–64 Gloucester St, The Rocks.
Map 1 B2. 9241 1893. *Sydney Explorer, 431, 432, 433, 434.* Jan: 10am–5pm daily; Feb–Dec: 10am–5pm Sat & Sun. Dec 25–26.

THIS 1844 TERRACE of four brick and sandstone houses has a rare history of continuous domestic occupancy from the 1840s right through to 1990. The museum now housed here examines this working-class domestic history, evoking the living conditions of its inhabi-

tants. Rather than recreating a single period, the museum retains the many renovations, however ramshackle, carried out by successive tenants.

Built for Edward and Mary Riley, who arrived from Ireland with their niece Susannah in 1838, these solid houses have basement kitchens and backyard outhouses. Connections to piped water and sewerage had probably arrived by the mid-1850s. The museum surveys the houses' development over the years, from wood and coal to gas and electricity, which enables the visitor to gauge the gradual lightening of the burden of domestic labor.

The terrace, including a corner grocer's shop, escaped the wholesale demolitions that occurred after the outbreak of bubonic plague in 1900, as well as later clearings of land to make way for the Sydney Harbour Bridge and the Cahill Expressway. In the 1970s, it was saved once again when the Builders Labourers' Federation, under the leadership of activist Jack Mundey, imposed a conservation "green ban" on The Rocks *(see p29)*, temporarily halting all demolition and redevelopment work.

Sailors' Home ❺

106 George St, The Rocks.
Map 1 B2. 9255 1788.
Sydney Explorer, 431, 432, 433, 434. 9am–5pm daily.

BUILT IN 1864 as lodgings for visiting sailors, the building now houses The Rocks Visitors Centre at street level, with exhibitions on the two upper levels. The L-shaped wing that fronts onto George Street was added in 1926.

At the time it was built, the Sailors' Home was a welcome alternative to the many seedy inns and brothels in the area, saving sailors from the perils of "crimping." "Crimps" would tempt newly arrived men into lodgings and bars providing much-sought-after entertainment. While drunk, the sailors would be sold onto departing ships, waking miles out at sea and returning home in debt.

Sailors used the home until 1980, when it was adapted for use as a puppet theater. In 1994, it opened as a heritage center and a tourist information and tour booking facility.

On the second level, a permanent exhibition outlines the archaeological, architectural and social heritage of The Rocks. The third level hosts temporary exhibitions that explore heritage issues. On the same level, at the eastern end, a recreation of a 19th-century sleeping cubicle gives visitors an impression of the spartan nature of the original sailors' accommodations.

Interior of the Sailors' Home, looking down to the shop

Façade of Cadman's Cottage, the oldest extant building in the city

Cadman's Cottage **6**

110 George St, The Rocks. **Map** 1 B2.
(9247 8861. **===** 431, 432, 433 434.
○ 10am–3pm Mon, 9am–4:30pm
Tue–Fri, 11am–4pm Sat & Sun.
● Good Fri, Dec 25.

DWARFED BY the adjacent
Sailors' Home, this simple
sandstone cottage now serves
as the city's information center
and shop for the New South
Wales National Parks & Wildlife Service. Built in 1816 as a
barracks for the crews of the
governor's boats, it is Sydney's
oldest surviving dwelling.
　The cottage is named after
John Cadman, a convict who
was transported in 1798 for
horse-theft. By 1813, he was
coxswain of a timber boat and
the following year received a
conditional pardon. In 1821,
he was appointed coxswain of
government craft and granted
a full pardon. Six years later,
he was made boat superinten-
dent and took up residence in
the four-room cottage that
now bears his name.
　Cadman married Elizabeth
Mortimer in 1830. She had also
arrived in Sydney as a convict,
sentenced to seven years transportation for the theft of one
hairbrush. The couple, along
with Elizabeth's two daughters,
lived in the cottage until 1846.
　When Cadman's Cottage was
built it stood on the foreshore
of Sydney Harbour. At high
tide, the water used to lap just
2.5 m (8 ft) from the door.

Now, as a result of successive
land reclamations such as the
filling-in of Circular Quay in
the 1870s, it is set well back
from the waterfront.

Westpac Museum **7**

6–8 Playfair St, The Rocks. **Map** 1 B2.
(9251 1419. **===** Sydney Explorer,
431, 432, 433, 434. **○** 1–4pm Mon,
10:30am–4pm Tue–Fri, 1–4pm Sat &
Sun. **●** Good Fri, Dec 25.

FROM 1817, WHEN the "holey"
dollar was in circulation and
Sydney's first bank opened, to
present-day plastic credit cards,
this museum traces the history
of banking in Australia.
　The exhibits include a Cobb
& Co. coach and a diorama of
the gold rush days, as well as
banking memorabilia. There
are also regular audiovisual
presentations and – perhaps
the highlight of the museum's
collection – a re-creation of a
working branch of the 1890s.

Argyle Centre **8**

18 Argyle St, The Rocks. **Map** 1 B2.
(9255 1788. **===** Sydney Explorer,
431, 432, 433, 434. **○** 9am–6pm
daily. **●** Good Fri, Dec 25. **◙ & ✔**

THE FORMER Argyle Bond
Stores consists of a number
of warehouses surrounding a
cobbled courtyard. They have
been converted into a retail
complex of mostly fashion and
accessories shops that retains
its period character and charm.
　Built between 1826 and the
early 1880s, the stores held
imported goods such as liquor.
All goods forfeited for the
non-payment of duties were
auctioned in the courtyard.
The oldest store was built for
Captain John Piper, but it was
confiscated and sold after his
arrest for embezzlement.

Argyle Centre from the courtyard

Garrison Church **9**

Cnr Argyle and Lower Fort Sts, Millers
Point. **Map** 1 A2. **(** 9247 2664.
=== 431, 433. **○** 8am–6pm daily.
◙ & ✔

OFFICIALLY NAMED the Holy
Trinity Church, this was
dubbed the Garrison Church
because it was the colony's
first military church. Officers
and men from various British

Bank of New South Wales one pound note from around 1830

regiments, stationed at Dawes Point fort, attended morning prayers here until 1870.

Henry Ginn designed the church, and the foundation stone was laid in 1840. In 1855, the architect Edmund Blacket was engaged to enlarge the church to accommodate up to 600 people. These extensions, minus the spire that Blacket proposed, were completed in 1878. Regimental plaques hanging along interior walls recall the church's military associations.

Other features to look out for are the brilliantly colored east window and the carved red cedar pulpit. The window was donated by the devout parishioner, Dr. James Mitchell, father of David Scott Mitchell, the principal benefactor of the State Library of New South Wales' Mitchell Library wing *(see p112)*.

East window, Garrison Church

Sydney Observatory ❿

Watson Rd, Observatory Hill, The Rocks. **Map** 1 A2. 🅒 9217 0485. 🚌 *Sydney Explorer, 431, 432, 433, 434.* 🅞 *2–5pm Mon–Fri, 10am–5pm Sat & Sun.* **Night viewings** 🅞 *Thu–Tue (nightly during school vacations).* ● *Good Fri, Dec 25.* 🅞 🅑 🅕

THIS DOMED BUILDING, which had been a center for astronomical observation and research for almost 125 years, became the city's astronomy museum in 1982. It has interactive equipment and games, along with night sky viewings; it is essential to book for these.

The building began life in the 1850s as a time-ball tower. At 1pm daily, the ball on top of the tower dropped to signal the correct time. Simultaneously at Fort Denison, a cannon was fired. This custom continues today *(see p107)*.

In the 1880s, some of the first astronomical photographs of the southern sky were taken here. From 1890–1962, the observatory mapped 750,000 stars as part of an international project that produced an atlas of the entire night sky.

Hero of Waterloo ⓫

81 Lower Fort St, Millers Point. **Map** 1 A2. 🅒 9252 4553. 🚌 *431, 432, 433, 434.* 🅞 *10am–11pm Mon–Sat, 10am–10pm Sun.* ● *Dec 25–26.* 🅞 🅑

THIS PICTURESQUE old inn is especially welcoming in the winter, when its log fires and cosy ambience offer respite from the chill outside. Built in 1844 from sandstone excavated from the Argyle Cut, this was a favorite drinking place for the nearby garrison's soldiers. Unscrupulous sea captains were said to use the hotel to recruit. Patrons who drank themselves into a stupor were pushed into the cellars through a trapdoor. From here they were carried along underground tunnels to the wharves close by and then onto waiting ships.

Wharf Theatre ⓬

Pier 4, Hickson Rd, Millers Point. **Map** 1 A1. 🅒 9250 1700. 🚌 *431, 432, 433, 434.* **Box office** 🅞 *10am–8:30pm Mon–Sat;* **Wharf** 🅞 *9am–11pm Mon–Sat.* 🅞 🅑 *See* **Entertainment** *p210.*

THE THEN RECENTLY formed Sydney Theatre Company took possession of this early 20th-century finger wharf at Walsh Bay in 1984. Pier 4/5 is

The corner façade of the Hero of Waterloo hotel in Millers Point

one of four finger wharves at Walsh Bay, reminders of the time when this was a busy part of the city's maritime industry.

Pier 4/5 fulfilled the Sydney Theatre Company's need for a base large enough to hold theaters, rehearsal rooms, and administration offices. The ingenious conversion of the once-derelict heritage building into a modern theater complex is recognized as an outstanding architectural achievement.

Since then, the main theater, a small and intimate space, has been a venue for many of the company's productions. It has seen premieres of plays from leading Australian playwrights such as Michael Gow and David Williamson, as well as performances of new works from overseas and plays from the standard repertoire.

At the tip of the wharf, the bar area and Wharf Restaurant *(see p189)* command superb harbor views across to the Harbour Bridge *(see pp70–71)*.

The Wharf Theatre, a former finger wharf, jutting on to Walsh Bay

Sydney Harbour Bridge ⓭

Ceremonial scissors

COMPLETED IN 1932, the construction of the Sydney Harbour Bridge was an economic feat, given the depressed times, as well as an engineering triumph. Prior to this, the only links between the city center on the south side of the harbor and the residential north side were by ferry or a circuitous 20-km (12½-mile) road route that involved five bridge crossings. The single-span arch bridge, colloquially known as the "Coathanger," took eight years to build, including the railroad line. The bridge was manufactured in sections on the site of the future Luna Park *(see p132)*. Loans for the total cost of approximately 6.25 million Australian pounds were eventually paid off in 1988.

The 1932 Opening
The ceremony was disrupted when zealous royalist Francis de Groot rode forward and cut the ribbon, in honor, he claimed, of King and Empire.

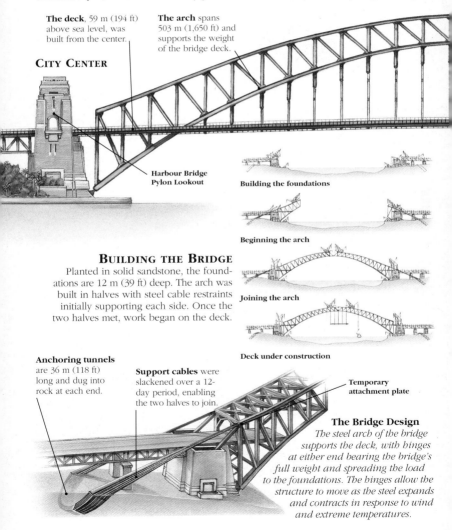

The deck, 59 m (194 ft) above sea level, was built from the center.

The arch spans 503 m (1,650 ft) and supports the weight of the bridge deck.

CITY CENTER

Harbour Bridge Pylon Lookout

Building the foundations

Beginning the arch

BUILDING THE BRIDGE
Planted in solid sandstone, the foundations are 12 m (39 ft) deep. The arch was built in halves with steel cable restraints initially supporting each side. Once the two halves met, work began on the deck.

Joining the arch

Deck under construction

Anchoring tunnels are 36 m (118 ft) long and dug into rock at each end.

Support cables were slackened over a 12-day period, enabling the two halves to join.

Temporary attachment plate

The Bridge Design
The steel arch of the bridge supports the deck, with hinges at either end bearing the bridge's full weight and spreading the load to the foundations. The hinges allow the structure to move as the steel expands and contracts in response to wind and extreme temperatures.

The Bridge in Curve *(1930)*
The bridge has inspired many artists. The huge structure towers over the nearby houses in this work by Grace Cossington Smith.

VISITORS' CHECKLIST

Map 1 B1. 9247 3408.
All routes to The Rocks.
Circular Quay. Circular
Quay, Milsons Point.
Harbour Bridge Pylon Lookout
10am–5pm daily. Dec 25.

Over 150,000 vehicles cross the bridge each day, about 15 times as many as in 1932.

Bridge Workers
The bridge was built by 1,400 workers, 16 of whom were killed in accidents during construction.

NORTH SHORE

Maintenance
Painting the bridge has become a metaphor for an endless task. Approximately 30,000 liters (7,925 gal) of paint are required for each coat, enough to cover an area equivalent to 60 football fields.

The vertical hangers support the slanting crossbeams that, in turn, carry the deck.

FATHER OF THE BRIDGE
Chief engineer Dr. John Bradfield shakes the hand of the engineer of the first train to cross the bridge. Over a 20-year period, Bradfield supervised all aspects of the bridge's design and construction. At the opening ceremony, the highway linking the harbor's south side and northern suburbs was named in his honor.

Paying the Toll
The initial toll of sixpence helped pay off the construction loan. The toll is now used for maintenance and to pay for the 1992 Sydney Harbour Tunnel.

Strolling along a section of the Writers' Walk at Circular Quay

Sydney Opera House 🄑

See pp74–7.

Writers' Walk 🄒

Circular Quay. **Map** 1 C2.
Circular Quay routes.

THIS SERIES OF PLAQUES is set in the pavement at regular intervals between East and West Circular Quay. It gives the visitor the chance to ponder the observations of famous Australian writers, both past and present, on their home country, as well as the musings of some noted literary visitors.

Each plaque is dedicated to a particular writer, with a quotation and a brief biographical note. Australian writers include novelists Miles Franklin and Peter Carey, poets Oodgeroo Noonuccal and Judith Wright, humorists Barry Humphries and Clive James, and the influential feminist writer Germaine Greer. Among visiting writers are Charles Darwin, Joseph Conrad, and Mark Twain.

Justice and Police Museum 🄖

8 Phillip St. **Map** 1 C3. 9252 1144.
Circular Quay routes. Jan: 10am–5pm Sun–Thu; Feb–Dec: 10am–5pm Sun. Dec 25.

THE BUILDINGS housing the museum were originally the Water Police Court, designed by Edmund Blacket in 1856; Water Police Station, designed

by Alexander Dawson in 1858; and Police Court designed by James Barnet in 1885. Here the rough-and-tumble underworld of waterfront crime, from the petty to the violent, was dealt swift and, at times, harsh justice. The museum exhibits bear vivid testimony to that turbulent period, as they document and recreate legal and criminal history. The formality of late-Victorian legal proceedings can be easily imagined in the fully restored courtroom.

Detail from Customs House

Menacing implements from brass knuckles to bludgeons are displayed as the macabre relics of violent and notorious crimes. Other aspects of policing and the justice system are highlighted in special exhibitions that change regularly.

The charge room, austere remand cell, prison uniforms, prison artifacts, and slideshow evoke powerful images of the penal code of the time.

Montage of criminal mug shots, Justice and Police Museum

Customs House 🄘

Alfred St, Circular Quay. **Map** 1 B3.
9247 2285. Circular Quay routes. to re-open December 1997.

COLONIAL ARCHITECT James Barnet designed this 1885 sandstone Classical Revival building on the same site as a previous Customs House. It recalls the days when trading ships berthed at the docks to load and unload their goods.

The building stands near the mouth of Tank Stream, the fledgling colony's fresh water supply. Among its many fine features are veranda columns in polished granite, a finely sculpted coat of arms, and an elaborate clock face, added in 1897, featuring a pair of tridents and dolphins. The stern face of Queen Victoria can be seen above the entrance doorway. The building is being refurbished as a cultural center that is due to open early in December 1997.

Macquarie Place 🄙

Map 1 B3. Circular Quay routes.

IN 1810 GOVERNOR Lachlan Macquarie created this park on what was once part of the vegetable garden of the first Government House. The sandstone obelisk, designed by convict architect Francis Greenway *(see p114)*, was erected in 1818 to mark the starting point for all roads in the colony. The gas lamps recall the fact that this was also the site of Sydney's first street lamp, installed in 1826.

Also in this little triangle of history are the remains of the bow anchor and cannon from HMS *Sirius*, flagship of the First Fleet. There is also a statue of Thomas Mort, a 19th-century industrialist whose vast business interests embraced gold, coal and copper mining, dairy and cotton farming, wool auctioning, and ship repair. These days his statue is a gathering place for the city's somewhat kamikaze bicycle couriers.

Façade of the Museum of Contemporary Art

Museum of Contemporary Art ⑲

Circular Quay West, The Rocks.
Map 1 B2. ⟦ 9252 4033. 🚌 *Sydney Explorer, 431, 432, 433 434.* ◯ *11am– 6pm daily.* ● *Dec 25.* 🎦 📷 ♿ ✓

SYDNEY'S SUBSTANTIAL collection of contemporary art has grown steadily, but largely out of public view, since 1943. This was the year John Power died, leaving his art collection and a financial bequest to the University of Sydney.

In 1991 the collection, which by then included works by Hockney, Warhol, Christo, and Lichtenstein, was transferred to this 1950s mock Art Deco former Maritime Services Board Building at Circular Quay West. As well as showing selections from its permanent collection, the museum hosts exhibitions by local and overseas artists. At the front of the building the MCA Café *(see p194)* spills out onto a terrace with superb views across to Sydney Opera House. The MCA Shop, in George Street, sells distinctive gifts by Australian designers.

National Trust Centre ⑳

Observatory Hill, Watson Rd, The Rocks.
Map 1 A3. ⟦ 9258 0123. 🚌 *Sydney Explorer, 343, 431, 432, 433, 434.*
◯ *9am–5pm Mon–Fri.* **Gallery**
◯ *11am–5pm Tue–Fri, noon–5pm Sat & Sun.* ● *public hols.* ♿

THE BUILDINGS that form the headquarters of conservation organization the National Trust of Australia date from 1815, when Macquarie chose the site on Observatory Hill for a military hospital.

Today they house tea rooms, a National Trust shop, and the SH Ervin Gallery, containing works by prominent 19th- and 20th-century Australian artists such as Thea Proctor, Margaret Preston, and Conrad Martens.

St. Philip's Church ㉑

3 York St. **Map** 1 A3. ⟦ 9247 1071. 🚌 *George St routes.* ◯ *9am–5pm Mon–Fri (apply at office).* ● *Jan 26, Apr 25.* 📷 ✓

DESPITE ITS ELEVATED SITE, this Victorian Gothic church seems overshadowed in its moden setting. Yet, when it was first built, the tall square tower with its decorative pinnacles was a local landmark.

Begun in 1848, St. Philip's is by Edmund Blacket, dubbed "the Christopher Wren of Australia" for the 58 churches he designed. In 1851, work was disrupted when its stonemasons left for the gold fields, but by 1856 the building was finally completed.

A peal of bells was donated in 1858, with another added in 1888 to mark Sydney's centenary. These bells still announce the services each Sunday.

The interior and pipe organ of St. Philip's Anglican church

The Founding of Australia* by Algernon Talmage, which hangs in Parliament House *(see pp112–13)

A FLAGPOLE ON THE MUDFLATS

It is easy to miss the modest flagpole in Loftus Street near Customs House. It flies a flag, the Union Jack, on the spot where Australia's first ceremonial flag-raising took place. On January 26, 1788, Captain Arthur Phillip came ashore to hoist the flag and declare the foundation of the colony. A toast to the King was drunk and a musket volley fired. On the same day, the rest of the First Fleet arrived from Botany Bay to join Phillip and his men. (On this date each year, the country marks Australia Day with a national holiday.) In 1788, the flagpole was on the edge of mudflats on Sydney Cove. Today, because of the large amount of land reclaimed to build Circular Quay, it is some distance from the water's edge.

Sydney Opera House ⑭

Advertising poster

No building on earth looks like the Sydney Opera House. Popularly known as the "Opera House" long before the building was complete, it is, in fact, a complex of theaters and halls linked beneath its famous shells. Its birth was long and complicated. Many of the construction problems had not been faced before, resulting in an architectural adventure that lasted 14 years *(see p77)*. An appeal fund was set up, eventually raising A$900,000, while the Opera House Lottery raised the balance of the A$102 million final cost. As well as being the city's most popular tourist attraction, the Sydney Opera House is also one of the world's busiest performing arts centers.

★ Opera Theatre
Mainly used for opera and ballet, this 1,547-seat theater is big enough to stage grand operas such as Verdi's Aida*.*

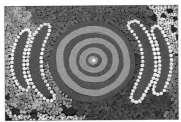

Detail of The Possum Dreaming *(1988)*
The mural in the Opera Theatre foyer is by Michael Nelson Tjakamarra, an artist from the central Australian desert.

The Opera Theatre
ceiling and walls are painted black to focus attention on the stage.

Opera House Walkway
Extensive public walkways around the building offer the visitor views from many different vantage points.

Northern Foyers
With spectacular views of the harbor, the Reception Hall and the large northern foyers of the Opera Theatre and Concert Hall can be rented for conferences, lunches, parties, and weddings.

Star Features
★ The Roofs
★ Concert Hall
★ Opera Theatre

★ Concert Hall
This is the largest hall, with seating for 2,690. It is used for symphony, choral, jazz, folk, and pop concerts, chamber music, opera, dance, and everything from body building to fashion shows.

VISITORS' CHECKLIST

Bennelong Point. **Map** 1 C2.
🎫 9250 7111. **Box office** 9250 7777. 🚌 Sydney Explorer, 324, 438, 440. 🚢 Circular Quay. 🚆 Circular Quay. 🕐 9am–8:30pm Mon–Sat, for tours and 2 hrs prior to 1st performance Sun. ⬤ Good Fri, Dec 25. 📷 ♿ limited. 🎧 9am–4pm. Check in advance (9250 7520). 🍴 🛍 🛗

The Monumental Steps
and forecourt are used for outdoor films and free entertainment.

Bennelong Restaurant
This dramatic and elegant venue is one of the finest restaurants in Sydney (see p188).

The Playhouse, seating almost 400, is ideal for intimate productions while also able to present plays with larger casts.

★ The Roofs
Although apocryphal, the theory that Jørn Utzon's arched roof design came to him while peeling an orange is appealing. The highest point is 67 m (221 ft) above sea level.

Curtain of the Moon *(1972)*
Designed by John Coburn, this and its fellow Curtain of the Sun were originally used in the Drama and Opera Theatres. Both have been removed for preservation, but they will eventually be put back on display.

Exploring Sydney Opera House

THE SYDNEY OPERA HOUSE covers almost 4.5 acres, and is the fourth building to stand on this prominent site. Underneath the ten spectacular roofs of varying planes and textures lies a complex maze of more than 1,000 rooms, some oddly shaped to fit into niches and nooks created by the angular exterior. The power supply alone could easily support a town of 25,000 people.

Coppelia in the Opera Theatre

OPERA THEATRE

THE RELATIVELY compact size of this venue is a bonus for patrons who savor intimacy. Stage designers continue to demonstrate the Opera Theatre's versatility for both opera and dance. The proscenium opening is 12 m (39 ft) wide, and the stage extends back 25 m (82 ft), while the pit accommodates 75 musicians. Box C regularly plays host to a resident ghost, an opera and dance aficionado.

CONCERT HALL

THE RICH concert acoustics under the vaulted ceiling of this venue are much admired. Sumptuous Australian wood paneling and the 18 acoustic rings above the stage clearly reflect back the sound. The 10,500 pipe Grand Organ was designed and built by Ronald Sharp from 1969–79.

DRAMA THEATRE AND PLAYHOUSE

THE DRAMA THEATRE was not in the original building plan, so jackhammers were brought in to hack it out of the concrete. Its stage is 15 m

Sydney Dance Company poster

(160 ft) square, and can be clearly viewed from every seat in the auditorium. Refrigerated aluminum panels in the ceiling control the temperature.

Fine Australian art hangs in the Playhouse foyer, notably Sidney Nolan's eye-catching *Little Shark* (1973) and a fresco by Salvatore Zofrea (1992–3), inspired by the play *Summer of the Seventeenth Doll.*

BACKSTAGE

ARTISTS PERFORMING at the Opera House have the use of five rehearsal studios, 60 dressing rooms and suites, and a green room complete with restaurant, bar, and lounge.

The scene-changing machinery works on very well-oiled wheels, most crucial in the Opera Theatre where there is regularly a nightly change of performance, with an average of 16 operas being performed in repertoire each year.

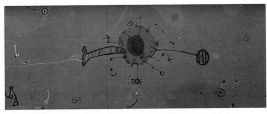

John Olsen's *Salute to Five Bells* (1973) in the Concert Hall foyer

TIMELINE

1945	1950	1955	1960	1965	1970

1955 International design competition announced

1948 Sir Eugene Goossens lobbies government and Bennelong Point is chosen as opera house site

1957 Utzon's design wins and a lottery is established to finance the building

1963 Building of roof shells begins

Roof in mid-construction

1973 Opera House officially opened by Queen Elizabeth II

Old trolley shed at Bennelong Point

1959 Construction begins

1963 Utzon opens Sydney office

1966 Utzon resigns. Australian architects appointed to complete interior design

1967 Concrete roof shells completed

1973 Prokofiev's opera *War and Peace* is the first public performance in Opera House

The Design of the Opera House

Jørn Utzon

IN 1957, JØRN UTZON won the international competition to design the Sydney Opera House. He envisaged a living sculpture that could be viewed from any angle – land, air, or sea – with the roofs as a "fifth façade." It was boldly conceived, posing architectural and engineering problems that Utzon's initial compendium of sketches did not begin to solve. When construction began in 1959, the intricate design proved impossible to execute and had to be greatly modified. The project remained so controversial that Utzon resigned in 1966, and an Australian design team completed the building's interior. Over the years, the Opera House has been variously described as "one of the modern wonders of the world" and "a ruck of nuns."

The Red Book, *as submitted for the 1957 design competition, contains Utzon's original concept sketches for the Sydney Opera House.*

Segmented globe

Segments separated

Roof comes into view

Several pieces *cut out of a globe were used in an ingenious manner by architect Jørn Utzon to make up the now familiar shell roof structure.*

UTZON'S OPERA HOUSE MODEL

Shell membrane roof

The northern foyers overlook Sydney Harbour.

Utzon visualized a building that "floated" on water.

The construction materials remain clearly exposed.

Stepped base

Utzon's original interiors *and many of his design features now exist only in model form. The architect donated his models and plans to the State Library of NSW (see p112).*

The pre-cast roof *has its inspiration in nature. The basic idea for the formwork of the roof was taken from the fanlike ribs of a palm. Realizing this deceptively simple idea took Utzon six years of design work.*

The roof tiles *were not fixed in place individually, but installed in panels to create the smooth and continuous roof surface.*

THE ARCHIBALD MEMORIAL FOUNTAIN

CITY CENTER

AUSTRALIA'S first thorough-fare, George Street, was originally lined with clusters of mud and wattle huts. The gold rushes brought bustling prosperity, and by the 1880s shops and the architecturally majestic edifices of banks dominated the area. The city's first skyscraper – Culwulla Chambers in Castlereagh Street – was completed in 1913, but the city council then imposed a 46-m (150-ft) height restriction that remained in place until 1956. Hyde Park, on the edge of the city center, was first used as a race-

Mosaic floor detail, St. Mary's Cathedral

course, attracting illegal betting and gambling taverns to Elizabeth Street. The park went on to host other amusements: wrestling matches, circuses, public hangings and, from 1804 onward, cricket matches between the army and the town. Today the park provides a surprisingly peaceful oasis, while the city's commercial center is an area of glamorous boutiques, department stores, extravagant arcades, and malls. There is excellent shopping and browsing for all budgets, with plenty of diversions to occupy the casual visitor.

SIGHTS AT A GLANCE

Historic Streets and Buildings
Marble Bar ❶
Queen Victoria Building ❷
Strand Arcade ❺
Martin Place ❻
Lands Department Building ❼
Sydney Town Hall ⓬

Museums and Galleries
Museum of Sydney ❽
Australian Museum
pp88–9 ⓮

Landmarks
Sydney Tower
p83 ❹

Cathedrals and Synagogues
St. Mary's Cathedral ❾
Great Synagogue ⓫
St. Andrew's Cathedral ⓭

Parks and Gardens
Hyde Park ❿

Theatres
State Theatre ❸

GETTING THERE
Town Hall, Wynyard, Martin Place, St. James and Museum railroad stations serve the area. There are frequent buses, particularly along Elizabeth and George Streets. Monorail stops are at City Center, Park Plaza, and World Square.

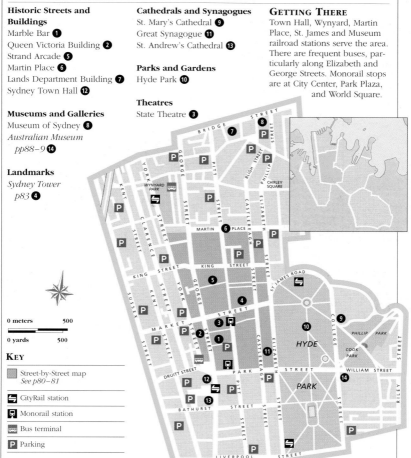

KEY

▨	Street-by-Street map *See p80–81*
🚇	CityRail station
Ⓜ	Monorail station
🚌	Bus terminal
Ⓟ	Parking

◁ **Mythological figures in the Archibald Fountain, Hyde Park**

Street-by-Street: City Center

Sculpture outside the MLC Centre

Aᴌᴛʜᴏᴜɢʜ ᴄʟᴏsᴇʟʏ ʀɪᴠᴀʟᴇᴅ by Melbourne, this is the business and commercial capital of Australia. Vibrant by day, at night the streets are far less busy when office workers and shoppers have gone home. The comparatively small city center of this sprawling metropolis seems to be almost jammed into a few city blocks. Because Sydney grew in such a haphazard fashion, with many of today's streets following tracks from the harbor originally made by bullocks, there was no allowance for the expansion of the burgeoning city into what has become a major international center. A colorful night scene of cafés, restaurants, and theaters is emerging, however, as more people return to the city center to live.

★ **Queen Victoria Building**
Taking up an entire city block, this 1898 former produce market has been lovingly restored and is now a shopping mall ❷

State Theatre
A gem from the era when the movies reigned, this richly decorated 1929 movie house was once hailed as "the Empire's greatest theater" ❸

To Sydney Town Hall

The Queen Victoria Statue was found after a worldwide search in 1983 ended in a small Irish village. It had lain forgotten and neglected since being removed from the front of the Irish Parliament in 1947.

STAR SIGHTS

★ **Queen Victoria Building**

★ **Sydney Tower**

★ **Martin Place**

0 meters	100
0 yards	100

KEY

– – – – Suggested route

Marble Bar
Once a landmark bar in the 1890 Tattersalls hotel, it was dismantled and reerected in the Sydney Hilton in 1973 ❶

Strand Arcade

A reminder of the late 19th century Victorian era when Sydney was famed as a city of elegant shopping arcades, this faithfully restored example is said to have been the finest of them all **5**

LOCATOR MAP
See Street Finder, *maps 1 & 4*

MLC Centre
(see p39)

★ Martin Place
Martin Place's 1929 Art Deco Cenotaph is the site of annual Anzac Day war remembrance services **6**

Theatre Royal

Skygarden is one of the city's newer arcades. It features elegant shops and boutiques with designer labels and a popular food court on the top level.

Hyde Park's northern end

★ Sydney Tower
The tower tops the city skyline, giving a bird's eye view of the whole of Sydney. It rises 305 m (1,000 ft) above the ground and can be seen from as far away as the Blue Mountains **4**

Entrance to the Marble Bar

The Marble Bar ❶

259 Pitt St. **Map** 1 B5. 🚈 *George St routes.* ⏰ *noon–11pm Mon–Wed, noon–midnight Thu, noon–2am Fri, 3pm–3am Sat.* ● *public hols.* 📷 *See Restaurants, Cafés and Pubs p197.*

THE MARBLE BAR, originally part of George Adams' Tattersalls Hotel built in 1893, is an inspired link with the Sydney of an earlier era. The bar, whose rich and decadent Italian Renaissance style had made it a local institution, was dismantled before the demolition of the hotel in 1969. Its colonnade entrance, fireplaces, and counters were reerected in the Sydney Hilton basement and reopened in 1973.

During the week, the bar attracts a broad range of city workers for lunch and after-work drinks. Toward the end of the week and on weekends, the atmosphere changes. If a band is playing, the bar bustles with a younger crowd who come to hear the mostly jazz and rhythm and blues music.

Queen Victoria Building ❷

George St. **Map** 1 B5. 📞 *9264 9209.* 🚈 *George St routes.* ⏰ *9am–6pm Mon–Wed, 9am–9pm Thu, 9am–6pm Fri & Sat, 11am–5pm Sun; 11am–5pm public hols.* 📷 ♿ *See Shops and Markets pp198 and 200.*

FRENCH DESIGNER Pierre Cardin called the Queen Victoria Building "the most beautiful shopping center in the world". Yet this spacious and ornate Romanesque building, better known as the QVB, began life as the Sydney produce market. The dust, flies, grime, and shouts, as horses struggled with their heavy loads on the slippery ramps, are now difficult to imagine. Completed to the design of City Architect George

Roof detail, Queen Victoria Building

McRae in 1898, the dominant features are the central dome, sheathed in copper (as are the 20 smaller domes) and the glass barrel-vault roof that lets in a flood of natural light.

The market closed at the end of World War I, and the building fell into disrepair. It had various roles during this time, including that of City Library. By the 1950s, after extensive remodeling and neglect, it was threatened with demolition.

Refurbished at a cost of over $75 million, the QVB reopened in 1986 as today's grand shopping gallery, housing over 190 shops and boutiques on four levels. At the Town Hall end a wishing well incorporates a

stone from Blarney Castle, Ireland, and a sculpture of Islay, beloved dog of Queen Victoria. In 1983, a worldwide search began for a statue of the queen herself. One was finally found in the village of Daingean, Republic of Ireland, where it had lain forgotten since its removal from the front of the Irish Parliament in 1947.

Now fully restored, the Queen Victoria Statue stands near the wishing well. Inside the QVB, suspended from the ceiling, is the Royal Clock. Weighing more than 1 ton and over 5 m (17 ft) tall, the clock was designed by Neil Glasser in 1982. The upper structure features part of Balmoral Castle above a copy of the four dials of Big Ben. At one minute to every hour, a fanfare is played, and there follows a parade depicting six scenes from the lives of various kings and queens of England.

State Theatre ❸

49 Market St. **Map** 1 B5. 📞 *9320 9050.* **Tours** *9231 4629.* 🚈 *George St routes.* **Box office** ⏰ *9am–6pm Mon–Sat.* ● *Good Friday, Dec 25.* ♿ 🎦 *9am–5pm Mon–Fri, bookings necessary.*

WHEN IT OPENED in 1929, this movie palace was hailed as the finest that local craftsmanship could achieve. The State Theatre is one of the best examples in Australia of the architectural fantasies used to entice people to the movies.

Its Cinema Baroque style is evident right from the Gothic foyer, with its vaulted ceiling, mosaic floor, richly decorated marble columns and statues. Inside the brass and bronze doors, the auditorium that seats over 2,000 people is lit by a 20,000-piece chandelier. The Wurlitzer organ rises from below stage just before performances. Now one of Sydney's premier concert, live theater, and special events venues, it is also the main base for the Sydney Film Festival, held in June of each year *(see p51).*

The ornately decorated Gothic foyer of the State Theatre

Sydney Tower ❹

The tallest public building in the Southern Hemisphere, Sydney Tower was conceived as part of the 1970s Centrepoint shopping center, but was not completed until 1981. More than a million people visit the turret each year to appreciate stunning 360-degree views, often stretching over 85 km (53 miles), and its intriguing bird's-eye perspective of familiar Sydney landmarks. A landmark in itself, it can be seen from almost anywhere in the city, and far beyond.

VISITORS' CHECKLIST

100 Market St. **Map** 1 B5.
9229 7430. Sydney Explorer, all city routes. Darling Harbour. St James, Town Hall. City Centre. 9:30am–9:30pm Mon–Fri & Sun, 9:30am–11:30pm Sat. **Last adm:** 15 mins before closing. Dec 25.

Observation Level
Views from Level 4 stretch to Pittwater in the north, Botany Bay to the south, westward to the Blue Mountains, and along the harbor out to the open sea.

The 30-m (98-ft) spire completes the total 305 m (1,000 ft) of the tower's height.

The water tank holds 162,000 liters (42,796 gallons) and acts as an enormous stabilizer on very windy days.

Level 4: Observation
Level 3: Coffee shop
Level 2: Buffet restaurant
Level 1: Dining room

The turret's nine levels, with room to hold almost 1,000 people at a time, include two revolving restaurants, a coffee shop, and the Observation Level.

The windows comprise three layers. The outer has a coating of gold dust. The frame design prevents panes falling outward.

The 56 cables weigh 7.7 tons each. If laid end to end, they would reach from New Zealand to Sydney.

The shaft is designed to withstand wind speeds expected only once in 500 years, as well as unprecedented earthquakes.

The stairs are two separate, fireproofed emergency escape routes. Each year in September or October Sydney's fittest race up the 1,474 stairs.

Construction of Turret
The eight turret levels were erected on the roof of the base building, then hoisted up the shaft using hydraulic jacks.

Double-decker elevators can carry up to 2,000 people per hour. At full speed, a lift takes only 40 seconds to ascend the 76 floors to the observation level.

New Year's Eve
Every year, fireworks are set off on top of Sydney Tower as part of the official public fireworks displays to mark the New Year.

Strand Arcade ❺

412–414 George St. **Map** 1 B5.
📞 9232 4199. 🚍 George St routes.
🕐 9:30am–5:30pm Mon–Wed,
9:30am–9pm Thu & Fri, 9:30am–
4pm Sat, 11am–4pm Sun. ● most
public hols. 📷 ♿ See **Shops and
Markets** pp198–201.

Vᴵᶜᵀᴼᴿᴵᴬᴺ ꜱʏᴅᴺᴇʏ was a city
of grand shopping arcades.
The Strand, joining George and
Pitt Streets and designed by
English architect John Spencer,
was the finest jewel in the city's
crown. The blaze of publicity
surrounding its opening in
April 1892 was equaled only
by the natural light pouring
through the glass roof and the
artificial glare from the chandeliers, each carrying 50 jets
of gas as well as 50 lamps.

The boutiques and shops in
the galleries make window
shopping a delight in this airy
building, which was restored
to its original splendor after a
fire in 1976. Be sure to stop,
as shoppers have done since
opening day, for light refreshments at Harris Coffee & Tea
near the Pitt Street entrance.

**The Pitt Street entrance to the
majestic Strand Arcade**

Martin Place ❻

Map 1 B4. 🚍 George St & Elizabeth
St routes.

Rᴜɴɴɪɴɢ ꜰʀᴏᴍ George Street
across Pitt, Castlereagh, and
Elizabeth Streets to Macquarie
Street, this plaza was opened
in 1891 and made a traffic-free
area in 1971. It is busiest at
lunchtime, when city workers
enjoy their sandwiches while
watching free entertainment

Interior of National Australia Bank, George Street end of Martin Place

sponsored by the Sydney City
Council, in an amphitheater
near Castlereagh Street.

Every Anzac Day, a national
day of war remembrance on
April 25, the focus moves to
the Cenotaph at the George
Street end. Thousands of past
and present servicemen and
women attend a dawn service
and wreath-laying ceremony,
followed by a parade. The
shrine, with bronze statues of a
soldier and a sailor on a granite
base, by Bertram MacKennal,
was unveiled in 1929.

On the southern side of the
Cenotaph is the symmetrical
façade of the Renaissance-
style General Post Office,
considered to be the finest
building by James Barnet,
Colonial Architect. Con-
struction of the GPO, as
Sydneysiders call it, took
place between 1866 and
1874, with additions in
Pitt Street between 1881
and 1885. Most contro-
versial were the relief
figures executed by
Tomaso Sani. Although   **Statue of explorer**
Barnet declared that   **Gregory Blaxland**
the figures represented
Australians in realistic form,
they were labeled "grotesque."

A stainless steel sculpture
of upended cubes, the Dobell
Memorial Sculpture stands
above a waterfall funded by

public contributions following
a donation by artist Lloyd
Rees. The sculpture, a tribute
to the artist William Dobell
(see p29), was created by Bert
Flugelman in 1979.

Lands Department
Building ❼

23 Bridge St. **Map** 1 B3. 🚍 325,
George St routes. 🕐 only 2 weeks in
the year, dates vary. ♿

Dᴇꜱɪɢɴᴇᴅ ʙʏ the Colonial
Architect James Barnet, the
three-story Classical Revival
sandstone edifice was built
between 1877 and 1890.
As in the GPO building,
Pyrmont sandstone was
used for the exterior.
Decisions about the sub-
division of much of rural
eastern Australia were
made in offices within.
Statues of explorers and
legislators who "pro-
moted settlement" fill
23 of the façade's 48
niches; the remainder
are still empty. The
luminaries include the
explorers Hovell and Hume,
Sir Thomas Mitchell, Blaxland,
Lawson and Wentworth (see
p136), Ludwig Leichhardt, Bass
and Matthew Flinders, and
the botanist Sir Joseph Banks.

Museum of Sydney ⑧

37 Phillip St. **Map** 1 B3. 🏧 *9251 5988.*
🚌 *Circular Quay routes.* ⏱ *10am–*
5pm daily. ⬤ *Good Fri, Dec 25.* 📷 ♿

Sᴵᴛᴜᴀᴛᴇᴅ ᴀᴛ the bottom of
Governor Phillip Tower, the
Museum of Sydney opened in
1995. The turbulent history of
Sydney from the 1788 arrival
of the British colonists until
1850 is recalled on the site of
the first Government House.
This served as the home, office,
and seat of authority for the
first nine governors of NSW
from 1788 until its demolition
in 1846. The design assimilates
the exhibition and preservation
of a valuable archaeological
site into a modern office block.

The Eora People
The first inhabitants of the
region now known as Sydney
(see pp18–19) made the hunting and fishing tools displayed
on Level 2. Men fished with
spears while women used
hook and line. The collectors'
chests on Level 3 hold items
of daily use such as flint and
ocher, each piece painstakingly
cataloged and evocatively
interpreted. Eora stories are
recounted by today's Sydney
Kooris – just some of the voices
in the whispering soundscape

**The Lookout, Level 3, overlooking
the piazza towards Circular Quay**

that permeates the museum.
In the square outside the
complex, the acclaimed *Edge
of the Trees* sculpture, with its
collection of 29 sandstone,
steel, and wooden pillars, sym-
bolizes the first
contact between
the Aboriginal
peoples and Euro-
peans. Haunting
voices in the Eora
tongue fill the
space. Inscribed
in the wood are
signatures of the
First Fleeters and
names of botani-
cal species in both
the indigenous language and
Latin. Incisions made in the
pillars are filled with organic
materials such as ash, feathers,
bone, shells, and human hair.

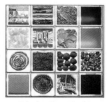

**Display from Trade
exhibition on Level 3**

European Settlement
Outside the museum a paving
pattern outlines the site of first
Government House. Original
foundations, lost under street
level for many years, can be
seen here through a window.
Inside the entrance a viewing
floor reveals more foundations.
A segment of wall has been
reconstructed using sandstone
excavated during archaeological exploration of the site.
Exhibits draw on pre-1850s
resources from both local and
overseas museums, ranging
from the Australian Museum
(see pp88–9) to the British
Natural History Museum.
The displays are brought to
life by the use of multimedia.
On Level 1, holographic ghosts
tell their stories, supported by
artifacts such as
dinner plates and
bone dominoes.
A video screen,
stretching up
through all three
levels, shows the
Sydney bush as it
was in 1788. Tales
of colonial places,
people, and events
are told through
the materials and
goods displayed, from bric-a-
brac to letter fragments, in the
collectors' chests. Panoramic
images of the developing city
provide a vivid backdrop.

Edge of the Trees **sculptural installation by Janet Laurence and Fiona Foley (1995)**

Terrazzo mosaic floor in the crypt of St. Mary's Cathedral

St. Mary's Cathedral ❾

Cathedral St. **Map** 1 C5.
9220 0400. Elizabeth St routes.
6:30am–6:30pm daily.

Although Catholics arrived with the First Fleet, the celebration of Mass was at first prohibited because of fears that the priests would provoke civil strife among the colony's large Irish Catholic population. It was not until 1820 that the first Catholic priests were offiially appointed and regular public services were allowed. In 1821, Governor Macquarie

laid the foundation stone for St. Mary's Chapel on this site, the first land granted to the Catholic Church in Australia.

The initial section of this Gothic Revival style cathedral was opened in 1882. In 1928, the building was completed, but without the twin southern spires originally proposed by the architect William Wardell. By the entrance steps are statues of Australia's first cardinal, Moran, and Archbishop Kelly who laid the cornerstone for the final stage in 1913. They

were sculpted by Bertram MacKennal, also responsible for the Martin Place Cenotaph *(see p84)* and the Shakespeare group outside the State Library *(see p112)*. The crypt's Celtic-inspired terrazzo mosaic floor took 15 years to complete.

Great Synagogue ⓫

187 Elizabeth St. **Map** 1 B5.
9267 2477. 394, 396, 380, 382. for services and tours only. public hols. noon Tue, Thu.

Candelabra from the Great Synagogue

The longest established Jewish congregation in Australia, consisting of more than 900 families, assembles in this synagogue, which was consecrated in 1878. Although Jews had arrived with the First Fleet, formal worship did not start until the 1820s. With its carved porch columns and wrought iron gates, the synagogue is perhaps the finest work of Thomas Rowe, the architect of Sydney Hospital *(see p113)*. Among interior features is a paneled ceiling, decorated with hundreds of tiny gold-leaf stars symbolizing God's command: "Let there be light."

Hyde Park ❿

Map 1 B5. Elizabeth St routes.

Fenced and named after its London equivalent by Governor Macquarie in 1810, Hyde Park marked the outskirts of the township. It was a popular exercise field for garrison troops and later incor-

Tomb of the Unknown Soldier in the Art Deco Anzac Memorial

porated a racecourse and a cricket pitch. Though much smaller today than the original park, it still provides a peaceful haven in the middle of the bustling city center.

Anzac Memorial
The 30-m (98-ft) high Art Deco memorial, reflected in the poplar-lined Pool of Remembrance, commemorates those Australians who were killed at war in the service of their country. Opened in 1934, the Anzac Memorial now includes a photographic and military artifact exhibition downstairs.

Sandringham Garden
In spring, the pergola in this sunken garden is a cascade of mauve-flowering wisteria. The garden, a memorial to the English kings George V and George VI, was opened by Queen Elizabeth II in 1954.

Diana, goddess of purity and the hunt, Archibald Fountain

Archibald Fountain
This bronze and granite fountain commemorates the French and Australian World War I alliance. It was completed by François Sicard in 1932 and donated by JF Archibald, one of the founders of the *Bulletin*, a popular literary magazine that encouraged the work of Henry Lawson and "Banjo" Paterson, among many others. It was Archibald's bequest that established the Archibald Prize for portraiture *(see p50)*.

The Grand Organ in Sydney Town Hall's Centennial Hall

Sydney Town Hall ⑫

483 George St. **Map** 4 E2.
[9265 9333. George St routes.
9am–5pm Mon–Fri. Jan 1,
Dec 25.

T HE STEPS of this sandstone
building, central to George
Street's Victorian architecture,
have been a favorite Sydney
meeting place since it opened
in 1869. Walled burial grounds
had originally covered the site.
It is a fine example of high
Victorian architecture, even
though the plans of the original
architect, JH Wilson, proved

beyond the builders' capabili-
ties. A rapid succession of
designers was brought in. The
vestibule – an elegant salon
with intricate plasterwork, lavish stained glass, and a crystal
chandelier – is the work of
Albert Bond. The Bradbridge
brothers completed the clock
tower in 1884. From 1888–9,
other architects were used for
the Centennial Hall, with its
coffered zinc ceiling and an
imposing 19th-century organ
with more than 8,500 pipes.
On the façade, you will see
numerous carved lion heads.
Just to the north of the main
entrance, facing George Street,
a lion has been
carved with one
eye shut. This
oddity appeared
because of the
head stone-
mason's habit of
checking the line
of the stonework
by closing one eye.
The sly joke was not
found until work was finished.
Some people have conclud-
ed that Sydney Town Hall
became the city's most elaborate building by accident, as
each architect strove to outdo
his predecessors. Today, it
makes a magnificent venue for
concerts, dances, and balls.

**The Great Bible,
St. Andrew's Cathedral**

St. Andrew's Cathedral ⑬

Sydney Square, Cnr George &
Bathurst Sts. **Map** 4 E3. [9265 1661.
George St routes. 8am–
5:30pm Mon–Fri, 9am–4pm Sat,
8am–8pm Sun.

W HILE THE FOUNDATION stone
for the country's oldest
cathedral was laid in 1819,
almost 50 years elapsed before
the building was consecrated
in 1868. The Gothic Revival
design is by Edmund Blacket,
whose ashes are interred here.
Inspired by York Minster in
England, the
twin towers were
completed in
1874. In 1949, the
main entrance
was moved to the
eastern end near
George Street.
Found inside are
memorials to Sydney
pioneers, including
Thomas Mort *(see p72)*. A 1539
bible and beads made from
olive seeds collected in the
Holy Land are among the display of religious memorabilia.
The southern wall incorporates stones from London's St.
Paul's Cathedral, Westminster
Abbey, and the House of Lords.

Obelisk
This monument was dubbed
"Thornton's Scent Bottle" after
the mayor of Sydney who had
it erected in 1857. The mock-
Egyptian edifice is in fact a
ventilator for a sewer.

Emden Gun
Standing at the corner of
College and Liverpool Streets,
this monument commemorates
a World War I naval action.
HMAS *Sydney* destroyed the
German raider *Emden* off the
Cocos Islands on November 9,
1914, and 180 crew members
were taken prisoner.

City Circle Railway
The park we see today bears
very little resemblance to the
Hyde Park of old. In fact, the
dictates of city railroad tunnels
have largely created its present
landscape. Tunnels were excavated through an open cut that

ran through the park, and after
the rail system was opened in
1926 the entire area had to be
remodeled and replanted.

Busby's Bore Fountain
This is a reminder of Busby's
Bore, the city's first piped
water supply opened in 1837.

John Busby, a civil engineer,
conceived and supervised the
construction of the 4.4-km (2¾-
mile) tunnel. It carried water
from bores on Lachlan Swamp,
now within Centennial Park
(see p127), to horse-drawn
water carriers on the corner
of Elizabeth and Park Streets.

Game in progress on the giant chessboard, near Busby's Bore Fountain

Australian Museum ⓮

Model head of
Tyrannosaurus rex

THE AUSTRALIAN MUSEUM, founded in 1827, was the first museum established in Australia and remains the premier showcase of Australian natural history. The main building, an impressive sandstone structure with a marble staircase, faces Hyde Park. Architect Mortimer Lewis was forced to resign his position when building costs began to far exceed the budget. Construction was completed in the 1860s by James Barnet. The collection provides a visual and audio journey across Australia and the near Pacific, covering prehistory, biology, botany, environment, and cultural heritage. Australian Aboriginal cultures and traditions are celebrated in a community access space also used for dance and other performances. Touring exhibitions are a regular and popular museum feature.

Museum Entrance
The façade features massive Corinthian square pillars or piers.

Planet of Minerals
This section features a walk-through re-creation of an underground mine with a display of gems and minerals.

Crocoite   **Azurite**

Agate   **Education Center**

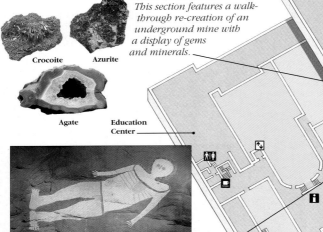

★ **Rock Painting, David Mowaljarlai**
In 1984, this Aboriginal artist painted an interpretation of the Wandjina, Ancestor Spirit of nature, rain-bearing clouds, and law, who can punish by cyclone and flood.

Skeletons

Ground floor

Main entrance

STAR EXHIBITS

- ★ **Afrovenator**

- ★ **"Eric," the Opalized Pliosaur**

- ★ **Rock Painting, David Mowaljarlai**

MUSEUM GUIDE

Aboriginal Australia is on the ground floor, as is the skeleton display. Mineral and rock exhibits are in two galleries on Level 1, with dinosaurs on Level 2. Birds and insects are also found on Level 2, along with human evolution, Indonesia, and marine invertebrate displays.

Aboriginal Australia
displays artifacts of daily use, like spears and grinding stones, as well as grave posts.

Search & Discover
Sydneysiders bring bugs, rocks, and bones to this area for identification. The public can also access CD-ROMS for research.

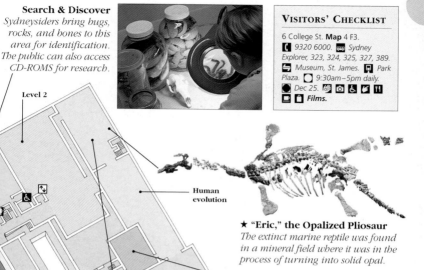

Level 2

VISITORS' CHECKLIST

6 College St. **Map** 4 F3.
☎ 9320 6000. 🚌 *Sydney Explorer, 323, 324, 325, 327, 389.*
🚇 *Museum, St. James.* 🅿 *Park Plaza.* ⏰ *9:30am–5pm daily.*
⬤ *Dec 25.* 📷 ⬤ ♿ ✎ 🍴
⬤ 🎬 *Films.*

Human evolution

★ "Eric," the Opalized Pliosaur
The extinct marine reptile was found in a mineral field where it was in the process of turning into solid opal.

Marine invertebrates

Discovery Space

Indonesia
The gamelan orchestra on display comprises xylophones for melody and gongs for rhythm. The gallery sometimes hosts performances.

Level 1

★ Afrovenator
The almost complete skeleton of the predatory "African hunter," Afrovenator, is about 9 m (30 ft) long. The dinosaur was discovered and subsequently unearthed in Niger, Africa, in 1993.

Birds and Insects
Australia's most poisonous spider, the male of the funnel-web species, dwells exclusively in the Greater Sydney region.

KEY TO FLOORPLAN

- ☐ Australian Environments
- ☐ Indonesia
- ☐ More than Dinosaurs
- ☐ Peoples of Australia
- ☐ Temporary exhibition space
- ☐ Nonexhibition space

"WELCOME STRANGER" GOLD NUGGET

In 1869, the largest gold nugget ever found in Australia was discovered in Victoria. It weighed 71.06 kg (156 lb). The museum holds a cast of the original in a display examining the impact of the gold rush, when the Australian population doubled in ten years.

◄— 67.5 cm (26½ in) wide —►

DARLING HARBOUR

NAMED IN HONOR of the seventh governor of New South Wales, Ralph Darling, this area was originally called Cockle Bay because of the mollusks early European settlers collected here. Darling Harbour was an unsavory place in the late 19th century, known for its thieves' dens and bawdy houses. Its docks, backed by a railroad yard, were an embarkation point for wool and other exports. The country's industrial age began here in 1815 with the opening of a steam mill. Darling

Horatio Nelson, National Maritime Museum

Harbour continued as, first, a grimy workplace and, later, with the industrial decline of Sydney Harbour, an obsolete and run-down backwater. In the 1980s, it was decided to make this prime city site a focal point of the 1988 Bicentenary. The project was the largest urban redevelopment ever carried out in Australia. Today Darling Harbour is an extension of the city center with a mixture of fine museums, shopping, and open space. It has become a popular and lively area of Sydney.

SIGHTS AT A GLANCE

Historic Districts and Buildings
Pyrmont Bridge **3**
Chinatown **7**

Museums and Galleries
National Maritime Museum pp94–5 **1**
Harris Street Motor Museum **4**
Powerhouse Museum pp100–101 **10**

Parks and Gardens
Chinese Garden **6**

Entertainment
Sydney Aquarium pp96–7 **2**
Convention and Exhibition Centre **5**

Theaters
Capitol Theatre **8**

Markets
Paddy's Market **9**

GETTING THERE
Harbourside, Convention, and Haymarket monorail stations are convenient. Ferries run to Darling Harbour wharf, while the most useful buses are the Sydney Explorer, 456, and 501.

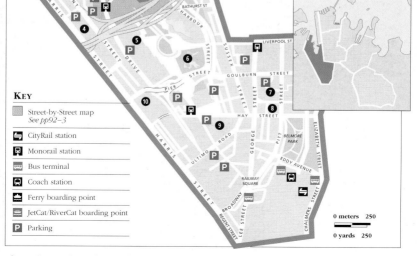

KEY

▣	Street-by-Street map *See pp92–3*
🚆	CityRail station
🚝	Monorail station
🚌	Bus terminal
🚍	Coach station
⛴	Ferry boarding point
🚤	JetCat/RiverCat boarding point
P	Parking

0 meters 250
0 yards 250

◁ **View from Harbourside Festival Marketplace shopping mall looking east toward the city**

Street-by-Street: Darling Harbour

DARLING HARBOUR was New South Wales' bicentennial gift to itself. This imaginative urban redevelopment covers a 133-acre site that was once a busy industrial center and international shipping terminal for the developing local wool, grain, timber, and coal trades. The advent of container shipping proved to be the end of the area's commercial viability, and it gradually fell into ruin. In 1984, however, the Darling Harbour Authority was formed to examine the area's commercial options. The resulting complex opened in 1988, complete with the National Maritime Museum and Sydney Aquarium, two of the city's tourist highlights. Free outdoor entertainment, appealing to children in particular, is a regular feature.

Carpentaria lightship, National Maritime Museum

The Harbourside Festival Marketplace offers a wide range of unusual gifts and Australian souvenirs. Clothing and record shops also vie for attention alongside busy restaurants.

Walkway to Harris Street Motor Museum

Convention and Exhibition Centre
This complex presents an alternating range of trade shows displaying everything from home decorating suggestions to bridal wear ❺

DARLING DRIVE

WESTERN DISTRIBUTOR

WESTERN DISTRIBUTOR

The Tidal Cascades sunken fountain was designed by Robert Woodward, also responsible for the El Alamein Fountain *(see p120)*. The double spiral of water and paths replicates the circular shape of the Convention Centre.

STAR SIGHTS

★ **Sydney Aquarium**

★ **National Maritime Museum**

The Dragon Boat Festival, which takes place each April, is now an international event. Over 2,000 people from around the world compete in a dragon boat race that accompanies other Chinese cultural and social events.

Pyrmont Bridge
The swingspan bridge opens for vessels up to 14 m (46 ft) tall. The monorail track running above the walkway also opens up to allow access for even taller boats ❸

LOCATOR MAP
See Street Finder, maps 3 & 4

Swingspan supports
for Pyrmont Bridge are sunk 10 m (33 ft) below the harbor floor.

★ National Maritime Museum
The seafaring history of the nation, both before and after European settlement, is recorded in a range of compelling exhibits ❶

The *Vampire*
destroyer (1959) is the largest in the vessel fleet moored outside the museum.

Wharf for harbor cruise departures

★ Sydney Aquarium
The aquatic life of Sydney Harbour, the open ocean, and the Great Barrier Reef can be seen in massive tanks that can be viewed from underwater walkways ❷

The flagpole in Cockle Bay was erected in 1988, the year of the Australian bicentennial. Every year in late July, these calm waters fill with all kinds of marine craft on display at the International Boat Show.

| 0 meters | 100 |
| 0 yards | 100 |

KEY

– – – Suggested route

National Maritime Museum ❶

1602 Willem Blaeu Celestial Globe

Ⓑ OUNDED AS IT IS by the sea, Australia's history is inextricably linked to maritime traditions. The museum displays material in a broad range of permanent and temporary thematic exhibits, many with interactive elements. As well as artifacts relating to the enduring Aboriginal maritime cultures, the exhibits survey the history of European exploratory voyages in the Pacific, the arrival of convict ships, successive waves of migration, water sports and recreation, and naval life. Historic vessels on display at the wharf include a flimsy Vietnamese refugee boat, sailing, fishing and pearling boats, a navy patrol boat, and a World War II commando raider.

Museum Façade
The billowing steel roof design by Philip Cox suggests both the surging sea and the sails of a ship.

First Australians traces the seafaring traditions of Aboriginal peoples and Torres Strait Islanders.

The Tasman Light was used in a Tasmanian lighthouse.

Passengers
The model of the Orcades *reflects the grace of 1950s liners. This display also charts harrowing sea voyages made by migrants and refugees.*

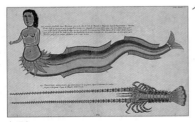

The *Sirius* anchor is from a 1790 wreck off Norfolk Island.

★ Discovery
This 1754 engraving of an East Indian sea creature is a European vision of the uncharted, exotic "great south."

Main entrance (sea level)

The Navy exhibit examines naval life in war and peace, as well as the history of colonial navies.

KEY TO FLOOR PLAN

☐	Discovery and First Australians
☐	Passengers
☐	Commerce
☐	Leisure
☐	Navy
☐	Linked by the Sea: USA Gallery
☐	Temporary exhibitions
☐	Nonexhibition space

STAR EXHIBITS

★ Discovery and First Australians

★ Leisure

★ Vampire

Linked by the Sea honors enduring links between the US and Australia. American traders stopped off in Australia on their way to China.

Commerce

This 1903 Painters' and Dockers' Union banner was carried by waterfront workers in marches. It shows the Niagara *entering the dry dock at Cockatoo Island* (see p106).

★ Leisure

The world's fastest boat, a 1.5 ton hydroplane named Spirit of Australia, *set the world water speed record in 1978, traveling at 511 km/h (317 mph). It was powered by an anti-submarine aircraft engine.*

Level 1

Mazda Gallery

A replica of Captain Cook's *Endeavour* moors at this dock when in Sydney.

Lighthouse

Sailors were guided by this 1874 lighthouse for over a century. It was rebuilt complete with original kerosene lamp.

Lightship *Carpentaria*

The fleet comprises an array of historic craft.

★ Vampire

The museum's largest vessel is the 1959 Royal Australian Navy destroyer, whose insignia is shown here. Tours of "The Bat" are accompanied by simulated battle action sounds.

MUSEUM GUIDE

The Leisure, Navy, and Linked by the Sea: USA Gallery exhibits are located on the main entrance level (sea level). The First Australians, Discovery, Passengers, and Commerce sections are found on the first level. There is access to the fleet from both levels.

Sydney Aquarium ❷

Tropical sea star

SYDNEY AQUARIUM contains the country's most comprehensive collection of Australian aquatic species. Over 5,000 animals from 600 species are held in a series of re-created marine environments. For many visitors, the highlight is a walk "on the ocean floor" through two floating oceanaria with 145 m (480 ft) of acrylic underwater tunnels. These allow close observation of sharks, stingrays, and schools of fish. Fur and harbor seals may be viewed above and below water in a special seal sanctuary. None of the displays is harmful to the creatures, and many of the tanks display practical information about marine environmental hazards.

Saltwater Crocodiles
The largest and most dangerous species of crocodile, "salties" live in the swamps and estuaries of Australia's north.

Entrance and gift shop

Café

Temporary exhibitions
focusing on particular species or marine environments are held here.

★ Great Barrier Reef Display
The world's largest coral reef extends along 2,300 km (1,430 miles) of Australia's coast and is home to a wealth of colorful fish such as this tang.

Blue-Spotted Stingray
This Great Barrier Reef-dweller feeds on mollusks and other invertebrates that thrive on the ocean floor.

Aquarium Building and Pier
The stark white design of the aquarium is Structuralist (see p39), an architectural style that dominates Darling Harbour.

Touch Pool
This area, resembling a rock pool, gives the visitor a rare chance to touch, with care, marine invertebrates found along the coastline. They include sea urchins, tubeworms, crabs, and starfish.

Mangrove habitat

Fishes of the Far North

Seal Sanctuary
Australian fur seals are carnivorous mammals that live in colonies in the cool waters of the southern Australian coast.

The underwater walk allows close-up viewing of the seals.

Pontoons surround the floating pool.

"Sails" form a roof over the two tanks.

Underwater viewing tunnel

Sydney Harbour Oceanarium
Underwater viewing tunnels pass through diverse saltwater habitats, showing some of the 570 species that inhabit Sydney waters.

★ The Open Ocean
The lone-hunting gray nurse shark, which has rows of fearsome, razor-sharp teeth, is clearly seen here. Giant stingrays are also a feature.

STAR EXHIBITS

★ **Great Barrier Reef Display**

★ **The Open Ocean**

Pyrmont Bridge ❸

Darling Harbour. **Map** 1 A5.
🚈 *Darling Park, Harbourside.* 📷
♿ 🚲

The architectural geometry of the Convention and Exhibition Centre

Pᴠʀᴍᴏɴᴛ ʙʀɪᴅɢᴇ opened in 1902. The world's oldest electrically operated swingspan bridge, it was fully functional even before Sydney's streets were lit by electricity. It was the second Pyrmont Bridge and provided access to what was then a busy international shipping terminal with warehouses for wool and other goods. Electricity for the bridge came from the Ultimo power station, the building which now houses the city's Powerhouse Museum *(see pp100–101)*.

Percy Allan, the bridge's designer, achieved overseas recognition for his two central steel swingspans and went on to design 583 more bridges in the course of his career. JJ Bradfield, the designer of the Sydney Harbour Bridge *(see pp70–71)*, was also involved in construction of this bridge.

The 369-m (1,200-ft) long Pyrmont Bridge has fourteen spans. The central swingspan is made of steel, while the other spans are made of iron-bark, an Australian hardwood. The bridge was permanently closed to road traffic in 1981, but reopened to pedestrians when the Darling Harbour complex opened in 1988. A portion of the monorail route travels along the bridge. The central steel swingspan is still driven by its original motor. The bridge is opened regularly to allow boats access to and from Cockle Bay.

The view from Pyrmont Bridge looking up toward the city center

Anthony Quinn's 1959 Cadillac, Harris Street Motor Museum

Harris Street Motor Museum ❹

320 Harris St, Pyrmont. **Map** 3 C3.
📞 9552 3375. 🚈 *Convention Centre.* ⏰ *10am–5pm Wed–Sun (school hols, daily).* ● *Good Fri, Dec 25.* 📷 ♿

Cᴇʟᴇʙʀᴀᴛɪɴɢ ᴀ ᴄᴇɴᴛᴜʀʏ of automotive history, the museum has more than 150 classic automobiles, commercial vehicles, and motorcycles on display, along with stories of the great car designers, their successes and failures. Exhibits include an Edwardian Gardener's Serpollet steam car, the unique Delorean, a Model T BP tanker, and actor Anthony Quinn's 1959 Cadillac. In the midst of the exotic cars are everyday vehicles such as the Morris, Vauxhall, and Buick.

Housed in a former 1890s warehouse, the museum also has the country's largest international standard slot car track. Two eight-lane tracks run over 67 m (220 ft), with the "driver" racing against the clock.

Convention and Exhibition Centre ❺

Darling Drive, Darling Harbour.
Map 3 C3. 📞 9282 5000.
🚈 *Convention.* ⏰ *7am–7pm Mon–Fri.* 📷 ♿

Tʜɪs ᴄᴜsᴛᴏᴍ-ʙᴜɪʟᴛ facility was completed in 1988. Major international and local conventions are held in the main auditorium. For trade shows and exhibitions, the Exhibition Centre's five halls can be combined to form a column-free area the size of five sports fields. The roof is supported by a system of sail-like masts and rigging that reflects the maritime history of Darling Harbour. Works of art by such noted Australian artists as Brett Whiteley and John Olsen hang inside.

Chinese Garden ❻

Darling Harbour. **Map** 4 D3.
🚈 *Haymarket.* ⏰ *9:30am–5pm (6:30pm daylight savings) daily.* 📷 ♿

Kɴᴏᴡɴ ᴀs the Garden of Friendship, the Chinese Garden was built in 1987. It is a tranquil refuge from the city streets. The garden's design was a gift to Sydney from its Chinese sister city of Guang-dong. The Dragon Wall is in the lower section beside the lake. It has glazed carvings of two dragons, one representing Guangdong province and the other the state of New South Wales. In the center of the wall, a carved pearl, symbolizing prosperity, is lifted by the waves. The lake is covered with lotus and water lilies for much of the year, and a rock monster guards against evil. On the other side of the lake is the Twin Pavilion. Waratahs (New South Wales's floral symbol) and flowering apricots are carved into its woodwork and also grow at its base.

A tea house, found at the top of the stairs in the Tea House Courtyard, serves traditional Chinese tea and cakes, as well as other light refreshments.

Chinatown ●

Dixon St Plaza, Sydney. **Map** 4 D4.
9281 1018. Haymarket.

ORIGINALLY concentrated around Dixon and Hay Streets, Chinatown is expanding to fill Sydney's Haymarket area, stretching west to Harris Street, south to Broadway and east to Castlereagh Street. It is close to the Sydney Entertainment Centre, where some of the world's best-known rock and pop stars perform and indoor sporting events are held.

For years, Chinatown was a run-down district at the edge of the city's produce markets where many Chinese migrants worked. Today Dixon Street, its main thoroughfare, has been

Chinatown entrance, Dixon Street

spruced up with street lanterns and archways, and a new wave of Asian migrants fills the now fashionable restaurants.

Chinatown is a distinctive area with greengrocers, traditional herbalists, and butcher shops with wind-dried ducks hanging in their windows. Jewelers, clothing stores, and confectioners fill the arcades. There are also two Chinese-language cinema complexes.

Capitol Theatre ●

13 Campbell St, Haymarket. **Map** 4 E4.
9320 5000. George St routes.
for performances only. **Box office**
9am–8pm Mon–Sat.

IN THE MID-1800s a cattle and corn market was situated here. It became Paddy's Market Bazaar with sideshows and an outdoor theater, which were in turn replaced by a circus

with a floodable ring. The present building was erected in the 1920s as a luxurious movie palace with 3,000 seats. In the mid-1990s, the theater was immaculately restored, in keeping with the original theme of a Florentine Garden.

The Capitol reopened as a theater for musicals with productions of *West Side Story* and *Miss Saigon* staged beneath its blue ceiling studded with twinkling stars representing the southern sky.

The lavishly renovated Capitol Theatre in Chinatown

Paddy's Market ●

Cnr Thomas & Hay Sts, Haymarket.
Map 4 D4. 9325 6200.
Haymarket. 9am–4:30pm
Sat–Sun. Apr 25, Dec 25.
See also **Shops and Markets** p203.

HAYMARKET, NEAR Chinatown, is home to Paddy's Market, Sydney's oldest and best-known market. It has been in this area, on a number of sites, since 1869 (with only one five-year absence). The origin of the name is uncertain, but is believed to have come from either the Chinese who originally supplied much of its produce, or the Irish who were their main customers.

Once the shopping center for the inner-city poor, Paddy's Market is now an integral part of an ambitious development including residential apartments, specialty retail fashion shops, and a five-screen cinema complex. Yet despite this transformation, the familiar clamor and chaotic bargain-hunting atmosphere of the original marketplace remain. Every weekend the market is filled with up to 800 stalls selling everything from fresh produce such as vegetables and flowers, to chickens, puppies, electrical products, and leather goods.

Pavilion in the grounds of the Chinese Garden

Powerhouse Museum ⑩

Thomas Hope Egyptian chair

THIS FORMER POWER STATION, completed in 1902 to provide power for Sydney's trolley system, was redesigned to cater to the needs of a modern, hands-on museum. Revamped, the Powerhouse opened in 1988. The early collection was held in the Garden Palace hosting the 1879 international exhibition of invention and industry from around the world *(see pp24–5)*. Few exhibits survived the devastating 1882 fire, and today's huge and ever-expanding holdings were gathered after this disaster. The buildings' monumental scale provides an ideal context for the epic sweep of ideas encompassed within: everything from the realm of space and technology to the decorative and domestic arts. The museum emphasizes Australian innovations and achievements celebrating both the extraordinary and the everyday.

★ Kings Cinema
Visitors can watch newsreels, early sound classics, and silent movies in this Art Deco theater that, with its many original furnishings, re-creates movie-going in the 1930s.

Soviet Organic Satellite Model
Replica spacecraft and a "habitation module," complete with kitchenette and sleeping area, detail the past and future of space exploration.

Level 3

Autogiro Aircraft
This rare 1934 precursor to the helicopter has a rotor powered by the movement of air rather than by a motor. The rotor's design provides vertical lift and controls direction.

MUSEUM GUIDE
The museum is in two buildings: the former power-house and the Neville Wran building. The 20 exhibits descend from Level 5, the restaurant level. The shop, entrance, and major exhibits are on Level 4. Level 3 has the-matic exhibits and the Kings Cinema. Level 2 has design, experiments, computer, space, and transportation exhibits.

KEY TO FLOOR PLAN

☐	Level 5: Decorative Arts Gallery
☐	Level 4: Decorative Arts and Innovation
☐	Level 3: Social History
☐	Level 2: Science and Technology
☐	Nonexhibition space

Level 2

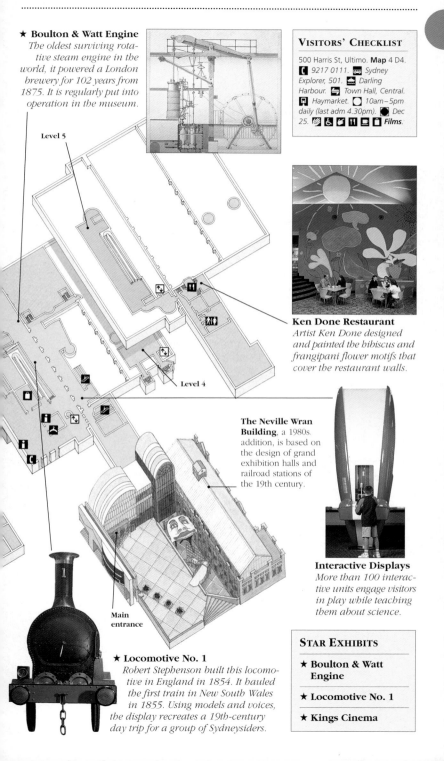

★ **Boulton & Watt Engine**
The oldest surviving rotative steam engine in the world, it powered a London brewery for 102 years from 1875. It is regularly put into operation in the museum.

Level 5

Ken Done Restaurant
Artist Ken Done designed and painted the hibiscus and frangipani flower motifs that cover the restaurant walls.

Level 4

The Neville Wran Building, a 1980s addition, is based on the design of grand exhibition halls and railroad stations of the 19th century.

Interactive Displays
More than 100 interactive units engage visitors in play while teaching them about science.

Main entrance

★ **Locomotive No. 1**
Robert Stephenson built this locomotive in England in 1854. It hauled the first train in New South Wales in 1855. Using models and voices, the display recreates a 19th-century day trip for a group of Sydneysiders.

STAR EXHIBITS

★ **Boulton & Watt Engine**

★ **Locomotive No. 1**

★ **Kings Cinema**

BOTANIC GARDENS AND THE DOMAIN

THIS TRANQUIL PART of Sydney can seem a world away from the bustle of the city center. It is rich in the remnants of Sydney's convict and colonial past: the site of the first farm, and the boulevard-like Macquarie Street where the barracks, hospital, church, and mint – bastions of civic power – are among the oldest surviving public buildings in Australia. This street continues to assert its dominance today as the home of the state government of New South Wales. The Domain, an open, grassy space, was originally set aside by the colony's first governor for his private use. Today it is a democratic place with joggers and touch footballers sidestepping picnickers. In January, during the Festival of Sydney, it hosts outdoor concerts with thousands of people enjoying fine music. The Botanic Gardens, which with The Domain was the site of Australia's first park, is a haven where visitors can stroll around and enjoy the extensive collection of native and exotic flora.

**Wooden angel,
St. James' Church**

SIGHTS AT A GLANCE

**Historic Streets and
Buildings**
Conservatorium of Music **2**
Government House **3**
Woolloomooloo Finger
   Wharf **6**
State Library of NSW **9**
Parliament House **10**
Sydney Hospital **11**
Sydney Mint Museum **12**
Hyde Park Barracks **13**

Museums and Galleries
*Art Gallery of New South
   Wales pp108–11* **7**

Churches
St. James' Church **14**

Islands
Fort Denison **5**

Monuments
Mrs. Macquaries Chair **4**

Parks and Gardens
*Royal Botanic Gardens
   pp104–5* **1**
The Domain **8**

GETTING THERE
Visit on foot, if possible. St. James and Martin Place train stations are close to most of the sights. The 311 bus from Circular Quay runs near the Art Gallery of NSW and past the Woolloomooloo Finger Wharf. The Sydney Explorer also stops at several sights.

0 meters   500

0 yards   500

KEY

Royal Botanic Gardens
See pp104–5

P Parking

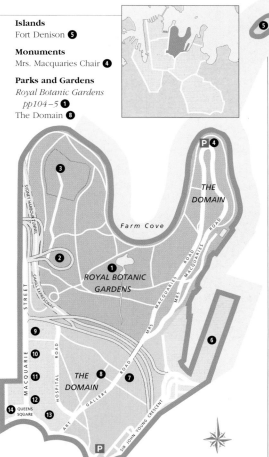

◁ **Succulents and cactus from the Succulent Garden in the Royal Botanic Gardens**

Royal Botanic Gardens ❶

Statue in the Botanic Gardens

THE ROYAL BOTANIC GARDENS, an oasis of about 74 acres in the heart of the city, occupy a superb position, wrapped around Farm Cove at the harbor's edge. Established in 1816 as a series of pathways through shrubbery, they are the oldest scientific institution in the country and house an outstanding collection of plants from Australia and overseas. A living museum, the gardens are also the site of the first farm in the fledgling colony. Fountains, statues, and monuments are today scattered throughout. Plant specimens collected by Joseph Banks on Captain James Cook's epic voyage along the east coast of Australia in 1770 are displayed in the National Herbarium of New South Wales, an important center for research on Australian plants.

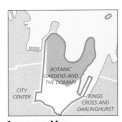

LOCATOR MAP
See Street Finder, maps 1 & 2

Government House (1897)

★ **Palm Grove**
Begun in 1862, this cool summer haven is one of the world's finest outdoor collections of palms. There are about 180 species. Borders planted with kaffir lilies make a colorful display in springtime.

★ **Herb Garden**
Herbs from around the world used for a wide variety of purposes – culinary, medicinal, and aromatic – are on display here. A sensory fountain and a sundial modeled on the celestial sphere are here also.

| 0 meters | 200 |
| 0 yards | 200 |

★ **Sydney Tropical Centre**
Two glasshouses contain tropical ecosystems in miniature. Native vegetation is displayed in the Pyramid, while the Arc holds plants not found locally, commonly known as exotics.

Mrs. Macquaries Chair, where the governor's wife liked to sit and watch the harbor, is marked by a carved rock ledge seat.

Mrs. Macquaries Road

Macquarie Wall
In 1810, work began on this 290-m (950-ft) long wall intended to separate the convict domain from the town's "respectable Class of Inhabitants." Only a small section remains standing today.

Choragic Monument *(1870)*
This replica of the eponymous statue of Lysicrates in Athens was carved in sandstone by Walter McGill.

The Fleet Steps met those disem- barking from ships in Farm Cove.

Andrew (Boy) Charlton Pool is a popular spot for inner-city swimming and sunbathing.

★ **Australia's First Farm**
It is claimed that some Middle Garden oblong beds follow the direction of the first fur- rows plowed in the colony.

National Herbarium of New South Wales
About one million dried plant specimens document biological diversity. Discovery and collection of new plants aims to slow down the extinction rate of entire species.

STAR SIGHTS

★ **Sydney Tropical Centre**

★ **Australia's First Farm**

★ **Palm Grove**

★ **Herb Garden**

Conservatorium of Music **2**

Macquarie St. **Map** 1 C3.
[📞] *9230 1222.* [🚌] *Sydney Explorer,
Circular Quay routes.* [🕐] *8:30am–
5pm Mon–Fri, 9am–4pm Sat.*
[⬤] *public hols, Easter Sat.* [♿]

W HEN IT WAS finished in
1821, this striking early
Gothic Revival building was
meant to be stables and servants' quarters for Government
House, but construction of
the latter was delayed for
almost 25 years. That stables
should be built in so grand a
style, and at such great cost,
brought forth cries of outrage
and led to bitter arguments
between the architect, Francis
Greenway *(see p114)*, and
Governor Macquarie – and a
decree that all future building
plans be submitted to London.
  Between 1908 and 1915,
"Greenway's folly" underwent
a dramatic transformation. A
concert hall, roofed in gray
slate, was built on the central
courtyard, and the building in
its entirety was converted for
the use of the new Sydney
Conservatorium of Music.
  The "Con" is still a training
ground for future musicians.
While undeniably picturesque,
it is not ideal for the needs of
the flourishing musical talent
of Sydney. The staff and students may eventually move to
more suitable premises, but at
present this idiosyncratic old
building continues to house the
city's premier music school.

THE HISTORY OF COCKATOO ISLAND

**HMS *Orlando* in dry dock at
Cockatoo Island in the 1890s**

Now completely deserted,
the largest of the 12 Sydney
Harbour islands was used to
store grain from the 1830s.
It was a penal establishment
from the 1840s to 1908, with
prisoners being put to work
constructing dock facilities.
The infamous bushranger
"Captain Thunderbolt" made
his escape from Cockatoo in
1863 by swimming across to
the mainland. From the 1870s
to the 1960s, Cockatoo
Island was a thriving naval
dockyard and shipyard, the
hub of Australian industry.

Government House **3**

Macquarie St. **Map** 1 C2.
[📞] *9931 5222.* [🚌] *Sydney Explorer,
Circular Quay routes.* **House** [🕐] *10am–
3pm Fri–Sun.* [⬤] *public hols.* **Garden**
[🕐] *10am–4pm.* [📷] [♿] [✓]

W HAT USED to be the official
residence of the governor
of New South Wales overlooks
the harbor from within the
Royal Botanic Gardens, but the
grandiose, somewhat somber,
turreted Gothic Revival edifice
seems curiously out of place
in its beautiful park setting.
  Modified by Mortimer Lewis
from an Edward Blore design,
it was built of local sandstone
and cedar from 1837–45. A
collection of 19th- and early
20th-century furnishings and
decoration is housed within.

**Resting on the carved stone seat
of Mrs. Macquaries Chair**

Mrs. Macquaries Chair **4**

Mrs. Macquaries Rd. **Map** 2 E2.
[🚌] *Sydney Explorer, 888.* [📷] [✓]

T HE SCENIC Mrs. Macquaries
Road winds alongside much
of what is now the city's Royal
Botanic Gardens, from Farm
Cove to Woolloomooloo Bay
and back again. The road was
built in 1816 at the instigation
of Elizabeth Macquarie, wife
of the Governor. In the same
year, a stone bench, inscribed
with details of the new road,
was carved into the rock at the
point where Mrs. Macquarie
would stop to admire the view
on her daily constitutional.
  Although today the outlook
from this famous landmark is
much changed, it is just as
arresting, taking in the broad
sweep of the harbor and beach
with all its landmarks.

The Conservatorium of Music at the edge of the Royal Botanic Gardens

Dilapidated old buildings on the historic Woolloomooloo Finger Wharf on the harbor beach

Fort Denison ❺

Sydney Harbour. **Map** 2 E1.
📞 9555 9844. 🚇 Circular Quay.
🚤 **Boat tours** from Circular Quay at
10am, noon, and 2pm daily. ⬤ Dec
25. 📷 📷 📷 📷

Fɪʀsᴛ ɴᴀᴍᴇᴅ Rock Island, this
prominent, rocky outcrop
in Sydney Harbour was very
quickly dubbed "Pinchgut."
This was probably because of
the meager rations given to
convicts who were confined
there as punishment. It had a
grim history of
incarceration in
the early years
of the colony.
   In 1796, con-
victed murderer
Francis Morgan
was hanged on
the island in
chains. His body
was left to rot on the gallows
for three years as a grisly warning to the other convicts.
   Between 1855 and 1857, the
Martello tower (the only one
in Australia), gun battery, and
barracks that now occupy the
island were built as part of
Sydney's defenses, and the site
was renamed after the governor of the time. The gun, still
fired at 1pm each day, was an
important aid for navigation,
allowing mariners to set their
ships' chronometers.
   Today the island is the perfect setting for watching the
many public harbor activities,

Fort Denison in 1907

such as fireworks displays. To
explore Fort Denison, book
on one of the daily boat tours
that leave from Circular Quay.

Woolloomooloo Finger Wharf ❻

Cowper Wharf Roadway, Woolloomooloo. **Map** 2 E4. 📞 9363 1688.
🚌 Sydney Explorer, 311. 📷

Tʜɪs ɪs ᴛʜᴇ ʟᴀʀɢᴇsᴛ of several
finger wharves that jut out
into the harbor. The wharf,
completed in
1914, was one
of the points of
embarkation for
soldiers bound
for both world
wars. Following
World War II, it
was a landing
place for many of
the thousands of immigrants
who came to Australia.
   The wharf was the subject of
public controversy in the late
1980s and early 1990s. Plans
to demolish it were thwarted
by the protests of conservation
groups. Together with its huge
cargo sheds, this important
maritime site has since been
earmarked for future, mainly
residential, development.

Art Gallery of New South Wales ❼

See pp108–11.

The Domain ❽

Art Gallery Rd. **Map** 1 C4.
🚌 Sydney Explorer, 888. 📷 📷

Pᴇᴏᴘʟᴇ ᴡʜᴏ sᴡᴀʀᴍ to the
January concerts and other
Festival of Sydney events in
The Domain (see p49) are part
of a long-standing tradition.
   This extensive public space
has long been a rallying point
for crowds of Sydneysiders
whenever emotive issues of
public importance have arisen,
such as the attempt in 1916 to
introduce military conscription
or the dismissal of the elected
federal government by the then
governor-general in 1975.
   Ever since the 1890s, part of
The Domain has also been
used as the Sydney version of
"Speakers' Corner." Here, on
any Sunday, visitors can watch
and listen as soapbox orators
hold forth about any subject
that takes their fancy.

A dramatic view of Sydney Opera House from The Domain

Art Gallery of New South Wales ❼

ESTABLISHED IN 1874, the art gallery has occupied its present imposing building since 1897. Designed by the Colonial Architect WL Vernon, the gallery doubled in size following 1988 building extensions. Two equestrian bronzes – *The Offerings of Peace* and *The Offerings of War* – greet the visitor on entry. The gallery itself houses some of the finest works of art in Australia. It has sections devoted to Australian, Asian, European contemporary and photographic works, along with a strong collection of prints and drawings. The Yiribana Gallery, the largest in the world to exclusively exhibit Aboriginal and Torres Strait Islander art and culture, was opened in 1994.

Cycladic figure (c. 2,500 BC)

Sofala *(1947)*
Russell Drysdale's visions of Australia show "ghost" towns laid waste by devastating natural forces such as drought.

Sunbaker *(1937)*
Max Dupain's iconic, almost abstract, Australian photograph of hedonism and sun worship uses clean lines, strong light, and geometric form. The image's power lies in its simplicity.

The Sculpture Terrace is a small outdoor area that has large-scale sculptures on display.

Madonna and Child with Infant St. John the Baptist
This oil on wood (c.1541) is the work of Siena Mannerist artist Domenico Beccafumi.

Level 5

Temporary exhibitions, often by much-acclaimed Australian artists, are held here throughout the year.

STAR EXHIBITS

★ **The Golden Fleece – Shearing at Newstead by Tom Roberts**

★ **Pukumani Grave Posts**

GALLERY GUIDE

The collection is housed on five descending levels. Level 5 displays photography. Level 4 contains many European and Australian features of the collection. Major temporary exhibitions are held on Level 3, 20th-century European prints are on Level 2, and the Yiribana Gallery is on Level 1.

Level 4

★ **Pukumani Grave Posts** *(1958)*
Carved by Tiwi people of Melville Island (north of Australia) and now in the Yiribana Gallery, these posts represent qualities of the deceased whose grave they solemnly surrounded.

Level 1

Nude in a Rocking Chair *(1956)*
Painted in Cannes when Pablo Picasso was 75, this oil vividly depicts the struggle between man and woman, artist and model. Although contorted, the figure is still recognizable as Jacqueline Roque, who was shortly to become the artist's second wife.

Melanesian art is exhibited in this gallery at the library entrance.

Level 2

Level 3

Guardians, Tang Dynasty
These 7th-century Chinese figures are part of a collection highlighting different traditions, periods, and cultures from the many countries of Asia.

★ **The Golden Fleece** *(1894)*
Also known as Shearing at Newstead, *this work by Tom Roberts marks the coming of age of Australian Impressionist art.*

The sandstone entrance was added in 1909.

KEY TO FLOOR PLAN

- Australian Art
- European Art
- Sculpture Terrace
- Photography
- Asian Art
- Prints, Drawings, and Watercolors
- Contemporary Art
- Yiribana Gallery
- Temporary exhibition space
- Nonexhibition space

Exploring the Art Gallery's Collection

ALTHOUGH LOCAL WORKS had been collected since 1875 the gallery did not seriously begin seeking Australian and non-British art until the 1920s, and not until the 1940s did it begin acquiring Aboriginal and Torres Strait Islander paintings. These contrasting collections are now its great strength. Major temporary exhibitions are also regularly staged, with the annual Archibald, Wynne, and Sulman prizes being most controversial and highly entertaining.

Grace Cossington Smith's 1955 *Interior with wardrobe mirror*

George Lambert's heroic *Across the black soil plains* (1899) impress with their huge size and complex compositions.

Australia was slow to take up Modernism. *Implement blue* (1927) and *Western Australian Gum Blossom* (1928), both by Margaret Preston, are her most assertive of the 1920s. Sidney Nolan's works range from *Boy in Township* (1943) to *Burke* (c.1962), exploiting myths of early Australian history. There are fine holdings of William Dobell and Russell Drysdale, as well as important collections of Arthur Boyd, Fred Williams, Grace Cossington Smith, and Brett Whiteley *(see p130)*.

Study for Self Portrait, a Francis Bacon painting from 1976

Hogarth, Turner, and Joshua Reynolds are represented, as are Neo-Classical works. *The Visit of the Queen of Sheba to King Solomon* (1884–90) by Edward Poynter has been on display since 1892. Ford Madox Brown's *Chaucer at the Court of Edward III* (1845–51) is the most commanding work in the Pre-Raphaelite collection.

The Impressionists and Post-Impressionists, represented by late-1880s Pissarro and Monet, are housed in the new gallery wing. Bonnard, Kandinsky, Braque, and many other well-known European artists are also here. *Old Woman in Ermine* (1946) by Max Beckmann and *Three Bathers* (1913) by Ernst Kirchner are strong examples of German Expressionism. The gallery's first Picasso, *Nude in a Rocking Chair* (1956), was purchased in 1981. Among distinguished sculptures is Henry Moore's *Reclining Figure: Angles* (1980), found resting by the side of the entrance.

AUSTRALIAN ART

AMONG THE MOST important colonial works is John Glover's *Natives on the Ouse River, Van Diemen's Land* (1838), an image of doomed Tasmanian Aborigines.

The old wing holds paintings from the Heidelberg school of Australian Impressionism. Charles Conder's *Departure of the Orient – Circular Quay* (1888) and Tom Robert's *The Golden Fleece – Shearing at Newstead* (1894) hang alongside fine works by Frederick McCubbin and Arthur Streeton. Rupert Bunny's sensuous *Summer Time* (c.1907) and *A Summer Morning* (c.1908) and

EUROPEAN ART

THE SCOPE OF the scattered European collection ranges from the medieval to the modern. British art from the late 19th to the early 20th century forms an outstanding component.

Among the Old Masters are some significant Italian works that reflect Caravaggio's influence. There are also several notable works from the Renaissance in Sienese and Florentine styles.

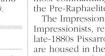

Henry Moore's *Reclining Figure: Angles* (1980)

PHOTOGRAPHY

AUSTRALIAN photography from 1975 to today, represented in all its various forms, is a major part of the collection. In recent years, however, the emphasis has been on building up a body of 19th-century Australian work in a range of early mediums. Nearly 3,000

Brett Whiteley's vivid *The Balcony (2)* from 1975

prints constitute this collection, with pieces by Charles Kerry, Charles Bayliss, and Harold Cazneaux, the latter a major figure of early 20th-century Pictorialism. Such international photographers as Muybridge, Robert Mapplethorpe, and Man Ray are also represented here.

ASIAN ART

THIS COLLECTION is one of the finest in Australia. Chinese art is represented by a chronological presentation of works from the pre-Shang dynasty (c.1600–1027 BC) to the 20th century. The Ming porcelains, earthenware funerary pieces *(mingqi)*, and the sculptures deserve close attention.

The Japanese painting collection contains fine examples by major artists of the Edo period (1615–1867). The Indian and Southeast Asian holdings consist of lacquer, ceramics, and sculptures, with painting exhibits changing regularly.

PRINTS AND DRAWINGS

AS SO MANY of the works in this collection are fragile, the exhibitions are changed frequently. The collection represents the European tradition from the High Renaissance to the 19th and 20th centuries, with work by Rembrandt, Constable, William Blake and Edvard Munch. A strong bias toward Sydney artists from the past 100 years has resulted in a fine gathering of work by Thea Proctor, Norman and Lionel Lindsay, and Lloyd Rees.

Egon Schiele's *Poster for the Vienna Secession* (1918)

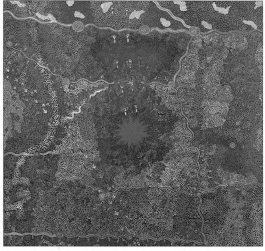

Warlugulong by Clifford Possum Tjapaltjarri and Tim Leura Tjapaltjarri

CONTEMPORARY ART

THE SIGNIFICANCE of the art of our time is reflected in the dynamic collection of recent work by international and Australian artists. The collection highlights the artistic themes that have been central to art practice of the last two decades. Works of Australian artists such as Imants Tillers, Ken Unsworth, and Susan Norrie are on display alongside pieces by notable international artists of the calibre of Cindy Sherman, Yves Klein, Philip Guston, and Anselm Kiefer. The gallery also has a contemporary project space that features temporary experimental installations.

Fruit Bats (1991) by Lin Onus

YIRIBANA GALLERY

DEVOTED TO the exhibition of Aboriginal and Torres Strait Islander artworks bought since the 1940s, traditional bark paintings hang alongside innovative works from both desert and urban areas. The ability of contemporary artists to apply traditional ceremonial body and sand painting styles to new media forms, and the endurance of "Aboriginality,"

are repeatedly demonstrated. The significant early purchases are mainly natural pigment paintings on bark and paper, often containing a simple, figurative motif of everyday life. Also of interest are two sandstone carvings by Queenslanders Linda Craigie and Nora Nathan, the only women artists in the collection until 1985. Topographical, geographical, and cultural mapping of the land is of intricate landscapes. The qualities and forms of the natural world, and the actions and tracks of Ancestral Beings, are coded within the images. These paintings are maps of Ancestral journeys and events. The bark painting *Three Mimis Dancing* (1964) by Samuel Wagbara examines the habitation of the land by Spirits and the recurrence of the Creation Cycles.

Pukumani Grave Posts Melville Island (1958) is a solemn ceremonial work dealing with death, while the eminent Emily Kame Kngwarreye honors the land from which she comes. The canvases of her intricate dot paintings, created using new tools and technology, appear to move and shimmer, telling stories of the animals and food to be found there.

Mosaic replica of the Tasman Map in the State Library of NSW

State Library of NSW ❾

Macquarie St. **Map** 4 F1.
📞 *9230 1414.* 🚌 *Sydney Explorer, Elizabeth St routes.* ⬤ *9am–9pm Mon–Fri, 11am–5pm Sat & Sun.* ⬤ *most public hols.* ♿ ✉

T HE STATE LIBRARY is housed in two separate buildings connected by a passageway and a glass bridge. The older building, the Mitchell Library wing (1906), is a majestic sandstone edifice facing the Royal Botanic Gardens. Huge stone columns supporting a vaulted ceiling frame the impressive vestibule. On the vestibule floor is a mosaic replica of an old map illustrating the two voyages made to Australia by Dutch navigator Abel Tasman in the 1640s. The original Tasman Map is held in the Mitchell Library as part of its large collection of historic Australian paintings, books, documents, and pictorial records.

The Mitchell wing's vast reading room, with its huge skylight and oak paneling, is just beyond the main vestibule. The newest section is an attractive contemporary structure that faces Macquarie Street. It houses the General Reference Library, open to anyone who wishes to use it.

Outside the library, also facing Macquarie Street, is a statue of explorer Matthew Flinders. Behind him on the windowsill is a statue of his co-voyager, his faithful cat, Trim.

Parliament House ❿

Macquarie St. **Map** 4 F1.
📞 *9230 2111.* 🚌 *Sydney Explorer, Elizabeth St routes.* ⬤ *when not in session: 9am–4:30pm Mon–Fri; when in session: 9am–7pm Mon–Fri.* ⬤ *most public hols.* ♿ ✉

T HE CENTRAL SECTION of this building, which houses the state parliament, is part of the original Sydney Hospital built from 1811–16. It has been a seat of government since the 1820s when the newly appointed Legislative Council first held meetings here. The building was extended twice during the 19th century and again during the 1970s and 1980s. The current building contains the chambers for both houses of state parliament, as well as parliamentary offices.

Malby's celestial globe, Parliament House

MACQUARIE STREET

Described in the 1860s as one of the gloomiest streets in Sydney, this could now claim to be the most elegant. Open on the northeastern side to the harbor breezes and the greenery of The Domain, a leisurely walk down this tree-lined street is one of the most pleasurable ways to view the architectural heritage of Sydney.

The new wing *of the library was built in 1988 and connected to the old section by a glass walkway.*

The Mitchell Library wing's portico (1906) has Ionic columns.

STATE LIBRARY OF NSW *(1906–41)*

The Legislative Assembly, *the lower house of state parliament, is furnished in the traditional green of the British House of Commons.*

Parliament House was once the convict-built Rum Hospital's northern wing.

PARLIAMENT HOUSE *(1811–16)*

Parliamentary memorabilia is on view in the Jubilee Room, as are displays showing Parliament House's development and the legislative history of New South Wales.

The corrugated iron building with a cast-iron façade tacked on at the southern end was a prefabricated kit from England. It was originally intended as a chapel for the gold fields, but was diverted from this purpose and sent to Sydney. In 1856, this dismantled kit became the chamber for the new Legislative Council. Its packing cases were used to line this chamber; the rough timber is still on view inside.

Stained glass at Sydney Hospital

Sydney Hospital ⑪

Macquarie St. **Map** 1 C4.
📞 9382 7111. 🚌 Sydney Explorer, Elizabeth St routes. ⏰ daily. 🎫 for tours. 📷 ♿ 🛍 upon request.

THIS IMPOSING COLLECTION of Victorian sandstone buildings stands on the site of what was once the central section of the original convict-built Sydney Hospital – known as the Rum Hospital because the

builders were paid by being allowed to import rum for resale. Both the north and south wings of the Rum Hospital survive as Parliament House and the Sydney Mint Museum. The central wing, which was in danger of collapsing, was demolished in 1879 and the new hospital, which still functions today, was completed in 1894.

The Classical Revival building boasts a Baroque staircase and elegant floral stained-glass windows in its entrance hall. Florence Nightingale approved the design of the 1868 nurses'

wing. In the inner courtyard, there is a brightly colored Art Deco fountain (1907), somewhat out of place among the surrounding heavy stonework.

At the front of the hospital sits *Il Porcellino*, a brass boar. It is a copy of a 17th-century fountain in Florence's Mercato Nuovo. Donated in 1968 by an Italian woman whose relatives had worked at the hospital, the statue is an enduring symbol of the close friendship between Italy and Australia.

Like his Florentine counterpart, *Il Porcellino* is supposed to bring good luck to all those who rub his snout. All coins tossed in the shallow pool at his feet for luck and fortune are collected for the hospital.

Il Porcellino, the brass boar in front of Sydney Hospital

The lamps hanging over the gateways of Parliament House are reproductions of the 19th-century gas lamps that used to stand here.

The Little Shop, a tiny corner store, currently resides in one of two domed former gatehouses.

The entrance stairs of Pyrmont sandstone have set the tone for all renovations. The stone, quarried in colonial times, must be matched exactly.

Corrugated iron and cast-iron façade

Arched sandstone bridges

Arcaded stone verandas with ornate balustrading

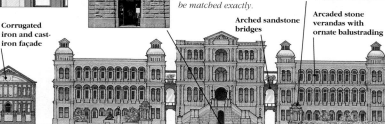

SYDNEY HOSPITAL (1868–94)

Sydney Mint Museum ⑫

Macquarie St. **Map** 1 C5.
📞 *9217 0311.* 🚌 *Sydney Explorer,
Elizabeth St routes.* ⏰ *10am–
5pm daily.* ⬤ *Dec 25.* 🎨 ◎ ♿

T HE GOLD RUSHES of the mid-
19th century transformed
colonial Australia. The Sydney
Mint opened in the 1816 Rum
Hospital's south wing in 1854
to turn recently discovered
gold into bullion and currency.
It was the first branch of the
Royal Mint established outside
London. The Mint was closed
in 1927, since it was no

longer competitive with the
Melbourne and Perth Mints.
The Georgian building went
into its own decline after it was
converted into government
offices. In the 1950s, the front
courtyard was even used as a
parking lot. In 1982, after
restoration, it opened as a
branch of the Powerhouse
Museum *(see pp100–101)*
and now houses exhibitions
on gold and the making of
Australian objects by gold
and silversmiths.
In the old coining factory,
visitors can press their own
souvenir $2 coin, a replica of
the Sydney sovereign that was
minted from 1855.

**Replica convict hammocks on the
third floor of Hyde Park Barracks**

FRANCIS GREENWAY, CONVICT ARCHITECT

Until recently, Australian $10 bills bore
the portrait of the early colonial architect
Francis Greenway, the only currency in
the world to pay tribute to a convicted
forger. Greenway was transported to
Sydney in 1814 to serve a 14-year sentence for his crime. Under the patronage
of Governor Macquarie, who appointed
him Civil Architect in 1816, Greenway
designed more than 40 buildings, of
which only 11 remain today. He
received a full pardon in 1819, but
soon fell out of favor because he
persisted in charging large fees
while still on government salary.
Greenway died in poverty in 1837.

**Francis Greenway
(1777–1837)**

Hyde Park Barracks ⑬

Queens Square, Macquarie St.
Map 1 C5. 📞 *9223 8922.* 🚆 *St
James, Martin Place.* ⏰ *10am–5pm
daily.* ⬤ *Good Fri, Dec 25.* ◎ ♿ ♿

D ESCRIBED BY Governor
Macquarie as "spacious"
and "well-aired," the beautifully proportioned barracks are
the work of Francis Greenway
and are considered his masterpiece. They were completed
in 1819 by convict labor and
designed to house 600 convicts

MACQUARIE STREET

Fine examples of Francis Greenway's Georgian
style are within an easy walk of one another at
the Hyde Park end of Macquarie Street. The
brick and sandstone of Hyde Park Barracks,
St. James' Church and the Old Supreme Court
Building form a harmonious group on the site
the governor envisaged as the city's civic center.

*Sydney Mint Museum,
like its twin, Parliament
House, has an unusual
double-colonnaded,
two-story veranda.*

The roof *of the Mint
Museum has now been
completely restored to
replicate the original
wooden shingles in
casuarina (she-oak).*

The stone wall
*of Hyde Park Barracks' north-
west pavilion still bears the
marks of the convicts' chisels.*

**Hyde Park
Barracks Café**

SYDNEY MINT MUSEUM *(1816)*

who until that time had been forced to find their own lodgings after their day's work. The building housed, in turn, Irish orphans and single female immigrants, before becoming courts and legal offices. Refurbished in 1990, it reopened as a museum on the history of the site and its occupants.

The displays include a room reconstructed as convict quarters of the 1820s, as well as pictures, models, and artifacts. Many objects recovered during archaeological digs at the site and now on display had been dragged away by rats to their nests; the scavenging rodents are acknowledged as valuable agents of preservation.

The Greenway Gallery on the second floor holds temporary exhibitions on history, ideas, and culture. From the Barracks Café, which incorporates the original confinement cell area, the visitor can gaze out over the now serene gravel courtyard, once the scene of brutal convict floggings.

Intermittently during school holidays, visitors can stay for a night in a convict dormitory, sleeping in a hammock and enjoying a convict-style breakfast in the morning.

Detail from the Children's Chapel mural in the St. James' Church crypt

St. James' Church ⓮

179 King St. **Map** 1 B5.
📞 9232 3022. 🚇 St. James, Martin Place. ⏱ 9am–5pm daily. 📷 ✔

THIS FINE GEORGIAN building, constructed with convict-made bricks, was designed as a courthouse in 1819. The architect, Francis Greenway, was forced to convert it into a church in 1820, when plans to build a grand cathedral on George Street were abandoned.

Greenway was unhappy about the change, but nevertheless designed a simple yet elegant church. Consecrated in 1824 by Samuel Marsden, the infamous "flogging parson," it is Sydney's oldest church. Many additions have been carried out, including designs by John Verge in which the pulpit faced toward high-rent pews, while convicts and the military sat behind the preacher where the service would have been inaudible. A Children's Chapel was added in 1930.

Prominent members of early 19th-century society, many of whom died violently, are commemorated in marble tablets. These tell the full and bloody stories of luckless explorers, the governor's wife dashed to her death from her carriage, and shipwreck victims.

This clock, dating from 1817 and one of Sydney's oldest, is on the Hyde Park Barracks façade.

L. MACQUARIE ESQ GOVERNOR 1817

Georgian sandstone façade

Statue of Prince Albert

The Land Titles Office, a WL Vernon building from 1908, has a Classical form with some fine Tudor Gothic detailing.

The stained-glass windows in St. James' Church are mostly 20th century and represent the union formed by air, earth, fire, and water.

Copper spire atop a square brick tower

HYDE PARK BARRACKS (1817–19) **LAND TITLES OFFICE** (1908–13) **ST. JAMES'** (1820)

KINGS CROSS AND DARLINGHURST

ITUATED ON the eastern fringe of the city, Kings Cross, known as "The Cross," and Darlinghurst are a couple of Sydney celebrities. Their allure is tarnished – or enhanced, perhaps – by trails of scandal and corruption. Kings Cross, particularly, is still regarded as a hotbed of vice; both areas still bear the taint of 1920s gangland associations. In fact, both are now cosmopolitan areas – among the most densely populated parts of

Façade detail, Del Rio (see p119)

Sydney, famed as much for their street life and thriving café culture as for their unsavory features. Kings Cross exudes a welcome breath of bohemia, in spite of the sleaze of Darlinghurst Road and the flaunting of its red light district. Darlinghurst comes brilliantly into its own every March, when the flamboyant Gay and Lesbian Mardi Gras parade, supported by huge crowds of spectators, makes its triumphant way along Oxford Street.

SIGHTS AT A GLANCE

Historic Streets and Buildings
Victoria Street **2**
Elizabeth Bay House **3**
Old Gaol, Darlinghurst **6**
Darlinghurst Court House **7**

Museums and Galleries
Sydney Jewish Museum **5**

Parks and Gardens
Beare Park **4**

Monuments
El Alamein Fountain **1**

GETTING THERE
Kings Cross train station serves the area. Bus number 311 travels through Kings Cross and Darlinghurst, and the 324, 325, and 389 are also useful. Buses 378, 380, and 382 travel along Oxford Street.

```
0 meters          100
0 yards           100
```

KEY

Street-by-Street map
See pp118–19

CityRail station

Parking

◁ **The large neon sign at the top of William Street marking the entrance to Kings Cross**

Street-by-Street: Potts Point

**Beare Park
fountain detail**

THE SUBSTANTIAL VICTORIAN houses filling the streets of this old suburb are excellent examples of the 19th-century concern with architectural harmony. New building projects were designed to enhance rather than contradict the surrounding buildings and general streetscape. Monumental structures and fine details of molded stuccoed parapets, cornices, and friezes, even the spandrels in herringbone pattern, are all integral parts of a grand suburban plan. (This plan included an 1831 order that all houses cost at least £1,000.) Cool and dark verandas extend the street's green canopy of shade, leaving an impression of cool drinks enjoyed on hot summer days in fine Victorian style.

The McElhone Stairs were preceded by a wooden ladder that linked Woolloomooloo Hill, as Kings Cross was known, to the estate far below.

Horderns Stairs

These villas, from the Georgian and Victorian eras, can be broadly labeled as Classical Revival and are fronted by leafy gardens.

**Kings Cross
Station**

★ **Victoria Street**
In 1972–4, residents of this historic street fought a sometimes violent battle against developers wanting to build high-rise office towers, motels, and blocks of flats ❷

Werrington, a mostly serious and streamlined building, also has flamboyant Art Deco detailing, now subdued under brown paint.

Tusculum Villa was just one of a number of 1830s houses subject to "villa conditions." All had to face Government House, be of a high monetary value, and be built within three years.

STAR SIGHTS

★ **Victoria Street**

★ **Elizabeth Bay House**

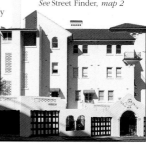

Challis Avenue is a fine and shady complement to nearby Victoria Street. This Romanesque group of terrace houses has an unusual façade, with arches fronting deep verandas and a grand ground floor colonnade.

LOCATOR MAP
See Street Finder, map 2

Rockwall, a symmetrical and compact Regency villa, was built to the designs of the architect John Verge (see p120) in 1830–7.

Del Rio is a finely detailed high-rise apartment block. It clearly exhibits the Spanish Mission influence that filtered through from California in the first quarter of the 20th century.

Landmark Hotel

CHALLIS AVENUE

STREET

MACLEAY

RICK AVENUE

ONSLOW PLACE

BILLYARD AVENUE

ONSLOW AVENUE

AVENUE

Y ROAD

The Arthur McElhone Reserve

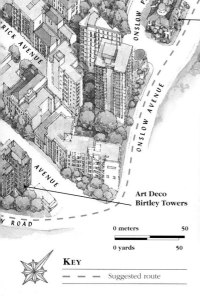

★ **Elizabeth Bay House**
A contemporary exclaimed over the beauty of the 1830s garden: "trees from Rio, the West Indies, the East Indies, China . . . the bulbs from the Cape are splendid" ❸

Art Deco Birtley Towers

| 0 meters | 50 |
| 0 yards | 50 |

KEY

– – – Suggested route

Elizabeth Bay was part of the original land grant to Alexander Macleay (see p120). He created a botanist's paradise with ornamental ponds, quaint grottoes, and promenades winding all the way down to the harbor.

El Alamein Fountain, commemorating the World War II battle

El Alamein Fountain **❶**

Fitzroy Gardens, Macleay St, Potts Point.
Map 2 E5. 🚌 *311.*

THIS DANDELION of a fountain in the heart of the Kings Cross district has a reputation for working so spasmodically that passers-by often murmur facetiously, "He loves me, he loves me not." Built in 1961, it commemorates the Australian army's role in the siege of Tobruk, Libya, and the battle of El Alamein in Egypt during World War II. At night, when it is brilliantly lit, the fountain looks surprisingly ethereal.

Victoria Street **❷**

Potts Point. **Map** 5 B2. 🚌 *311, 324, 325.*

AT THE POTTS POINT end, this street of 19th-century terrace houses, interspersed with a few incongruous-looking high-rise blocks, is, by inner-city standards, almost a boulevard. The gracious street you see today was once at the center of a bitterly fought conservation struggle, one which almost certainly cost the life of a prominent heritage campaigner.

In the early 1970s, many residents, backed by the "green bans" *(see p29)* put in place by the Builders' Labourers Federation of New South Wales, fought to prevent demolition of old buildings for high-rise

Juanita Nielsen

development. Juanita Nielsen, publisher of a local newspaper and heiress, vigorously took up the conservation battle. On July 4, 1975, she disappeared without trace. A subsequent inquest into her disappearance was unable to reach a verdict.

As a result of the actions of the union and residents, most of Victoria Street's superb old buildings still stand. Ironically, they are now occupied not by the low-income residents who fought to save them, but by the well-off professionals who eventually displaced them.

Elizabeth Bay House **❸**

7 Onslow Ave, Elizabeth Bay.
Map 2 F5. 📞 *9356 3022.* 🚌 *Sydney Explorer, 311.* 🕐 *10am–4:30pm Tue–Sun.* ⬤ *Good Fri, Dec 25.* 🚫📷

ELIZABETH BAY HOUSE *(see pp22–3)* contains the finest colonial interior on display in Australia. It is a potent expression of how the depression of the 1840s cut short the 1830s' prosperous optimism. Designed in the Greek Revival style by John Verge, it was built for Colonial Secretary Alexander Macleay, from 1835–39. The domed oval saloon with its cantilevered staircase is recognized as Verge's masterpiece. The exterior is less satisfactory, as the colonnade and portico were not finished because of a crisis in Macleay's financial affairs. The present portico dates from 1893. The

interior is furnished to reflect Macleay's occupancy from 1839–45, and is based on inventories drawn up in 1845 for the transfer of the house and contents to Macleay's son, William Sharp. He took the house as payment of his father's debts, leading to a rift that was never resolved.

The original 54-acre land grant was subdivided for apartments and houses in the 1880s. In the 1940s, the house itself was divided into 15 apartments. In 1942, the artist Donald Friend, standing on the balcony of his apartment – the former morning room – saw the ferry *Kuttabul* hit by a torpedo from a Japanese submarine.

The house was restored and opened in 1977 and is a property of the Historic Houses Trust of NSW.

The sweeping staircase under the oval dome, Elizabeth Bay House

Beare Park **❹**

Ithaca Rd, Elizabeth Bay. **Map** 2 F5. 🚌 *311, 350.*

ORIGINALLY A PART of the Macleay Estate, Beare Park is now circled by apartment buildings. A refuge from hectic Kings Cross, it is one of a handful of parks serving a densely populated area. In the shape of a natural amphitheater, the park puts Elizabeth Bay on glorious view.

The family home of JC Williamson, a theatrical entrepreneur who came to Australia from America in the 1870s, formerly stood at the eastern end of the park.

Star of David in the lobby of the Sydney Jewish Museum

Sydney Jewish Museum ❺

148 Darlinghurst Rd, Darlinghurst.
Map 5 B2. ☎ *9360 7999.* 🚌 *Sydney Explorer, Bondi & Bay Explorer, 311, 378.* ⭘ *10am–4pm Mon–Thu, 10am–2pm Fri, 11am–5pm Sun.* ⬤ *Sat, Jewish hols.* 🛍 ♿ 🛒

Sixteen Jewish convicts were on the First Fleet and many more were to be transported before the end of the convict era. As with other convicts, most would endure and some would thrive, seizing all the opportunities the colony had to offer for those wishing to make something of themselves.

The Sydney Jewish Museum relates stories of Australian Jewry within the context of the Holocaust. The ground floor display explores present-day Jewish traditions and culture

within Australia. Ascending the stairs to mezzanine levels 1–6, the visitor passes through chronological and thematic exhibitions which unravel the history of the Holocaust.

From Hitler's rise to power and *Kristallnacht*, through the evacuation of the ghettos and the Final Solution, to the ultimate liberation of the infamous death camps and Nuremberg Trials, the harrowing events are graphically documented. Photographs and relics, some exhumed from mass graves, as well as audiovisual exhibits and oral testimonies recall this horrific period.

Holocaust survivors act as guides on each level. Their presence, bearing witness to the recorded events, lends considerable power and moving authenticity to the exhibits throughout the museum.

Old Gaol, Darlinghurst ❻

Cnr Burton & Forbes Sts, Darlinghurst.
Map 5 A2. ☎ *9339 8666.*
🚌 *378, 380, 382* ⭘ *7:30am–10pm Mon–Fri.* ⬤ *public hols.* 📷 ♿

Originally known as the Woolloomooloo Stockade and later as Darlinghurst Gaol, this complex is now part of the Sydney Institute of Technology. It was constructed over a 20-year period from 1822.

Surrounded by walls almost 7 m (23 ft) high, the cell blocks radiate from a central roundhouse. The jail is built of stone

quarried on the site by convicts that was then chiseled by them into blocks.

No fewer than 67 people were executed here between 1841 and 1908. Perhaps the most notorious hangman was Alexander "The Strangler" Green, after whom Green Park, outside the jail, is thought to have been named. Green lived near the park until public hostility forced him to live in relative safety inside the jail.

Some of Australia's most noted artists, including Frank Hodgkinson, Jon Molvig and William Dobell, trained or taught at the art school that was established here in 1921.

The former Governor's house, Old Gaol, Darlinghurst

Darlinghurst Court House ❼

Forbes St, Darlinghurst. **Map** 5 A2.
☎ *9368 2947.* 🚌 *378, 380, 382.*
⭘ *Feb–Dec: 10am–4pm Mon–Fri & Sun.* ⬤ *Jan, public hols.* ♿ 🛒

Abutting the grim old jail, to which it is connected by underground passages, and facing tawdry Taylors Square, this unlikely gem of Greek Revival architecture was begun in 1835 by Colonial Architect Mortimer Lewis. He was responsible only for the central block of the main building with its splendid six-columned Doric portico with fine Greek embellishments. The balancing side wings were not added until the 1880s.

The court house is still used by the state's Supreme Court mainly for criminal cases, and these are open to the public.

Beare Park, a quiet inner-city park with harbor views

PADDINGTON

**Clock tower on
Paddington Town Hall**

PADDINGTON IS JUSTLY celebrated for its handsome terraces, but this "village in the city," as it is often dubbed, is also famed for its interesting specialty shops full of oddities and collectables, fine restaurants, small hotels, fashionable art galleries, and antique dealers' shops. Paddington boasts a lively street culture, especially on Saturdays when people from far and wide flock to the famous weekly Paddington Bazaar, spilling out into the streets, pubs, and cafés of the surrounding area. Stretching from the Victoria Barracks at its western end, along Oxford Street to the green haven of Centennial Park, Paddington slopes away from this bustling central thoroughfare into the narrow lanes and elegant, leafy streets. The suburb has undergone a series of radical transformations. The first Paddington was built in the 1830s as a Georgian weekend retreat for the moneyed class. These gracious homes had a short life, before being torn down and subdivided. The terraces succeeding them fell into ruin by the 1920s, but are now admired as finely restored Victorian homes with their distinctive wrought-iron "lace" verandas. The glimpses of harbor found in the quiet streets make Paddington one of Sydney's most sought-after residential areas.

SIGHTS AT A GLANCE

Historic Streets and Buildings
Paddington Street ❶
Five Ways ❸
Juniper Hall ❹
Paddington Town Hall ❺
Paddington Village ❻
Victoria Barracks ❼

Parks and Gardens
Centennial Park ❽

Markets
Paddington Bazaar ❷

GETTING THERE
The best way to travel to and around this area is by bus. Buses 378, 380, and 382 run along Oxford Street on their way between the city and beach suburbs, while bus 389 cuts through the back streets.

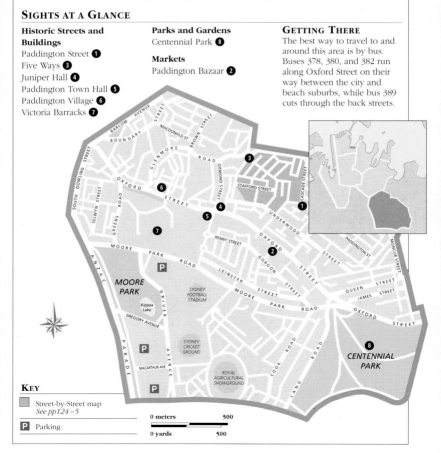

KEY

- Street-by-Street map
  See pp124–5
- **P** Parking

0 meters 500
0 yards 500

◁ **The front entrance to a lovingly restored Victorian terrace house in Paddington**

Street-by-Street: Paddington

PADDINGTON BEGAN TO FLOURISH in the 1840s, when the decision was made to build the Victoria Barracks. At the time much of it was "the most wild looking place . . . barren sand-hills with patches of scrub, hills and hollows galore." The area began to fill rapidly, as owner builders bought into the area and built short rows of terrace houses, many extremely narrow because of the lack of building regulations. After the Depression, most of Paddington was threatened with demolition, but was saved and restored by the large influx of postwar migrants.

Victorian finial in Union Street

★ **Five Ways**
This shopping hub was established in the late 19th century on the busy Glenmore roadway trodden out by cattle ❸

Duxford Street's terrace houses in pastel shades constitute an ideal of town planning: the Victorians preferred houses in a row to have a pleasingly uniform aspect.

"Gingerbread" houses can be seen in Broughton and Union Streets. With their steeply pitched gables and fretwork barge-boards, they are typical of the rustic Gothic Picturesque architectural style.

The London Tavern opened for business in 1876, making it the suburb's oldest pub. Like many of the pubs and delicatessens in this well-serviced suburb, it stands at the end of a row of terraces.

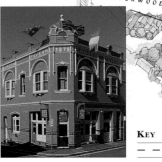

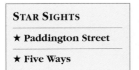

STAR SIGHTS

★ **Paddington Street**

★ **Five Ways**

KEY

– – – Suggested route

The Sherman Gallery is housed in a strikingly modern building. It is designed to hold Australian and international contemporary sculpture and paintings. Suitable access gates and a special in-house crane enable the movement of large-scale artworks, including textiles.

The Sotheby's Gallery is a renowned gallery and auction house. It is housed in a typical Paddington corner building, with an iron-lace balcony.

LOCATOR MAP
See Street Finder, *maps 5 & 6*

Warwick, built in the 1860s, is a minor castle lying at the end of a row of humble terraces. Its turrets, battlements, and assorted decorations, in a style somewhat fancifully described as "King Arthur," even adorn the garages at the rear.

Windsor Street's terrace houses are, in some cases, a mere 4.5 m (15 ft) wide.

Street-making in Paddington's early days was often an expensive and complicated business. A cascade of water was dammed to build Cascade Street.

★ Paddington Street
Under the established plane trees, some of Paddington's finest Victorian terraces exemplify the building boom of 1860–90. Over 30 years, 3,800 houses were built in the suburb ❶

0 meters　　　50

0 yards　　　50

Paddington Street terrace house

Paddington Street ❶

Map 6 D3. 🚌 *378, 380, 382.*

W ITH ITS HUGE PLANE trees shading the road and fine two-, three-, and four-story terrace houses on each side, Paddington Street is one of the oldest, loveliest, and at the same time most typical of the suburb's streets.

Paddington grew rapidly as a commuter suburb in the late 19th century, and most of the terraces were built for renting to the city's artisans. They were cheaply decorated with iron lace (some of which had arrived in ships as ballast), as well as Grecian-style friezes, worked parapets, swagged urns, lions rampant, cornices, pilasters, scrolls, and other fancy plastering. Façades were proudly emblazoned with the house and terrace names.

By the 1900s, these terraces had become unfashionable as people who could afford to moved farther out of the city to newly emerging "garden suburbs" such as Haberfield, Croydon, and Strathfield.

In the 1960s, however, tastes changed once more: the architectural appeal of the terraces, as well as the many advantages of living near the city, came to be appreciated. Paddington experienced a renaissance.

Paddington Street now offers the perennial browser plenty of opportunities to indulge. Small art galleries and interior design studios operate out of store-fronts both quaint and grand.

Paddington Bazaar ❷

395 Oxford St. **Map** 6 D4.
📞 *9331 2646.* 🚌 *378, 380, 382.*
🕐 *10am–4pm (5pm daylight saving)*
Sat. ⬤ *Dec 25.* 📷 ⬤ *See Shops and Markets p203.*

T HIS MARKET, which began in 1973, takes place every Saturday, come rain or shine, in the grounds of Paddington Village Uniting Church. It is probably the most colorful and varied in Sydney: a place to meet and be seen as much as to shop. Stallholders come from all over the world, and many young designers, hoping to launch their careers, display their wares. Among the myriad offerings are jewelry, pottery, and an array of other arts and crafts, as well as both new and secondhand clothing.

Whatever you are looking for, from organic bananas to a full Oriental massage, you are likely to find it here.

Five Ways ❸

Cnr Glenmore Rd & Heeley St.
Map 5 C3. 🚌 *389.*

A T THIS PICTURESQUE junction, where three streets cross on Glenmore Road, a busy shopping hub developed by the trolley line that ran from the city to Bondi Beach. On the five corners stand Victorian and early 20th-century shops, one now a restaurant.

Occupying another corner is the impressive, three-story Royal Hotel *(see p196)*, which was completed in 1888. This mixed Victorian and Classical

Revival building, with its intricately worked cast-iron "lace" screen balcony offering distant harbor views, is typical of the hotel architecture found in Sydney at that time.

Balcony of the Royal Hotel

Juniper Hall ❹

250 Oxford St. **Map** 5 C3.
📞 *9258 0123.* 🚌 *378, 380, 382.*
🕐 *twice yearly (dates vary).* ✉

T HE GIN DISTILLER Robert Cooper built this superb example of Colonial Georgian architecture for his third wife Sarah. He named it after the main ingredient of the gin that made his fortune.

Completed in 1824, the two-story home is the oldest still standing in Paddington and is probably the largest house ever built in the suburb. It had to be: Cooper already had 14 children when he declared that Sarah would have the finest house in Sydney, and he subsequently fathered 14 more.

Juniper Hall was saved from demolition in the mid-1980s and restored in fine style. Now under the auspices of the National Trust, the building is used as private office space.

The Colonial Georgian façade of the superbly restored Juniper Hall

Paddington Town Hall ❺

Cnr Oxford St & Oatley Rd. **Map** 5 C3.
🚌 *378, 380, 382.* ⏰ *10am–4pm
Mon–Fri.* ⬤ *public hols.* 📷

THE PADDINGTON Town Hall
was completed in 1891.
An international competition
that, in a spirit of Victorian
self-confidence, was intended
to produce the state's finest
town hall, was won by local
architect JE Kemp. His Classical Revival building, to which
a clock tower was later added,
still dominates the surrounding
area, although it is no longer
a center of local government.

The building now houses
Chauvel Cinema *(see p210),*
run by the Australian Film
Institute, Paddington Library,
a radio station, commercial
offices, and a large ballroom
that is available for rent.

Paddington Town Hall

Paddington Village ❻

Cnr Gipps & Shadforth Sts. **Map** 5 C3.
🚌 *378, 380, 382.*

PADDINGTON BEGAN life as a
working-class suburb. The
community was comprised of
the carpenters, quarrymen, and
stonemasons who supervised
the convict gangs that built
Victoria Barracks in the 1840s.

The artisans and their families occupied a tight huddle of
spartan houses, a few of which
remain, crowded into the
narrow streets nearby. Like
the barracks, these dwellings
and surrounding buildings
were built mainly of locally
quarried stone.

The lush green expanse of Centennial Park

Victoria Barracks ❼

Oxford St. **Map** 5 B3. 📞 *9339 3000.*
🚌 *378, 380, 382.* **Museum**
⏰ *10am–3pm Thu & alternate Sun.*
⬤ *summer school vacation.* 📷 ♿
🚩 **Parade & tour:** *10am Thu.*

VICTORIA BARRACKS is the
largest and best-preserved
group of late Georgian architecture in Australia, covering
almost 29 acres. It is widely
considered to be one of the
best examples of a military
barracks in the world.

Designed by the Colonial
Engineer, Lt. Col. George
Barney, the barracks were
built between 1841 and 1848
using local sandstone quarried by mainly convict labor.
Originally intended to house
800 men, it has been in
continuous military use ever
since, and still operates as a
center of military planning,
administration, and command.

The main block is 225 m
(740 ft) long and has symmetrical two-story wings with
cast-iron verandas flanking a
central archway. The perimeter
walls, which are designed to

**The archway at the Oxford Street
entrance to Victoria Barracks**

repel surprise attacks, have
foundations 10 m (40 ft) deep
in places. Occupying a former
jail block, the museum traces
Australia's military heritage.

Centennial Park ❽

Map 6 E5. 🚌 *Clovelly, Coogee,
Maroubra, Randwick, Bronte, City,
Bondi Beach & Bondi Junction routes.*
⏰ *8am–6pm daily (8pm daylight
savings).* ♿

ENTERING THIS 544-acre park
through one of its sand-
stone and wrought-iron gates,
the visitor may wonder how
such an extensive and idyllic
place has survived so close to
the center of the city.

Formerly a common, it was
dedicated "to the enjoyment
of the people of New South
Wales forever" on January 26,
1888, the centenary of the
foundation of the colony. On
January 1, 1901, more than
100,000 people gathered here
to witness the Commonwealth
of Australia come into being,
when Australia's first federal
ministry was sworn in by the
first governor-general.

Today picnickers, painters,
runners, and those on horses,
bikes, and inline skates (all of
which can be rented nearby)
make enthusiastic use of this
vast recreation area.

Once the source of Sydney's
water supply, the swamps are
now home to many water
birds. In the park are ponds,
cultivated gardens, an Avenue
of Palms with 400 trees, an
athletic field, and a café *(see
p194)* serving breakfast,
lunch, and light snacks.

FARTHER AFIELD

BEYOND THE INNER CITY, numerous places vie for the visitor's attention. Around the harbor shores are picturesque suburbs, secluded beaches, scenic outlooks, and cultural and historic sights. Taronga Zoo is worth a visit as much for its incomparable setting as for its birds and animals. Manly, stretching between harbor and ocean,

Mr. and Mrs. Luna Park

is the city's northern playground, while Bondi is its eastern counterpart. In Balmain, Glebe, and Surry Hills, the visitor can experience the character of the inner suburbs. Out west at Parramatta, there are sights that recall and evoke the first days of European settlement and the colony's initially unsteady steps toward agricultural self-sufficiency.

SIGHTS AT A GLANCE

Historic Districts and Buildings
University of Sydney **3**
Balmain **6**
Kirribilli Point **8**
North Head **12**
Vaucluse House **13**
Watsons Bay **15**
Macquarie Lighthouse **16**
Captain Cook's Landing Place **18**
Elizabeth Farm **19**
Hambledon Cottage **20**
Experiment Farm Cottage **21**
Old Government House **23**

16 km = 10 miles

Parks and Gardens
Nielsen Park **14**

Museums and Galleries
Brett Whiteley Studio **1**
Nutcote **9**

Entertainment
Luna Park **7**
Taronga Zoo pp134–5 **10**

Beaches
Manly **11**
Bondi Beach **17**

Restaurants and Pubs
Surry Hills **2**
Glebe **4**

Markets
Sydney Fish Market **5**

Cemeteries
St. John's Cemetery **22**

KEY

	Main sightseeing areas
	Park or preserve
✈	Airport
③	Metroad route
══	Freeway or highway
══	Major road
══	Minor road

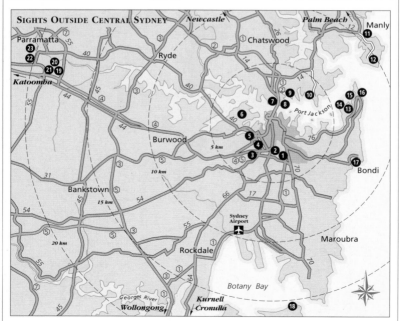

SIGHTS OUTSIDE CENTRAL SYDNEY

Newcastle · Palm Beach · Manly · Parramatta · Chatswood · Ryde · Katoomba · Port Jackson · Burwood · Bondi · Bankstown · Maroubra · Sydney Airport · Rockdale · Botany Bay · Georges River · Kurnell · Cronulla · Wollongong

◁ **The majestic clock tower rising above the main quadrangle at the University of Sydney**

Brett Whiteley Studio ❶

2 Raper St, Surry Hills. **Map** 5 A4.
📞 9225 1881. 🚌 343, 372, 393.
🕙 10am–4pm Sat & Sun. ⬛ Easter
Sun. ⬛ 📷

I N JUNE 1992, Brett Whiteley,
enfant terrible of Australian
contemporary art, died unex-
pectedly at the age of 53. An
internationally acclaimed and
prolific artist, he produced
some of the most sumptuous
images of Sydney and its distinctive harbor ever painted.

In 1985, Whiteley bought a
former factory and converted
it into a studio and residence.
The studio is now a public
museum and art gallery. It
features the work of Whiteley
and other artists. Visitors have
the opportunity to gain an
insight into Whiteley's life and
work through changing exhibitions and displays of personal
effects and memorabilia. The
studio is under the administration of the Art Gallery of New
South Wales *(see pp108–11).*

Surry Hills ❷

Map 5 A3. 🚌 301, 302, 303, 304,
339, Oxford St routes. See **Shops
and Markets** pp200–201.

T HIS WAS ONCE one of the
more depressed areas of
the inner city. In the 1920s,
Surry Hills was a haunt of the
razor gangs that terrorized
inner-city Sydney. The 1940s
slums were vividly described in
Ruth Park's celebrated novels
Poor Man's Orange and *The*

Shop in Crown Street, Surry Hills

Harp in the South. In the postwar years, the low property
and rental prices attracted a
large number of new migrants
to the already-hectic district.

In recent decades, young
professionals have moved into
the area, lured by the charm
of its Victorian terraces and
closeness to the city. Many
of the suburb's traditional
inhabitants have since
been displaced.

Today Surry Hills
is a curious mixture
of fashion and seedi-
ness. Newly renovated
houses stand alongside
dilapidated dwellings,
while streets of elegant
Victorian terraces abut
modern high-rise apart-
ments and factory
warehouses.

For the visitor, the
suburb offers a wide range of
ethnic cuisines, often at bargain prices. It is famed for the
Lebanese and Turkish restaurants that cluster near the
intersection of Cleveland and
Elizabeth Streets. You will

also find Indian, Chinese, Thai,
French, and numerous Italian
eateries scattered around the
suburb, along with casual
cafés and stylish pubs.

Once the center of Sydney's
garment trade, it still has factory outlets where clothing,
lingerie, and accessories can
be purchased at below retail
prices. Alternative fashion and
retro clothing shops are found
at the Oxford Street end of
Crown Street.

University of Sydney ❸

Parramatta Rd, Camperdown.
Map 3 B5. 📞 9351 2222. 🚌 343,
Parramatta Rd & City Rd routes.
🕙 daily. 📷 ⬛ 📷 of university by
arrangement, bookings essential.

I NAUGURATED IN 1850, this is
Australia's oldest university.
The campus is a sprawling
hodgepodge of buildings
from different eras, of
often dubious architec-
tural merit. However,
the original Victorian
Gothic main building
still stands on its ele-
vated site, dominating
its surroundings. The
work of the Colonial
Architect Edmund
Blacket, it is scrupulously
modeled on the
architecture of Cam-
bridge and Oxford.
It features intricate stone
tracery, a clock tower with
carved pinnacles, gargoyles
(one, in the quadrangle, represents a crocodile), and a
cloistered main quadrangle.

**Statue of Hermes,
Nicholson Museum**

The gem of the complex,
and probably Blacket's finest
work, is the Great Hall at the
main building's northern end.
This grandly somber hall, with
its carved cedar ceiling and
stained-glass windows depicting famous philosophers and
scientists, is often used for
public concerts as well as for
university ceremonies.

The Nicholson Museum of
antiquities, the natural history
Macleay Museum, and the War
Memorial Art Gallery, which
houses the university's art
collection, are all within the
grounds. They are open to the
public on most weekdays.

Brett Whiteley Studio: former artist's studio, now a museum

Corner view of Badde Manors Café on Glebe Point Road, Glebe

Glebe ❹

Map 3 A4. 🚌 *431, 433. See* **Shops and Markets** *p203.*

THE WORD "GLEBE" means land assigned to a clergyman as part of his holdings. In 1789, Governor Phillip granted 400 acres to Richard Johnson, the First Fleet chaplain, and his wife Mary. Almost all of the present suburb was once part of that Glebe Estate. Many of its streets wind down to the working harbor and contain terrace houses with Sydney wrought-iron "lace" in varying states of repair.

The once-grand residences of the 19th-century elite were mostly towards the harbor end of Glebe Point Road, with workers' cottages clustered nearer Parramatta Road. It is a mix that survives to this day. Glebe is partly a gentrified member of the café society and partly a humble address, while also being a dormitory suburb for students at the nearby University of Sydney.

It is densely populated and lively, with many restaurants and cafés in all price ranges, traditional and trendy pubs, good bookstores, an art-house movie theater, and shops selling everything from antique clocks to New Age goods. Glebe Market is held every Saturday and has stalls ranging from second-hand clothing and silver jewelry to bric-a-brac.

Sydney Fish Market ❺

Cnr Pyrmont Bridge Rd & Bank St, Blackwattle Bay. **Map** 3 B2. 📞 9660 1611. 🚌 *501.* 🕐 *7am–4pm daily.* ⬤ *Dec 25.* 📷 ♿ 🚻 *See* **Shops and Markets** *pp202–3.*

EVERY WEEKDAY, about 200 seafood retailers and other dealers arrive at this cooperative fish market to bid for the previous day's catch. It is sold by Dutch auction, with prices starting high and decreasing, which halves the sale time. The catch consists of a quantity and variety of fish and other seafood species many times that offered at the London or San Francisco markets.

A fair amount of this catch ends up, later in the morning, in the fish market's numerous large retail outlets that, for the general public, are its main attraction. As well as fresh fish, these retailers sell smoked salmon and roe, sushi, marinated baby octopus, and many other ready-to-eat delicacies. Visitors watch the experts as they tenderize octopus and squid in cement mixers. As well as fish sellers, there are a number of other fresh food shops, several restaurants, and, of course, purveyors of fish and chips for the connoisseur.

Balmain ❻

🚌 *433, 434, 442. See* **Shops and Markets** *p203 and* **Four Guided Walks** *pp142–3.*

BALMAIN WAS ONCE one of Sydney's most staunchly working-class areas, with shipyards, a dry dock and repair yards, a coal mine, numerous rough-and-ready pubs, and an intimidating criminal element. Its late 19th-century town hall, post office, court house and fire house on Darling Street reflect the civic pride of the suburb in the Victorian era.

In recent years, the many stone and timber cottages of what had become a slum have transformed into a charming, bustling suburb that still retains its village character, with interesting shops, galleries, cafés, restaurants, and pubs.

The quietness of the Balmain peninsula, its proximity to the city, and its bohemian ambience perhaps account for the many prominent writers – including the novelist Kate Grenville and playwright David Williamson – who live and work here.

The Saturday market, held at St. Andrews Congregational Church in Darling Street, is one of Sydney's best. Antiques, estate jewelry, and ingenious art and craft items are on sale.

Imposing entrance to Balmain court house on Darling Street

The Colorful Faces of Luna Park

The gateway to Luna Park is the gaping mouth of a huge laughing face, flanked by two 36-m (129-ft) Art Deco towers. Between 1935 and 1945, four successive canvas, wire and plaster faces fell to the ravages of time. Built in the 1950s, the fifth face was replaced in 1973 with one designed by the Sydney artist Martin Sharp. The seventh, from the 1980s, is now at the Powerhouse Museum (see pp100–101). Today's face is made of polyurethane and painted fiberglass.

The present Luna Park face, crossing the harbor by barge

The Big Dipper at Luna Park

Luna Park ❼

1 Olympic Drive, Milsons Point.
📞 9922 6644. 🚊 Luna Park.
🕒 8:30am–5pm daily. 📷 🚻 ♿

THIS FAMOUS amusement park, built on the site of former Harbour Bridge construction workshops, was modeled on Luna Park at Coney Island. Built in South Australia, Sydney's Luna Park was dismantled and re-erected on its present site in 1935. For the next 43 years it was one of the most conspicuous landmarks on the harbor shores. Except during the blackouts of World War II, its brilliant illuminations were a feature of the city's night scene.

In 1979, seven people were killed in a ghost-train fire, a tragedy that led to the park's eventual closure in April 1988. In the early 1990s, Luna Park was refurbished. In 1995, it

reopened as an amusement park, but this has since closed down. Although rides are no longer operating, visitors can still wander through the area.

Luna Park retains many of its extravagant features. Las Vegas glitz and 1940s Futurism are just two of the styles decorating one of Sydney's most treasured icons. The old-style fun house Coney Island, Crystal Palace, and the gateway face are all protected by heritage listing.

Kirribilli Point ❽

Kirribilli Ave, Kirribilli. 🚊 Kirribilli
North Sydney.

THE TWO HOUSES occupying this prominent headland, in their delightful garden settings, are typical of the magnificent homes in sprawling grounds that once ringed the harbor. Most have been demolished

now and the land subdivided for apartment living. Kirribilli, meaning "place for fishing," is the most densely populated suburb in Australia.

The larger, more dominant of the two houses is Admiralty House, built as a single-story residence in 1843. Between 1885 and 1913 it served as the residence of the commanding officer of Britain's Royal Navy Pacific Squadron, which was based in Sydney. Fortifications on the shoreline recall its military history. Now the official Sydney home of Australia's governor-general, it is said that even its shed could be considered the city's best address.

In 1855, the charming Gothic Kirribilli House, with its steep gables and decorative fretwork, was built in the grounds of Admiralty House. Today it is the official Sydney residence of Australia's prime minister.

Nutcote ❾

5 Wallaringa Ave, Neutral Bay.
📞 9953 4453. 🚊 Kurraba Point,
Neutral Bay. 🕒 11am–3pm Wed–Sun.
⬤ Good Fri, Dec 25–26. 📷 🎫

ONE OF THE CLASSICS of Australian children's literature, Snugglepot and Cuddlepie, was published in 1918. Since then, these two characters – known as the "gumnut" babies along with the cartoon creatures Bib and Bub – have been loved by countless young Australians.

Nutcote was, for 44 years, the home of their creator, illustrator and author May Gibbs. Saved from demolition, then

Admiralty House and Kirribilli House, near Sydney Harbour Bridge

Shop façades featuring decorative gables along Manly's Corso

restored and refurbished in the style of the 1930s, it opened in 1994 as an historic house museum. Visitors can view the author's painstakingly kept notebooks and other memorabilia (including the table at which she worked), as well as original editions of her books. There is a garden tea room, with views across the harbor and a shop that sells a range of May Gibbs' souvenirs.

May Gibbs' studio at Nutcote

Taronga Zoo ❿

See pp134–5.

Manly ⓫

🚢 Manly. **Oceanworld** West Esplanade. 📞 9949 2644. ⏰ 10am–5:30pm daily. ⛔ Dec 25. 🅿 📷 ♿
🎫 See **Four Guided Walks** pp146–7.

LONG AFTER Australia's conversion to the metric system, the slogan "seven miles from Sydney and a thousand miles from care" is still current. It refers to Manly and the 7-mile (11-km) journey from Circular Quay by harbor ferry. If asked to suggest a single excursion,

most Sydneysiders would nominate a ferry ride to Manly. This narrow stretch of land lying between the harbor and the ocean was named by Governor Phillip, even before the township of Sydney got its name, for the impressive bearing of the Aboriginal men.

As the ferry pulls in to the rejuvenated Manly wharf you will notice, on the right, the amusement park that occupies the adjacent pier, and on the left, the tranquil harborside beach known as Manly Cove.

At the far end of Manly Cove is Oceanworld, where visitors can see sharks, giant stingrays, and other species in an underwater viewing tunnel. You can also dive with the sharks here if you are brave enough.

The Corso is a lively pedestrian thoroughfare of souvenir shops and fast food outlets. It leads to Manly's ocean beach, with its promenade lined by towering Norfolk pines. Nearby stands a monument to a local newspaper proprietor who, in 1902, defied bans on daytime

swimming and promptly found himself arrested. The next year Australia's swimming laws were liberalized.

In October each year, Manly plays host to the prestigious Manly Jazz Festival (see p48).

North Head ⓬

📞 9977 6522. 🚢 Manly.
Quarantine Station ⏰ 1:10pm daily, or as arranged. Bookings essential.
Ghost tours Wed, Fri, Sun. Bookings essential (starting times vary).
⛔ public hols. 🅿 📷 ♿ 🎫
See **Parks and Reserves** pp44–7.

THE MAJESTIC CLIFFS of North Head afford the finest views in Sydney Harbour National Park, providing vistas along the coastline, across to Middle Harbour and toward the city. North Head is also the ideal place for observing the movements of harbor and seagoing craft and especially for seeing off the yachts at the start of the annual Sydney to Hobart race (see p49).

The Quarantine Station nestles just above Spring Cove within the national park. Here, between 1832 and the 1960s, many ships with their crews and passengers were quarantined to protect Sydneysiders from the spread of epidemic diseases such as smallpox, plague, influenza, and typhoid fever. Over 500 people died here, leading some people to believe the area is haunted.

Countless migrants spent their first months in Australia in this place of splendid isolation. Many of its internees left poignant messages and poems carved in the sandstone.

First-class quarters at the Quarantine Station, North Head

Taronga Zoo ❿

Red kangaroo

THIS FAMOUS HARBORSIDE ZOO is home to almost 4,000 animals, with a special emphasis placed on unique Australian wildlife exhibits. Conspicuous iron bars and fences have been dispensed with, as many of the large enclosures use moats to separate the wandering public from the curious animal onlookers contained in environments closely resembling their natural habitat. The zoo is involved in the breeding of endangered animals, and readily donates or exchanges animals to capitalize on the worldwide gene pool.

Asian Elephant
This relatively large enclosure encourages more natural behavior as the elephants are able to interact freely.

Australian Birds

Athol Wharf Road

Bradleys Head Road

Lower entrance

Athol Wharf Rd

0 meters _____ 100
0 yards _____ 100

The platypus is one of only three species of egg-laying mammals.

Common Wombat
This ground-dwelling animal is a powerful burrower able to move quickly if disturbed. It feeds on roots and has a pouch for carrying its young.

Bradleys Head Road

Upper entrance

Performing seal theater

STAR DISPLAYS

★ **White Tiger**

★ **Orangutan Rain Forest**

★ **Koala House**

Upper Entrance
This edifice has greeted visitors since the opening in 1916. By 1917, more than half of Sydney's population had paid a visit.

★ Orangutan Rain Forest
Threatened by widespread destruction of their natural habitat in the Sumatra and Borneo rain forests, these primates are on the world's endangered species list.

Visitors' Checklist

Bradleys Head Rd, Mosman.
☎ *9969 2777.* 🚌 *238, 247, 250.* ⛴ *Taronga Zoo.* 🕘 *9am–5pm daily (last adm 4:30pm).*
👋 📷 ♿ ✋ ☕ 🛍 ***Concerts, talks, performances.***

Ferry to Circular Quay
Cable car
Taronga Zoo
Birds of Prey
15
16
17
18
19
20
21
22
23
24
26
27

★ White Tiger
Chester the white tiger is not an albino, but the result of a mating between tigers carrying a recessive white gene.

Meerkat
This southern African mongoose always forages in groups, with a guard alert for signs of danger.

African Waterhole
Savanna waterholes are visited by a great variety of species each day. The zoo recreates that environment as giraffes, zebras, and pygmy hippopotami roam together.

The golden lion tamarin is the most endangered primate in the world today.

The Serpentaria has amphibians, invertebrates, and reptiles.

★ Koala House
Visitors can see the koalas in their eucalypt habitat at tree level. The spiral ramp allows you to get close to feeding and sleeping animals.

Key to Animal Enclosures

African Waterhole 24
Asian elephant 10
Australian Birds 13
Australian Walkabout 3
Australia's Night Life 5
Birds of Prey 18
Chimpanzee Park 23
Dingo & Tasmanian devil 7
Echidna & platypus 4
Golden lion tamarin 26
Jungle Cats 12
Koala House 28
Lion 21
Meerkat 19
Orangutan Rain Forest 25
Otter 16
Penguin 8
Red panda 17
Saltwater crocodile 9
Seals and sea-lions 14
Serpentaria 27
Snow leopard 22
Sun bear 15
Walk-through Rain Forest 6
Wetlands 1
White tiger 20
Wombat 2
Yellow-footed rock wallaby 11

Façade of Vaucluse House, with its garden and fountain

Vaucluse House ⑬

Wentworth Rd, Vaucluse.
📞 9388 7922. 🚌 325. ⏰ 10am–
4:30pm Tue–Sun. ⚫ Good Fri,
Dec 25. ♿ 📷

Tradition has it that the
most riotous party colonial
Sydney ever saw took place
on the Vaucluse House lawns
in 1831. WC Wentworth and
4,000 of his political cronies
gathered there to celebrate the
recall to England of Governor
Ralph Darling, the arch-enemy.
  WC Wentworth was a major
figure in the colony, being one
of the first three Europeans to
cross the Blue Mountains *(see
pp160–61)*. He was the son of
a female convict and a physi-
cian forced to "volunteer" his
services to the new colony in
order to avoid conviction on
a highway robbery charge.
  The younger Wentworth
became an author, lawyer, and
statesman who stood for the
Australian-born "currency" lads
and lasses against the "sterling"
English-born. He lived here
with his family from 1829–53,
during which time he drafted
the Constitution Bill, giving
self-government to the state.
  Vaucluse House was begun
in 1803 by Sir Henry Browne
Hayes, a knight of the realm
transported for kidnapping a
Quaker heiress. Sitting comfortably in 27 acres of parkland, natural bush, and
cultivated gardens, this Gothic
Revival house, with its many
idiosyncratic additions, has
been compared to a West
Indian plantation house. The
interior and grounds have been
restored to 1840s style, and the

house contains some furniture
that originally belonged to the
Wentworth family. A popular
tea house is on the grounds.

**Greycliffe House, in the tranquil
grounds of Nielsen Park**

Nielsen Park ⑭

🚌 325. ⏰ 5am–10pm daily.

Part of the Sydney Harbour
National Park, Nielsen Park,
with its grassy expanses, sandy
beach, and fenced swimming
pool, is the perfect spot for a
family picnic. Here visitors can

savor the unusual peace that
descends on many harbor
beaches on an endless sunny
day. It is also an ideal vantage
point from which to enjoy a
spectacular summer sunset or
simply to observe the coming
and going of ferries and the
meandering harbor traffic.
  In the midst of this tranquil
setting, enhancing its charm,
stands Greycliffe House with
its decorative gables and ornate
chimneys. This Victorian
Gothic mansion was completed
in 1852 for WC Wentworth's
daughter and now offers local
national park information.

Watsons Bay ⑮

📞 9391 7100. ⛴ Watsons Bay.
See **Four Guided Walks** pp148–9.

As the base for the boats
that take the pilots out to
arriving ships, this pretty bay
has long been a vital part of
the working harbor. It is also
the home of Doyle's famous
waterfront seafood restaurant,
long a magnet for Sydneysiders
and visitors alike.
  Just up the hill and almost
opposite the bay on the ocean
side is The Gap, a spectacular
cliff with tragic associations.
Many troubled people have
taken a suicidal leap from this
rugged cliff onto the wave-
lashed rocks below.
  It was here that the ill-fated
ship *Dunbar* was wrecked in
1857, with the loss of all but
one of its 122 passengers and
crew. Treacherous conditions
had led to miscalculation of
the ship's distance from the
Heads. All hands were ordered

View over Watsons Bay, looking southwest toward the city

The crescent-shaped Bondi Beach, Sydney's most famous beach, looking toward North Bondi

on deck as The Gap's rock walls loomed. The recovered anchor is now set into the cliff near the shipwreck site.

The 1883 Macquarie Lighthouse overlooking the Pacific Ocean

Macquarie Lighthouse **16**

📷 324, 325. 📷 ♿

THIS IS THE SECOND lighthouse on this windswept site that is attributed to the convict architect Francis Greenway *(see p114)*. He supervised the construction of the first tower, which was completed in 1818 and described by Governor Macquarie as a "noble magnificent edifice." The colony's first lighthouse, it replaced the previous system of bonfires lit up along the headland and earned Greenway a conditional pardon. When the sandstone

eventually crumbled away, the present lighthouse was built. Although designed by Colonial Architect James Barnet, it was based on Greenway's original and was illuminated for the first time in 1883.

Bondi Beach **17**

📷 380, 382, 389, 321. See **Four Guided Walks** *pp144–5.*

THIS LONG CRESCENT of golden sand, so close to the city, has long been a mecca for the sun and surf set *(see pp54–5)*. Throughout the year, surfing enthusiasts visit from far and wide in search of the perfect wave, and inline skaters hone their skills on the promenade. But the beach life that once defined many Australians has declined in recent times, partly as a result of growing awareness of the dangers of sun exposure *(see p223)*, but also because of a shift in cultural attitudes and preoccupations.

People now seek out Bondi for its trendy seafront cafés and cosmopolitan milieu as much as for the beach. The pavilion, built in 1928 as changing rooms, has been a community center since the 1970s. It is now a busy venue for festivals, plays, films, and craft displays.

BONDI SURF BATHERS' LIFE SAVING CLUB

The founding of the surf lifesaving club at Bondi Beach in 1906 gave impetus to the formation of other local clubs, and ultimately to a global movement. An early club member demonstrated his new lifesaving reel, designed using hair pins and a thread spool. Now updated, it is standard equipment on beaches worldwide. In 1938, Australia's largest surf rescue was mounted at Bondi, when more than 200 people were washed out to sea by freak waves. Five died, but lifesavers rescued more than 180, establishing their well-earned reputation.

Bondi surf lifesaving team at the Bondi Surf Carnival, 1937

Captain Cook's Landing Place ⑱

Captain Cook Drive, Kurnell.
☎ 9668 9111. 🚌 987. **Toll Gate**
🅿 7am–7:30pm daily. **Discovery**
Centre 🕐 11am–3pm Mon–Fri,
10am–4pm Sat & Sun. ● Dec 25.
🌳 📷 ♿ 🅿

ALTHOUGH THIS PLACE may be
difficult to get to, visitors
will find it worth the effort. It
is, after all, one of Australia's
most important European historic sites. Here James Cook,
botanists Daniel Solander, and
Joseph Banks and the crew of
HMS *Endeavour* landed on
April 29, 1770. Aboriginal
peoples waving spears at the
invaders were shot at. One,
hit in the legs, returned with
a shield in an effort to defend
himself from attack.

Now, people can cast a fishing line from the rock where

Pampas grass and banana plants in the garden at Elizabeth Farm

the Europeans stepped ashore.
Nearby are the site of a well
where a shore party "found
fresh water sufficient to water
the ship" and a monument that
marks the first recorded European burial in Australia, the
grave site of Forby Sutherland.

There are also monuments
to Solander, Banks, and Cook,
but it is the peaceful ambience
that is most impressive. Now
part of Botany Bay National
Park, Captain Cook's Landing
Place has lovely walks, some
accessible to wheelchairs,
where visitors may roam and
observe the flora that led to
the naming of Botany Bay.

The Discovery Centre in the
park focuses on a number of
themes: the bay's wetlands and
the importance of their conservation; an exhibition detailing
Cook's exploration of the area,
"Eight Days That Changed the
World"; and an introduction to
Aboriginal customs and culture.

**Cook's Obelisk, overlooking Botany
Bay, Captain Cook's Landing Place**

Elizabeth Farm ⑲

70 Alice St, Rosehill. ☎ 9635 9488.
🚆 Harris Park. 🕐 10am–4:30pm
Tue–Sun. ● Good Fri, Dec 25. 🌳
📷 ♿ 🅿

THE DISCOVERY OF fertile land
at Parramatta, and the har-
vesting of its first successful
grain crop in 1790, helped save
the fledgling colony from starvation and led to the rapid
development of the area.

In 1793, John Macarthur was
granted 100 acres of land at
Parramatta. He named the
property after his wife and
this was to be Elizabeth's
home for the rest of her life.
Macarthur was often absent, as
the center of his wool opera-
tions had moved to Camden.

Part of the house, a simple
stone cottage built in 1793, still
remains, and it is the oldest
European building in Australia.
As it was added to over the

JOHN MACARTHUR

John Macarthur did not, as he claimed, introduce
the merino sheep to New South Wales. He did,
however, cross it with hardier breeds, improving
the strain and thus creating the staple export so
vital to Australia's prosperity. Macarthur held vast
landholdings and became the leading member of a
pastoral elite. With his wife Elizabeth, he arrived in
Sydney in 1790 aboard the Second Fleet as a lieutenant in the New South Wales Corps. He quickly
rose to prominence, but his temper brought him
into conflict with successive governors. In 1808,
Macarthur led the "Rum Rebellion" that deposed
Governor Bligh. As secretary to the colony, he was,
for six months, virtually its ruler. Banished from
the colony in 1809 for his actions against Bligh,
he pursued business interests in London before
returning in 1817, a champion of free enterprise.

John Macarthur, 1766–1834

next 50 years, it developed into a substantial home with many features of a typical Australian homestead. Simply furnished to the period of 1820–50, with reproductions of paintings and other Macarthur possessions, the house is now a museum strongly evoking the original inhabitants' life and times.

The kitchen, Hambledon Cottage

Hambledon Cottage ⑳

63 Hassall St, Parramatta. ☏ 9635 6924. 🚆 Parramatta. ⏰ 11am–4pm Wed–Thu, Sat–Sun. ⬤ public hols. ♿ &

THIS DELIGHTFUL cottage, with its painted plasterwork walls, was built in 1824 as the retirement home for Penelope Lucas, governess to the Macarthur daughters. It is set in a park containing trees brought to Australia in 1817 by John Macarthur.

Visitors can wander through rooms that have been restored to the period 1820–50. An 1830 Broadwood piano is one of the furniture exhibits. The kitchen has walls of convict-made bricks. It contains such original appliances and utensils as a handmill for grinding wheat and a bread oven.

Experiment Farm Cottage ㉑

9 Ruse St, Parramatta. ☏ 9635 5655. 🚆 Parramatta. ⏰ 10am–4pm Tue–Thu, 11am–4pm Sun. ⬤ Good Fri, Dec 18–31. ♿ &

WHEN HIS SENTENCE expired in 1789, convict farmer James Ruse was given 1½ acres of land at Parramatta on which to start a farm, along with a hut, grain for sowing, vital farming tools, two sows and six hens. Ruse successfully planted and harvested a substantial wheat crop with the assistance of his wife, Elizabeth, the first female convict to be emancipated in New South Wales. They were rewarded in 1791 with a grant of 30 acres, the colony's first land grant. Arthur Phillip, the governor of the time, called the land Experiment Farm.

In 1793, Ruse sold this farm to surgeon John Harris for the sum of £40. The date of the cottage is not certain, but it is believed to be early 1830s. The woodwork throughout is Australian red cedar and the cottage is furnished according to an 1838 inventory.

Medicine chest (c.1810),
Experiment Farm

St. John's Cemetery ㉒

O'Connell St, Parramatta. ☏ 9635 5904. 🚆 Parramatta. 📷 &

THIS WALLED cemetery – the oldest in Australia – houses the graves of many convicts and settlers who arrived on the First Fleet in 1788. The oldest grave that can be identified is the flat sandstone slab simply inscribed "H.E. Dodd 1791." Henry Edward Dodd, known to be Governor Phillip's butler, was the tenth person buried in the cemetery, but the location of the other nine graves is unknown. The first recorded burial was of a child on January 31, 1790. One prominent grave here is that of pioneer churchman Samuel Marsden, who earned the unfortunate title of the "flogging parson" during his period as magistrate general because of his harsh judgments. The merchant Robert Campbell *(see p66)* and the father of the explorer and patriot William Charles Wentworth *(see p136)*, D'Arcy Wentworth, are also buried here.

Old Government House ㉓

Parramatta Park (entry by Macquarie St gates), Parramatta. ☏ 9635 8149. 🚆 Parramatta. ⏰ 10am–4pm Tue–Fri, 11am–4pm Sat & Sun. ⬤ Good Fri, Dec 25. ♿ & limited.

THE CENTRAL BLOCK of Old Government House is the oldest intact public building in Australia. This elegant brick structure, plastered to resemble stone, was built by Governor Hunter in 1799 on the site of a cottage constructed in 1790 for Governor Phillip. Wings at the side and rear were added between 1812 and 1818. The Doric porch, added in 1816, has been attributed to Francis Greenway *(see p114)*.

Australia's finest collection of early 19th-century furniture is now housed inside. A structure on the site, once thought to be a dairy, has been identified as an early worker's cottage.

The drawing room of Old Government House, Parramatta

FOUR GUIDED WALKS

YDNEY'S TEMPERATE CLIMATE and natural beauty make it an ideal city for walking. The following walks have been chosen for their distinct character; they all capture a view of the essential Sydney. You can follow the paths that trace the headlands and inlets around Watsons Bay; enjoy an invigorating clifftop walk at Bondi; catch glimpses of the original landscape in Manly's unspoiled bushland; or explore the narrow streets of historic Balmain. Three of the walks incorporate ocean or harborside beaches, so be prepared in warmer weather by packing a swimsuit, towel

Mural on a Manly surf shop

and hat, and wearing a reliable sunscreen. Please remember when in Sydney's national parks and bushland that all the indigenous flora and fauna is protected. The best sign of appreciation is to leave the bush as you found it. The *Tips for Walkers* provide practical information about each walk, listing accessibility by bus, train, or ferry and estimated distance of the walk, along with scenic rest areas, picnic spots, cafés, and restaurants en route. The NSW Travel Centre *(see p218)* can supply visitors with information on the many guided walking tours available in Sydney.

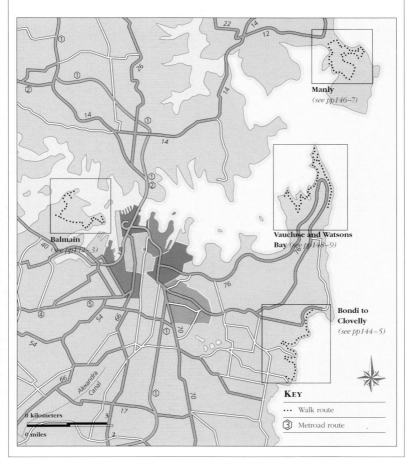

Manly
(see pp146–7)

Vaucluse and Watsons Bay *(see pp148–9)*

Balmain *(see pp142–3)*

Bondi to Clovelly
(see pp144–5)

Alexandra Canal

0 kilometers   3

0 miles   2

◁ **A lookout rising high above the treacherous waters of the Pacific Ocean at The Gap (*see p148*)**

A Two-Hour Walk Around Balmain

HISTORIC BALMAIN VILLAGE was named after William Balmain, a ship's surgeon on the First Fleet. In 1800, he was granted rights to about 550 acres of the peninsula, which he later sold for a paltry 5 shillings in a dubious business transaction. From the mid-1800s, much of the land was subdivided for housing to support the then flourishing mining and maritime industries. Today, grand colonial and Victorian buildings stand side by side with tiny workers' cottages, adding variety to every street.

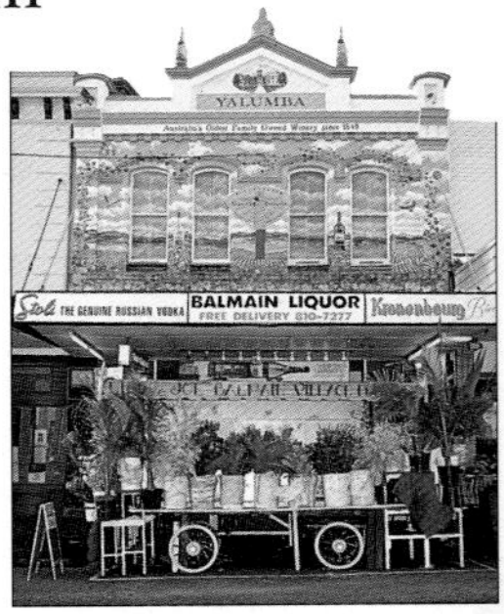

Colorful shopfront on Darling Street, Balmain

The Waterman's Cottage ③

East Balmain

Begin from the Darling Street Wharf ①. By the 1840s, when the ferry service began, shipyards dotted these shores. The sandstone building at No. 10 Darling Street ②, once the Dolphin Hotel then the Shipwright's Arms, was a watering hole for sailors and ferrymen. On the opposite corner is The Waterman's Cottage (1841) ③, home to Henry McKenzie, whose boat ferried residents to and from Sydney Town.

Turn left into Weston Street and walk through the Illoura Reserve for views of the city and Darling Harbour. Leave the park via William and Johnston Streets, stopping in the latter to view Onkaparinga ④, the colonial residence at No. 12. When building started in 1860, mussel shells from Aboriginal feasts stood in mounds on the harbor shore beyond.

Turn left onto Darling Street then right into Duke Street. Gilchrist Place then leads down to Mort Bay Reserve ⑤. Ship's propellers stand as monuments to the area's working past. A path leads up to The Avenue's timber workers' cottages.

Back on Darling Street, turn left down Killeen Street. Take the path across Ewenton Park to Ewenton ⑥ (c.1854). Past the park, Hampton Villa ⑦ at 12B Grafton Street was home to state premier Henry Parkes.

Turn right into Ewenton Street and then left into Wallace Street, with its variety of early Australian architecture. The rough stone home at No. 1 is known as the Railway Station as its narrow frontage makes it look like one. Charming Clontarf ⑧ is found at No. 4, and the symmetry of Maitland House ⑨ is well worth a second glance. Return to Darling Street.

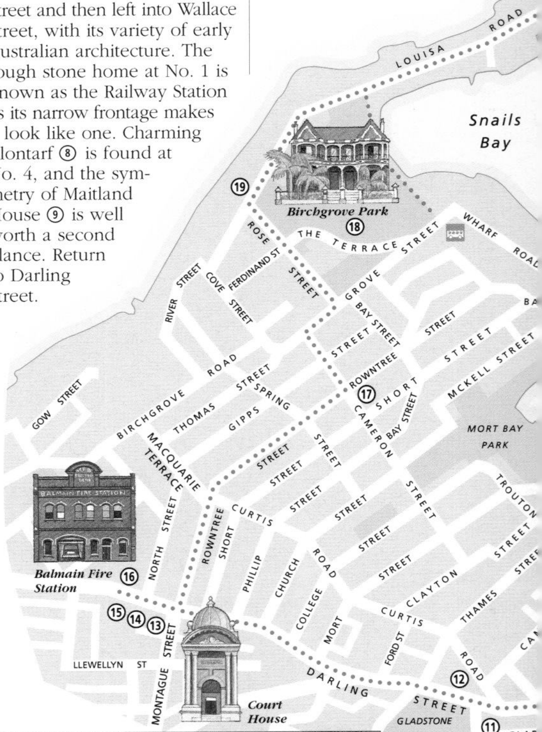

The domestic grandeur of Louisa Road

Historic Links

Sydney's oldest extant lock-up, The Watch House (1854) ⑩ at No. 179 Darling Street, has been restored, but a ghostly female form remains. Farther along, enjoy a drink at The London Hotel (1870) ⑪, where the balcony stools are made of old-fashioned tractor seats.

After the traffic circle, visit St. Andrew's Church ⑫ before losing yourself to the bookshops, cafés, and delicatessens of Balmain. Every Saturday, the Balmain Market fills the churchyard *(see p203)*. At the far end of the shops, the Victorian Post Office (1887) ⑬ and neighboring Court House ⑭ reflect the prosperity of 1880s' Sydney. The Town Hall ⑮ dome was removed during World War II for fear of air raids. Across the street is the Fire Station ⑯ (1894). Set on the crest of a hill, its horse-drawn vehicles always traveled downhill on their outward journey.

Distant views of the city and Sydney Harbour Bridge from Snails Bay

Balmain to Birchgrove

Retrace your steps to Rowntree Street. Turn left and wander down to Birchgrove (about 10 minutes' walk). From Birchgrove shops ⑰, take Cameron Street left and Grove Street right, to Birchgrove Park ⑱ and Snails Bay. Walk down Rose Street to Louisa Road. Two of the most notable homes are Nos. 12 and 14, Keba (1878) and Vidette (1876) ⑲, where the deep verandas and iron-lace balconies hint at the opulence of colonial lifestyles. A poem in praise of the nearby park is inscribed on a plaque at Keba's entrance while, amid the formal greenery of Vidette, a deep well is still fed by a natural spring.

Balmain War Memorial

There is a wealth of interest in the homes that follow: a tiny porch, Victorian entrance tiles, ornate iron lace – plus occasional glimpses of water frontage and private moorings. At the road's end, the preserve at Yurulbin Point ⑳ marks the mouth of Parramatta River. A fishing nook on its eastern corner is a perfect vantage point for taking in the city skyline and passing harbor traffic.

MINI MARKET

Shops nestled in the quiet Birchgrove village ⑰

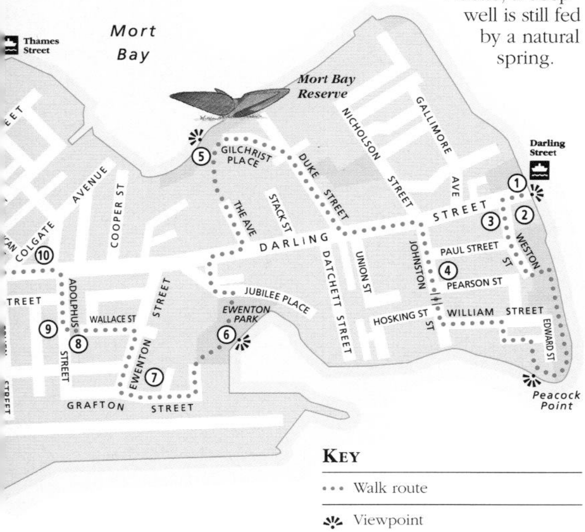
Yurulbin Point
Thames Street
Mort Bay
Mort Bay Reserve
Darling Street
Peacock Point
GILCHRIST PLACE
DUKE STREET
NICHOLSON STREET
GALLIMORE AVE
THE AVE
STACK ST
DARLING STREET
PAUL STREET
WESTON ST
JOHNSTON ST
PEARSON ST
UNION ST
DATCHETT STREET
JUBILEE PLACE
EWENTON PARK
HOSKING ST
WILLIAM STREET
EDWARD ST
AVENUE
COOPER ST
COLGATE
ADOLPHUS STREET
WALLACE ST
EWENTON STREET
GRAFTON STREET
0 meters 250
0 yards 250

Key

- ••• Walk route
- Viewpoint
- Bus stop
- Ferry boarding point

Tips for Walkers

Starting point: *Darling Street Wharf.*
Length: *5.5 km (3½ miles).*
Getting there: *Ferries regularly leave Circular Quay for Darling Street Wharf. The 442 bus from the Queen Victoria Building stops in Darling Street. To return, there is a 15-minute ferry ride at hourly intervals from Yurulbin Point (pick up a schedule at Circular Quay). Alternatively, take Bus 441 from Grove Street (Snails Bay) back to the city (weekdays only).*
Stopping-off points: *Darling Street, in particular, has many good delicatessens, pâtisseries, restaurants, and cafés. Places to picnic include Mort Bay Reserve, Gladstone Park, Birchgrove Park, and Yurulbin Point.*

A Two-Hour Walk from Bondi Beach to Clovelly

THIS INVIGORATING OCEANSIDE and clifftop walk explores the beautiful shoreline and surfing beaches of eastern Sydney. The local color along this scenic trail is at its most vibrant on weekends, when people flock to the cafés and beaches. The Victorian cemetery at the walk's end bears witness to Sydney's multicultural heritage.

Pool at North Bondi Beach

A Seaside Community

Walk north along Campbell Parade [1], passing a colorful array of hotels, beachwear shops, and lively cafés that give the street a raffish atmosphere. The stylish Gelato Bar at No. 140 makes an indulgent pit-stop. Keep walking until the Hotel Bondi [2], the parade's most significant building and easily spotted by its pretty clock tower. Opened as a first-class hotel in 1920, it initially stood quite alone by what was then a bush-fringed beach. Turn right, crossing the road in front of the hotel, and walk down to Queen Elizabeth Drive leaving the traffic and noise of Campbell Parade behind as you reach Sydney's most famous beach, Bondi.

Statue of lifesaver near Bondi Pavilion

Bondi's popularity dates back to the 1880s. Although daylight swimming was banned at the time, the beach was considered a fashionable place to stroll. Bondi trams came into use shortly after and, by the time swimming restrictions were lifted in 1902, the red and white trams were filled with beachgoers. Just ahead you will see Bondi Pavilion [3]. Built in 1928 to replace a modest wooden building, it was designed on a large scale and originally housed a ballroom, gymnasium, restaurant, café, Turkish baths, and open-air theater. Although decidedly less glamorous today, the complex is still a thriving local community center hosting cultural events. Photographs inside recall the romance of Bondi Beach in earlier times.

Next to the Pavilion is the home of Australia's oldest surf life saving club, the Bondi Surf Bathers [4] *(see p137)*. Follow the sweep of the beach to its southern end.

Climb a flight of steps to continue on Notts Avenue, above Bondi Baths [5] and alongside the Bondi Icebergs clubhouse. Prospective members must swim every Sunday, regardless of weather, 50 weeks of the year for four years, to join.

TIPS FOR WALKERS

Starting point: *Campbell Parade, southern end.*
Length: *4 km (2½ miles).*
Getting there: *Take the train to Bondi Junction, then Bus 380 to Bondi Beach. Bus 339 runs from Clovelly Beach to Circular Quay. Waverley Cemetery is open from 8am to dusk every day.*
Stopping-off points: *Public toilets, showers, food, and refreshments are available at Bondi, Tamarama and Bronte Beaches. Take-out cuisine can be bought along Bondi's Campbell Parade as the walk begins. Tamarama's beach café serves refreshing drinks. In warm weather, make the most of four of Sydney's best beaches by packing your swimming gear.*

Tamarama Surf Life Saving Club, at the beach's northern end

Bronte's swimming pools

Bondi to Bronte

Veer left off Notts Avenue as the path drops down and skirts sharp rock formations, the result of years of erosion. Take the steep steps to Mackenzies Point lookout [6] on the headland. The magnificent view stretches for 180 degrees from Ben Buckler in the north to Malabar in the distant south.

KEY

- ••• Walk route
- Viewpoint
- Bus stop
- [P] Parking

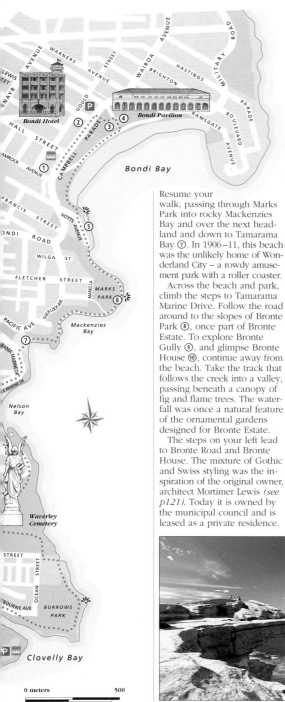

Bondi Hotel

Bondi Pavilion

Bondi Bay

Mackenzies Bay

Nelson Bay

Waverley Cemetery

Burrows Park

Clovelly Bay

0 meters   500

0 yards   500

Bronte to Waverley

Continue down Bronte Road toward the southern end of Bronte Beach. After passing Bronte's cafés, walk through the parking lot and follow the road uphill, through a cutaway originally dug for trams. As the road winds through the cutting and veers right, take the steps through Calga Reserve. Walk down Trafalgar Street to the Waverley Cemetery ⑪.

In grand displays of Edwardian and Victorian monumental masonry, English, Italian, and Irish residents have been laid to rest. Among notable Australians buried here are writers Henry Lawson and Dorothea Mackellar; Fanny Durack, the

Irish Memorial, Waverley Cemetery

first woman to win an Olympic gold medal (in 1912) and do the Australian crawl swimming stroke; and aeronautical pioneer Lawrence Hargrave.

The Irish Memorial honors the 1798 Irish Rebellion and its leader Michael Dwyer, who was transported to Australia for his part in the uprising.

Leave the cemetery at the southern end and walk through Burrows Park. Hug the coast around to Eastbourne Avenue, which leads down to Clovelly Beach ⑫ and the walk's end.

Resume your walk, passing through Marks Park into rocky Mackenzies Bay and over the next headland and down to Tamarama Bay ⑦. In 1906–11, this beach was the unlikely home of Wonderland City – a rowdy amusement park with a roller coaster.

Across the beach and park, climb the steps to Tamarama Marine Drive. Follow the road around to the slopes of Bronte Park ⑧, once part of Bronte Estate. To explore Bronte Gully ⑨, and glimpse Bronte House ⑩, continue away from the beach. Take the track that follows the creek into a valley, passing beneath a canopy of fig and flame trees. The waterfall was once a natural feature of the ornamental gardens designed for Bronte Estate.

The steps on your left lead to Bronte Road and Bronte House. The mixture of Gothic and Swiss styling was the inspiration of the original owner, architect Mortimer Lewis *(see p121)*. Today it is owned by the municipal council and is leased as a private residence.

Lookout at Mackenzies Point, a popular spot for watching surfers ⑥

A Three-Hour Walk Around Manly

THIS WALK TAKES IN THE holiday atmosphere of downtown Manly and its splendid surf beach, before passing along quieter shorelines and clifftop streets, and through unspoiled bushland replete with native flora and fauna. It features marvelous views, the commanding architecture of Manly's most significant building, St. Patrick's Seminary, and the charm of Collins Beach and Fairy Bower.

Houses rising above Fairy Bower

Brass band plays in The Corso

From Harbor to Ocean

Start at Manly Wharf ①. This suburb was little more than a cozy fishing village until 1852, when entrepreneur Henry Gilbert Smith's vision of a resort, similar to fashionable Brighton in his native England, started to take shape. The ferry service began in 1855, operating from the same spot in use today.

Leaving Manly Cove, cross The Esplanade and walk down The Corso, a pedestrian mall. At the end of The Corso, to the left, stands the New Brighton Hotel ② in striking Egyptian Classical Revival Style. In 1926, it replaced the original New Brighton, built in 1880 as the resort's first attraction.

Head toward the rolling surf and sweeping sands of Manly Beach ③ then continue south along the promenade. From the 1950s-style Surf Pavilion, follow Marine Parade walkway around to Cabbage Tree Bay. The pretty area around the rock pool was named Fairy Bower ④ for the delicate wildflowers and maidenhair ferns that once grew on the hillside. Beyond the rock pool, continue on the pathway around to Shelly Beach ⑤, a secluded scuba diving and snorkeling spot, which is also ideal for child swimmers. The 1920s beach kiosk has now been stylishly restored and converted into the smart Le Kiosk restaurant.

Detail on the New Brighton Hotel

Shelly Beach to St. Patrick's Seminary

Across the park, take the steps to your left to Shelly Beach Headland. A path farther left loops around the headland. Viewing platforms ⑥ overlook the vast South Pacific Ocean.

Take the parking lot exit into Bower Street. Follow the road as it rounds high above Fairy Bower, passing by homes of diverse architectural styles, from Spanish Mission to Neo-Georgian. Turn left into College Street, then right into Reddall Street, and left again

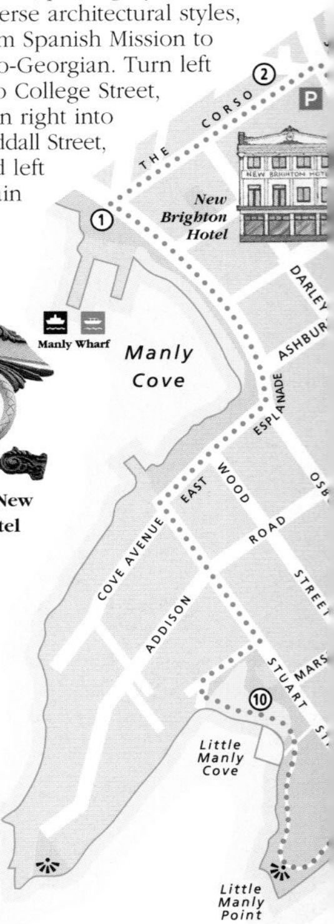

> **TIPS FOR WALKERS**
>
> ***Starting point:*** *Manly Wharf*
> ***Length:*** *7.5 km (4½ miles).*
> ***Getting there:*** *Regular ferry and JetCat services depart from Wharf 2 at Circular Quay.*
> ***Stopping-off points:*** *The wide range of fresh food counters at Manly Pier make it an ideal place to stock up on picnic fare. Restaurants and cafés line The Corso and Manly Beach Promenade. A kiosk at Shelly Beach offers the choice of a smart restaurant, barbecue, or snack bar. In warm weather, come prepared with a swimsuit, hat, towel, and sunscreen.*

The clear waters of sheltered Shelly Beach ⑤

into Addison Road. Opposite the Victorian buildings at Nos. 97–99 and 95, a lane into Fairy Bower Road leads to views of St. Patrick's Seminary ⑦. Both Neo-Gothic and Romanesque architectural principles are in evidence in this 1885 Catholic seminary, built only after much deliberation by the essentially Protestant government.

Leave Fairy Bower Road by Vivian Street to turn left into Darley Road and arrive at the seminary. On the opposite side of the road, the Archbishop's House stands partly hidden by Norfolk Island pines. Known as the Cardinal's Palace for its lavish interiors, it is, sadly, not open to the public.

The grand Victorian architecture of St. Patrick's Seminary ⑦

North Head Reserve
At the top of Darley Road, turn right beneath the Parkhill Sandstone Arch ⑧ into North Head

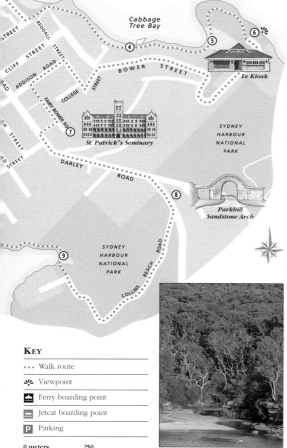

KEY

••• Walk route

⚡ Viewpoint

🚢 Ferry boarding point

🚤 Jetcat boarding point

🅿 Parking

0 meters   250

0 yards   250

Collins Beach ⑨ on the edge of Sydney Harbour National Park

Reserve. Follow the right-hand fork onto Collins Beach Road down through bushland, alive with bird calls. Paperbarks, Sydney red gums, and banksias are just some of the native flora growing in abundance.

At the road's end, follow the track to your right across two footbridges, then down steps to Collins Beach ⑨. A stone cairn between the second foot-bridge and the beach marks where Governor Arthur Phillip was speared by the Aboriginal Wil-ee-ma-rin after a misunderstanding. The quiet waterfall and dense bushland make it possible to imagine this beach in precolonial days.

Leave this peace and quiet via a rough hillside track onto a concrete pathway, then out into Stuart Street. Beyond the street, Little Manly Point gently nudges out into the harbor.

Back to the Present
For memorable harbor views, follow the direction of Stuart Street through Little Manly Point Reserve, passing by the pools of Little Manly Cove ⑩. If you are reluctant to end this charming walk, turn left and proceed to the end of Addison Road. Manly Point Peace Park offers a quiet place to take in a panorama of the distant city.

Return down Addison Road, making your way back to the wharf via Stuart Street and the East Esplanade. With its boat sheds and bleached wood yacht clubs, the East Esplanade Park has a nautical atmosphere and is a relaxing place to meander. Continue past the attractions of the amusement pier to Manly Wharf, which was your starting point.

A Three-Hour Walk in Watsons Bay and Vaucluse

Tracing the perimeters of spectacular South Head, this walk touches on the area's colonial connections and takes in a variety of ocean and harborside terrain, from headlands with sweeping views and crashing waves, to secluded coves, white sandy beaches, and the streets of one of Sydney's most desirable neighborhoods.

Signal Station ② at Dunbar Head

Macquarie Lighthouse to Camp Cove

The start of this walk is majestic Macquarie Lighthouse (1883) ①. A copy of the country's first lighthouse built in 1818 *(see p137)*, it stands on the same site.

Take the walk northward, passing by the Signal Station ② following Old South Head Road. Before the station was built in 1848, a flag was hoisted to warn the colony of ships entering the harbor.

Continue along the footpath, where a plaque marks the location of Australia's worst maritime disaster. It was here that the migrant ship *Dunbar* crashed onto the rocks in a gale in 1857 *(see pp136–7)*. The only survivor was hauled to safety up the treacherous cleft in the cliff face known as Jacob's Ladder ③. From here, follow the descending path, arriving at the turbulent seas and jutting stony ledges of The Gap ④. The *Dunbar*'s anchor is here set into concrete, while salvaged personal effects are displayed at the National Maritime Museum *(see pp94–5)*.

Taking the steps down from The Gap, bear right into the entrance of Sydney Harbour National Park. This single-lane roadway leads through natural bushland into HMAS *Watson* Military Reserve. Follow the road up to visit the Naval Memorial Chapel ⑤. A large clear window inside the chapel offers spectacular views of North Head and the Pacific Ocean. Resume your walk by taking the road out of the preserve, and then turn right into Cliff Street. Passing a row of weatherboard cottages on your left, follow the street to its end and onto Camp Cove Beach ⑥. It was here in 1788 that Captain Arthur Phillip first stepped ashore after leaving Botany Bay to explore the coastline.

Bust, Macquarie Lighthouse ①

Camp Cove to Watsons Bay

Take the wooden steps at the northern end of the cove to make the 40-minute return walk to South

Nudist Lady Bay Beach

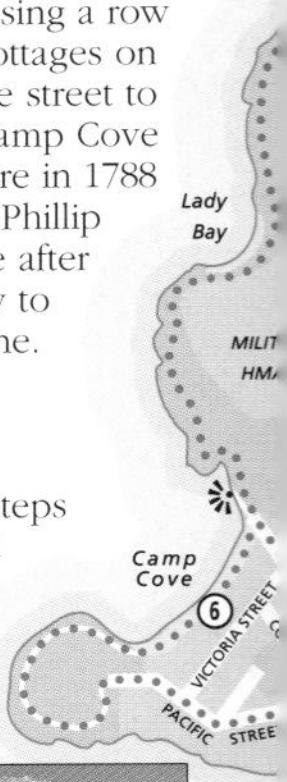

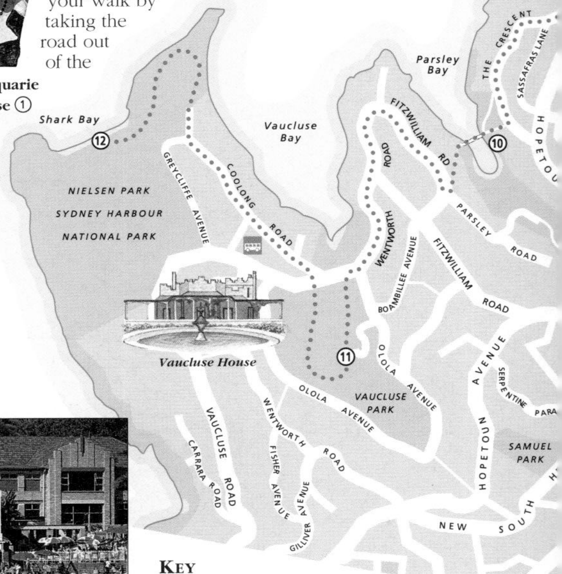

Doyle's well-known restaurant at Watsons Bay ⑧

Key

- ••• Walk route
- Viewpoint
- Bus stop
- Ferry boarding point

Suspension bridge across Parsley Bay ⑩

Macquarie Lighthouse

SYDNEY HARBOUR
NATIONAL PARK

④ Dunbar's Anchor

THE GAP PARK

③

0 meters 500

0 yards 500

Head. Above the steps are signs of colonial defenses: a firing wall with rifle slots; a cannon lying farther along. After passing Lady Bay Beach, you will reach Hornby Light-house ⑦, which marks the harbor's entrance. Retrace your steps to Camp Cove Beach. Climb the western-end stairs to Laings Point, a defense post in World War II. A net stretching across the harbor mouth was anchored here to prevent enemy ships entering.

Follow Pacific Street to Cove Street, then along to Marine Parade and Wharf Beach in Watsons Bay ⑧ *(see pp136–7)*. Named after Robert Watson of the First Fleet's *Sirius*, this was once first port of call for ships entering the harbor. Nearby, Doyle's restaurant offers sea-food with a view. Follow the parade past the pools and tea rooms. Pilot boats ⑨ moored close by guide cruise and con-tainer ships into the harbor.

Watsons Bay to Vaucluse

Continue to secluded Gibsons Beach, taking the footpath left through native shrubbery, then right onto Hopetoun Avenue. Turn into The Crescent, trac-ing the curve of this exclusive street around to Parsley Bay Reserve. A short descent opens

Children's bedroom, one of the exhibits at Vaucluse House ⑪

onto a suspension bridge hung across the waters of tranquil Parsley Bay ⑩. Crossing the bridge, follow the pathway between two houses to arrive on Fitzwilliam Road. Continue right along Fitzwilliam Road, turning left into Wentworth Road to reach the extravagant Vaucluse House ⑪, surrounded by exotic gardens *(see p136)*.

To finish your walk, make your way along Coolong Road to Nielsen Park *(see p136)* and Shark Bay ⑫. Protected from its namesake by a netted enclosure, the natural setting and safe waters of this beach make it a favorite for picnics.

Dramatic rock cleft known as Jacob's Ladder ③ **near The Gap**

TIPS FOR WALKERS

Starting point: Macquarie Lighthouse.
Length: 8 km (5 miles).
Getting there: Take Bus 324 from Circular Quay, or Bus 387 from Bondi Junction. Return by Bus 325 from Nielsen Park.
Stopping-off points: There are public toilets and showers at Camp Cove, Watsons Bay, Parsley Bay, and Nielsen Park. Food and refreshments are available throughout the walk at Watsons Bay, Parsley Bay, Vaucluse, and Nielsen Park. The tea rooms at Vaucluse House offer views of the gardens, and the café at Nielsen Park sells homemade food in generous portions. The walk covers several harbor beaches where you can swim safely. In warm weather, bring a swimsuit, towel, hat, and sunscreen, and allow time for swimming, sun-bathing, and picnicking.

BEYOND SYDNEY

EXPLORING BEYOND SYDNEY 152–153
PITTWATER AND KU-RING-GAI CHASE 154–155
HAWKESBURY TOUR 156–157
HUNTER VALLEY 158–159
BLUE MOUNTAINS 160–161
SOUTHERN HIGHLANDS TOUR 162–163
ROYAL NATIONAL PARK 164–165

Exploring Beyond Sydney

To the east, Sydney is bounded by the Pacific Ocean; to the west, by the Great Dividing Range. To the north and south, within easy distance of the city, are superb beaches and stretches of coastal scenery, while inland, you will encounter waterfalls, deep valleys, and fascinating flora and wildlife. On the Hawkesbury River, to the north and west of the city, are settlements of historical as well as scenic interest while, farther north, the Hunter River meanders through sloping vineyards. The excursions on pages 154–65 offer the visitor the chance to sample the rich variety of Sydney landscapes from the exhilarating to the tranquil.

Pioneer Village on the Hawkesbury River

Façade of Rothbury Estate in the Hunter Valley

SIGHTS AT A GLANCE

Blue Mountains ❹
Hawkesbury Tour ❷
Hunter Valley ❸
Pittwater and Ku-ring-gai Chase
    National Park ❶
Royal National Park ❻
Southern Highlands Tour ❺

GETTING AROUND

All the areas covered in these excursions can be easily reached by road from Sydney. Freeways and highways take travelers part of the way to the Southern Highlands, Blue Mountains, and Hunter Valley, while the other areas are accessible on paved, well-marked major roads. A number of tour operators offer guided one-day, or longer, tours to the Blue Mountains, Hunter Valley, Southern Highlands and South Coast, and parts of the Hawkesbury region. CityRail has regular train services to the Blue Mountains, Royal National Park, and to parts of the area covered by the Southern Highlands Tour. Ferries offer access to some parts of the Hawkesbury River.

0 kilometers   50

0 miles   25

Grand old house in Kiama, near the Southern Highlands

Mudgee

Orange,
Dubbo

BATHURST

Fish River

LITHGOW

BLUE
MOUNTAINS ❹

KANANGRA BOY
NATIONAL PARK

MOSS VALE

Canberra

MORTON
NATIONAL PA

Bege

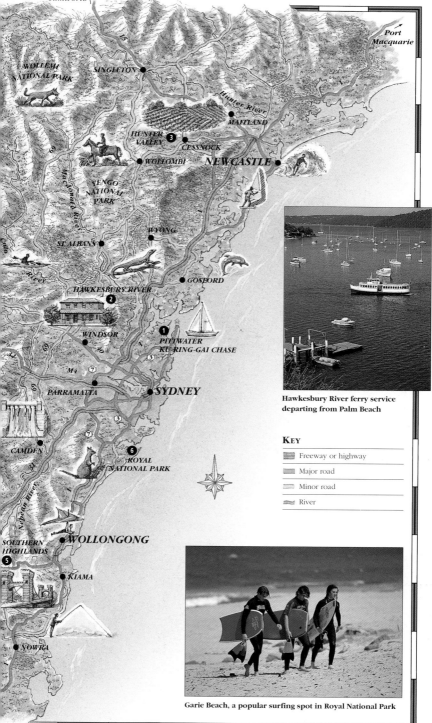

Hawkesbury River ferry service departing from Palm Beach

KEY

▨	Freeway or highway
▨	Major road
▨	Minor road
〰	River

Garie Beach, a popular surfing spot in Royal National Park

Pittwater and Ku-ring-gai Chase ❶

Barrenjoey Lighthouse

PITTWATER AND THE ADJACENT Ku-ring-gai Chase National Park lie on Sydney's northernmost outskirts. They are bounded to the north by Broken Bay, at the mouth of the Hawkesbury River *(see pp156–7)*. Sparkling waterways and golden beaches are set against the unspoiled backdrop of the national park. Picnicking, bushwalking, surfing, boating, sailing, and windsurfing are popular pastimes with visitors. The Hawkesbury River system curls around an ancient sandstone landscape rich in Aboriginal rock art, and flora and fauna.

Coal and Candle Creek
The pretty inlet is typical of eroded valleys formed during the last Ice Age. Water melted from the ice caps flooded the valleys to form the bays and creeks of Broken Bay.

Akuna Bay
The isolated marina, general store and café serve the Hawkesbury River boating fraternity.

ABORIGINAL ART IN KU-RING-GAI CHASE

Ku-ring-gai Chase has literally hundreds of Aboriginal rock art sites, providing an insight into one of the world's oldest cultures. The most common are rock engravings, generally made in groups with as many as 100 individual figures. They include whales up to 8 m (26 ft) long, fish, sharks, wallabies, echidnas, and Ancestral Spirits such as Daramulan, who created the land, its people, and animals.

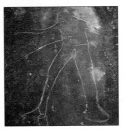

Aboriginal rock art near the Basin, Ku-ring-gai Chase

KEY

▬▬	Major road
═══	Secondary road
━━	Minor road
▢	National Park
– –	Ferry route
‑ ‑	Walk route
🚤	Boat rental
🔱	Aboriginal rock art
✲	Viewpoint

Map labels: BRISBANE WATER NATIONAL PARK · Patonga · Hawkesbury River · Juno Point · Gunyah Beach · Hungry Beach · Flint and Steel · Challenger Head · Refuge Bay · Cowan Creek · Cowan Point · West Head Road · KU-RING-GAI CHASE NATIONAL PARK · Coal and Candle Creek · Cottage Point · Smith's Creek · Akuna Bay · General San Martin Drive · McCarrs Creek Road · RYDE, CHATSWOOD

Palm Beach Wharf

Palm Beach, a haven for sea birds such as pelicans, is popular with sunseekers. It is also the base for the boats that visit and deliver supplies to the isolated communities on Pittwater and the Hawkesbury.

Pittwater

This graceful finger of water separates Palm Beach from Ku-ring-gai Chase. Pittwater boasts secluded beaches, picnic areas, and several hamlets that can only be reached by water.

Whale Beach

Spectacular houses seem to hug the cliffs overlooking this fine surf beach. The Palm Beach Peninsula's beaches are often less congested than those closer to the city.

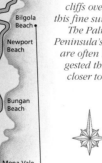

Bilgola Beach

A small community of residents backs this patrolled surf beach set against a pretty rainforested valley. Wooden steps lead down from the ridge above through coastal heathland.

Broken Bay

Lion Island

West Head

Barrenjoey Head

Great Mackerel Beach

Palm Beach

Pittwater

Whale Beach

Careel Bay

Basin

Longnose Point

Towlers Bay

Barrenjoey Road

Avalon Beach

BILGOLA PLATEAU

It Bay

Scotland Island

Bilgola Beach

Church Point

Newport Beach

Bungan Beach

Mona Vale Road

Mona Vale Beach

Pittwater Road

RYDE, CHATSWOOD

DEE WHY, MANLY

0 kilometers   2

0 miles   1

TIPS FOR TRAVELERS

Distance from Sydney: *About 30 km (19 miles).*
Duration of journey: *About 45 minutes to Mona Vale Beach.*
Getting there: *Take Military Rd on the city's North Shore and cross the Spit Bridge. Follow Pittwater Rd to Mona Vale Beach.*
When to go: *The Christmas holiday period is the peak season, and beaches can be crowded. Ku-ring-gai Chase offers everything from shoreline to bushwalks and can be enjoyed year round.*
Where to stay and eat: *Contact the visitors' information center for full details of facilities.*
Tourist information: *Pittwater Visitors Information Centre is at 1 Park St, Mona Vale.* 9979 8717. 10am–4pm Thu–Sun.

Hawkesbury Tour ❷

AUSTRALIA'S LONGEST eastward-flowing river, the Hawkesbury–Nepean, forms Sydney's northern and western boundaries. It was at first thought to be two separate rivers until further exploration revealed that they were in fact one. The section known as the Hawkesbury runs from the Colo River Valley to Broken Bay in the north *(see pp154–5)*.

Settled in 1794, by 1799 the Hawkesbury Valley's small farms produced three-quarters of the colony's grain. Its riverscape has changed little since then and much of the area remains a quiet backwater. It is an area rich in relics of the early colonial period, including towns and villages established during the Macquarie era of 1810–19 *(see p22)*. It is also a place of great scenic grandeur, with magnificent vistas of one of Australia's most beautiful rivers.

Tizzana Winery ⑤
A touch of Tuscany on the banks of the Hawkesbury, this sandstone winery was built in 1887 by Dr. Thomas Fiaschi. It is open to visitors on Saturdays and public holidays.

Ebenezer Uniting Church ④
Built in 1809, the church and its 1817 schoolhouse have been superbly restored. The tree under which services were first held still stands.

Portland Reach ⑥
On the river, pleasure craft have replaced the grain barges of the past, but the area's farming community survives.

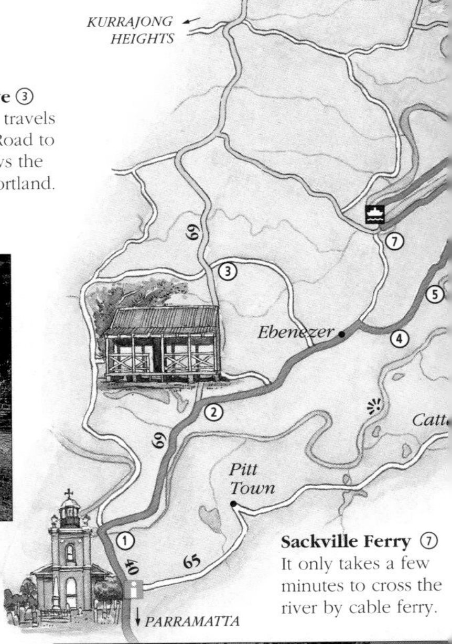
SINGLETON
Colo River
69
KURRAJONG HEIGHTS
69
Ebenezer
Catt
69
Pitt Town
40
65
PARRAMATTA

Colo River Drive ③
This pretty route travels along the Putty Road to Colo, then follows the river to Lower Portland.

Australiana Pioneer Village ②
This collection of original pioneer buildings recreates an early colonial village. At the center is Rose Cottage (1811), built of ironbark slabs with she-oak shingle roofing.

Sackville Ferry ⑦
It only takes a few minutes to cross the river by cable ferry.

Windsor ①
Built in 1815, the Macquarie Arms Hotel is just one of Windsor's fine early colonial buildings. Many others, including several by architect Francis Greenway *(see p114)*, remain from the town laid out in 1810.

MACQUARIE ARMS

Settlers Arms Inn ⑩
Once an overnight stop for stage coaches to the Hunter Valley (*see pp158–9*), this atmospheric 1836 hotel is in the largely unchanged village of St. Albans.

Webbs Creek Ferry ⑨
Opened in 1908, this cable ferry gives access to the western bank of the Hawkesbury for the drive beside the Macdonald River.

Old General Cemetery ⑪
A stark reminder of the hardships and tragedies of early settlement, this is the resting place of six First Fleeters (*see p20*).

Portland Ferry ⑧
If taking the Colo River Drive, cross the river here by ferry for the River Road to Wisemans Ferry.

Macdonald River

Hawkesbury River

GOSFORD

Old Great North Road ⑫
The convict-built road with its massive buttresses was completed in 1828. Part of it still remains.

Maroota

65

36

Cornelia

HORNSBY

Wisemans Ferry ⑬
This small village on a bend in the Hawkesbury River is where ex-convict Solomon Wiseman started his ferry service, Australia's oldest, in 1827.

TIPS FOR DRIVERS

Distance from Sydney: 55 km (35 miles) to Windsor.

Duration of tour: About 3½ hours, excluding stops.

Getting there and back: Follow M4 to James Ruse Drive (53) just before Parramatta, then Windsor Rd (40). To return from Wisemans Ferry, take the Old Northern Rd (36) to Middle Dural, then Galston Rd to Hornsby. From here, follow Pacific Hwy south.

When to go: Peak season is from December to February. The river, national parks, and small towns can be enjoyed all year.

Where to stay and eat: Cafés, restaurants, and accommodations can be found at Windsor and Wisemans Ferry. The Settlers Arms Inn at St. Albans has a few rooms, a bar, and restaurant.

Tourist information: There is a visitors' center at Hawkesbury Museum, Thompson Square, Windsor. ☎ (045) 77 2310.

KEY

▬▬ Tour route

══ Scenic route

═══ Other road

⛴ Cable ferry

ℹ Tourist information

⋇ Viewpoint

0 kilometers 5

0 miles 3

Hunter Valley ❸

Cheese made by local producer

Sᴏᴍᴇ ᴏꜰ ᴛʜᴇ ᴇᴀʀʟɪᴇꜱᴛ vineyards to be planted in Australia were on the fertile flats of the Hunter River in the 1830s, when a thriving industry in fortified wine grew up in the area. Since the 1970s, one of the country's premium table wine districts has evolved *(see pp182–3).*
With more than 50 wineries and 30 restaurants, the Hunter Valley is a popular trip for Sydneysiders. Hot air ballooning, golf courses, horseback riding, and cycling supplement vineyard visits. Most large wineries open daily for sales and tastings. Smaller establishments open on weekends or by appointment.

SINGLETON, UPPER HUNTER

Lindemans
In 1842, Dr. Henry John Lindeman resigned his naval commission to establish a vineyard in the Hunter. His company has been a major producer in the Australian wine industry ever since.

ROSEMOUNT ESTATE, UPPER HUNTER

Golden Grape Estate
A popular tour bus stop, the winery has a gallery showing grape varieties found around the world. There is also a museum which features early wine-making equipment.

Hunter Estate
Marsh Estate
Deaseys Road
Broke Road
Tyrrell's Wines
Brokenwood
Tambu
Pokolbin
Tull
Debeyers Rd
Pok
Oakey
McWilliam's
Marrow
Petersons

PERSONALITIES OF THE HUNTER VALLEY

The wine industry seems to attract or create characters that are larger than life. Among the current generation of living legends is Len Evans, writer, wine judge, *bon vivant,* and founder of the ambitious Rothbury Estate and Evans Family Wines. His contemporaries include Max Lake, a Sydney surgeon who started Lake's Folly as a weekend winery, and Murray Tyrrell, patriarch of a wine-making family that produced its first Hunter vintage in 1864 and proudly retains its independence.

Len Evans checking grape vines

Wyndham Estate

Established in the 1830s, this pioneering vineyard on the Wyndham family's property has a Georgian sandstone homestead that has been restored to its original condition.

Rothbury Estate

The grand inspiration of Len Evans, this winery is dedicated to wine excellence and education. Dinners and concerts held in the winery's cask hall are popular events.

Lake's Folly

Australian growers stopped planting Cabernet Sauvignon vines in the 19th century, but in the 1960s, Max Lake reintroduced the variety, and his success has been repeated across Australia.

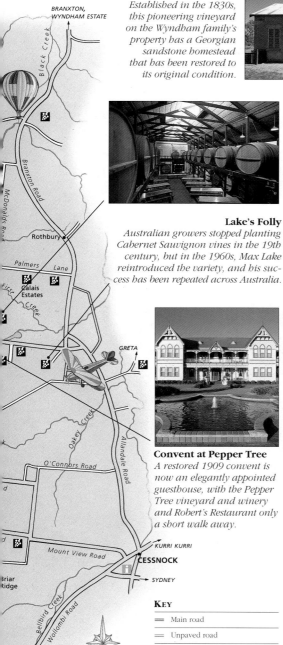

Convent at Pepper Tree

A restored 1909 convent is now an elegantly appointed guesthouse, with the Pepper Tree vineyard and winery and Robert's Restaurant only a short walk away.

TIPS FOR TRAVELERS

Distance from Sydney: *130 km (81 miles).*
Duration of journey: *About 2 hours from the center of Sydney.*
Getting there and back: *Take the Sydney–Newcastle freeway north of Sydney and follow the signs to Cessnock. An alternative route is through the picturesque Wollombi Valley. Allow about 3 hours as this is a scenic route with some unpaved roads.*
When to go: *Year round. Vintage is Jan – Mar.*
Where to stay and eat: *There is a wide variety of motels, guesthouses, rental cottages and cabins, cafés, and restaurants.*
Tourist information: *Visitor Information Centre, Turner Park, Aberdare Rd, Cessnock.*
((049) 90 4477.
Farther afield: *The Upper Hunter vineyards are about 40 minutes by car northwest of Pokolbin.*

KEY

═══	Main road
═══	Unpaved road
🏭	Winery
ℹ	Tourist information
☼	Viewpoint

Map labels:
BRANXTON, WYNDHAM ESTATE
Black Creek
Branxton Road
McDonalds Road
Rothbury
Palmers Lane
Calais Estates
Fless Creek
GRETA
Oakey Creek
Allandale Road
O'Connors Road
Mount View Road
KURRI KURRI
CESSNOCK
SYDNEY
Briar Ridge
Bellbird Creek
Wollombi Road
Bellbird
WOLLOMBI, SYDNEY

0 kilometers 2
0 miles 1

Blue Mountains ❹

FOR A QUARTER OF A CENTURY after European settlement, the Blue Mountains prevented the colony's westward expansion. In 1813, an expedition led by the explorers Gregory Blaxland, William Lawson, and William Charles Wentworth found a way across. The magnificent scenery, characterized by rugged cliffs and rock formations, ravines, and waterfalls, is best appreciated on the bushwalks that wind along cliff tops and through valleys. The restaurants, cafés, and antique shops will tempt the less energetic. The mountains are named for the perennial blue haze, caused by light striking eucalyptus oil particles in the air.

Zig Zag Railroad
A steam train travels through cuts and tunnels, and over three impressive viaducts built from 1866–9.

Grose Valley from Govetts Leap
Considered by many to be the most imposing view in the Blue Mountains, a great panorama with a series of ridges stretches into the far distance.

The Grose River
flows between the two roads crossing the mountains.

Victoria Falls

Mount York

ZIG ZAG RAILWAY

JENOLAN CAVES

Three Sisters
This giant rock formation near Echo Point takes its name from an Aboriginal legend. The story tells of three sisters turned to stone by their witch-doctor father to keep them safe from an evil bunyip, or monster.

JENOLAN CAVES

About 55 km (34 miles) south-west of Mount Victoria is a magical series of spectacular underground limestone caves with icy blue rivers and fleecy limestone formations. They are surrounded by an extensive wildlife preserve. People have been making the trek here since the caves were discovered in 1838, staying originally in the Grand Arch cave and later in the Edwardian splendor of Jenolan Caves House, which still operates today.

The vividly colored Pool of Cerberus at Jenolan Caves

KEY

——	Major road
	Other road
•••	Suggested walk
🚶	Starting points for other walks
🅰	Campsite
🏕	Picnic area
ℹ	Tourist information
☀	Viewpoint

Mount Wilson
A picturesque village with cultivated gardens and exotic trees, it has been called a "little corner of the northern hemisphere." Some gardens are open to the public in spring and autumn.

The Cathedral of Ferns is a remnant of the temperate rain forest that once covered this area.

Mount Tomah Botanic Gardens
This superbly landscaped garden, specializing in cool-climate plants, has sweeping views over the Grose Valley.

RICHMOND

Mount Banks

Yester Grange
The beautifully restored Victorian country house at Wentworth Falls has tea rooms and a restaurant, as well as a collection of antiques and crafts.

Wentworth Falls
An impressive double water-fall is the starting point for the National Pass track, a challenging four-hour return walk to the next valley.

Kings Tableland

Jamison Valley

Leura village is classified by the National Trust. Nearby are Leura Cascades, floodlit at night and one of the prettiest sights in the mountains.

0 kilometers 5

0 miles 3

TIPS FOR TRAVELERS

Distance from Sydney: *About 105 km (65 miles).*
Duration of journey: *About 90 minutes to Wentworth Falls.*
Getting there and back: *Follow Metroad route 4 and the Great Western Highway to Wentworth Falls. Return by Bells Line of Road to Windsor. State Rail has regular services to the area. An Explorer Bus runs from Katoomba railroad station at 9:30am on weekends and public holidays.*
When to go: *Year-round. Always be prepared for the cold, especially when hiking, since the weather can change rapidly in all seasons.*
Where to stay and eat: *Contact the visitor information center.*
Tourist information: *Blue Mountains Visitors' Information Centre, Echo Point, Katoomba.*
(047) 82 0756.

Southern Highlands Tour [5]

Common wombat

THIS EASILY ACCESSIBLE area to the south of Sydney is often said to be more typical of Great Britain, particularly Scotland, than Australia. It is actually a delightful combination of both: Australian high country and coastal hinterland with many European qualities. It is a land of abrupt hills and valleys, waterfalls and fast-running streams; of quaint villages, cozy restaurants and cafés, antique shops, and elegant places to stay. The tour takes in spectacular Seven Mile Beach and the pretty town of Berry before heading to Kangaroo Valley, sleepy Bundanoon, and the antique shops of Berrima and Bowral. An exhilarating adjunct to the tour is nearby Minnamurra Falls with its boardwalk through rain forest.

Bowral [8]
This highlands town holds a famous spring tulip festival every year and is home to cricket's Bradman Museum.

Berrima [7]
Bypassed by the railroad in the 19th century, the only Georgian village in the highlands remains one of the most picturesque.

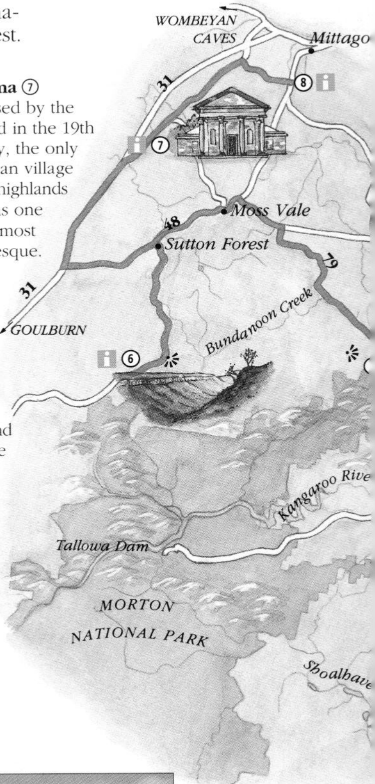
WOMBEYAN CAVES
Mittago
31
8
7
Moss Vale
48
Sutton Forest
79
31
GOULBURN
Bundanoon Creek
6
Kangaroo Rive
Tallowa Dam
MORTON NATIONAL PARK
Shoalhave

Bundanoon [6]
Romantic guesthouses and a glow worm cave make this town a popular weekend destination.

Fitzroy Falls [5]
Part of Morton National Park, the falls plunge 80 m (262 ft) into the subtropical rain forest below. The falls lookout has access for the disabled and walking trails with stunning views.

0 kilometers 10

0 miles 5

KEY

- Tour route
- Scenic route (alternative)
- Other roads
- Tourist information
- Viewpoint

Kangaroo Valley [4]
Hampden Bridge, a castellated suspension bridge, crosses the Kangaroo River at this small village. The river is an idyllic place for canoeing.

BERRIMA GAOL

Completed in 1839 by convict labor, this Georgian sandstone jail is featured in Rolf Boldrewood's classic 1888 bushranging novel *Robbery Under Arms*. The fictitious character Captain Starlight, who escapes from Berrima, describes it as "the largest, most severe, the most dreaded of all prisons in New South Wales."

Kiama ①
The historic town began life in the 1820s as a port for shipping cedar. Its blowhole can spurt water as high as 60 m (200 ft).

Seven Mile Beach ②
Part of a national park and best seen from Gerroa's Black Head, the beach is flanked by dunes and hardy coastal vegetation, including forest and swamp. It is a great fishing, swimming, and picnicking spot.

TIPS FOR DRIVERS

Distance from Sydney: *120 km (75 miles).*
Duration of tour: *About 3½ hours, excluding stops.*
Getting there and back: *Take Metroad route 1, then follow the F3 freeway and Princes Hwy (1) to Kiama. Return via the F5 freeway (31) from Mittagong, then Metroad route 5 into the city.*
When to go: *Year-round. The beaches are best in summer, the gardens in spring and autumn. Traditional Christmas fare is offered at local restaurants and hotels during "Christmas in July."*
Where to stay and eat: *Eating places, hotels and guesthouses are found all over the South Coast and Southern Highlands.*
Tourist information: *Kiama Visitors Centre, Blowhole Point, Kiama.* **☎** *(042) 32 3322. Southern Highlands Visitors Information Centre, Hume Hwy, Mittagong.* **☎** *(048) 71 2888.*

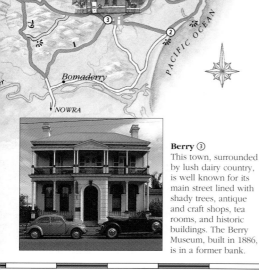

Berry ③
This town, surrounded by lush dairy country, is well known for its main street lined with shady trees, antique and craft shops, tea rooms, and historic buildings. The Berry Museum, built in 1886, is in a former bank.

Royal National Park ❻

DESIGNATED AS A NATIONAL PARK in 1879, the "Royal" is the second oldest in the world after Yellowstone in the United States. It covers about 37,100 acres of landscape typical of the Sydney Basin sandstone. To the east, waves from the Pacific Ocean have undercut the sandstone and produced majestic coastal cliffs broken occasionally by small creeks and some spectacular beaches. Streams flowing north and east have incised deep river valleys. Heath vegetation on the plateaus merges with woodlands on the upper slopes. The park is ideal for bushwalking, picnicking, camping, swimming, and birdwatching.

Waratah

Hacking River
Boating, fishing, and canoeing are common water sports.

Audley
A popular picnic area since the Edwardian era, its pavilion was built in 1901. The visitors' center is housed in a 1920s dance hall.

Heathcote

Lady Carrington Drive
Named after a governor's wife and now closed to vehicles, the road is crossed by 15 creeks and is delightful to walk or cycle. It also leads to the track to Palona Cave.

KEY

—	Main road
⋯	Walking track
🚆	CityRail station
⛴	Ferry boarding point
⊞	Picnic area
Ⓐ	Campsite
≋	Swimming
℗	Parking
☀	Viewpoint

The Forest Path follows a circular route, passing through subtropical rain forest.

Garie Beach is a patrolled surf beach accessible by road.

Werrong

Figure Eight Pool

0 kilometers   4

0 miles   2

Bundeena
Enclosed by national park on three sides, the small settlement at the mouth of the Hacking River may be reached by ferry from Cronulla or by road through the national park.

Cronulla

Jibbon Head
Aboriginal rock carvings such as this Jibbon Beach kangaroo may be up to 5,000 years old.

Jibbon Lagoon

Deer Pool
One of many freshwater pools in the park, this sheltered spot is on the track from Bundeena Drive to Marley and Little Marley.

Little Marley Beach

Wattamolla Lagoon
This pretty picnic spot has a lagoon with a waterfall at its edge and a protected ocean beach.

Curracurrang
This rock formation is about halfway along the two-day Coast Walk. Sea eagles and terns nest in caves at the base of this rocky cove, which also has a secluded swimming hole and waterfall.

TIPS FOR TRAVELERS

Distance from Sydney: 34 km (21 miles).
Duration of journey: About 1 hour from the center of Sydney.
Getting there: Follow Metroad route 1 south to Sutherland, then follow the signs to Heathcote and Wollongong. The turn-off to Farnell Avenue and the park entrance is shortly after Sutherland and well marked.
When to go: Year-round, but conditions for walking in summer can be hot, so allow for this. If bushwalking, carry fresh water at all times and check on the fire danger at the Visitors' Center before setting off.
Where to stay and eat: There are kiosks at Audley, Garie Beach, and Wattamolla, but it is best to bring your own food. Camping information can be obtained at the Visitors' Center.
Tourist information: National Parks & Wildlife Service Visitors' Centre, Sir Bertram Stevens Drive, Audley. 9542 0648.

TRAVELERS' NEEDS

WHERE TO STAY 168–177

RESTAURANTS, CAFÉS, AND PUBS 178–197

SHOPS AND MARKETS 198–207

ENTERTAINMENT IN SYDNEY 208–215

WHERE TO STAY

WITH AUSTRALIA's recent emergence as a major tourist destination, the urgent need for more high-quality and good-value accommodations became apparent. Previously, most Sydney hotels and guesthouses had been regarded as expensive and of varying standard. There has since been an enormous improvement in both quality and value, and there are excellent choices ranging from five-star luxury to the homeyness of a small, unpretentious hotel. In addition to hotels, Sydney has apartments,

Observatory Hotel doorman (p174)

accommodations in private homes, and budget and backpacker hostels for travelers on a budget. Information on these alternatives is given below. From a survey of various types of accommodations in different areas and price brackets, we have selected those offering good value for their money. The chart *Choosing a Hotel* on pages 172–3 will help you to find the best to suit your needs. When you have selected the most likely hotels, you will find a more detailed description of of one on pages 174–7.

A view of the rooftop pool at the Sydney Hilton Hotel (see p175)

WHERE TO LOOK

MOST OF the expensive hotels are in or near the city center, but it is possible to find accommodations within most price ranges throughout Sydney. The city center has the advantage of having many of the larger theaters, galleries, and shops nearby, as well as convenient transportation to more distant sights and attractions.

Budget accommodations can be found in the vibrant Kings Cross district. Choices here range from backpacker hostels to the small "boutique" hotels where the emphasis is on quality and personal service.

In The Rocks area, with its beautifully restored colonial buildings, you can choose from bed and breakfast in a traditional Sydney pub or the opulence of a five-star luxury hotel with good views of the Sydney Opera House.

The hotels around Darling Harbour and Chinatown offer good values for shoppers and

are also within easy reach of the city center. Paddington has smaller hotels and apartments; to the east are the fashionable hotels of Double Bay. On the other side of Sydney Harbour Bridge, the North Shore provides a relaxed look at Sydney, and you can travel to and from the city center by ferry.

The popular beachside suburbs of Bondi and Manly are a little way out of the center of Sydney, but some visitors like the opportunity to be close to superb beaches and yet still be near to the city.

You should also remember that in Australia a hotel can be a pub or a place to drink *(see pp196–7)*. Pubs do not always provide accommodations.

HOW TO BOOK

IT IS ADVISABLE to book well in advance, especially for the Christmas school vacation in December and January, the Gay and Lesbian Mardi Gras

Festival in February and Mardi Gras Parade in early March, the Easter holiday, and July and September school vacation.

Reservations can be made by letter, phone, fax or through your local international travel agent. A credit card number or bank check in Australian dollars is usually required to secure your booking. Check cancellation requirements in case you have to change your plans, and reconfirm before you arrive in Sydney.

The **NSW Travel Centre** provides a reservation service and also has a useful booklet on Sydney hotels, and the **NRMA** (National Roads and Motorists' Association) will arrange accommodations for members of motoring organizations, such as the AAA. The **Countrylink** agencies at the larger railroad stations offer a comprehensive service, and AFTA travel agencies, situated throughout the city, will book most hotels. Some travel

The indoor pool at the Observatory Hotel in The Rocks (see p174)

The curvilinear shape of the Hotel Nikko in Darling Harbour *(see p176)*

agencies specialize in specific areas. Tourist information centers can also offer valuable advice about where to stay in Sydney.

DISCOUNT RATES

WITH FEWER visitors staying in Sydney from April to October (except during school vacation periods), some of the more expensive hotels may be willing to negotiate a better rate. This is particularly so if they think you will look elsewhere for accommodations. It is worth asking for the corporate rate where hotels give discounts for group or company bookings. Most hotels give these without question.

Stained glass at Simpsons Hotel *(see p176)*

Weekends, there are fewer business clients around so this is the time when prices are cheaper in the top hotels. Money can also be saved by booking for a week at a time. Asking for a room without a harbor or ocean view is another good way of reducing costs.

The NSW Travel Centre and the **Travellers Information Service** in the city can often arrange up to 50 percent off regular hotel accommodation rates (this does not normally apply to budget hotels) to those who book in person on the day a room is required.

HIDDEN EXTRAS

BREAKFAST is usually charged on top of the room rate in the more expensive hotels. It is best to avoid consuming any of the contents of the minibar until you have checked the price. Alcohol is usually much more expensive here than in liquor stores. Also, be wary of the telephone charges. There will almost certainly be a considerable mark-up on any calls you make from your room. In general, tipping is not widespread, but it is expected in the more expensive hotels. You should make a note of the check-out time when you arrive, or negotiate a late check-out, as a surcharge may be incurred if you stay late.

SPECIAL OFFERS

HOTELS OFTEN cooperate with airlines, rail services, bus companies, theaters, and entertainment promoters to provide package deals that include discounted accommodations. Booking agencies will have brochures with details of these seasonal offers, or ask the hotel for information on any special deals.

"Special occasion" packages (such as for anniversaries or honeymoons) are available at the top end of the market.

DISABLED TRAVELERS

THE INFORMATION regarding wheelchair access that is given on pages 174–7 relies very much on each hotel's own assessment of its facilities.

ACROD NSW supplies a handbook for people who have mobility problems, and **Barrier Free Travel** has a *Guide to Sydney for Travellers with Disabilities*. The **Centre for Leisure and Tourism Studies** also has information on accessible accommodation for those with disabilities.

TRAVELING WITH CHILDREN

IT IS WORTH inquiring about special rates and facilities or deals that allow children to stay in their parents' room for no extra cost. Refer to *Choosing a Hotel* on pages 172–3 for hotels that cater to children.

APARTMENTS

ACCOMMODATION including full kitchen and laundry facilities offers the traveler greater independence. It is also a bargain as the living space is larger than standard hotel rooms and the prices are competitive. The choice ranges from one- to three-bedroom luxury apartments in the inner city to basic flats at the beach. In *Choosing a Hotel* on pages 172–3, all the "apartment" hotels listed offer efficiency facilities.

Woolloomooloo Waters serviced apartments *(see p176)*

A luxurious room at the Regents Court Hotel in Potts Point *(see p176)*

PRIVATE HOMES

EUROPEAN-STYLE bed-and-breakfast accommodation in a private home can be an ideal way to experience a city. It is fast becoming a popular alternative to more impersonal hotel rooms for many people who choose to visit Sydney.

People from all walks of life offer rooms in a wide variety of house styles and locations. Agencies such as **Bed and**

Breakfast Sydneyside and the **Homestay Network** make every effort to match the host and guest if possible, so call to discuss any preferences before making a reservation.

BUDGET ACCOMMODATIONS

As A FAVORED destination for many young travelers, Sydney has a large number of hostels that cater specifically to their needs. Despite fierce competition, standards vary widely. At their best, hostels offer excellent value.

While it is necessary to book in advance at some hostels, others do not take bookings, and beds are on a first come, first served basis. Apartments,

---

DIRECTORY

DISCOUNT AGENCIES

Travellers Information Service
Sydney Coach Terminal,
Eddy Ave, Sydney
NSW 2000. **Map** 4 E5.
[9281 9366.

USEFUL BOOKING ADDRESSES

Countrylink
Central Railway Station
Map 4 E5. [132232.

NRMA
151 Clarence St, Sydney
NSW 2000. **Map** 1 A4.
[9260 9122.
FAX 9260 8765.

NSW Travel Centre
11–31 York St, Sydney
NSW 2000. **Map** 1 A4.
[132077.
Also: International Arrivals
Hall, Kingsford Smith
Airport. [9667 6050.

DISABLED ASSISTANCE

ACROD NSW
55 Charles St, Ryde
NSW 2112. [9809 4488.

Barrier Free Travel
36 Wheatley St, North
Bellingen NSW 2454.
[(066) 55 1733.

Centre for Leisure and Tourism Studies
PO Box 222, Lindfield
NSW 2070. [9330 5100.
FAX 9330 5195.

APARTMENT AGENCIES

Bondi Beach Serviced Apartments
25 Wallis Parade,
North Bondi NSW 2060.
[9388 1477.

Medina on Crown
359 Crown St, Surry Hills
NSW 2010. **Map** 5 A3.
[9360 6666.
FAX 9361 5965.
*Also at Elizabeth Bay,
Double Bay, Paddington.*

Metro Serviced Apartments City
132–136 Sussex St, Sydney
NSW 2000. **Map** 1 A4.
[9290 9200.
FAX 9262 3032.

BED-AND-BREAKFAST AGENCIES

Bed and Breakfast Sydneyside
PO Box 555, Turramurra
NSW 2074. [9449 4430.

Homestay Network
5 Locksley St, Killara NSW
2071. [9498 4400.
FAX 9498 8324.

HOSTELS

Alishan Guesthouse
100 Glebe Point Rd, Glebe
NSW 2037. **Map** 3 A5.
[9660 1001.

Forbes Terrace
153 Forbes St,
Woolloomooloo
NSW 2011. **Map** 5 B1.
[9358 4327.

Hereford Lodge YHA
51 Hereford St, Glebe
NSW 2037. [9660 5577.

Highfield House
166 Victoria St, Potts Point
NSW 2010. **Map** 2 E5.
[9358 1552.

Lamrock Hostel
7 Lamrock Ave,
Bondi Beach NSW 2026.
[9365 0221.

NSW YHA
176 Day St, Sydney NSW
2000. **Map** 4 D3.
[9267 3044.
Central reservations
[9261 5727.

University of Sydney
Arundel House
[9660 4881.
International House
[9950 9800.
St. John's College
[9394 5200.

Sancta Sophia
[9519 7123.
Wesley College
[9565 3333.
Women's College
[9557 1195.

Wattle House Hostel
44 Hereford St, Glebe
NSW 2037. [9692 0879.

GAY AND LESBIAN ACCOMMODATIONS

AGLTA and IGTA
Lyn Hocking, Level 10,
130 Elizabeth St, Sydney
NSW 2000. **Map** 4 F3.
[9268 2111.

Breakout Tours
GPO Box 3801,
Sydney NSW 2001.
[9558 8229.

Destination Downunder
PO Box A2494,
Sydney South NSW 2000.
[9268 2111.

CAMPING

Blue Mountains National Park
[(045) 885 247.

Ku-ring-gai Chase National Park
[9451 8124.

Royal National Park
[9542 0648.

Striking sculpture in the lobby of L'otel, Darlinghurst *(see p176)*

rooms, and dormitories are all available, but dormitories are often mixed sex; check before arriving. The backpacker scene changes quickly, so ask other travelers for the latest developments. Potts Point and Glebe have the largest concentration of cheap accommodations.

HALLS OF RESIDENCE

STUDENT ROOMS, with shared bathroom facilities, are available at the University of Sydney over the summer break from December to February. The university is conveniently close to the city and to public transportation, and the moderate price includes breakfast.

GAY AND LESBIAN ACCOMMODATION

LESBIAN AND GAY visitors are welcome in all of Sydney's hotels. In fact, quite a number of them cater primarily, if not exclusively, to same-sex

couples. Many of the small hotels in the inner city areas of Darlinghurst, Paddington, Newtown, and Surry Hills are geared specifically towards gay and lesbian visitors, although most of them also welcome heterosexual guests.

The **AGLTA** (Australian Gay and Lesbian Travel Association) produces an accommodation guide which is available at no cost. There is a small charge for postage and handling if you are inquiring from overseas.

Travel agencies such as **Destination Downunder** and **Breakout Tours** specialize in vacations and accommodations for gay and lesbian travelers.

CAMPING

ALTHOUGH NOT AN option in the city itself, camping is available in several national parks close to Sydney. This can be a cheap and idyllic way of enjoying the natural beauty and wildlife of the bushland.

The **Royal National Park** *(see pp164–5)* has a campsite with facilities at Bonnie Vale. Advance booking is required all year round. Free bush or "walk-in" camping is allowed in several other places, but first call the park to obtain the necessary camping permit.

At The Basin in **Ku-ring-gai Chase National Park** *(see pp154–5)*, reservations should be made and all fees paid before your stay or on arrival. There are toilets, cold showers, barbecues, and phones.

There are basic campsites near Glenbrook, Woodford, Blackheath, and Wentworth

Falls in the **Blue Mountains National Park** *(see pp160–61)*. You will need to book if you want to camp at the Euroka Clearing near Glenbrook, but this is not necessary for the other sites. Bush camping is also permitted in the park, but there are some restrictions. Contact the national park for more details before you visit.

USING THE LISTINGS

Hotels are listed on pages 174–5. Each hotel is listed according to area and price category. The symbols summarize the facilities available at each of them.

⬛ all/number of rooms with bath and/or shower

1️⃣ single-rate rooms available

⬛ rooms for more than two people available

👶 children welcome (eg babysitting service, cots, etc)

📺 television in all rooms

▤ air conditioning in all rooms

🖼 rooms with good views

♨ hotel swimming pool or beach

♿ wheelchair access

⬆ elevator

🅿 hotel parking available

🌿 garden or grounds

🍴 restaurant

💳 credit and charge cards accepted:
AE American Express
DC Diners Club
MC MasterCard/Access
V Visa
JCB Japanese Credit Bureau

Price categories for a double room, including continental breakfast and service, in Australian dollars:
ⓢ under $120
ⓢⓢ $120–$200
ⓢⓢⓢ $200–$280
ⓢⓢⓢⓢ $280–$380
ⓢⓢⓢⓢⓢ over $380

Manly Pacific Parkroyal *(see p177)*, overlooking Manly's ocean beach

Choosing a Hotel

THE HOTELS AND RENTAL APARTMENTS on the following pages have all been chosen and inspected specifically for this guide. This chart shows the selected hotels at a glance and lists some of the factors that will help you to make an informed choice. A detailed description of each hotel appears on pages 174–7. They are listed by area of the city, and all entries appear alphabetically within their price categories.

		Number of Rooms	Apartment Hotels	Children's Facilities	Business Facilities	Recommended Restaurant	Close to Shops and Restaurants	Quiet Location	24-Hour Room Service
The Rocks and Circular Quay *(see p174)*									
Lord Nelson Brewery Hotel	$	5		●		●		●	
Russell	$$	29		●		●	●		
Stafford	$$	61	●	●	●		●	●	
Old Sydney Parkroyal	$$$	174		●	●	●	●		●
ANA Hotel Sydney	$$$$	573		●	●	●	●	●	●
Observatory	$$$$	100		●	●	●	●	●	●
Regent Sydney	$$$$	594		●	●	●	●		●
Sydney Renaissance	$$$$	579		●	●	●	●		●
Park Hyatt Sydney	$$$$$	158		●	●	●	●	●	●
City Center *(see pp174–5)*									
Castlereagh Inn	$	84		●	●	●	●		
All Seasons Menzies	$$	446		●	●	●	●	●	●
Hyde Park Plaza	$$	182	●	●	●	●	●	●	●
Savoy Serviced Apartments	$$	70	●	●			●		
Sydney Marriott	$$$	244		●	●	●	●	●	●
Wentworth	$$$	423		●	●	●	●		●
York Apartment Hotel	$$$	133	●	●	●	●	●	●	
Sheraton on the Park	$$$$	559		●	●	●	●		●
Sydney Hilton	$$$$	585		●	●	●	●		●
Darling Harbour *(see pp175–6)*									
Sydney Travellers Rest	$	86	●	●			●		
West End	$	91		●		●			
Country Comfort Sydney Central	$$	114		●	●		●	●	●
Golden Gate	$$	251		●	●		●	●	●
Novotel Sydney on Darling Harbour	$$$	527		●	●	●	●	●	●
Parkroyal at Darling Harbour	$$$	295		●	●	●	●	●	●
Waldorf Apartment Hotel	$$$	70	●	●			●	●	
Hotel Nikko Darling Harbour	$$$$	645		●	●	●	●		●
Botanic Gardens and The Domain *(see p176)*									
Hotel Inter-Continental Sydney	$$$	497		●	●	●	●	●	●
Ritz Carlton	$$$	140		●	●	●	●	●	●
Kings Cross and Darlinghurst *(see p176)*									
Dorchester Inn	$	15	●	●	●	●	●		
Madison's	$	40		●			●	●	
Crescent on Bayswater	$$	70	●	●		●	●	●	
L'otel	$$	16				●	●		
Regents Court	$$	30	●	●			●	●	
Simpsons of Potts Point	$$	14		●			●	●	
Sebel of Sydney	$$$	165		●	●	●	●		●
Woolloomooloo Waters	$$$	80	●	●	●	●			●

Price categories for a double room (not per person), including continental breakfast and service:
$ under A$120
$$ A$120–$200
$$$ A$200–$280
$$$$ A$280–$380
$$$$$ Over A$380

FAMILY ROOMS
Rooms equipped for two adults and two children.

CHILDREN'S FACILITIES
Cribs, a babysitting service, children's menu, high chairs in the breakfast room or restaurant.

BUSINESS FACILITIES
Conference rooms, desks, fax, and computer service for guests.

CLOSE TO SHOPS AND RESTAURANTS
Within a 5-minute walk of a good center for shops and restaurants.

QUIET LOCATION
Quiet residential neighborhood or quiet street in a busy area.

		NUMBER OF ROOMS	APARTMENT HOTELS	CHILDREN'S FACILITIES	BUSINESS FACILITIES	RECOMMENDED RESTAURANT	CLOSE TO SHOPS AND RESTAURANTS	QUIET LOCATION	24-HOUR ROOM SERVICE
PADDINGTON *(see p176–7)*									
Grand National	$	20				●	●	●	
Hughenden	$	35		●		●	●	●	
Sullivans	$	62		●			●		
FARTHER AFIELD *(see p177)*									
Periwinkle Guesthouse	$	18		●			●	●	
Savoy Double Bay	$	34		●			●	●	
Harbourside Apartments	$$	82	●	●				●	
Hotel Lawson	$$	96		●	●	●	●		●
McLaren	$$	28		●	●		●	●	
Ravesi's on Bondi Beach	$$	16		●	●	●	●		
Sir Stamford Double Bay	$$	72		●	●	●	●	●	
Manly Pacific Parkroyal	$$$	169		●	●	●	●	●	●
Medina Executive Apartments	$$$	48	●	●			●	●	
Ritz Carlton Double Bay	$$$	140		●	●		●	●	●

THE ROCKS AND CIRCULAR QUAY

Lord Nelson Brewery Hotel

19 Kent St, The Rocks NSW 2000. **Map** 1 A2. **☎** 9251 4044. **FAX** 9251 1532. **Rooms:** 5. 🛏 🔧 📺 🍴 🎫 *AE, DC, MC, V.* Ⓢ

For 150 years, bar-room banter has resounded off the thick sandstone slab walls of this celebrated pub, famous for its home brews. On the top floor, stone walls and rustic furnishings are a feature of the cozy bedrooms, and there are shared bathrooms and a breakfast kitchenette for guests. This is a great place to meet the locals.

Russell

143a George St, The Rocks NSW 2000. **Map** 1 B2. **☎** 9241 3543. **FAX** 9252 1652. **Rooms:** 29. 🛏 18. ① 🔧 🎫 ⓣ 🍴 🎫 *AE, DC, MC, V, JCB.* ⓈⓈ

The interior of this late 19th-century building is appealingly decorated, with chintz fabrics, pretty wallpaper, country-style antiques and fresh flowers in abundance. A welcoming and intimate hotel, it has a rooftop garden, which is the perfect spot for a quiet drink after a hectic day in the city.

Stafford

75 Harrington St, The Rocks NSW 2000. **Map** 1 B2. **☎** 9251 6711. **FAX** 9251 3458. **Rooms:** 61. 🛏 ① 🔧 🎫 📺 🍴 🎫 🎫 🎫 *AE, DC, MC, V.* ⓈⓈ

In this unusual apartment complex, guests are housed in either the central custom-made property or in seven charmingly restored 1870 terrace houses nearby. All of the apartments have well-equipped kitchens but, if you prefer, room service breakfast can be arranged. There are a heated spa, swimming pool, sauna, and gym for guests.

Old Sydney Parkroyal

55 George St, The Rocks NSW 2000. **Map** 1 B2. **☎** 9252 0524. **FAX** 9251 2093. **Rooms:** 174. 🛏 🔧 🎫 📺 🍴 🎫 🎫 🎫 🍴 🎫 *AE, DC, MC, V.* ⓈⓈⓈ

The hotel is big enough to offer all the facilities found in a large establishment, but small enough to offer personal attention. The decor is a little dated, but this may not be a consideration given the great location within the historic Rocks area and the proximity to Circular Quay and the Opera House.

ANA Hotel Sydney

176 Cumberland St, The Rocks NSW 2000. **Map** 1 A3. **☎** 9250 6000. **FAX** 9250 6250. **Rooms:** 573. 🛏 🔧 🎫 📺 🎫 🎫 🎫 🎫 🍴 🎫 *AE, DC, MC, V, JCB.* ⓈⓈⓈⓈ

Clever use of marble, glass, modern art, and lush greenery gives this plush hotel a light and airy atmosphere. Service is exemplary and the spacious guest rooms and suites all have harbor views. Guests on the Executive Floor enjoy additional perks, but anyone can sip cocktails high up in the Horizon Bar where the glittering lights of the harbor at night are a magical backdrop.

Observatory

89–113 Kent St, Millers Point NSW 2000. **Map** 1 A2. **☎** 9256 2222. **FAX** 9256 2233. **Rooms:** 100. 🛏 🔧 🎫 📺 🎫 🎫 🎫 🎫 🍴 *AE, DC, MC, V, JCB.* ⓈⓈⓈⓈ

Although relatively new, this smart boutique hotel blends successfully with the surrounding 19th-century buildings. It has been lavishly but tastefully furnished with original antiques, fine tapestries, and paintings. All the guest rooms have luxurious marble bathrooms. The indoor pool has special lighting in the ceiling, which makes it sparkle like a starry night sky.

Regent Sydney

199 George St, Sydney NSW 2000. **Map** 1 B3. **☎** 9238 0000. **FAX** 9251 2851. **Rooms:** 594. 🛏 ①  🔧 🎫 📺 🎫 🎫 🎫 🎫 🍴 🎫 *AE, DC, MC, V, JCB.* ⓈⓈⓈⓈ

The imposing modern grandeur of the vast lobby is reflected in the elegant guest rooms. The superb location offers wonderful views of the harbor and city, while the state-of-the-art equipment in the Health Club gives you the chance to work up an appetite, which can easily be sated at one of the three first-class restaurants.

Sydney Renaissance

30 Pitt St, Sydney NSW 2000. **Map** 1 B3. **☎** 9259 7000. **FAX** 9252 1999. **Rooms:** 579. 🛏 🔧 🎫 📺 🎫 🎫 🎫 🎫 🍴 🎫 *AE, DC, MC, V, JCB.* ⓈⓈⓈⓈ

The three-tiered lobby, with an elaborate Italian mosaic centerpiece and sweeping staircase, sets a scene of some magnificence, but the hotel is surprisingly unstuffy. The rooms are large and offer all the features expected of a five-star hotel. The Renaissance Club, for those staying on the top four floors of the hotel, has a private lounge where breakfast, afternoon tea, and cocktails are on the house.

Park Hyatt Sydney

7 Hickson Rd, The Rocks NSW 2000. **Map** 1 B1. **☎** 9241 1234. **FAX** 9256 1555. **Rooms:** 158. 🛏 🔧 🎫 📺 🎫 🎫 🎫 🍴 🎫 *AE, DC, MC, V, JCB.* ⓈⓈⓈⓈ

This deluxe hotel, which hugs the harbor shore and is almost in the shadow of the Harbour Bridge, appears to be carved in sandstone. It is quiet, opulent, and splendidly furnished in richly colored fabrics and works of art. The guest rooms have every luxury, including a 24-hour butler service. The picture windows of the Art Deco lobby and the excellent restaurant are classy settings for watching the bustle of activity at Circular Quay.

CITY CENTER

Castlereagh Inn

169–171 Castlereagh St, Sydney NSW 2000. **Map** 1 B5. **☎** 9264 2281. **Rooms:** 84. 🛏 ① 🔧 📺 🎫 🎫 🍴 🎫 *AE, DC, MC, V.* Ⓢ

The magnificently restored grand dining room is a special feature of this old-fashioned hotel. Crystal chandeliers illuminate crisp, white linen and furnishings reminiscent of a past era. Morning paper and continental breakfast are included in the affordable price.

All Seasons Menzies

14 Carrington St, Sydney NSW 2000. **Map** 1 A4. **☎** 9299 1000. **FAX** 9290 3819. **Rooms:** 446. 🛏 🔧 🎫 📺 🎫 🎫 🎫 🍴 *AE, DC, MC, V, JCB.* ⓈⓈ

For decades, the "Menzies" has been proud of its traditional, elegant atmosphere and the recent renovations retain the ambience of a gentlemen's club, with sumptuous green leather sofas on rich carpets over dark granite floors. Sports enthusiasts will revel in the Sporters Bar and Bistro where 15 monitors continuously show sports events.

Hyde Park Plaza

38 College St, Sydney NSW 2010. **Map** 4 F3. **☎** 9331 6933. **FAX** 9331 6022. **Rooms:** 182. 🛏 🔧 🎫 📺 🎫 🎫 🎫 🍴 *AE, DC, MC, V, JCB.* ⓈⓈ

The hotel has a great location opposite the southern end of Hyde Park. The foyer is rather unprepossessing and dated, but the wide variety of self-contained suites, from studios to three-bedroom "flexi-suites," are roomy, comfortably furnished, and fitted with every convenience, right down to an ironing board.

Savoy Serviced Apartments

37–43 King St, Sydney NSW 2000. **Map** 1 A5. ☎ *9267 9211.* FAX *9262 2023.* ***Rooms:*** *70.* 🛁 ⊞ 🚸 [TV] ☰ ⇅ [P] 💳 *AE, DC, MC, V, JCB.* $$

These one-bedroom apartments can accommodate up to four adults; the sofa converts to a double bed. Rooms are decorated in either frilly country-cottage style or a more modern design. The Savoy Deli is handy for stocking the fully equipped kitchens.

Sydney Marriott

36 College St, Sydney NSW 2000. **Map** 4 F3. ☎ *9361 8400.* FAX *9361 8599.* ***Rooms:*** *244.* 🛁 [1] ⊞ 🚸 [TV] ☰ ☀ ≋ ♿ ⇅ [P] 🌿 🍴 💳 *AE, DC, MC, V, JCB.* $$$

This elegant hotel, overlooking Hyde Park, suits the business traveler very well, with its conference rooms, business center, and an executive lounge. The tastefully decorated rooms are fully appointed and even include microwave ovens. Some suites have hot plates, spa baths, and fax lines.

Wentworth

61 Phillip St, Sydney NSW 2000. **Map** 1 B4. ☎ *9230 0700.* FAX *9227 9133.* ***Rooms:*** *423.* 🛁 ⊞ 🚸 [TV] ☰ ☀ ♿ ⇅ [P] 🍴 💳 *AE, DC, MC, V.* $$$

Since 1966, this has been one of Sydney's most distinguished hotels. Now elegantly refurbished to expected international standards, the rooms have excellent facilities and all include a valet service. There are four no-smoking floors.

York Apartment Hotel

5 York St, Sydney NSW 2000. **Map** 1 A3. ☎ *9210 5000.* FAX *9290 1487.* ***Rooms:*** *133.* 🛁 ⊞ 🚸 [TV] ☰ ☀ ≋ ♿ *limited.* ⇅ [P] 🌿 🍴 💳 *AE, DC, MC, V, JCB.* $$$

There is an understated elegance throughout this well-located hotel. All of its apartments, from studio to penthouse, are individually designed, beautifully furnished, and have generous balconies, modern kitchens, and large bathrooms.

Sheraton on the Park

161 Elizabeth St, Sydney NSW 2000. **Map** 1 B5. ☎ *9286 6000.* FAX *9286 6686.* ***Rooms:*** *559.* 🛁 ⊞ 🚸 [TV] ☰ ☀ ≋ ♿ ⇅ [P] 🍴 💳 *AE, DC, MC, V, JCB.* $$$$

Another relative newcomer in the city, there has been no expense spared on the interior design and furnishings of this hotel. Centrally placed, it is convenient for both business and shopping, with the major department stores a short walk away. The peaceful oasis of Hyde Park is just across the road.

Sydney Hilton

259 Pitt St, Sydney NSW 2000. **Map** 1 B5. ☎ *9266 0610.* FAX *9265 6065.* ***Rooms:*** *585.* 🛁 [1] ⊞ 🚸 [TV] ☰ ☀ ≋ ♿ ⇅ [P] 🍴 💳 *AE, DC, MC, V, JCB.* $$$$

This *grande dame* of the central city's five-star hotels has the usual Hilton high standard of service and facilities, particularly for business people. There is a wide range of cuisine at the four hotel restaurants and a good choice of bars – do not miss the ornately decorated and historic Marble Bar *(see p82)*. Check out the small art gallery, which sometimes has special exhibitions.

Darling Harbour

Sydney Travellers Rest

37 Ultimo Rd, Haymarket NSW 2000. **Map** 4 D4. ☎ *9281 5555.* FAX *9281 2666.* ***Rooms:*** *86.* 🛁 [1] ⊞ 🚸 [TV] ♿ ⇅ [P] 🍴 💳 *AE, DC, MC, V.* $

This hotel offers apartments, rooms with en suite bathrooms, and budget rooms with shared facilities. The decor is predominantly mushroom pink, with rather bland, although serviceable, furnishings, but you can overlook that for the price and the central location. An airport bus will call at the hotel on request.

West End

412 Pitt St, Sydney NSW 2000. **Map** 4 E4. ☎ *9211 4822.* FAX *9281 9570.* ***Rooms:*** *91.* 🛁 [1] 🚸 [TV] ☰ ♿ ⇅ 🍴 💳 *AE, DC, MC, V, JCB.* $

Within walking distance of Central Railway Station, this older style hotel offers great value. Almost outside the door is Chinatown, while the city center is just up the road. All rooms have a refrigerator and tea- and coffee-making facilities.

Country Comfort Sydney Central

Cnr George & Quay Sts, Sydney NSW 2000. **Map** 4 D5. ☎ *9212 2544.* FAX *9281 3794.* ***Rooms:*** *114.* 🛁 ⊞ 🚸 [TV] ☰ ≋ ♿ ⇅ [P] 🍴 💳 *AE, DC, MC, V, JCB.* $$

Situated opposite Central Railway Station, the hotel is popular with visitors from country towns. The rooms, varying in style from standard to luxury spa suites, have been refurbished recently. Helpful staff maintain the Country Comfort reputation for friendly service.

Golden Gate

169–179 Thomas St, Haymarket NSW 2000. **Map** 4 D5. ☎ *9281 6888.* FAX *9281 6688.* ***Rooms:*** *251.* 🛁 ⊞ 🚸 [TV] ☰ ☀ ≋ ♿ ⇅ [P] 🌿 🍴 💳 *AE, DC, MC, V, JCB.* $$

The entrance, reception area and stairways are all part of the original 1902 Infants' Hospital building, now incorporated into an imposing façade for this modern hotel. All rooms and suites are extraordinarily large with excellent services for guests – including a rooftop pool, barbecue area, and putting green.

Novotel Sydney on Darling Harbour

100 Murray St, Pyrmont NSW 2009. **Map** 3 C2. ☎ *9934 0000.* FAX *9934 0099.* ***Rooms:*** *527.* 🛁 ⊞ 🚸 [TV] ☰ ☀ ≋ ♿ ⇅ [P] 🍴 💳 *AE, DC, MC, V, JCB.* $$$

This modern superstructure towers above Darling Harbour. With the monorail station virtually on the doorstep, the city center is just a few minutes away. The rooms are good four-star quality and have views across the city, while pool, tennis court, sauna, and gym are all on hand for energetic guests.

Parkroyal at Darling Harbour

150 Day St, Darling Harbour NSW 2000. **Map** 4 D3. ☎ *9261 4444.* FAX *9261 8766.* ***Rooms:*** *295.* 🛁 ⊞ 🚸 [TV] ☰ ☀ ♿ ⇅ [P] 🍴 💳 *AE, DC, MC, V, JCB.* $$$

A funnel-like atrium rises skyward through the center of the lobby, and swirls of vivid color through the murky greens almost create the sensation of swimming under water. The stylish guest rooms look out over the city skyline and Darling Harbour, which, with its myriad lights reflecting on the water at night, seems almost to glitter.

Waldorf Apartment Hotel

57 Liverpool St, Sydney NSW 2000. **Map** 4 E3. ☎ *9261 5355.* FAX *9261 3753.* ***Rooms:*** *70.* 🛁 [1] ⊞ 🚸 [TV] ☰ ☀ ≋ ♿ ⇅ [P] 💳 *AE, DC, MC, V, JCB.* $$$

Everything is included in these spacious one- and two-bedroom apartments, from hair dryers and clock radio alarms to in-house movies and a rooftop pool. With a choice of over 50 restaurants in the area, the well-equipped kitchen may not be used much during a short stay. The balcony overlooking the city is a nice spot to relax with a drink after a day's sightseeing.

Hotel Nikko Darling Harbour

161 Sussex St, Sydney NSW 2000. **Map** 4 D2. ☎ *9299 1231.* [FAX] *9299 3340.* ***Rooms:*** *645.* 🛏 ⊞ 🏃 [TV] ≣ ☀ ♿ ⇅ [P] 🍃 🍴 💳 *AE, DC, MC, V, JCB.* $$$$

Sleek modern design marries well with several restored 19th-century maritime buildings. A classic old pub, the Dundee Arms, is now the hotel's bar. All rooms are beautifully appointed, some with views over Darling Harbour. The top four executive floors offer the privacy and services of a hotel within a hotel.

Botanic Gardens and The Domain

Hotel Inter-Continental Sydney

117 Macquarie St, Sydney NSW 2000. **Map** 1 C3. ☎ *9230 0200.* [FAX] *9240 1240.* ***Rooms:*** *497.* 🛏 🏃 [TV] ≣ ☀ ≋ ♿ ⇅ [P] 🍴 💳 *AE, DC, MC, V, JCB.* $$$

The ingenious design of this hotel blends colonial heritage with contemporary architecture. Part of the old 1851 Treasury Building now forms the foyer and lower stories. The dramatic lobby is constructed beneath impressive vaulted sandstone arches reaching three levels above the marble floor. Here, small music ensembles frequently perform while guests sip tea or cocktails.

Ritz Carlton

93 Macquarie St, Sydney NSW 2000. **Map** 1 C3. ☎ *9252 4600.* [FAX] *9252 4286.* ***Rooms:*** *104.* 🛏 ⊞ 🏃 [TV] ≣ ☀ ≋ ⇅ [P] 🍴 💳 *AE, DC, MC, V, JCB.* $$$

There is a refined but relaxed air in this intimate hotel. Features include open fireplaces, oriental carpets, marble floors, and 18th- and 19th-century antiques. Enjoy cocktails in the old-world atmosphere in The Bar. The rooftop pool and deck have wonderful views.

Kings Cross and Darlinghurst

Dorchester Inn

38 Macleay St, Potts Point NSW 2011. **Map** 2 E5. ☎ *9358 2400.* [FAX] *9257 7579.* ***Rooms:*** *15.* 🛏 [1] ⊞ 🏃 [TV] ≣ [P] 🍃 🍴 💳 *AE, DC, MC, V, JCB.* $

Hidden away in the quiet, leafy part of Kings Cross is this charming 1886 hotel. Recently refurbished, the colonial atmosphere has been retained; the roomy, self-contained serviced apartments are absolutely up-to-date, but have kept those elegant high ceilings and quaint Victorian decorative features that have such historic appeal.

Madison's

6–8 Ward Ave, Elizabeth Bay NSW 2011. **Map** 5 C1. ☎ *9357 1155.* [FAX] *9357 1193.* ***Rooms:*** *40.* 🛏 ⊞ 🏃 [TV] ≣ ⇅ [P] 💳 *AE, DC, MC, V.* $

A tropical garden courtyard separates two modern blocks of small rooms and suites. Nothing fancy here, but the rooms are clean with standard fittings, modern furniture, and small bathrooms. It is also close to all the action of Kings Cross.

Crescent on Bayswater

33 Bayswater Rd, Potts Point NSW 2011. **Map** 5 C1. ☎ *9357 7266.* [FAX] *9357 7418.* ***Rooms:*** *70.* 🛏 ⊞ 🏃 [TV] ≣ ≋ ⇅ [P] 🍴 💳 *AE, DC, MC, V, JCB.* $$

The wrought-iron balconies of this modern hotel have been designed to blend harmoniously with the graceful Victorian terraces nearby. The French château-like staircase sweeping up to the excellent restaurant from street level is much more interesting than the basic lobby. The guest rooms are self-contained with kitchenettes and balconies.

L'otel

114 Darlinghurst Rd, Darlinghurst NSW 2010. **Map** 5 B1. ☎ *9360 6868.* [FAX] *9331 4536.* ***Rooms:*** *16.* 🛏 [TV] [P] 🍴 💳 *AE, DC, MC, V.* $$

Situated in the heart of Sydney's café culture, this European-style small hotel has individually styled suites, either with French provincial decor or a more modern 1950s Retro feel. The hallways provide a fascinating art gallery, displaying canvasses by young local artists. Room service is available from the bar and restaurant downstairs.

Regents Court

18 Springfield Ave, Potts Point NSW 2011. **Map** 2 E5. ☎ *9358 1533.* [FAX] *9358 1833.* ***Rooms:*** *30.* 🛏 ⊞ 🏃 [TV] ≣ ⇅ [P] 🍃 💳 *AE, DC, MC, V, JCB.* $$

An innovative design team has created one of Sydney's more stylish and individual small hotels. The serviced apartments have lots of room and are equipped with high-quality kitchen appliances – even a Parmesan cheese grater. The collection of 20th-century designer furniture used throughout belongs to the owners, who make every effort to ensure friendly service.

Simpsons of Potts Point

8 Challis Ave, Potts Point NSW 2011. **Map** 2 E4. ☎ *9356 2199.* [FAX] *9356 4476.* ***Rooms:*** *14.* 🛏 [1] ⊞ 🏃 [TV] ≣ [P] 💳 *AE, DC, MC, V, JCB.* $$

Built in 1892 as a family residence, this historical hotel has been exquisitely and expertly restored, retaining the atmosphere of past times with spacious and elegantly designed rooms, grand hallways, and splendid stained-glass windows. The hotel itself provides the same impressive attention to detail, offering every comfort to guests.

Sebel of Sydney

23 Elizabeth Bay Rd, Elizabeth Bay NSW 2011. **Map** 2 F5. ☎ *9358 3244.* [FAX] *9357 1926.* ***Rooms:*** *165.* 🛏 [1] ⊞ 🏃 [TV] ≣ ☀ ≋ ⇅ [P] 🍃 🍴 💳 *AE, DC, MC, V.* $$$

This sophisticated hotel has been a favorite for years and has always attracted visiting rock and film celebrities, probably because of the discrete and clublike atmosphere. All the guest rooms have excellent facilities – some even have their own balconies and dressing rooms. The suites have mini-kitchens, sitting rooms, and spas. The rooftop pool is set in a Mediterranean-style garden.

Woolloomooloo Waters

88 Dowling St, Woolloomooloo NSW 2011. **Map** 2 E5. ☎ *9358 3100.* [FAX] *9356 4839.* ***Rooms:*** *80.* 🛏 ⊞ 🏃 [TV] ≣ ☀ ≋ ⇅ [P] 🍴 💳 *AE, DC, MC, V, JCB.* $$$

Clever reconstruction of a huge warehouse in former docklands has created a well-designed modern hotel in a slightly offbeat area. The large studios and apartments, comfortably and tastefully furnished in gray and peach tones, have full kitchen and laundry facilities. The somewhat claustrophobic effect of the indoor pool has been minimized by an imaginative design.

Paddington

Grand National

161 Underwood St, Paddington, 2021. **Map** 6 D4. ☎ *9363 3096.* [FAX] *9363 3542.* ***Rooms:*** *20.* [1] ☀ 🍴 💳 *AE, DC, MC, V.* $

Once just another of the back-street Paddington pubs, this 100-year-old building has been fixed up with the help of an architect with a flair for theater design. The stylish dining room and cocktail bar are

popular with the trend-setting locals. The accommodations are a great value for those who don't mind packing their bathrobes for trips to the shared bathrooms.

Hughenden

14 Queen St, Woollahra NSW 2025. **Map** 6 E4. ☎ *9363 4863.* [FAX] *9362 0398.* ***Rooms:*** *35.* 🛏 [1] ▦ 🚸 [TV] [P] 🌿 🍴 💳 *AE, DC, MC, V.* $

After a checkered history, from being a family home in 1876 to a girls' school in later years and a boarding house for artistic types after World War II, this rambling old building is now restored to its original grandeur with beautifully carved staircases and marble fireplaces. The rooms are all quite comfortably furnished, and the hotel has a very good restaurant.

Sullivans

21 Oxford St, Paddington NSW 2021 **Map** 5 B3. ☎ *9361 0211.* [FAX] *9360 3735.* ***Rooms:*** *62.* 🛏 🚸 [TV] ☰ 🏊 ⇅ [P] 🌿 💳 *AE, DC, MC, V.* $

An uninspiring exterior belies the attractive minimalist interior of this family-owned small hotel. The rooms are not large, but are comfortable with good facilities. The central courtyard in terra-cotta tones has an inviting pool. Bicycles are available for guests to ride.

FARTHER AFIELD

Periwinkle Guesthouse

19 East Esplanade, Manly NSW 2095. ☎ *9977 4668.* [FAX] *9977 6308.* ***Rooms:*** *18.* [1] ▦ 🚸 [TV] ☀ 🏊 [P] 🌿 💳 *MC, V.* $

Stylish rooms with high ceilings, wrought-iron verandas, and a leafy courtyard are features of this very pretty family-run guesthouse. The rooms all have ceiling fans and cane furniture, but bathrooms are shared. There are private outdoor areas where guests can enjoy the tranquillity of Manly Cove.

Savoy Double Bay

41–45 Knox St, Double Bay NSW 2028. ☎ *9326 1411.* [FAX] *9327 8464.* ***Rooms:*** *34.* 🛏 ▦ 🚸 [TV] ☰ [P] 🌿 💳 *AE, DC, MC, V.* $

The rooms may be small and somewhat blandly furnished, but this small hotel, set among the outdoor cafés, exclusive shops and chic restaurants of upscale Double Bay, offers excellent value. Room rates include a continental breakfast and also complimentary newspapers and coffee, which are available to guests in the atrium.

Harbourside Apartments

2a Henry Lawson Ave, McMahons Point NSW 2060. ☎ *9963 4300.* [FAX] *9922 7998.* ***Rooms:*** *82.* 🛏 ▦ 🚸 [TV] ☀ 🏊 ⇅ [P] 🌿 💳 *AE, DC, MC, V.* $$

Most of the executive- and family-serviced apartments in this 16-story building close to the waterfront have what are probably some of the best views in Sydney. While the two-bedroom apartments are huge, the studios are a bit pokey, but all the apartments are comfortably furnished and have good kitchen facilities. The pool has a wonderful position right by the harbor's edge.

Hotel Lawson

383–389 Bulwara Rd, Ultimo NSW 2007. **Map** 3 C4. ☎ *9211 1499.* [FAX] *9281 3764.* ***Rooms:*** *96.* 🛏 ▦ 🚸 [TV] ☰ ♿ [P] 🌿 💳 *AE, DC, MC, V, JCB.* $$

This is a modern hotel but the use of stained wood throughout the rooms is reminiscent of an old country pub. The place is friendly and relaxed and the rooms are a bargain. The prints and memorabilia of 19th-century poet and short-story writer, Henry Lawson, give a real Australian flavor.

McLaren

25 McLaren St, North Sydney NSW 2060. ☎ *9954 4622.* [FAX] *9922 1868.* ***Rooms:*** *28.* 🛏 ▦ 🚸 [TV] ☰ ♿ [P] 🌿 💳 *AE, DC, MC, V, JCB.* $$

The original stately mansion, now protected by National Trust listing, blends pleasingly with a new wing connected by the Atrium Garden. Here, cane furniture, hanging ferns, and a glass ceiling evoke a seaside resort setting. All the facilities of a large hotel (including room service) are offered, with the friendly approach of a more intimate hotel.

Ravesi's on Bondi Beach

Cnr Campbell Parade & Hall St, Bondi Beach NSW 2026. ☎ *9365 4422.* [FAX] *9365 1481.* ***Rooms:*** *16.* 🛏 ▦ 🚸 [TV] ☰ ☀ 🏊 ♿ *limited.* ⇅ 🍴 💳 *AE, DC, MC, V.* $$

Smart, laid-back, and trendy, this busy small hotel epitomizes the relaxed style of beach life at Bondi. The rooms are furnished in cane and wood, and some of the suites have private balconies overlooking the surf of Bondi Beach. The hotel's restaurant is regarded as one of the best in the area *(see p189)*, but you will need to book ahead as it is always very popular with the local residents.

Sir Stamford Double Bay

22 Knox St, Double Bay NSW 2028. ☎ *9363 0100.* [FAX] *9327 3110.* ***Rooms:*** *72.* 🛏 ▦ 🚸 [TV] ☰ 🏊 ♿ ⇅ [P] 🍴 💳 *AE, DC, MC, V, JCB.* $$

The lobby is sumptuously furnished and decorated in midnight blue and gold. The use of deep, rich colors continues in the bold design of the guest rooms, featuring exquisite furnishings, billowing silk curtains, and canopied beds, or else New York loft-style rooms complete with mezzanine bedrooms. The elegant Romanesque-style pool is open to guests 24 hours a day.

Manly Pacific Parkroyal

55 North Steyne, Manly NSW 2095. ☎ *9977 7666.* [FAX] *9977 7822.* ***Rooms:*** *169.* 🛏 ▦ 🚸 [TV] ☰ ☀ 🏊 ♿ ⇅ [P] 🌿 🍴 💳 *AE, DC, MC, V, JCB.* $$$

Situated right on Manly's ocean beach, the hotel has unbeatable views of sand and surf. All the rooms are light and spacious, with balconies and every modern convenience. There are bars, restaurants, a nightclub, and a rooftop pool, and also plenty of local pubs and cafés just a short stroll away.

Medina Executive Apartments

400 Glenmore Rd, Paddington NSW 2113. **Map** 6 D2. ☎ *9361 9000.* [FAX] *9361 5965.* ***Rooms:*** *48.* 🛏 ▦ 🚸 [TV] ☰ ♿ [P] 🌿 💳 *AE, DC, MC, V.* $$$

Set in landscaped gardens in a peaceful residential area, these huge two- and three-bedroom modern apartments offer all the conveniences of home, combined with hotel-style services. It is only a short walk to the supermarket to stock the refrigerator. Buses going directly to the beach or to the city are close by on New South Head Road.

Ritz Carlton Double Bay

33 Cross St, Double Bay NSW 2028. ☎ *9362 4455.* [FAX] *9362 4744.* ***Rooms:*** *140.* 🛏 ▦ 🚸 [TV] ☰ ☀ 🏊 ♿ ⇅ [P] 🌿 🍴 💳 *AE, DC, MC, V, JCB.* $$$

This hotel reeks of sophistication, from the first-floor lounge and reception area to the classically decorated rooms and suites. The central courtyard is in the style of a Mediterranean villa garden, while the rooftop heated pool has fabulous views of Sydney Harbour.

For key to symbols *see p171*

RESTAURANTS, CAFÉS, AND PUBS

SYDNEYSIDERS are justifiably proud of their dining scene. Australia's largest city has been populated by successive waves of migrants, all of whom have added something of their home countries to the communal table. These influences have spilled over into contemporary cuisine, which is often called "modern Australian." This term covers just about any ethnic style the chef may fancy, loosely based on French cuisine. The result is that, in terms of ethnic diversity, Sydney is able

Fresh seafood, Chinese style

to offer many dining options. For a summary of key features and prices of restaurants included in this guide, turn to *Choosing a Restaurant* on pages 186–7. There is a more detailed description of each restaurant in the listings on pages 188–93. Casual eating places, where you can often enjoy food that is as good as at a restaurant but cheaper, are featured on pages 194–7; here you will also find mention of pubs that have recommended bistros and dining areas.

WHERE TO EAT

CIRCULAR QUAY, The Rocks, Darlinghurst, Potts Point, and Paddington are the areas where you will find the widest choice of places to eat. Just outside the city center, and not covered in depth in these listings, are the inner-city "eat streets" of Glebe Point Road, Glebe *(see p131)*, and King Street, Newtown.

On the lower North Shore is Military Road, which extends from Neutral Bay to Mosman. It would be difficult to walk along any of these streets and not find a café or restaurant to suit your taste and budget.

All of the major hotels have at least one restaurant and a few of these, such as Kable's in the Regent Sydney *(see p174)*, serve some of the finest food that Sydney has to offer. Signature restaurants that are recommended in the grander

hotels include Raphael at the Sydney Renaissance, Unkai, a splendid Japanese dining room in the ANA Hotel, and the very Venetian Galileo in the Observatory Hotel *(see pp174–7)*. They aim at the well-heeled diner on an expense account, but nonetheless offer a high standard of dining for people who want the best and are prepared to pay for it.

HOW MUCH TO PAY

COMPARED WITH other major world capitals, dining out in Sydney is relatively inexpensive. The cost of a three-course meal in an average restaurant is probably 25 percent lower than its equivalent in, say, New York or London. The cost is further reduced if you choose a BYO restaurant where you can avoid paying the marked-up price of restaurant wine by taking your own alcohol.

Understated chic at Darley Street Thai, Kings Cross *(see p191)*

OPENING TIMES

MOST RESTAURANTS serve lunch from noon to 3pm and dinner from 6pm to about 11pm, though last orders are often at 10:30pm. Cheap and cheerful ethnic kitchens may close earlier, around 9:30pm, but this largely depends on demand. Many restaurants close on some, if not all, public holidays *(see p51)*. This is particularly true of Christmas Day, Dec 26, and Good Friday.

RESERVATIONS

BOOKING IS recommended in most places – earlier in the day is usually adequate. If, you want to be sure of a table for Friday or Saturday in a spot that is currently fashionable, however, you may need to make a reservation at least a week in advance. The more casual brasseries and bistros

The popular Fez Café in Victoria Street, Darlinghurst *(see p193)*

are the exceptions. Many are open all through the day and, as they aren't the sort of place where people linger over their meal, they do not take bookings. You may have to wait a few minutes for a table if you arrive at a busy time.

LICENSING LAWS

SYDNEY RESTAURANTS must be licensed to sell food, but when a place is described as licensed, this usually refers to its license to sell alcohol. BYO (bring your own) restaurants are not licensed to sell liquor and you will need to buy it beforehand if you want to drink alcohol with your meal. A small amount will probably be charged for "corkage."

BYO restaurants not only reduce the cost of dining out, but also allow wine buffs to choose exactly the wines they wish to drink with their meal. At fashionable establishments such as Claude's *(see p193)*, it is a good idea to inquire about the day's menu, so you can choose your wine accordingly.

Relaxing in a café at the top end of Oxford Street, Paddington

DRESS CODES

DRESS STANDARDS in Sydney restaurants are really quite relaxed, even in the more fashionable establishments. Most restaurants will draw the line, however, at patrons in beachwear and flip flops.

Neat and tidy is the general rule. Neat casual dress is the safest option when considering

Surf watching from the balcony at Ravesi's on Bondi Beach *(see p190)*

what to wear. Jackets and ties are a rare sight unless the wearer has come straight from the office or is conducting a business meeting over a meal.

TAX AND TIPPING

AS IN THE REST of Australia, there are no government taxes or service charges added to the check in Sydney. While tipping is not compulsory, 10 to 15 percent of the total is customary as a reward for good service. You can leave a cash tip on the table after you have paid or simply add it to the total if paying by charge or credit card.

EATING WITH CHILDREN

MOST RESTAURANTS accept children who can sit still throughout a meal, although you may feel more comfortable in either Chinese restaurants or the cheap pasta eateries in East Sydney, where children are always welcome.

Hamburger chains such as McDonald's and Hungry Jacks have branches throughout the city. For families wanting to dine rather than snack, chains such as Pizza Hut and the Black Stump steakhouses offer special menus for children as well as alcohol for the adults.

The Hard Rock Café *(see p194)* in Darlinghurst has enough of a buzz to drown out any noise young children may make and the menu and upbeat atmosphere are popular with older kids. Perhaps the best spots to dine out with

children are those where they can play safely outside after they have eaten. The Bathers Pavilion *(see p188)* is right on Balmoral Beach *(see pp54–5)*, a sheltered harbor beach that has a fenced swimming pool, while Centennial Park Café *(see p194)* is within supervisory range of grassy lawns and a children's playground.

USING THE LISTINGS

Key to symbols in the listings on pp188–93.

▯❶	fixed-price menu
▱	bring your own bottle
🚹	children's portions
V	vegetarian dishes available
♿	wheelchair access
▤	air conditioning
▦	tables outside
▨	tables with good views
⤧	nonsmoking section
♟	good wine list
★	highly recommended
▤	credit cards accepted:

AE   American Express
DC   Diners Club
MC   MasterCard/Access
V   Visa
JCB Japanese Credit Bureau

Price categories for a three-course evening meal for one person including cover charge and service (but not wine):
Ⓢ under A$25
⒮Ⓢ A$25–35
⒮⒮Ⓢ A$35–50
⒮⒮⒮Ⓢ A$50–70
⒮⒮⒮⒮Ⓢ Over A$70

What to Eat in Sydney

Meat pie with tomato sauce

SYDNEYSIDERS take for granted the quality and variety of produce offered. The ordinary fare has been pushed aside as restaurateurs seek out regional specialties. From New South Wales, you may sample Sydney rock oysters, honey from Mudgee, mushrooms from Orange, lamb from Illabo, and the Southern Highlands' gourmet potatoes. From other states, try the olive oil of South Australia, salmon farmed in Tasmania, soft fruit and dairy produce from Victoria, reef fish and exotic fruit from Queensland, and Western Australian farmhouse cheeses.

Eucalypt Honey
Imported bees seem to love the eucalypts. Leatherwood, light in color, has the strongest flavor.

Potato Wedges
Coated with a spicy seasoning then fried in a two-step process, these variations on the humble French fry are usually served with sour cream and chili sauce.

Yum Cha
Literally "drinking tea," this Chinese feast includes dim sum, or steamed dumplings stuffed with meat, fish, or vegetables.

Focaccia
This Italian-inspired sandwich has gourmet antipasto, salad, and meat slices between toasted slabs of crusty flat bread.

Lebanese Mezes
Expect an array of appetizers from bean and vegetable dips, marinated and grilled vegetables, and filled pastries.

Crab

Balmain bug

Rock oysters

Scallops

Lobster

King prawns

Mussels

Seafood Platter
Coming from comparatively clean waters, Australian seafood is both abundant and of extremely high quality.

Mixed Leaf Salad
Garden-fresh salad features on most menus. It is served here with feta cheese and grilled vegetables.

Char-grilled Kangaroo Fillet
A relatively recent addition to butchers' shelves, low-fat kangaroo steak is usually served rare.

Thai Green Curry
Chicken is the favorite variety, but a tasty vegetarian version is also commonly served.

Kebabs

Chicken wings

Baby octopus

Seared Beef Steak
Australian beef, here wrapped in paperbark, is usually served with the season's vegetables.

Barbecue
Char-grilled meat, poultry, and fresh seafood, such as baby octopus, are served by themselves or in combination, usually accompanied by bread and green salad.

Freshwater Crayfish
Also known as "yabbies," this main dish is usually served simply on a bed of greens with a dipping sauce such as aïoli.

Blue-eyed Cod
Although known as cod, it is in fact trevalla, a deep sea fish of meaty texture and mild flavor. It is often served in thick steaks.

Lamb Loin Fillet
Thick slices of tender seared lamb served on a salad of arugula and fresh snow peas are ideal Sydney summer eating.

Baked Ricotta Cake
Indigenous Australian ingredients such as rosella buds may appear in contemporary desserts.

Pavlova
This meringue dessert is topped with fresh cream and summer fruit, such as passionfruit.

Mixed Berry Ice Cream
Homemade ice creams, such as raspberry or honey, are often served with seasonal fruit.

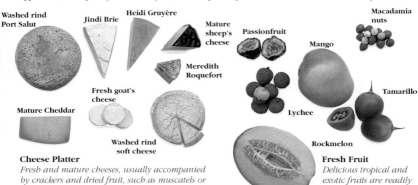

Washed rind Port Salut

Jindi Brie

Heidi Gruyère

Mature sheep's cheese

Passionfruit

Macadamia nuts

Mango

Meredith Roquefort

Fresh goat's cheese

Tamarillo

Mature Cheddar

Lychee

Washed rind soft cheese

Rockmelon

Cheese Platter
Fresh and mature cheeses, usually accompanied by crackers and dried fruit, such as muscatels or figs, are the perfect way to finish a meal.

Fresh Fruit
Delicious tropical and exotic fruits are readily available all year.

What to Drink in Sydney

Semillon Chardonnay

THE DEFINITION OF a seven-course Australian meal, the old joke runs, is a meat pie and a six-pack (of beer, that is). It is true that Australians do love their beer, with a wide range of local products from which to choose. They can also select from some of the most acclaimed and best-value wines in the world, produced by both local small businesses and corporate wineries. Imported wines, beers, and spirits are also readily available.

SPARKLING WINE

WITH PINOT NOIR and Chardonnay – the two classic Champagne varieties – responding well to the injection of expertise and capital from France in the 1980s, the sparkling wine shelves are stacked with premium products at affordable prices.

Pinot Noir Chardonnay

MAJOR WINE REGIONS

1. Hunter Valley
2. Mudgee
3. Riverina
4. Yarra Valley
5. Geelong
6. Northeastern Victoria
7. Clare Valley
8. Barossa Valley and Adelaide Hills
9. Coonawarra and Padthaway
10. Margaret River
11. Tasmania

South Australia is the country's largest producer of wine.

Grange Hermitage

WHITE WINE

Rhine Riesling   **Botrytis Semillon**

WHEN AUSTRALIANS first adopted table wines in the 1960s and 1970s, their preference was for a Moselle-type wine, or Riesling and Gewürztraminer. Later, they embraced drier varieties such as Semillon, Chardonnay, and Sauvignon Blanc, and showed a passion for wood-matured wines. Today, they can also choose from lesser known grapes such as Marsanne and *muscat à petits grains*. One of the most prized whites is Rosemount Estate's Roxburgh Chardonnay but, unfortunately, much of it is exported. In 1982, the De Bortolis made their first Botrytis Semillon, which started the dessert wine revolution. It remains the leader in this field.

Grape picking by hand in the Hunter Valley, north of Sydney

The Chardonnay grape lends its buttery, honeyed, rich notes to many of Australia's premium still and sparkling wines. It is regarded as the leading white wine grape worldwide.

GRAPE TYPE	BEST REGIONS	BEST PRODUCERS
Chardonnay	Barossa Valley	Penfolds, Saltram
	Hunter Valley	Petersons, Rosemount Estate, Scarborough, Tyrrell's
	Yarra Valley	Coldstream Hills, St. Huberts
Riesling (Rhine Riesling)	Barossa Valley	Leo Buring, Orlando
	Clare Valley	Jud's Hill, Petaluma, Pikes
Semillon	Hunter Valley	Brokenwood, McWilliam's, Rothbury Estate
	Margaret River	Evans & Tate, Moss Wood
Semillon Chardonnay	Hunter Valley	Rosemount Estate
Semillon (dessert)	Riverina	De Bortoli
Muscat/Tokay	Northeastern Victoria	Baileys, Campbells, Chambers, Morris

RED WINE

A USTRALIA'S BENCHMARK RED is Grange Hermitage, an invention of the late Max Schubert, in the 1950s. He preferred wines that required at least a decade's cellaring. In contrast, Wolf Blass, an architect of the current style, champions the "drink-now" approach with quickly maturing wines. Both men have created blends of varieties from different districts, with oak barrels an integral part of the process. Lighter reds, which may be served slightly chilled, have recently been introduced.

Vast vineyards of Leeuwin Estate, Margaret River

Shiraz   **Pinot Noir**

GRAPE TYPE	BEST REGIONS	BEST PRODUCERS
Cabernet Sauvignon	Barossa Valley	Henschke, Penfolds, Wolf Blass
	Coonawarra	Bowen Estate, Lindemans, Rouge Homme, Wynns
	Margaret River	Leeuwin Estate, Vasse Felix
Shiraz (Hermitage)	Barossa Valley	Henschke, Penfolds, Wolf Blass
	Hunter Valley	Brokenwood, Lindemans
	Margaret River	Cape Mentelle
Pinot Noir	Geelong	Bannockburn, Scotchman's Hill
	Hunter Valley	Calais, Rothbury Estate
	Yarra Valley	Coldstream Hills, Diamond Valley
Cabernet Shiraz	Barossa Valley	Penfolds, Wolf Blass
	Coonawarra	Leconfield, Lindemans, Mildara
	Margaret River	Cape Mentelle

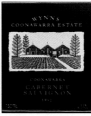

Cabernet Sauvignon from the Coonawarra district is one example of this increasingly popular quality red grape.

BEER

M OST AUSTRALIAN BEER is vat fermented, or pilsener, and consumed chilled. Full-strength beer has an alcohol content of around 4.8 percent, mid-strength beers have around 3.5 percent while "light" beers have less than 3 percent. Traditionally heat sterilized, cold filtration is now popular. Aficionados of traditional ale should seek out the city's pub breweries. Beer is ordered by glass size and brand. A schooner is a 426 ml (15 fl oz) glass, while a middy is 284 ml (10 fl oz).

Tooheys Red Bitter   **A local pilsener**

Middy   **Schooner**

FRUIT JUICES

W ITH THE FABULOUS fresh fruit at their disposal all year, cafés concoct an astonishing array of fruit-based nonalcoholic drinks. They include frappés of fruit pulp and juice blended with crushed ice; smoothies of fruit blended with milk or yogurt; and pure juices, extracted from everything from carrots to watermelons.

Pear and kiwi frappé   **Banana smoothie**   **Strawberry juice**

OTHER DRINKS

T AP WATER in Sydney is fresh and clean, but local and imported bottled water is fashionable. The cola generation has graduated to alcoholic soft drinks and soda drinks. One brand, Two Dogs alcoholic lemonade, was born when a glut of lemons flooded the fruit market.

Alcoholic soda

COFFEE

S YDNEY'S PASSION for coffee means that short black, macchiato, caffe latte, cappuccino, and flat white (with milk) are now available at every neighborhood café.

Flat white coffee

Caffe latte

Sydney's Best: Restaurants, Cafés, and Pubs

SYDNEY IS THRICE BLESSED when it comes to restaurants. Not only are their quantity and quality staggering, but they are also a remarkably good value when compared with other world centers. Even at the grandest establishment it is possible to enjoy a single course and a glass of wine for under A$25. Within the areas covered by this guide, there is something for every taste, pocket, and occasion. Full restaurant listings are on pages 188–93, while the more casual eating places are covered on pages 194–7.

Bennelong Restaurant
This is a grand dining experience with dramatic harbor views from the Opera House. (See p189.)

Rockpool
Asian flavors and splendid seafood are featured on the much-praised menu. (See p190.)

THE ROCKS AND
CIRCULAR QUAY

Customs House Bar
The crowds at this tiny business district haunt spill outside and under the trees. (See p196.)

BOTANI
GARDEN
AND TH
DOMAIN

CITY CENTER

DARLING
HARBOUR

Il Edna's Table
Contemporary Australian dishes with "bush tucker" ingredients are the specialty here. (See p188.)

Restaurant Manfredi
Classic Italian cuisine is updated using new ingredients and combinations. (See p192.)

Silver Spring
Diners hail passing carts laden with dim sum *in the lunchtime ritual known as* yum cha *(to take tea) at this bustling Chinatown restaurant.* (See p191.)

Botanic Gardens Restaurant
Wisteria frames the view of the duck pond and gardens from the deck of this restaurant, which serves Mediterranean food. (See p188.)

Darley Street Thai
Considered the best Thai restaurant in Sydney, its chef was trained in Thailand and is renowned for his depth of knowledge of this complex cuisine. (See p191.)

Bayswater Brasserie
This brasserie is especially noted for its Sunday brunch. Some of the patrons have dined here daily since its 1982 opening. (See p189.)

Bar Coluzzi
Captains of industry, media types, and anybody who is serious about coffee gravitate to this tiny café. (See p194.)

KINGS CROSS
AND
DARLINGHURST

Claude's
An elegant dining option for people who appreciate fine French-influenced fare, it has service to match. (See p193.)

PADDINGTON

Royal Hotel
This busy pub bistro has veranda seating for watching the street life below. (See p196.)

0 meters   500

0 yards   500

Choosing a Restaurant

THE RESTAURANTS IN THIS GUIDE have been chosen for their good value or exceptional food. This chart, arranged by area and price category, highlights some of the factors which may influence your choice. Full restaurant reviews, arranged according to cuisine, are on pages 188–93. Information on cafés and pubs is given on pages 194–7.

		Page Number	Fixed-Price Menu	Good Views	Tables Outside	Vegetarian Specialties	Seafood Specialties	BYO	Children's Facilities	Late Opening
THE ROCKS AND CIRCULAR QUAY										
Rock Fish Café (Seafood)	$$	190				■	●		●	
The Wharf Restaurant (Bistros and Brasseries)	$$	189	■	●		■	●		●	
Sailor's Thai (Asian)	$$$	191			●		●			
Merrony's (Contemporary) ★	$$$$	188		■		■	●			■
Bennelong Restaurant (Contemporary) ★	$$$$$	189		■			●			■
Rockpool (Seafood) ★	$$$$$	190					●			
CITY CENTER										
Casa Asturiana (Mediterranean)	$$	193				■	●			
The Edge (Bistros and Brasseries)	$$	189			●	■	●		●	
Grand Taverna (Mediterranean)	$$	193			●	■	●			
Sharwarma Grill House (Middle Eastern)	$$	193	●			■		■		
Beppi's (Italian)	$$$	192				■	●			■
Criterion (Middle Eastern)	$$$	193		■	●	■	●			
Il Edna's Table (Contemporary) ★	$$$	188				■	●			
Sino Jin Jiang (Chinese)	$$$	191				■	●			
Forty One (Contemporary) ★	$$$$	188	●	■		■	●			
Restaurant Suntory (Asian)	$$$$	192				■	●			
DARLING HARBOUR										
Golden Century (Chinese) ★	$	190				■	●			■
Kampung (Asian)	$	191				■	●		●	
Malaya (Asian)	$	191				■	●		●	
Regal (Chinese)	$	190				■	●		●	■
Golden Harbour (Chinese)	$$	190				■	●			■
Marigold (Chinese)	$$	191					●		●	
Silver Spring (Chinese) ★	$$	191				■	●			
Jordons Seafood Restaurant (Seafood)	$$$	190	●	■	●		●			
Kamogawa (Asian)	$$$$	192					●			
BOTANIC GARDENS AND THE DOMAIN										
Botanic Gardens Restaurant (Contemporary) ★	$$$	188		■	●	■	●		●	
Claudine's French Restaurant (French)	$$$	193				■	●	■		
KINGS CROSS AND DARLINGHURST										
No Names (Italian)	$	192						■		
Fez Café (Middle Eastern)	$$	193				■	●	■		
Fishface (Seafood)	$$	190			●	■	●	■		
Lime & Lemongrass (Asian)	$$	191	●		●	■				■
Macleay Street Bistro (Bistros and Brasseries)	$$	189			●		●	■		
Oh! Calcutta! (Asian)	$$	191			●	■	●	■		
Bayswater Brasserie (Bistros and Brasseries) ★	$$$	189		■		■	●			
Cicada (Contemporary)	$$$	188			●		●			

Price categories for a three-course evening meal for one person including cover charge and service (but not wine):
$ under A$25
$$ A$25–$35
$$$ A$35–$50
$$$$ A$50–$70
$$$$$ Over A$70

★ Means highly recommended.

FIXED-PRICE MENU
A menu of two to three courses for a set price that includes coffee but excludes wine and other drinks.

BYO
Bring your own alcohol. A small charge is often made for corkage.

LATE OPENING
Orders will still be accepted at or after 11pm.

	Price	Page Number	Fixed-Price Menu	Good Views	Tables Outside	Vegetarian Specialties	Seafood Specialties	BYO	Children's Facilities	Late Opening
Cosmos (Mediterranean)	$$$	193				●	●	●		●
Mezzaluna (Italian) ★	$$$	192		●	●	●	●			
Darley Street Thai (Asian) ★	$$$	191				●	●			
Wockpool (Asian) ★	$$$	192			●	●	●			●
Paramount (Contemporary) ★	$$$$	189				●				
PADDINGTON										
Bistro Moncur (French)	$$	193			●	●	●			
Lucio's (Italian)	$$$	192					●			
Claude's (French) ★	$$$$$	193	●			●	●	●		●
FARTHER AFIELD										
Meera's Dosa House (Asian)	$	191	●		●	●		●	●	
Sports Bard (Bistros and Brasseries)	$	189	●			●	●			●
Barnaby's Riverside (Contemporary)	$$	188	●		●	●	●		●	
Frattini (Italian)	$$	192				●	●	●		
Gastronomia Chianti (Italian)	$$	192				●				
Mohr Fish (Seafood)	$$	190	●				●			
Armstrong's Manly (Bistros and Brasseries)	$$$	189	●		●	●	●		●	
Bathers Pavilion (Contemporary) ★	$$$	188		●			●		●	●
Courtney's Brasserie (Bistros and Brasseries)	$$$	189			●	●	●			
Darling Mills (Contemporary)	$$$	188			●		●	●		●
Gotham Bar & Brasserie (Bistros and Brasseries)	$$$	189	●			●	●	●		
Le Kiosk (Contemporary)	$$$	188	●		●	●	●			
Ravesi's on Bondi Beach (Bistros and Brasseries)	$$$	190	●		●		●			
Restaurant Manfredi (Italian) ★	$$$	192			●	●	●			
Riberries (Contemporary)	$$$	188	●			●	●	●		●
The Pier (Seafood) ★	$$$$	190	●				●			

CONTEMPORARY

In the 1980s, Sydney chefs started to embrace the multiculturalism of contemporary Australian society. Culinary influences from the many migrant countries were at last infiltrating the kitchens. At the same time, a movement began toward a lighter, fresher approach to both cooking and presentation. Now imaginative chefs, using superb ingredients, successfully produce delicious and unusual flavors while a few of the bolder ones experiment with formerly obscure native Australian or "bush tucker" foods.

Barnaby's Riverside

66 Phillip St, Parramatta.
(9633 3777. **○** noon–midnight
Mon–Sat, noon–5pm Sun. ✦ ▮ ▤
▦ ▮ ⬛ AE, DC, MC, V. $$

This colonial cottage overlooking the Parramatta River is a great setting for sampling a menu that combines Asian, Mediterranean, and North African influences. Try the kangaroo with plum sauce, *sashimi* of Atlantic salmon, or baby squid with preserved lemon on couscous. Save room for the buffalo chips (French fries), whose only relationship to the animal is their chunky size.

Bathers Pavilion

4 The Esplanade, Balmoral.
(9968 1133. **○** noon–3pm Mon–Fri, 9am–3pm Sat & Sun, 6:30pm–
midnight daily. ✦ ▮ ▦ ▥ ▮ ★
⬛ AE, DC, MC, V, JCB. $$$

On a sunny day or moonlit night, the setting of this old Spanish-Mission-style beach pavilion in parkland at Balmoral Beach *(see pp54–5)* is quite magical, with its views across Middle and North Harbours to the open sea. The furniture may look a little faded, but the food is always fresh and inventively prepared in a variety of ethnic styles. In the more casual and laid-back Refreshment Room, you can order wine by the glass, cakes, coffee, and herbal teas.

Botanic Gardens Restaurant

Royal Botanic Gardens, Mrs Macquaries Rd. **Map** 2 D4. **(** 9241 2419.
○ noon–2:30pm Mon–Sat, noon–
3pm Sun. ✦ ▮ ▦ ▥ ▦ ▥ ★
⬛ AE, DC, MC, V. $$$

The wisteria-covered balcony looks out over the lovely Royal Botanic Gardens *(see pp104–5)* in this lunchtime spot, where the food has a Mediterranean accent. The combination of fine location and fine food is not lost on the business

people from nearby Macquarie Street. If you plan to stop by when visiting the gardens, be sure to reserve to ensure a table.

Cicada

29 Challis Ave, Potts Point. **Map** 2 E4.
(9358 1255. **○** noon–2:30pm
Wed–Fri, 6:30–10pm Mon–Sat. ▤
▦ ▮ ⬛ AE, DC, MC, V. $$$

Robust Mediterranean and Middle Eastern flavors are given a subtle interpretation in this very popular restaurant with its vine-covered terrace for outdoor eating. The menu changes seasonally, but the *escalivada* (eggplant) terrine with *tapenade* and black olive bread is a perennial favorite. There is an excellent wine list.

Darling Mills

134 Glebe Point Rd, Glebe. **Map** 3 A4.
(9660 5666. **○** 6pm–midnight
Mon, noon–midnight Tue–Sat, noon–
11pm Sun. ▦ ▥ ▮
⬛ AE, DC, MC, V. $$$

This spacious sandstone building, completed in 1857 by Colonial Architect Edmund Blacket, was restored in the 1970s as a restaurant. A rooftop greenhouse means that the kitchen can harvest the freshest possible produce. Naturally the house salad should not be missed, but salmon, smoked on the premises, is another specialty.

Il Edna's Table

Lobby Level, MLC Centre, Martin Place. **Map** 1 B4. **(** 9231 1400.
○ noon–3pm Mon–Fri, 6–10pm
Tue–Sat. ▤ ▤ ▮ ★ ⬛ AE, DC,
MC, V. $$$

Restaurant manager Jennice Kersh and her chef brother, Raymond, are ever-so-gently converting even the most conservative palates to the tastes of the outback with the menu they offer in this stylish space right in the heart of the city. Aboriginal art on the walls sets the scene for dishes such as ocean trout wrapped in ky choy and paperbark, and served with bush tomato *aïoli.* Aboriginal dancers and musicians perform here occasionally.

Le Kiosk

1 Marine Parade, Shelly Beach, Manly.
(9977 4122. **○** noon–2:30pm
Mon–Fri, noon–3pm Sat, noon–
3:30pm Sun, 6:30–9pm Mon–Thu,
6:30–9:30pm Fri, 6:30–10pm Sat,
7–9pm Sun. ▤ ▮ ▤ ▦ ▦
▮ ⬛ AE, DC, MC, V. $$$

It would be hard to find a more pleasant way to punctuate a day at beachside Manly *(see p133)* than by strolling along the waterfront

walkway to lunch in this charming sandstone cottage with outdoor tables set in a subtropical garden. Try the excellent seafood platter for two and a crisp white wine from the all-Australian list. Sunday breakfast is the full English extravaganza, buffet-style, starting with a glass of chilled sparkling wine.

Riberries

411 Bourke St, Darlinghurst.
Map 5 A3. **(** 9361 4929. **○** 7pm–
late Mon–Sat. ▮ ▥ ▤ ▥ ▮
⬛ AE, DC, MC, V. $$$

Jean-Paul Bruneteau began introducing native foods to his classical French cuisine in the early 1980s. Since moving to the Victorian sandstone premises, he concentrates on using more and more native ingredients, such as bunya nuts, warrigul greens, and lemon aspen (a citrus with flavor similar to grapefruit). Kangaroo, emu, and *witjuti* grubs are on the menu, but there is also plenty to interest vegetarians. The riberry, which is a native clove, is used in both sweet and savory dishes.

Forty One

Level 41, Chifley Tower, Chifley Square. **Map** 1 B4. **(** 9221 2500.
○ noon–2pm Mon–Fri, 6:30–10pm
Mon–Sat. ▮⬤▮ ▤ ▮ ▤ ▦ ▥ ▮
★ ⬛ AE, DC, MC, V. $$$$

With impressive vistas of the city and Sydney Harbour, the view from this elegant establishment invites superlatives. So does the menu, which is French-based with occasional Asian influences. The crown roast of hare is a great treat when available and even the restaurant's most *soigné* clientele cannot resist the "variations on a theme," a chance to sample each of about five delectable desserts.

Merrony's

2 Albert St, Circular Quay. **Map** 1 C3.
(9247 9323. **○** noon–2:30pm
Mon–Sat, 5:45–11:45pm Mon–Sat.
▤ ▮ ▤ ▦ ▥ ▦ ▥ ★ ⬛ AE, DC,
MC, V. $$$

Chef Paul Merrony worked his way through the Michelin stars of France and England before bringing his classical French training home. At this restaurant, which overlooks Circular Quay and the passing trains, the menu changes with the marketplace and has a strongly French influence. Duck *confit* with sorrel and fried parsley, grilled sirloin with great French fries and shrimp or seafood bisque are near constants, all served with a very impressive range of Australian wines. This is a good place for supper after the opera.

Paramount

73 Macleay St, Potts Point. **Map** 2 E5. ☎ *9358 1652.* 🕐 *6:30–11pm daily.* [V] ☰ 🚭 🍷 ★ 💳 *AE, DC, MC, V.* $$$$

The interior of this restaurant has been described as the sensuous equivalent of sitting in a mother-of-pearl shell. Certainly, the molded fiberglass interior, glass bar, and white lighting create an impressive backdrop for the complex flavors of the refined fare the chef Chris Manfield dishes up. The menu changes monthly, as does the wine list, but regulars find it hard to pass up the duck and shiitake mushroom pie with ginger glaze or molded ice desserts made from fruits in season. In fact, Paramount is accustomed to welcoming guests just for their delicious desserts.

Bennelong Restaurant

Sydney Opera House, Bennelong Point. **Map** 1 C2. ☎ *9250 7578.* 🕐 *7–10pm Mon–Sat.* [V] ♿ *on request.* ☰ ❄ 🚭 🍷 ★ 💳 *AE, DC, MC, V.* $$$$$

Located in one of the shells of the Sydney Opera House *(see pp74–7)*, this restaurant has arguably the best location in Sydney, with its views across Circular Quay and the harbor. Dining here is almost as much of a drama as the daily performances at the nearby theaters. There are no flowers, music, or art to distract from the creations of the celebrated duo Gay Bilson and Janni Kyritsis. The serious dining area is at the lower end of the space with a mezzanine bar separating it from the more casual section. In the main dining area, roast pigeon with liver stuffing and broth or ocean trout with bone marrow and red wine butter may be offered. The other menu, aimed at pre- and post-theater goers, has reinvented classics such as shrimp cocktail, *tripes Lyonnaise*, and even the humble steak and kidney pie.

Bistros and Brasseries

Sydney's dining-out pattern has changed in recent years, and there is now a demand for restaurants where people can drop in for just one dish – and perhaps a glass of house wine. Often styled along the lines of a French bistro or brasserie, these places are generally open throughout the day and evening. Diners can expect good food which has been imaginatively prepared, moderate prices, and a bright and casual atmosphere. Kings Cross and Darlinghurst have a large concentration of bistros and brasseries.

Sports Bard

32 Campbell Parade, Bondi Beach. ☎ *9130 4582.* 🕐 *6pm–midnight Mon, noon–midnight Tue–Fri, 10am–midnight Sat & Sun.* [V] ☰ ❄ 🚭 💳 *AE, MC, V.* $

Somehow this upbeat spot on the southern end of Sydney's most famous beach *(see p137)* manages to hold as much appeal for families as it does for trendy young couples. Perhaps it is the house special risottos, or the decadent desserts, or the breakfast of poached egg, smoked salmon, and spinach on a potato pancake. Maybe it is the pool room out back. Whatever the attraction, lots of people want to share it, so be prepared to wait for a table on the weekend.

The Edge

60 Riley St, Darlinghurst. **Map** 5 A1. ☎ *9360 1372.* 🕐 *noon–11pm daily.* 🚸 [V] ⛱ 🚭 💳 *AE, MC, V.* $$

The setting, with its wooden floors and marble bars, may seem austere, but 1930s French posters, friendly service, and the almost clubby relationship between the staff and regulars lighten the atmosphere. With extensive vegetarian options, this is a place meat eaters can bring their vegetarian friends. The pizzas from the wood-fired ovens are delicious and have numerous imaginative toppings.

Macleay Street Bistro

73a Macleay St, Potts Point. **Map** 2 E5. ☎ *9358 4891.* 🕐 *noon–3pm Fri–Sun, 6–11pm daily.* 🍾 ♿ ⛱ 💳 *AE, DC, MC, V.* $$

The French-style menu sits quite comfortably with the former bohemian tradition of Kings Cross. Those who are particular about their steak tartare and brandade of salt cod all swear by the versions served here. Frequently nominated as Sydney's best BYO, this place is busy so make sure you get there early on Fridays and at weekends, since they do not take bookings.

The Wharf Restaurant

Pier 4, Hickson Rd, Millers Point. **Map** 1 A1. ☎ *9250 1761.* 🕐 *noon–3pm Mon–Sat, 6–10:30pm Mon–Sat.* [V] ♿ ⛱ ❄ 💳 *AE, DC, MC, V.* $$

The perfect place for a meal either before or after a performance, this restaurant, at the end of the wharf that is home to the Sydney Theatre Company *(see p69)*, is worth a visit in its own right. It has dress-circle views of the harbor – ask for an outdoor table on a warm day – and good simple fare, such as pasta, risotto, and grilled seafood.

Armstrong's Manly

Manly Wharf, Manly. ☎ *9976 3835.* 🕐 *noon–9:30pm Sun–Thu, noon–10pm Fri & Sat.* 🚸 [V] ♿ ☰ ⛱ ❄ 🚭 💳 *AE, DC, MC, V, JCB.* $$$

The harbor views from the Manly ferry wharf, a relaxed atmosphere and the best of produce with an emphasis on superb seafood make this a quintessential Sydney dining experience. You may order a full three-course meal with wine – the fish and chips here are second to none – a substantial snack, such as the mountainous Armstrong's Burger, or just coffee and a slice of cake. All will be excellent.

Bayswater Brasserie

32 Bayswater Rd, Potts Point. **Map** 5 B1. ☎ *9357 2749.* 🕐 *noon–11pm Mon–Thu, noon–11:30pm Fri & Sat, 10am–10pm Sun.* [V] ♿ ☰ ⛱ 🚭 🍷 ★ 💳 *AE, DC, MC, V.* $$$

The Thai chicken curry has been everyone's favorite since 1982, but the chef also recommends the river rock oysters or Pacific oysters from Tasmania's clear waters, the succulent Illabo lamb from the west of New South Wales, and the South Australian squid with black ink pasta. The bread, pastries, and ice cream, all made on the premises, are superb, and Sunday brunch has become an institution.

Courtney's Brasserie

2 Horwood Pl, Parramatta. ☎ *9635 3288.* 🕐 *noon–10:30pm Mon–Fri, 6–10:30pm Sat.* [V] ♿ ☰ ⛱ 🚭 💳 *AE, DC, MC, V.* $$$

This convict-brick building first opened its doors in 1830 as a soldiers' mess. Located in the business center of Sydney's west, this spot has a loyal clientele. It is well worth a visit during or after a busy day touring Parramatta's historic buildings *(see pp138–9)*.

Gotham Bar & Brasserie

135 Rowntree St, Balmain. ☎ *9555 8008.* 🕐 *noon–3pm Mon–Sat, 11am–3pm Sun, 6–11pm daily.* 🍾 [V] ☰ ❄ 🚭 💳 *AE, DC, MC, V.* $$$

Friendly service from staff who know their food and wine is the hallmark of this former pub, built in 1863, and restored to its original condition. The atmosphere in the main dining room is buzzy, but there are three quieter rooms available with views toward the Harbour Bridge. The menu ranges through Mediterranean, Asian, and Creole with a classical French finish. On weekends, people willingly line up for brunch.

For key to symbols *see p179*

Ravesi's on Bondi Beach

Cnr Campbell Parade & Hall St, Bondi Beach. **[** 9365 4422. **○** 7:30am–9:30pm Mon–Thu & Sun, 7:30am–10:30pm Fri & Sat. **⟨icons⟩** AE, DC, MC, V. **$$$**

Sit on the balcony to catch the sea breeze, beachfront life, and uninterrupted views of the surf. The house special, fish and chips with *aïoli*, the tuna with avocado, corn and Spanish onion salsa, and the mango brûlée are particularly delicious. Breakfast is a specialty, and snacks are served all day.

SEAFOOD

Sydney is blessed when it comes to seafood – not only with abundance but also with quality and freshness *(see p202)*. Most restaurants have daily seafood specials, and a handful have exclusively seafood menus. The traditional purveyors of fish and chips in the city are the Doyle family – their Watsons Bay beachfront establishment is almost an institution *(see p136)*. They also have branches at Circular Quay and the Sydney Fish Market *(see p131)*.

Fishface

132 Darlinghurst Rd, Darlinghurst. **Map** 5 B1. **[** 9332 4803. **○** noon–3pm Thu–Sun, 6–11pm daily. **⟨icons⟩** $$

The menu changes daily in this tiny café, where patrons sit on bar stools at high tables to eat some of the best-value seafood on offer. Seafood risotto is always popular as, of course, is the fish of the day. You cannot make a reservation, but staff will collect diners from the bar of the nearby hotel when a table becomes available.

Mohr Fish

202 Devonshire St, Surry Hills. **[** 9318 1326. **○** 7am–10pm Mon–Fri, 9am–10pm Sat & Sun. **⟨icons⟩** $$

Regulars happily repair to the bar of the pub across the road to wait for one of the four tables at this superior seafood café, which also does a roaring takeout trade. Fish of the day in beer batter and bouillabaisse are firm favorites.

Rock Fish Café

14 Loftus St. **Map** 1 B3. **[** 9252 3114. **○** 11:30am–3pm Mon–Fri, 5:30–10pm Mon–Fri. **⟨icons⟩** AE, DC, MC, V. $$

The city's Gallipoli Club for war veterans may seem an unlikely location for this bustling seafood

bistro, but the suits from the city know good value and brisk service when they find it and always keep the place packed at lunchtime. The blackboard menu changes often, but green chili curry and Parmesan-crumbed sardines are frequently listed because of demand.

Jordons Seafood Restaurant

Harbourside Festival Marketplace, Darling Harbour. **Map** 3 C2. **[** 9281 3711. **○** noon–3pm Mon–Fri, noon–11pm Sat & Sun. **⟨icons⟩** AE, DC, MC, V $$$

"Seafood as fresh as this morning" the menu proclaims at this venue overlooking Darling Harbour *(see pp90–101)*. Sushi, *sashimi*, and char-grilled baby octopus sit alongside deep-fried snapper and salmon. The indecisive can opt for the deluxe platter for two, a hot and cold selection of the market's best.

The Pier

594 New South Head Rd, Rose Bay. **[** 9327 6561. **○** noon–3pm daily, 6–10pm Mon–Sat, 6–9pm Sun. **⟨icons⟩** ★ AE, DC, MC, V. $$$$

An elegant harborside restaurant where the menu, with its Asian and Mediterranean influences, is almost as impressive as the stunning water views. Simplicity is the keynote – from classic fish and chips to a whole John Dory baked with ginger, chili, and green onions. Dine here on a sunny day and you will gain an inkling of why some fervently patriotic T-shirts proclaim Sydney the "best address on earth."

Rockpool

107 George St, The Rocks. **Map** 1 B3. **[** 9252 1888. **○** noon–2:30pm Mon–Fri, 6–11pm Mon–Sat. **⟨icons⟩** ★ AE, DC, MC, V. $$$$$

The modish lounge bar at the front of the restaurant sets the scene for seriously good food with a particular emphasis on Asian-influenced seafood. Although the menu changes seasonally, herb- and spice-encrusted tuna steaks and John Dory in Indian pastry with cardamom sauce are regulars. It is said Sydney's first taste of sticky date tart took place here, and many will claim it is still the best.

CHINESE

Sydney's Chinatown spreads from Darling Harbour to Central Railway Station, but Chinese restaurants can be found throughout the city and suburbs. Hot and spicy food

from the western province of Sichuan, delicate Shanghai-style dishes and Peking-style food are all available, but Cantonese cuisine remains the dominant tradition. *Yum cha (dim sum)*, the brunch-type dumplings and snacks enjoyed with tea, is among the most reasonably priced dining in town.

Golden Century

393–399 Sussex St. **Map** 4 E4. **[** 9212 3901. **○** noon–4am daily. **⟨icons⟩** ★ AE, DC, MC, V, JCB. $

Eight tanks brimming with live scallops, pippies, shrimp, lobster, abalone, King Island crab, parrot fish, coral trout, perch, and barramundi tell the story of this excellent Cantonese restaurant. Customers usually select their dinner from the tank then discuss with the waiter how it should be prepared. Shift workers, hotel staff, taxi drivers, night owls, and jet-lagged overseas visitors also appreciate the Golden Century because it is one of the few spots in the city where they can be sure of a fine meal at 3am.

Regal

347 Sussex St. **Map** 4 E3. **[** 9261 8988. **○** 10am–3pm daily, 5:30pm–midnight daily. **⟨icons⟩** AE, DC, MC, V, JCB. $

The glittering chandeliers, private rooms downstairs, people lining up, and waiters dashing everywhere to make this place reminiscent of the *yum cha* palaces of Hong Kong. The pace is somewhat gentler at dinner. Cantonese seafood is the star, and King Island crab is available for those who fancy a real indulgence. Best ordered by groups of six or eight people, these massive crustaceans – they start at about 5 kg (11 lb) – are served in several appetizing guises.

Golden Harbour

31–33 Dixon St. **Map** 4 D3. **[** 9212 5987. **○** 10am–4pm Mon–Fri, 9am–4pm Sat & Sun, 5:30–11pm Mon–Thu, 5:30pm–1am Fri–Sun. **⟨icons⟩** AE, DC, MC, V, JCB. $$

On Sundays the lines for *yum cha* wind out into Dixon Street. Regulars say it is worth the wait for the splendid dumplings filled with snowpea leaves or garlic chives, "silky noodles" (pan-fried rice noodles), pippies in black bean sauce, or barbecued pork pastries. In the evenings, the Cantonese menu emphasizes seafood fresh from the tanks with specials such as succulent king prawns steamed whole with garlic, squid in spicy salt, and curried mud crab.

Marigold

299–305 Sussex St. **Map** 4 D3. ☎ *9264 6744.* 🕐 *10am–3pm daily, 5:30–11pm daily.* 🧒 📋 💳 *AE, DC, MC, V, JCB.* $$

This restaurant is the original of a triumvirate that includes the Marigold Citymark and the Regal. It was an innovator on the Chinatown landscape when it was opened in the early 1980s, with its daily *yum cha* and seafood taken live from the tanks. It is now more of a fixture, but there is still an inclination to set the pace and try out new ingredients, such as crocodile meat (served either with chili or on a sizzling plate with satay sauce).

Silver Spring

1st Floor, Sydney Central, Cnr Hay & Pitt Sts. **Map** 4 E4. ☎ *9211 2232.* 🕐 *10am–11pm Mon–Fri, 9am–11pm Sat & Sun.* 🧒 [V] 📋 🚭 ★ 💳 *AE, DC, MC, V, JCB.* $$

Waiters communicate by walkie-talkies when they are busy turning over the tables to new diners at this multiroomed upstairs restaurant. On an average Saturday or Sunday morning, *yum cha* will be served to 1,500 people. The scene is more sedate at night, with Cantonese specialties such as barbecued suckling pig, shark's fin soup, and beef in black pepper sauce.

Sino Jin Jiang

Level 2, Queen Victoria Building. **Map** 4 E2. ☎ *9261 3388.* 🕐 *noon–3pm daily, 5:30–10pm Mon–Wed & Sun, 5:30–11pm Thu–Sat.* [V] 📋 💳 *AE, DC, MC, V.* $$$

In a city where Cantonese cuisine rules, this stylish dining room stands apart. A black lacquer and turquoise interior sets the scene for dishes from the western province of Sichuan and the central seaport of Shanghai. The former may supply green tea smoked duck with pancakes while the latter provides lion's head dumplings – pork balls wrapped in Chinese cabbage and poached in chicken soup.

Other Asian

The growing number of Korean, Thai, Japanese, Indonesian, Indian, Vietnamese, and Malaysian restaurants reflects the successive waves of migration into Australia. The restaurants here are all highly recommended, but you will also find authentic fare in most of the many population centers, such as Thai and Vietnamese in Marrickville and Cabramatta *(see pp40–43)*, Malay and Indonesian in Randwick, and Korean in Campsie.

Kampung

Royal Garden International Hotel, 431–439 Pitt St. **Map** 4 E4. ☎ *9281 6999.* 🕐 *noon–2:30pm daily, 6–10pm daily.* 🧒 [V] ♿ 📋 💳 *AE, DC, MC, V, JCB.* $

This second-floor hotel restaurant in the heart of Chinatown serves predominantly Malaysian cuisine. There are *halal* and vegetarian dishes, along with the popular house special of chili crab, beef *rendang, nasi lemak, nasi goreng,* and *laksa.* A special menu for children is also available.

Malaya

761 George St. **Map** 4 E5. ☎ *9211 0946.* 🕐 *noon–3pm Mon–Fri, 5–10pm Mon–Sat.* 🧒 [V] ♿ 📋 🚭 💳 *AE, DC, MC, V.* $

Located a short distance from three major media offices and close to Central Railway Station, this bustling two-level restaurant has, for more than 30 years, served as an alternative staff canteen for Sydney's journalists. The low-priced menu includes Indonesian, Malaysian, Sichuan, Singaporean, and *halal* dishes, along with the ever-popular *laksas, sambals, rendang,* and a delicious fish head curry.

Meera's Dosa House

567 Crown St, Surry Hills. ☎ *9798 7205.* 🕐 *6:30–10:30pm Tue–Sat.* 🍾 [V] ♿ ⛱ 🚭 💳 *MC, V.* $

This tiny shopfront celebrates the *dosa,* a southern Indian rice and lentil flour pancake with a variety of meat, vegetarian, and even fruit fillings. The savory ones are a meal in themselves, served with salad, homemade chutney, and *raita.* However, if you have room for something extra, there are also *panir* (fresh cheese) *pakoras, dhal kachori* (fried lentil dumplings), and *idlis* (spicy steamed rice cakes served with soup).

Lime & Lemongrass

42 Kellett St, Potts Point. **Map** 5 B1. ☎ *9358 5577.* 🕐 *6:30–11pm Mon–Thu & Sun, 6:30–11:30pm Fri & Sat.* 🍴 [V] 📋 ⛱ 🚭 $$

Sunthree Pancharoen has been a leader of Sydney's Thai revolution since the early 1980s. She now spreads the word from this stylish terrace house with balcony and courtyard seating in the heart of the Kings Cross district. Sunthree's menu is drawn from all over Thailand. Special dishes are the tapioca balls with peanuts and vegetable pickles and freshly steamed spring rolls, packed with cucumber, sprouts, eggs, and Chinese sausage, served with tamarind sauce.

Oh! Calcutta!

251 Victoria St, Darlinghurst. **Map** 5 B2. ☎ *9360 3650.* 🕐 *noon–3pm Fri, 6–10pm daily.* 🍾 [V] 📋 ⛱ 🚭 💳 *AE, MC, V.* $$

There are no Indian clichés in this modern, sparsely decorated restaurant with its bentwood chairs, stainless steel fittings, white linen, and stylish sandstone sculptures. The menu here is similarly nonconformist and changes constantly. It spans the entire subcontinent from Pakistan and Afghanistan to Sri Lanka and India. Afghani *mantu* (steamed dumplings filled with ground lamb and celery) are a very popular dish, and Goan mussels with chili and coriander are also recommended if available.

Darley Street Thai

30 Bayswater Rd, Potts Point. **Map** 5 B1. ☎ *9358 6530.* 🕐 *noon–2:30pm Tue–Sun, 6:30–11pm daily.* [V] ♿ *limited.* 🚭 ★ 💳 *AE, DC, MC, V.* $$$

Even when the names are familiar, the dishes are head and shoulders above their peers at this respected establishment. The chef David Thompson is well known for the research he has done into the Thai table using centuries-old cookbooks. His dishes, emanating as they do from the households of the wealthy, are much more complicated than those normally served at Thai restaurants. The chef also pays scant regard to the cost of the labor involved. The coconut cream, for example, takes three days to prepare. The water is first smoked using a jasmine candle, then infused with flowers before being combined with fresh coconut flesh. The cost of such indulgence may make this restaurant more expensive than the average Thai eatery, but the resulting excellence is definitely worth every cent.

Sailor's Thai

106 George St, The Rocks. **Map** 1 B2. ☎ *9251 2466.* 🕐 *noon–2:30pm Mon–Fri, 6–10pm Mon–Sat.* **Noodle Bar** 🕐 *noon–6pm daily.* 📋 ⛱ 🚭 💳 *AE, DC, MC, V.* $$$

This restaurant located in the heart of The Rocks has a canteen noodle bar with one long communal dining table upstairs where your neighbor may be an actress or a judge. An offshoot of the renowned Darley Street Thai, it serves great Thai food at less expensive prices. The chef learned his trade from a Bangkok matriarch, and the food he offers here, at prices more suited to a budget, is Thai cuisine of a standard that would certainly be a cut above most.

For key to symbols *see p179*

Wockpool

155 Victoria St, Potts Point. **Map** 2 E5.
 9368 1771. 6:30–11:30pm
Mon–Sat. V 🖂 ⚌ 🍷 ★ AE,
DC, MC, V. $$$

Malaysian *laksas*, Vietnamese *phos*, and other noodle dishes are prominent on the menu at the laid-back little brother of the Rockpool restaurant *(see p190)*. This is where chef Neil Perry offers the rustic dishes he cannot serve at the more sophisticated venue in The Rocks. The Thai-style pork and seafood sausages are always in favor, as is a Chinese-inspired duck *confit* served with Pekingese pancakes.

Kamogawa

1st Floor, 177 Sussex St. **Map** 1 A5.
 9299 5533. 6–10:30pm
daily. ⚌ 🍷 AE, DC, MC, V, JCB.
$$$$

Stately *kaiseki* menus, in which the presentation is almost as important as the food, range from seven to 12 courses in this elegant establishment. Ten private *tatami* rooms, where you sit on the floor, cater to groups of two to 20. With a large Japanese clientele, lobster, and *awabi* (abalone) *sashimi* are popular choices from the main dining room's extensive à la carte menu.

Restaurant Suntory

529 Kent St. **Map** 4 E3. 9267 2900.
 noon–2pm Mon–Fri, 6:30–10pm
Mon–Sat, 6–9pm Sun. V ⚌
🍷 AE, DC, MC, V, JCB. $$$$

Here, the outlook onto a tranquil Japanese garden provides a welcome break from the bustle out on the city streets. The restaurant has a *teppanyaki* (barbecue at table) room, an à la carte section, and four *tatami* rooms for groups of four to 16. *Shabu shabu* and *sukiyaki* are firm favorites, along with the hot rock barbecue, which features beef specially selected from a Victorian producer.

ITALIAN

Italians were prominent among postwar migrants to Australia, and one of their legacies has been the large number of Italian eateries to be found all over Sydney. They range from the cheap and cheerful spaghetti houses of Darlinghurst to the home-style pizza, pasta, and veal-based menus found in the restaurants of the inner western suburb of Leichhardt, Sydney's Little Italy. A growing number of city-smart dining rooms also present the refined fare and suave service of Italy's northern regions.

No Names

1st Floor, 81 Stanley St, Darlinghurst.
Map 5 A1. 9360 4711.
 noon–2:30pm daily, 6–10pm
daily. 🍷 ⚌ 🍷 $

Despite there being no sign, you will have little trouble finding this spaghetti canteen. Just look for the line on the stairs waiting for some of the best-value food in town. A few grills and *gelati* have been added to the basic spaghetti *bolognese* or *napoletana* choice, but little else has altered – the bread and cordial are still free. Be prepared to share a table if you are in a hurry.

Frattini

122 Marion St, Leichhardt.
 9569 2997. noon–3pm Mon–
Fri & Sun, 6–10pm daily. 🍷 V
🍷 limited. ⚌ 🍷 AE, MC, V. $$

One of the outstanding restaurants in Sydney's Little Italy, this trattoria's approach could not be farther removed from many of its neighbors, who still seem to be caught in a spaghetti-and-garlic-bread time warp. The salmon *carpaccio* is always popular, as are *neonata* (fritters of New Zealand whitebait) and asparagus with Parmesan. Try to leave room for mascarpone-filled crêpes with liqueur-poached strawberries. There never seems to be a quiet day here, so be sure to reserve well in advance.

Gastronomia Chianti

444 Elizabeth St, Surry Hills. **Map** 4 E5.
 9319 4748. 10:30am–5pm
Mon–Thu, 10:30am–10:30pm Fri &
Sat. V ⚌ 🍷 AE, DC, MC, V. $$

Doreen Orsatti has been a part of the Surry Hills *(see p130)* scene since she and her late husband, Francesco, opened Chianti in 1955. In the early 1990s, she remodeled her place as a delicatessen, café, and restaurant. Patrons range from local workers stocking up on their salami or *antipasti*, footsore bargain shoppers grabbing a filled *focaccia* and coffee while touring the area's factory outlets, to people simply in search of three imaginative courses. The mushroom risotto is a menu constant, and there will always be chunky Italian sausages, grilled liver, fish, and pasta specials.

Beppi's

Cnr Stanley & Young Sts, Darlinghurst.
Map 4 F3. 9360 4558. noon–
3:30pm Mon–Fri, 6pm–late Mon–
Sat. V ⚌ 🍷 AE, DC, MC, V,
JCB. $$$

In 1956, when Beppi Polese took over a humble Yugoslav café, he gradually set about introducing the Italian dishes that would transform it into a Sydney landmark. In those days, Beppi would get up to catch the low tide and harvest mussels from the pylons of the then wooden Spit Bridge. Today, mussels are readily available at the markets, but Beppi is still known as a man who will go to the most extraordinary lengths to give his diners the best. His cellar is quite exemplary, and the outstanding wine list is supplemented by a selected vintage wine list that offers Australian reds dating back to 1952. A visit to this temple of gastronomy is a real treat for anyone who is serious about good food, wine, and service.

Lucio's

47 Windsor St, Paddington. **Map** 6 D3.
 9380 5996. 12:30–3pm Mon–
Sat, 6:30–11pm Mon–Sat. 🍷
🍷 🍷 AE, DC, MC, V. $$$

Phone a day ahead and order *pesce al sale* (fish baked in a rock salt mold) at this institution famed for the consistency of its upscale northern Italian menu. It is also famed for the professionalism of its waiting staff, who are accustomed to dealing with some of this city's barons of industry. There are always several varieties of ravioli available, and the grilled Atlantic salmon from Tasmania is another constant. However, regulars say you should not pass up the *gamberi e fagioli* (shrimp, cannellini beans, and caviar with olive oil).

Mezzaluna

123 Victoria St, Potts Point. **Map** 2 E5.
 9357 1988. noon–3pm Tue–Fri
& Sun, 6–11pm Tue–Sun. ⚌ 🍷 🖂
★ AE, DC, MC, V, JCB. $$$

The chance to dine here should not be missed if possible: the finest of northern Italian cuisine, excellent wines and wonderful views of the city skyline from the covered terrace. This is the perfect place to eat on a balmy summer's evening or a sunny winter's day. Norma and Marc Polese (wife and son of the owner of Beppi's) are in charge in these modernized twin stone houses, producing the almost faultless cuisine for which Sydney is becoming known.

Restaurant Manfredi

88 Hackett St, Ultimo. **Map** 3 C4.
 9211 5895. noon–3pm Wed–
Fri, 6:30–10pm Tue–Sat. V ⚌ 🖂
🍷 ★ 🍷 AE, DC, MC, V. $$$

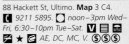

Chef Stefano Manfredi has deemed his establishment a "true Italian/ Australian restaurant" with dishes such as the warm smoked salmon lasagne or spinach and yabbie (freshwater crayfish) *gnocchi* that you would never find in Italy. The menu, along with the pared-down, contemporary interior and sail-covered courtyard, provides one of the city's best dining experiences. Its location is a little out of the way in an area not noted for its restaurants, but you can ask for directions when making a reservation.

FRENCH

These days, Sydney's dining public is notoriously fickle, embracing Vietnamese noodle dishes one day and Moroccan *tagines* the next. Yet the French tradition just seems to go on forever, and even the most ardent supporters of the best contemporary Australian cooking probably have a firm grounding in classical French cuisine. Francophiles are lucky, though, since the city has a number of purists who use wonderful fresh produce to provide excellent French fare.

Bistro Moncur

Woollahra Hotel, 116 Queen St, Woollahra. **Map** 6 E4. 9363 2782. noon–3pm Tue–Sat, 9am–noon Sun, 6–10:30pm Tue–Sat, 6–9pm Sun. V 🅴 📷 ♿ AE, DC, MC, V. $$

Damien Pignolet uses the term *habitué* (regular) to describe the clientele he aims to attract to his bistro. One wall is covered by an amusing Michael Fitzjames mural of people who like to lunch. However, the absence of "attitude" and, more importantly, food that you would consider yourself lucky to find in a classic Parisian bistro have helped Pignolet achieve his goal. Officially, you cannot book to enjoy the *tripes Lyonnaise*, classic Provençal fish soup, and *entrecôte café de Paris*, but if you phone ahead a table will usually be held for 30 minutes.

Claudine's French Restaurant

151 Macquarie St. **Map** 1 C4. 9241 1749. 7:30am–3pm daily, 5:30–8:30pm daily. 📷 V ♿ 🅴 ⚡ 🍴 🍽 AE, DC, MC, V, JCB. $$$

This well-patronized haunt opposite the Botanic Gardens is in the heart of the city's medical district. It serves authentic Gallic fare and there are levels of dining – serious at the front, bistro in the middle, and takeout at the back. The excellent food covers a gamut of tastes from crispy duck breast Parmentier with sautéed quince to simple but delicious filled baguettes. The wine list is one of the best in the city, and the ambience in the evenings is warm and intimate.

Claude's

10 Oxford St, Woollahra. **Map** 6 D4. 9331 2325. 7:30pm–late Tue–Sat. 🍴 📷 📶 ⚡ ★ 🍽 AE, MC, V. $$$$$

Discretion and fine service are the bywords in this dining room that has gained its renown from the skills of the chef Tim Pak Poy. The wine you bring will be treated with the same degree of reverence accorded the preparation of the superlative dishes, and you may possibly feel you have accidentally joined a very serious gathering of a very serious epicurean society.

MEDITERRANEAN AND MIDDLE EASTERN

The bold flavors and relaxed style of the Mediterranean fit well with Sydney's climate, waterfront, and outdoor lifestyle. The readily available prime-quality seafood also lends itself easily to Greek and Spanish cuisine. For decades, the city's Little Lebanon has been at the western end of Cleveland Street in Surry Hills *(see p130)*, where diners were introduced to the delights of the *meze* platter of appetizers, grilled meats, sausages or meatballs for main courses, and pastry desserts rich in honey and nuts.

Casa Asturiana

77 Liverpool St. **Map** 4 E3. 9264 1010. noon–10:30pm Tue–Fri, 5:30–10:30pm Sat, noon–10pm Sun. 🍴 V ♿ limited. 🍽 🍴 AE, DC, MC, V. $$

With more than 20 choices, *tapas*, or tasting portions, are the main attraction in this two-story former warehouse that has a traditional Castilian ground floor and a modernist space with marble bar above. It is family run, and the recipes are reworkings of well-known northern favorites such as *paella*, squid cooked in its own ink, and stuffed sardine fillets. There are *sangría*, Asturian cider, and Tío Pepe to wash it all down and *casadiellas* or little walnut pastries to go with stiff black coffee and "cognac."

Grand Taverna

Sir John Young Hotel, 557 George St. **Map** 4 E3. 9267 3608. noon–3pm Mon–Sat, 5:30–10pm Mon–Wed, 5:30–11pm Thu–Sat. V 🍽 🍴 🍽 AE, DC, MC, V. $$

You can sit at the bar or at a table inside or outside in this popular pub bistro with all the traditional Spanish dishes. Shrimp come in garlic or tomato-based sauces; octopus, fish, and *chorizo* sausage

come from the barbecue. Dishes for two include mixed seafood Sevillana (tomato and garlic sauce) and *paella*. A jug of *sangría* from the bar, for which you pay beforehand, will complete the meal.

Fez Café

247 Victoria St, Darlinghurst. **Map** 5 B1. 9360 9581. 7am–10:30pm Mon–Sat, 8am–10:30pm Sun. 📷 V ♿ $$

On weekends, patrons line up to sip thick coffee on the cushioned window seats and to breakfast on couscous, compote of spiced dried fruit with nuts, and yogurt. The menu spans the crescent from Turkey to Morocco, beginning with a *meze* platter of dips and pickled vegetables with Turkish bread, and travels through to Moroccan *tagines* and duck in pomegranate sauce.

Shawarma Grill House

44 Park St. **Map** 4 E2. 9267 9636. 7am–9pm daily. 🍴 📷 V ♿ $$

As the name suggests, grilled beef, lamb, or chicken on flat bread with *homous*, *tabouli*, and salad is the house special in this Lebanese café. Vegetarians are not neglected with other Lebanese offerings, such as *falafel*, lentils, and stuffed vine leaves. Few can resist the sticky nut and honey-laden pastries.

Cosmos

185a Bourke St, Darlinghurst. **Map** 5 A1. 9331 5306. noon–2:30pm Fri, 6:30pm–late Mon–Sat. 📷 V ♿ ⚡ 🍽 AE, DC. $$$

A setting as bold as an Aegean sunset, matched by an enticing Greek menu, has earned the owner–chef Peter Conistis a chorus of fans. His parents come from central Greece, where food is kept simple to emphasize pure flavors. You can sample his translations to contemporary cuisine with offerings such as pies filled with rabbit and black olives, smoked eggplant and oysters, or *moussaka* of eggplant, scallops, and *taramasalata*.

Criterion Brasserie

Lobby Level, MLC Centre, Martin Place. **Map** 1 B4. 9233 1234. 10am–late Mon–Fri, 6pm–late Sat. V ♿ 🍽 🍴 ⚡ 🍽 AE, DC, MC, V. $$$

This restaurant manages a rare combination of slick city good looks with old-fashioned Lebanese family service. The house special *meze* platter, with yogurt balls, marinated vegetables, and pastries, will appeal to vegetarians. *Saluna*, a Moroccan spice-encrusted fish with basmati rice, date syrup, and green tomatoes, is another delicious dish.

For key to symbols *see p179*

Light Meals and Snacks

SYDNEY'S CASUAL EATING SCENE is extremely competitive, and wherever you choose to take a break you will probably enjoy good-value food that approaches the high standards set by more formal establishments. The eateries listed here all have a staunch local following and are particularly recommended for those hungry travelers whose time and budget are limited.

CAFÉS

FOOD COLUMNISTS frequently note the mercurial nature of Sydney's dining scene by chronicling the multitude of establishments that open and close each year. With cafés, this situation is magnified and, as a result of this competition, the standards are quite high.

Most places serve breakfast in either the eggs-and-bacon or croissant-and-pastry guises, and then move into the day with a menu offering burgers, cheese melts, *focaccia* and salads, pasta and risotto. The night owls can enjoy cakes and desserts and choose from espresso coffee, *caffe latte*, and *cappuccino*, or from a range of teas, juices, milk shakes, fruit *frappés*, and smoothies.

COFFEE AND TEA

DARLINGHURST is the caffeine kingdom of Sydney and **Bar Coluzzi**, with its boxing pictures on the walls, is its capital. Media heavies, lawyers, and taxi drivers throng here both for the company and the coffee. Across the road at the **Tropicana Coffee Lounge**, the clientele is more likely to be involved in the theater or the film industry. At **Café Hernandez**, aficionados flock in for a Spanish short black and supplies of coffee beans.

Xocoalt may be tiny, but the bitter hot chocolate that gives the café its Aztec name and its excellent coffee have a huge following, as do the amazing chocolate truffles. Everything shines at **The Box,** from the stainless steel floor and the mirror at the back with a menu written in lipstick, to the glittering clientele. **Barfly**, in the city center, is for those who know their coffee, and so too is the popular Paradiso family of cafés, which includes **Bar Paradiso** in Macquarie Place, another **Bar Paradiso** in the MLC Centre, and the **Paradiso Lunch Bar** in Darling Park, close to Chinatown.

Good-quality reading matter is on hand for all the customers at **New Edition Tea Rooms**, which is located in a small bookshop on Oxford Street, Paddington. There has been a **Roma Caffè Ristorante** near Central Railway Station since the early 1970s and, while the address may have changed, the winning formula of good Italian coffee, pasta, pastries, and great gelato has not.

SNACKS AND LIGHT MEALS

SHOULD YOU want to start the day in a sun-drenched spot, **Bill's** is a favorite place. You can breakfast on ricotta hot cakes with honeycomb butter or lunch on a delicious steak sandwich. There is a similar mood at **La Passion du Fruit** in Surry Hills, which has a big following for its fruit *frappés*, fresh salads, and the hot olive bread pockets filled with any selection from the *antipasto* table. Just a few blocks away, on Crown Street, **Prasit's Northside** (actually on the southern side of the Harbour Bridge) offers imaginative and aromatic Thai fare from a tiny easy to miss shopfront.

Shoppers in Paddington usually fit in a lunch at one of the cafés – but on Saturdays there may be lines since this is when the Paddington Bazaar is held *(see p126)*. The **Hot Gossip Coffee Lounge** has a delicatessen adjacent, where you can buy healthy fare to take out **Sloane Rangers** is a real home away from home, with lots to keep vegetarians happy and a small courtyard in the back. For a quick snack before seeing a movie at the Academy Twin, try the nearby **Flicks Café**. Farther along Oxford Street, in Darlinghurst, the pool table at the **Spanish Deli** is a big attraction, while the menu at **Dov** is a mixture of Mediterranean Jewish and Middle European cuisine.

At **Una's Coffee Lounge**, the regular clientele are often joined by homesick Germans longing for *schnitzel*, soup, and *spaëtzle* (noodles). The **Hard Rock Café** remains true to its international formula, but weekend crowds suggest that the demand for burgers and T-shirts has not lessened. **Le Petit Crème** is an oasis of *brioche* and *croque madame* (toasted cheese sandwich with chicken). In Potts Point, vegetarian food and changing art on the walls are the order of the day at **Roy's Famous**.

GALLERIES AND GARDENS

THESE DAYS, most of the city's galleries, museums, and larger parks have good cafés or restaurants – the following are a cut above the average.

Most of the clientele at the **Centennial Park Café** are there to take in the passing parade of joggers, horseback riders, and cyclists as they tuck into pasta, risotto, salad, or a roasted tuna steak with African spices. Wine is available by the bottle or the glass. At the **Concourse Restaurant** in the forecourt of the Opera House, Mediterranean fare is on the menu. Directly across Circular Quay, the **MCA Café** is run by the same team as at the upscale Rockpool restaurant *(see p190)*. The menu here is also strongly Mediterranean.

The food is often influenced by visiting exhibitions at the **Art Gallery Restaurant**, and this café is worth a visit even if you do not have time to see the collections. The **Hyde Park Barracks Café** has seating in the courtyard. Dishes such as potted goat's milk cheese with slow-roasted garlic on toast and delicious open sandwiches stir up the appetite. You can enjoy sandwiches, soups, and cream teas in the palm-studded surrounds of **Vaucluse House Tea Rooms**, in the garden of the former home of statesman and explorer, WC Wentworth.

TAKE-OUT FOOD

THE FILLED baguettes practically march out the door of the city's **Deli on Market**. There is also good coffee and a selection of their own cakes, chutneys, cheeses, and vinaigrettes to take out. For a far more down-to-earth dining experience, you can drop in to **Harry's Café de Wheels** in Woolloomooloo, to sample an Aussie meat pie and sauce

from the stand-up bar at this diner. This Sydney institution has been satisfying the late-night food cravings of both locals and visitors for decades and is particularly popular with the sailors from the adjacent naval dockyard. An entirely different sort of treat can be found at the **Maya Indian Sweets Centre** in Surry Hills, where a particularly luscious array of desserts and cakes is available – there are a few tables for tea if you are desperate to eat.

At the opposite end of the spectrum are the food courts in the basements or ground floors of major city buildings.

These serve the city's office workers at lunchtime with a grand assortment of foods to take out or eat at tables nearby. Australia Square, the MLC Centre, Chifley Tower, the Mid City Centre, and the American Express Tower all have food courts with shops offering everything from Asian noodles and Mexican nachos to pizza and sushi.

Most of Sydney's markets *(see p203)* have food stalls where a large mixed plate of Indian, Mexican, or Asian food will cost only a few dollars. Paddington Bazaar has good, cheap vegetarian food in the hall at the back of the market.

DIRECTORY

THE ROCKS AND CIRCULAR QUAY

Bar Paradiso
7 Macquarie Pl. **Map** 1 B3.
📞 9241 2141.

Concourse Restaurant
Sydney Opera House.
Map 1 C2. 📞 9250 7300.

MCA Café
Museum of Contemporary Art, Circular Quay.
Map 1 B2. 📞 9241 4253.

Rossini Café
5 Alfred St, Circular Quay.
Map 1 B3. 📞 9247 8026.

CITY CENTER

Bar Paradiso
MLC Centre, Martin Place.
Map 1 B4. 📞 9221 0527.

Barfly
102 Bathurst St. **Map** 4 E3.
📞 9267 2480.

Deli on Market
30–32 Market St.
Map 4 E2. 📞 9262 6906.

DARLING HARBOUR

Paradiso Lunch Bar
Darling Park, 201 Sussex St.
Map 4 D2. 📞 9264 1729.

Roma Caffè Ristorante
Sydney Central,
181 Hay St. **Map** 4 E4.
📞 9211 3909.

BOTANIC GARDENS AND THE DOMAIN

Art Gallery Restaurant
Art Gallery Rd, The Domain.
Map 2 D4. 📞 9232 5425.

Hyde Park Barracks Café
Queens Square,
Macquarie St. **Map** 1 C5.
📞 9223 1155.

KINGS CROSS AND DARLINGHURST

Bill's
433 Liverpool St,
Darlinghurst. **Map** 5 B2.
📞 9360 9631.

Bar Coluzzi
322 Victoria St,
Darlinghurst. **Map** 5 B1.
📞 9380 5420.

The Box
28a Bayswater Rd,
Potts Point. **Map** 5 B1.
📞 9358 6418.

Café Hernandez
60 Kings Cross Rd,
Potts Point. **Map** 5 C1.
📞 9331 2343.

Dov
252 Forbes St,
Darlinghurst. **Map** 5 A2.
📞 9360 9594.

Hard Rock Café
121–129 Crown St,
Darlinghurst. **Map** 5 A1.
📞 9331 1116.

Harry's Café de Wheels
Cowper Wharf Rd,
Woolloomooloo.
Map 2 E5. 📞 9357 3074.

Le Petit Crème
118 Darlinghurst Rd,
Darlinghurst. **Map** 5 B1.
📞 9361 4738.

Roy's Famous
176 Victoria St,
Potts Point. **Map** 5 B1.
📞 9357 3579.

Spanish Deli
88 Oxford St,
Darlinghurst. **Map** 5 A2.
📞 9380 6459.

Tropicana Coffee Lounge
227b Victoria St,
Darlinghurst. **Map** 5 B1.
📞 9360 9809.

Una's Coffee Lounge
340 Victoria St,
Darlinghurst. **Map** 5 B1.
📞 9360 6885.

Xocoalt
197 Victoria St, Potts Point.
Map 5 B1. 📞 9358 4625.

PADDINGTON

Centennial Park Café
Cnr Grand & Parkes Drives,
Centennial Park.
Map 6 E5. 📞 9360 3355.

Flicks Café
3 Oxford St, Paddington.
Map 5 B3. 📞 9331 7412.

Hot Gossip Coffee Lounge
438 Oxford St, Paddington.
Map 6 D4. 📞 9332 4358.

New Edition Tea Rooms
328 Oxford St, Paddington.
Map 6 D3. 📞 9361 0744.

Sloane Rangers
312 Oxford St, Paddington.
Map 5 C3. 📞 9331 6717.

FARTHER AFIELD

La Passion du Fruit
633 Bourke St, Surry Hills.
Map 5 B3. 📞 9690 1894.

Maya Indian Sweets Centre
470 Cleveland St, Surry Hills.
Map 5 A5. 📞 9699 8663.

Prasit's Northside
395 Crown St, Surry Hills.
Map 5 A3. 📞 9332 1792.

Vaucluse House Tea Rooms
Wentworth Rd, Vaucluse.
📞 9388 8188.

Sydney Pubs and Bars

CONFUSINGLY for the overseas visitor, Australian pubs and bars are more commonly known as hotels. This is because licensing laws originally required any place serving alcohol to provide accommodations too. In the cities, at least, hotels have changed radically, and what were once the domains of beer-swilling males have now evolved into far more civilized spots.

Pub menus have also undergone a metamorphosis. In place of the former meat pie and sauce, most pubs now offer hearty snacks, such as *nachos, focaccia*, pasta, grills, and salads, at remarkably low prices. All pubs serve basic mixed alcoholic drinks and often wine by the glass, but cocktails tend to be the preserve of the more upscale places. Pubs are also often good venues for entertainment ranging from rock to jazz *(see pp214–15)*.

RULES AND CONVENTIONS

IN THEORY, pubs are open from 10am to 10pm every day. This often extends to midnight closing on Fridays and Saturdays, and even to 3am when live entertainment is provided. Some pubs, in areas where there are large numbers of shift workers, will open at 6am and are known as "early openers." Others, particularly in tourist hang-outs, have a 24-hour license. You must be at least 18 years old (and able to provide the proof) to buy or consume any alcohol. However, children under 18 may accompany adults into beer gardens and into hotel restaurants. Dress requirements are purely at the discretion of the owner, and the management always has the right to refuse service.

One aspect of traditional pub culture is the custom of "shouting," or buying drinks for your companions. It can be very expensive to become involved in buying "rounds" – when someone buys you a drink, it is considered bad form if you do not return the favor. If you are on a budget and do not want to offend, simply explain that you are only staying for one drink or make some other excuse.

Apart from being very good places to soak up some local atmosphere, pubs are also ideal spots for watching any televised major international or local sports matches in the company of like-minded people. Many hotels broadcast matches on a big screen and locals gather to watch.

Pubs are also excellent spots for live entertainment – many Australian rock music names first performed in hotels. The daily newspapers are a good source of information on dates, times, and places *(see p221)*.

JOIN THE LOCALS

PUBS PROVIDE the chance to observe Sydney at play. At Circular Quay, the **Customs House Bar** has been serving drinks since 1826. On Friday nights, up to 2,000 people spill out into Macquarie Place to talk shop and gossip under the trees. **Miro Tapas Bar** is an equally trendy destination, with floor-to-ceiling murals and Spanish-style snacks to go with the *sangría* and melon and peach "shooters." The **Dendy Bar** is in the Dendy cinema complex *(see p210)*; here office workers mix with film-goers and coffee is served alongside cocktails.

Cowboy boots and country music set the scene at the **Arizona Bar & Restaurant**, where American beers and margaritas wash down New Mexican spiced ribs and grills. Situated close to the State Theatre *(see p82)*, it is a very popular haunt of film-festival patrons. A little farther afield in Surry Hills, the **Elephant's Foot Hotel** boasts everything from cocktails and coffee to cake and pasta, plus a pool table. There are also pool tables at the busy **Palace Hotel**

in Darlinghurst, which has a popular restaurant, and the **Green Park Hotel**, which does not offer any bar food apart from potato chips.

There are plenty of "locals" in Paddington, most of which serve above-average bar food to their discerning clientele. The **London Tavern** opened in 1876 and claims to be the suburb's oldest pub. The sign outside welcomes all except for dogs, giraffes, elephants, and children under 18 for drinks. Five Ways *(see p126)* is dominated by the **Royal Hotel**, an 1880s three-story corner establishment, where cocktails are served in the upstairs Elephant Bar and the restaurant below extends out onto an iron-lace encrusted veranda. Both the bistro at the **Paddington Inn** and the dining room of the **Bellevue Hotel** offer good contemporary Mediterranean-style fare.

Just about any Sydneysider who has partied through the night has ended up at the **Bourbon & Beefsteak** in the wee hours. This bar undergoes an amazing transformation around dawn. The cigarette smoke clears to reveal a full breakfast room extravaganza, with the signed portraits of famous patrons on the walls, masses of fresh flowers and starched white table linen.

UPSCALE BARS

IF YOU ARE looking for a more elegant atmosphere, head for **Horizon's Bar** at the top of the ANA Hotel *(see p174)*. You can admire views extending from Botany Bay to Manly while you sip a Toblerone (liquid chocolate with a kick). Or drop into **The Cortile** in the glamorous lobby of the Hotel Inter-Continental and sip a cocktail in the comfort of the cane armchairs. There are always about 25 Australian wines sold by the glass, plus four or five of the imported Champagnes at **Charlies**. This bar also has a short bar menu and eight types of beer on tap.

The **Regent Club Bar** in the Regent Sydney *(see p174)* is another hotel lounge that is ideal either for pre- or post-theater drinks and nibbles. The stylish **L'otel** *(see p176)* has a cocktail bar, where the staff especially recommend the margaritas, and quite a decent restaurant. Try the delicious crispy squid with chili salt.

HISTORIC PUBS

A WALK ALONG George Street will reveal some of The Rocks' old pubs, but two of the more significant ones are a few streets back. The **Hero of Waterloo**, built in 1843, has a maze of stone cellars underneath, which testifies to its nefarious past *(see p69)*. The **Lord Nelson Brewery Hotel** was first licensed in 1841 and is now a "pub brewery" with a range of ales brewed on the premises. It also has Nelson's Bistro and, upstairs, six guest rooms *(see p174)*.

The **Sydney Cove Oyster Bar**, on the eastern side of Circular Quay, operates from

a remodeled tram terminal. Its outdoor tables are certainly a treat in fine weather, as is the range of Australian wines and beers. The latter includes Coopers and Redback wheat beer. Enjoy a glass with the small but satisfying seafood menu, which offers oysters prepared in five ways (there is steak for die-hard meat eaters).

At the **Marble Bar** *(see p82)*, the sumptuous decoration on its walls is Italian Renaissance in style with hunting scenes, exotic flora and fruit complementing the cocktail list.

ENTERTAINMENT

A S A VENUE for poetry and prose readings, comics, and other literati gatherings, the **Harold Park Hotel** in Glebe stands alone. There is a bistro in the evenings, but the food may be overshadowed by the stimulating company.

Also in Glebe is the **Nag's Head**, where soloists and duettists perform everything from Neil Diamond to Pearl Jam, Wednesday to Sunday nights. The pub bistro serves a variety of grills and salads.

In Surry Hills, there are live bands every Saturday night at the **Hopetoun Hotel** and there is a DJ playing old funk, jazz and blues on Friday and Sunday evenings. The bar menu has *focaccia*, pies, and pasta. In Rozelle, there is folk and blues on weekends and a bistro serving pasta and grills at the **Rose, Shamrock and Thistle**. The **Orient Hotel** in the heart of The Rocks is very popular with both locals and tourists. On New Year's Eve, it practically bursts at the seams. There are cover bands daily and jazz on weekends, plus a restaurant and a cook-your-own barbecue, which has an accompanying pianist.

DIRECTORY

THE ROCKS AND CIRCULAR QUAY

Customs House Bar
Sydney Renaissance Hotel, Macquarie Place.
Map 1 B3.
9259 7000.

Hero of Waterloo
81 Lower Fort St, Millers Point. **Map** 1 A2.
9252 4553.

Horizon's Bar
Level 36, ANA Hotel, 176 Cumberland St, The Rocks. **Map** 1 A3.
9250 6000.

Lord Nelson Brewery Hotel
19 Kent St, Millers Point.
Map 1 A2.
9251 4044.

Orient Hotel
Cnr George & Argyle Sts, The Rocks. **Map** 1 B2.
9251 1255.

Regent Club Bar
The Regent of Sydney, 199 George St. **Map** 1 B3.
9238 0000.

Sydney Cove Oyster Bar
1 Circular Quay East.
Map 1 C2. 9247 2937.

CITY CENTER

Arizona Bar & Restaurant
247 Pitt St. **Map** 1 B5.
9261 1077.

Charlie's
90 Pitt St. **Map** 1 B4.
9231 2054.

Dendy Bar
19 Martin Place. **Map** 1 B4.
9221 1243.

Marble Bar
Sydney Hilton Hotel, 259 Pitt St. **Map** 1 B5.
9266 0610.

Miro Tapas Bar
76 Liverpool St. **Map** 4 E3.
9267 3126.

BOTANIC GARDENS AND THE DOMAIN

The Cortile
Hotel Inter-Continental, 117 Macquarie St.
Map 1 C3. 9230 0200.

KINGS CROSS AND DARLINGHURST

Bourbon & Beefsteak Bar
24 Darlinghurst Rd, Kings Cross. **Map** 5 B1.
9358 1144.

Green Park Hotel
360 Victoria St, Darlinghurst. **Map** 5 B2.
9380 5311.

L'otel
114 Darlinghurst Rd, Darlinghurst. **Map** 5 B1.
9360 6868.

PADDINGTON

Bellevue Hotel
159 Hargrave St, Paddington. **Map** 6 E3.
9363 2293.

London Tavern
85 Underwood St, Paddington. **Map** 6 D3.
9331 1637.

Paddington Inn
338 Oxford St, Paddington. **Map** 6 D4.
9380 5277.

Royal Hotel
237 Glenmore Rd, Paddington. **Map** 5 C3.
9331 2604.

FARTHER AFIELD

Elephant's Foot Hotel
Cnr Devonshire & Crown Sts, Surry Hills.
9319 6802.

Harold Park Hotel
115 Wigram Rd, Glebe.
9552 2999.

Hopetoun Hotel
416 Bourke St, Surry Hills. **Map** 5 A3.
9361 5257.

Nag's Head Hotel
162 St Johns Rd, Glebe.
Map 3 A5.
9660 1591.

Palace Hotel
122 Flinders St, Darlinghurst. **Map** 5 A3.
9361 5170.

Rose, Shamrock & Thistle
193 Evans St, Rozelle.
9555 7755.

SHOPS AND MARKETS

For most travelers, shopping can be as much of a voyage of discovery as sightseeing. The variety of shops in Sydney is wide and the quality of merchandise is usually good. The city has many elegant arcades and shopping galleries, with plenty of nooks and crannies to explore. The range of goods for sale is

Souvenir boomerangs

vast – most international labels are imported and local talent in many fields, notably jewelry, fashion, and indigenous arts and crafts, is promoted. Nor does the most interesting shopping stop at the city center; there are several "satellite" alternatives. The best shopping areas are highlighted on pages 200–201.

The Tin Shed, a junk-shop-café in Balmain *(see p131)*

SHOPPING HOURS

Most shops are open from 9am to 5:30pm during the week, and from 9am to 4pm on Saturdays. On Thursdays, many shops stay open until 9pm. Some are open late every evening and most of these also open on Sundays.

HOW TO PAY

Major credit cards are accepted at many shops, but there may be a minimum purchase requirement. You will need identification, such as a valid passport or driver's

licence, when using traveler's checks. Shops will generally exchange goods or refund your money if you are not satisfied, provided you have some proof of purchase. This does not usually apply to items bought on sale. Australia has no sales or service tax – the price you see is what you pay.

SALES

Many shops conduct sales all year round. The big department stores of **David Jones** and **Grace Bros** have two clearance sales a year. The post-Christmas sales start on December 26, and last into January. Avid bargain-hunters line up from dawn for substantial savings. The other major sale time is during July, after the end of the financial year.

TAX-FREE SALES

Duty-free shops are found in the center of the city as well as at Kingsford Smith Airport. Some shops also have branches in the larger suburbs.

Overseas visitors can save around 30 percent on goods such as perfume, jewelry, cameras, and alcohol at shops

that offer duty-free shopping. You must show your passport and onward ticket when the goods are collected.

Most duty-free merchandise must be kept in its sealed bag until you leave. Cameras and video cameras are exceptions. Some duty-free shops in the city will deliver your goods to the airport where you can pick them up on your departure.

Chifley Tower, with the Chifley Plaza shopping arcade at its base

ARCADES AND MALLS

Arcades and shopping malls in Sydney range from the ornately Victorian to modern marble and glass. The **Queen Victoria Building** *(see p82)* is Sydney's most palatial shopping space. Four levels contain more than 200 shops. The top level, Victoria Walk, is devoted to merchandise such as silver, antiques, designer knitwear, and high-quality souvenirs.

The elegant **Strand Arcade** *(see p84)* was originally built in 1892. Jewelry, lingerie, high fashion, fine antiques, and gourmet coffee shops and tea rooms are its stock in trade.

Pitt Street Mall is home to several other shopping centers. **Skygarden** is the place for

Interior design shop on William Street in Paddington *(see p124)*

houseware, classy fashion from Australian and international designers, and art galleries of distinction. A spacious food gallery offers everything from antipasto to Thai take-out. The bustling **Mid City Centre** is home to the huge HMV music store and shops selling clothes, accessories, and gifts. **Centrepoint** has more than 140 speciality shops that stock everything from avant-garde jewelry to leather goods.

Nearby in Pitt Street, the marble and glass of **Piccadilly** houses flashy boutiques, good shoe shops (including Bruno Magli and Raymond Castles), quality jewelers and cafés.

Both the **MLC Centre** and the nearby **Chifley Plaza** cater to the prestige shopper. Gucci, Cartier, Tiffany & Co., Kenzo, and Moschino are just some of the shops found in these arcades.

The **Harbourside Festival Market-place** has dozens of shops, plus several waterfront restaurants. The atmosphere is festive and the merchandise includes fine arts, jewelry, duty-free shopping, beachwear, and Australiana.

Greengrocer's display of fresh fruit and vegetables

Gowings menswear store logo

BEST OF THE DEPARTMENT STORES

THE SPRING and Mother's Day floral displays in the **David Jones** Elizabeth Street store are legendary, as is the luxurious perfumery and cosmetics hall on the ground

floor. The building has seven floors of quality merchandise, including women's clothing, lingerie, baby goods, toys, and stationery. The Market Street store nearby specializes in menswear, furniture, furnishing fabrics, kitchenware, china, crystal, and silver. The food hall situated on the lower ground floor is famous for its range of gourmet food and fine wines. **Grace Bros** is a good stop for the visitor in need of cosmetics, hats, sunscreen for the Sydney climate, casual T-shirts and jeans, Australian fashion, lingerie, or hosiery.

Gowings, which has operated continuously since 1868, is a Sydney institution. This unpretentious, family-owned and family-run menswear store also sells such things as sunglasses, watches, Swiss army knives, fishing gear, miners' lamps, and genuine Australiana such as kangaroo leather wallets and plaited leather belts.

SHOPPING FARTHER AFIELD

GOOD SHOPPING is also found outside central Sydney. Other areas well worth visiting include Double Bay, with its sophisticated, village-style shopping, to the east, and the Left Bank-style student haunts of Newtown to the south and Glebe to the west. Bargains can be found at the clothing and homeware factory outlets at Surry Hills and Redfern to the south of the city (east of Redfern railroad station).

Part of the spring floral display, David Jones department store

---

ARCADES, SHOPPING MALLS, AND DEPARTMENT STORES

Centrepoint
Cnr Pitt, Market & Castlereagh Sts.
Map 1 B5. [9229 7444.

Chifley Plaza
Chifley Square. **Map** 1 B4.
[9221 4500.

David Jones
Cnr Elizabeth & Castlereagh Sts.
Map 1 B5. [9266 5544.
Also: Cnr Market & Castlereagh
Sts. **Map** 1 B5. [9266 5544.

Harbourside Festival Marketplace
Darling Harbour. **Map** 3 C2.
[9281 3999.

Gowings
Cnr George & Market Sts.
Map 1 B5. [9264 6321.

Grace Bros
436 George St. **Map** 1 B5.
[9238 9111.

Mid City Centre
Pitt Street Mall. **Map** 1 B5.
[9221 2422.

MLC Centre
Cnr King & Castlereagh Sts.
Map 1 B5. [9224 8333.

Piccadilly
210 Pitt St. **Map** 1 B5.
[9267 3666.

Queen Victoria Building
Cnr George, Market & York Sts.
Map 1 B5. [9264 9209.

Skygarden
77 Castlereagh St. **Map** 1 B5.
[9231 1811.

Strand Arcade
Pitt Street Mall. **Map** 1 B5.
[9232 4199.

Sydney's Best: Shopping Streets and Markets

SYDNEY'S BEST SHOPPING AREAS range from galleries, arcades, and department stores selling expensive gifts and jewelry *(see pp198–9)*, to boutiques of extroverted or elegant cutting-edge fashion and its accessories. The range of styles is impressive – both international couture brands and acclaimed local designer labels *(pp204–5)*. The city's hip fringe areas are alive with street fashion and its accoutrements.

Colorful markets are a delight for collectors and bargain-hunters alike *(p203)*, while those who seek out quirky and one-of-a-kind items are well catered to, as are those looking to take home quality crafts and indigenous art as mementos of their visit. Expert browsers will find a tempting selection of book and music stores *(pp206–7)* from which to choose.

The Rocks Market
On weekends, the stalls offer affordable arts and crafts and jewelry. (See p203.)

Queen Victoria Building
This elegant shopping gallery offers four floors of designer wear, gifts, and specialty stores amid cafés.

Darling Harbour
Quality Australiana, surf and beach wear, souvenir ideas, children's clothes, colorful knits, and art and craft shops abound.

Sydney Fish Market
You can buy fresh seafood daily in the colorful fish sellers' halls or order from the cafés that spill out onto the sunny terrace alongside the marina. (See p202.)

Chinatown
This is the place to find discounts on watches, gold jewelry, opals, and even fabrics. There are also Chinese butcher shops, herbalists, and supermarkets.

THE ROCKS AND CIRCULAR QUAY

CITY CENTER

DARLING HARBOUR

0 meters   500
0 yards   500

City Center
Dazzling shopping arcades and malls are dotted throughout the city center, notably Pitt Street Mall, Strand and Piccadilly Arcades, and Centrepoint.

Castlereagh Street
The city's designer row is home to Chanel, Moschino, Gucci, and Hermès. The most exclusive names cluster near the King Street intersection.

BOTANIC
GARDENS AND
THE DOMAIN

**Darlinghurst
and Surry Hills**
These suburbs are the youth culture barometer: young designers, leather à la mode, gay fashion, hot music, and gifts for those who love quirky collectibles.

KINGS CROSS AND
DARLINGHURST

PADDINGTON

Paddington and Woollahra
Fashionable clothing, housewares, and jewelry are on display. Bookshops, cafés and galleries add to the allure. Queen Street, Woollahra, is the antique shop strip.

Paddington Bazaar
Considered by many to be Sydney's best market and a showcase for the up-and-coming fashions, it is held every Saturday. (See p203.)

Sydney Fish Market

Each year, 16 million kilograms (35 million pounds) of fresh fish and other seafood are sold at the Fish Market's Dutch Clock auction. In this system, prices start high and gradually descend on a computerized "clock," until a buyer puts in a bid. At this point, no other bids are accepted, and the deal is made. This unusually quiet auction starts at 5:30am every Monday to Friday and runs for two to three hours until all the seafood is sold. Members of the public can follow the auction proceedings from a viewing area.

Balmain bug

The waterfront cafés offering fine seafood at reasonable prices make dining here a rare treat.

Blue swimmer crabs have a mild flavor and are found all around the Australian coastline.

About 30 wholesalers, many of them family concerns, buy bulk quantities of the day's catch; some also have retail outlets at the market itself.

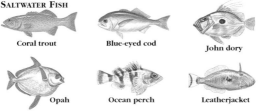

Local fishermen arrive at the market between 4pm the previous day and 8am on the day of the auction. About 80 percent of the catch is from the far coasts of New South Wales.

SELECTING YOUR FISH

SHELLFISH

Freshwater crayfish	Cuttlefish	Blue swimmer crab	Tiger shrimp

FRESHWATER FISH

Rainbow trout	Golden perch	Murray cod	Barramundi

SALTWATER FISH

Coral trout	Blue-eyed cod	John dory	Flounder
Opah	Ocean perch	Leatherjacket	Red emperor

Markets

SCOURING MARKETS FOR THE CHEAP, the cheerful, and the chic has become a popular weekend pastime in Sydney. Weekly or monthly markets that suit both the bargain-hunter and the serious shopper have sprung up all over Sydney's suburbs. Caps, souvenir T-shirts, bargain leather jackets, high-class art – there is bound to be something to suit every taste. Just as popular are the Sydney Fish Market and the produce markets, which have turned shopping for staples into a big day out.

Balmain Market

Cnr Darling St and Curtis Rd, Balmain. 442, 434. 7:30am–4pm Sat.

Held in the grounds of the Balmain Congregational Church, in the shade of a fig tree said to be more than 150 years old, this compact, high-caliber market attracts both locals and tourists. Fees from stallholders contribute to the ongoing restoration of the church, which was built in 1853. As well as children's wear, second-hand books, modern and antique jewelry, arty mirrors, recycled stationery, stained-glass mobiles, and Chinese healing balls, there's a food hall where you can find fresh and aromatic Japanese, Thai, Indian, and vegetarian dishes cooking.

Bondi Market

Bondi Beach Public School, Campbell Parade, North Bondi. 380, 382, 389. 10am–5pm Sun in summer (4pm in winter).

Arrive early (some of the stalls are all set up by 9am) for the best second-hand clothing buys; funky 1970s gear is particularly popular. The best bargain clothes are near the back of the market. Expect to see the odd pop star and stars of Australian television soap operas among the browsers. The market is also noted for its cactus plants, glassware, and tourist art – scenes of Bondi Beach are a specialty.

Glebe Market

Glebe Public School, Glebe Point Road, Glebe. **Map** 3 B5. 431, 433. 9am–5pm Sat in summer (4:30pm in winter).

A treasure-trove for the junk shop enthusiast and canny scavenger, this market is bright, changeable, and popular with the inner-city grunge set. Best buys are bric-a-brac (get there early for bargain porcelain and, if you're lucky, the odd undervalued lithograph) and crafts made from recycled wood, metal, and glass. Eccentricities include patchwork velvet jesters' caps, suitcases full of amber and turquoise beads, and handpainted light bulbs. Second-hand clothes are a good buy here, as are leather wallets, silver rings and pendants, amulets and plaited friendship bands, books, CDs, and records.

Paddington Bazaar

(See p126.)

Like Paddington itself, this market reflects the latest trends and fashions in the contents of its stalls. From nouveau to novelties, there is always something tempting here, and it is unlikely you will come away empty-handed. You can preview clothes and fashion trends before they hit the shops. Silver jewelry is abundant, so prices are very competitive; there are also stylish children's clothes, leather goods, unusual buckles, belts, stationery, candles, handcrafts, and oddities such as babies' baseball caps and rubber novelty masks.

Paddy's Market

(See p99.)

In the 19th century, Paddy's in the Haymarket was the city's fringe market and also the location of fairgrounds and circuses. Today it has between 500 and 800 stalls under one roof. Early birds will get the best flowers, fruit, vegetables, and seafood. There are also good buys in caneware, luggage, leather goods, tools, housewares, ornaments, gifts, souvenirs, and toys . . . not to mention pet rabbits, puppies, kittens, and cockatoos.

The Rocks Market

George St, The Rocks. **Map** 1 B2. 431, 432, 433, 434. 10am–6pm Sat & Sun (5pm in winter).

On weekends, rain or shine, a sail-like canopy is erected at the top end of George Street, transforming the area into an atmospheric marketplace. Get there early to beat the afternoon crowds. The market was established with Sydneysiders in mind, but it has now become just as popular with visitors. There are about 140 stalls, whose wares are unique rather than inexpensive. Quality is a priority here. Look out for wind chimes, pewter picture frames, pub poster prints, stained-glass for the home, lace, oils, leather goods, wooden toys, gold-plated leaves, and jewelry made from wood, shell, silver, or crystal. There are also new paperbacks for sale at half price. You can watch a sculptor making art out of stone, immortalize your visit with a calico "Sydney" bag or have your portrait sketched in charcoal.

Sydney Fish Market

(See p131.)

Sydney is famous for its fresh seafood, and the Sydney Fish Market is the ideal place to buy it. You can choose from over 100 species, both live and prepared, in the fish sellers' halls. The displays of seafood are arresting, with coral reds, marble pinks, blacks, grays and iridescent yellows to take your mind off the sloshy floors and the smell of the sea. The market also has sushi bars; fish cafés (where you can sit inside or outside on the waterfront); a bakery; a fine foods delicatessen (their chutneys and olives are delicious); a poultry and game specialist; a shop selling fine wines to complement the gourmet meal you are planning; and a fresh fruit and vegetable shop. The Sydney Seafood School operates above the market, offering lessons in preparing and serving seafood.

The Tarpeian Market

Western Boardwalk, Sydney Opera House. **Map** 1 C2. 438. 10am–sunset Sun.

Sir Joseph Banks named what is now the southern rock face and walkway of the Opera House after the Tarpeian Rock in Rome, hence this market's unusual name. Under calico market umbrellas, you will find arts and crafts in a spectacular setting. Some call this a distillation of the best, and certainly you won't find T-shirts and cheap souvenirs, but rather goods that have been either hand-made or hand-finished. It is an eclectic mix: from English porcelain thimbles to welded art (such as miniature motorcycles), ornate wooden smoking pipes, framed prints of Sydney, jewelry, groovy hats, and healing crystals. If you are lucky, you can catch performance artists – who are often happy to pose for pictures. The morning may be a more pleasant time to go in summer, but you will miss the afternoon entertainment.

Clothes and Accessories

SMART CASUAL IS A TERM often heard in Sydney, applied to both dress and occasion. Particularly in summer, the style is visibly relaxed with warm weather encouraging dressing down rather than dressing up. Shops do not neglect the formal dresser, however, and stylish Australian labels vie with the international designer names for sale.

WOMEN'S CLOTHES

STYLISH DAYWEAR and casual clothes in classic, if a little unadventurous, styles are the province of **Country Road**, which has shops throughout Sydney. **Carla Zampatti** is an Australian designer whose specialty is elegant day and evening wear. **David Jones** stocks innovative Australian names such as Robert Burton, Leonie Levy, and Jodie Boffa, while international labels such as Sonia Rykiel, Donna Karan, and Missoni are to be found on the exclusive seventh floor. **Grace Bros.** carries impressive Australian designers such as Jane Lamerton, Covers, Anthea Crawford, and Trent Nathan.

Emporio Armani can also be found in Sydney, with its trademark quality fabric, cut, and design excellence. The **Sportsgirl** stores are great for bright accessories and up-to-the-minute fashions. **Collette Dinnigan** uses Italian and French lace, silk, and tulle to make exquisite lingerie that includes teddies, bustiers, and decadent pyjamas.

MEN'S CLOTHES

THE EXCELLENT menswear department in **David Jones** stocks everything from casual to formal dress. **Ralph Lauren Polo** has shoes, sweaters, jackets, shirts, and accessories for the designer-orientated.

Josephs Men's Store also stocks upscale men's labels, including Bally, Zegna, and Gant. **Marcs** is locally-made clothing (for both men and women), from T-shirts to suits, and top imports such as Yohji Yamamoto and Issey Miyake.

For men who do not enjoy fussy shopping, **Gowing Bros.** is the answer. This department store stocks absolutely everything imaginable from socks, shirts, and detachable collars to made-to-measure suits, pyjamas, hats, and even regulation whites for lawn bowling – all at very competitive prices.

AVANT-GARDE AND STREET FASHION

PADDINGTON, Darlinghurst, Surry Hills, and King Street in Newtown are the places to find some of Sydney's best street fashion. **Bracewell** and **Morrissey Edmiston** design for women and men. Their clothes are in demand by rock stars, models, and everyone in between. **Lisa Ho** and **Black Vanity** also cater to the style-conscious woman.

Skin Deep has retro gear for men – Hollywood-style shirts, suits from the 1940s and 1950s, old silk ties, and great tie pins. Watch the markets, Glebe and Paddington in particular (*see p203*), for the up-and-coming designers. **Aussie Boys**, popular with the gay crowd, stocks

cheeky casual clothes for men and women, as well as trendy gym gear and the latest party wear. **Dangerfield** is another shop filled with funky fashion.

ESSENTIALLY AUSTRALIAN

AUSTRALIAN "outback fashion," from elastic-sided riding boots and Akubra hats to the stylish Driza-bone oilskin coats, are found at **R. M. Williams**. Beach- and surfwear labels to look for are Hot Tuna, 100% Mambo, Rip Curl, Speedo, and Brian Rochford. Shops carrying these brands include **Hot Tuna**, **Surf Dive 'n Ski**, and major department stores. The **Mambo Friendship Store** carries Mambo label surf and street wear and accessories. **General Pants Co.** is another retail outlet for Mambo.

KNITWEAR

CHUNKY HANDKNITS adorned with Australian motifs are sold at **Dorian Scott**, alongside children's wear, hats, and an eclectic range of casual wear. You will also find the rainbow-colored Coogi knits here. The **Great Australian Jumper Company** has classic knitwear

SIZE CHART

Women's clothes

Australian	6	8	10	12	14	16	18	20
American	4	6	8	10	12	14	16	18
British	6	8	10	12	14	16	18	20
Continental	38	40	42	44	46	48	50	52

Women's shoes

Australian	6–6½	7	7½–8	8½	9–9½	10	10½–11
American	5	6	7	8	9	10	11
British	3	4	5	6	7	8	9
Continental	36	37	38	39	40	41	42

Men's suits

Australian	44	46	48	50	52	54	56	58
American	34	36	38	40	42	44	46	48
British	34	36	38	40	42	44	46	48
Continental	44	46	48	50	52	54	56	58

Men's shirts

Australian	36	38	39	41	42	43	44	45
American	14	15	15½	16	16½	17	17½	18
British	14	15	15½	16	16½	17	17½	18
Continental	36	38	39	41	42	43	44	45

Men's shoes

Australian	7	7½	8	8½	9	10	11	12
American	7	7½	8	8½	9½	10½	11	11½
British	6	7	7½	8	9	10	11	12
Continental	39	40	41	42	43	44	45	46

designed by Adele Weiss and made from Australian wool. **Vivian Chan Shaw** specializes in feathery evening knits made from superfine wool.

SHOES

THE SHOE FETISHIST is very well served in Sydney, with shops like **Edward Meller**, **Evelyn Miles**, and **Raymond Castles** appealing to all tastes. **Bally** and **Bruno Magli** have top-notch styles at matching prices. **Grace Bros.** and **David Jones** carry the chic designs of Elle Effe, as well as a good range of men's shoes. **Josephs Shoe Store** stocks top-quality shoes for men, including Bally.

HATS

SYDNEY'S MARKETS *(see p203)* have hats galore, ranging from raffia to plush velvet. Maya Neumann sells original designs at Paddington Bazaar and **Wrights on Piccadilly**. The **Strand Hatters** stocks a wide range of styles for men and women, from typical bush hats to wide-brimmed straw creations. **Mario Bravo** also sells casual and formal hats.

Vic Cooper Hats is where fashion magazines go for hats for their photo shoots. Helen Kaminski's distinctive raffia and felt hats are sold at David Jones and Dorian Scott.

DIRECTORY

WOMEN'S CLOTHES

Carla Zampatti
143 Elizabeth St. **Map** 1 B5.
9264 3257.

Collette Dinnigan
39 William St, Paddington.
Map 6 D3. 9360 6691.

Country Road
142 Pitt St. **Map** 1 B5.
9394 1818.
One of several branches.

David Jones
See p199.

Emporio Armani
4 Martin Place. **Map** 1 B4.
9231 3655.

Grace Bros.
See p199.

Sportsgirl
Skygarden. **Map** 1 B5.
9223 8255.
One of several branches.

MEN'S CLOTHES

David Jones
See p199.

Gowing Bros
See p199.

Josephs Men's Store
Sheraton Wentworth Hotel, Phillip Street.
Map 1 B4.
9221 2203.

Marcs
Mid City Center.
Map 1 B5.
9221 5575.
One of several branches.

RALPH LAUREN POLO
Queen Victoria Building.
Map 1 B5.
9267 1630.

AVANT-GARDE AND STREET FASHION

Aussie Boys
102 Oxford St,
Darlinghurst. **Map** 5 A2.
9360 7011.

Black Vanity
400 Oxford St,
Paddington. **Map** 6 D4.
9360 5130.
One of three branches.

Bracewell
264 Oxford St,
Paddington. **Map** 5 C3.
9360 6192.
One of two branches.
Menswear
274 Oxford St,
Paddington. **Map** 5 C3.
9331 5844.

Dangerfield
330 Crown St, Surry Hills.
Map 5 A2.
9380 6294.

Lisa Ho
2a–6a Queen St,
Woollahra. **Map** 6 E4.
9360 2345.

Morrissey Edmiston Man
Strand Arcade. **Map** 1 B5.
9221 5616.

Morrissey Edmiston Woman
Strand Arcade. **Map** 1 B5.
9232 7606.

Skin Deep
141 Elizabeth St.
Map 1 B5. 9264 1239.

ESSENTIALLY AUSTRALIAN

General Pants Co.
391 George St. **Map** 1 B5.
9299 3565.
One of several branches.

Hot Tuna
180 Oxford St,
Paddington. **Map** 5 C3.
9361 5049.

Mambo Friendship Store
17 Oxford St,
Paddington. **Map** 5 B3.
9331 8034.

R. M. Williams
389 George St. **Map** 1 B5.
9262 2228.
One of three branches.

Surf Dive 'n Ski
462 George St. **Map** 1 B5.
9267 3408.
One of several branches.

KNITWEAR

Dorian Scott
105 George St, The Rocks.
Map 1 B2.
9247 4090.

Great Australian Jumper Company
Chifley Plaza. **Map** 1 B4.
9231 3511.
One of three branches.

Vivian Chan Shaw
Queen Victoria Building.
Map 1 B5. 9264 3019.

SHOES

Bally
Queen Victoria Building.
Map 1 B5.
9267 3887.

Bruno Magli
Piccadilly. **Map** 1 B5.
9267 4712.

David Jones
See p199.

Edward Meller
St. James Arcade.
Map 1 B5. 9232 1807.
One of three branches.

Evelyn Miles
MLC Centre. **Map** 1 B4.
9233 1569.

Grace Bros.
See p199.

Josephs Shoe Store
Strand Arcade. **Map** 1 B5.
9233 1879.

Raymond Castles
Centrepoint. **Map** 1 B5.
9232 2147.
One of three branches.

HATS

David Jones
See p199.

Dorian Scott
See Knitwear.

Mario Bravo
Queen Victoria Building.
Map 1 B5.
9264 1798.

Strand Hatters
Strand Arcade. **Map** 1 B5.
9231 6884.

Vic Cooper Hats
Royal Arcade, 255 Pitt St.
Map 1 B5.
9267 3713.

Wrights on Piccadilly
210 Pitt St. **Map** 1 B5.
9267 7663.

Specialty Shops and Souvenirs

SYDNEY OFFERS AN EXTENSIVE RANGE of gift and souvenir ideas, from unset opals and jewelry to Aboriginal art and hand-crafted souvenirs. Museum shops, such as at the Museum of Sydney (see p85) and the Art Gallery of NSW (see pp108–11), often have specially commissioned items that make great presents or reminders of your visit.

ONE-OF-A-KIND

SPECIALTY SHOPS abound in Sydney – some practical, some eccentric, others simply indulgent. **Ausfurs** sells everything from luxurious sheepskin coats and jackets to pure wool handknits and mohair rugs.

Red Earth sells reasonably priced natural oils, vegetable soaps, skincare products, and cosmetics. **Mug Mania** has all kinds of crazy, colorful mugs, plates, and cups on its shelves. It is worth visiting just to see the vast display of stock. **Wheels & Doll Baby** is a rock'n'roll heaven – loads of leather, belts, shoes, and rocker accessories. For unusual telephones and hip watches with a high-tech look, explore **Hello Darling**. **The Watch Gallery** stocks more traditional watches. Designer sunglasses can be found at both branches of **The Looking Glass**.

AUSTRALIANA

AUSTRALIANA has become more than just a souvenir genre; it is now an art form in itself. **Australian Craftworks** sells souvenirs as desirable art, including woodwork, pottery, and leather goods.

Done Art and Design has distinctive prints by Ken and Judy Done on a wide range of clothes, swimwear, and accessories, and at **Weiss Art** you will find tasteful, mainly black and white, minimalist designs on clothes, umbrellas, baseball caps, and cups. **Makers Mark** is a showcase for exquisite work by artisans in wood, glass, and silver. The Queen Victoria Building's Victoria Walk (see p82) is dominated by shops selling Australiana: souvenirs, silver, antiques, art, and crafts.

The **Australian Museum** (see pp88–9) has a small shop on the ground floor. It sells slightly unusual gift items such as native flower presses, bark paintings and Australian animal puppets, puzzles, and games.

BOOKS

THE LARGER CHAINS such as **Dymocks** and **Angus & Robertson's Bookworld** have a good range of guide books and maps of Sydney. For more eclectic browsing, **Abbey's Bookshop**, **Ariel** (open until midnight), **New Edition Bookshop**, and **Gleebooks**. **The Bookshop** specializes in gay and lesbian fiction and non-fiction. The **State Library of NSW** (see p112) bookshop has a good choice of Australian books, particularly on history.

MUSIC

SEVERAL SPECIALTY music shops of international repute can be found in Sydney. **Red Eye Records** is for the streetwise, with its collectibles, rarities, alternative music, and concert tickets. At **Timewarp Records** the vinyl comeback is heralded. Classic jukebox-style vinyl 45s are a speciality here, as are reissues on CD from the 1950s, 1960s, and 1970s. **Central Station Records and Tapes** has mainstream grooves, plus rap, hip hop, and cutting edge dance music. **Birdland** stocks blues, jazz, soul, and avant-garde. **Folkways** specializes in world music, **Waterfront** independent rock and grunge, and **Utopia Records** heavy metal. **Michael's Music Room** sells classical music only.

ABORIGINAL ART

TRADITIONAL PAINTINGS, fabric, jewelry, boomerangs, carvings, and cards can be bought at the **Aboriginal and Tribal Art Centre**. At **New Guinea Primitive Arts** you will find a range of tribal artifacts from Aboriginal Australia, Papua New Guinea, and Oceania, from masks to totem poles. Purchases can be shipped or mailed overseas if you wish.

The **Coo-ee Aboriginal Art Gallery** boasts a large selection of limited edition prints, hand-printed fabrics, books, and Aboriginal music. The long-established **Hogarth Galleries Aboriginal Art** has a fine reputation and usually has work by Papunya Tula and Balgo artists and respected painters such as Clifford Possum Tjapaltjarri and Emily Kame Kngwarreye (see p111).

OPALS

SYDNEY OFFERS a variety of opals in myriad settings. Both **Flame Opals** and **Opal Fields** sell opals from all the major Australian opal fields. At **The Rocks Opal Mine** you can board a mine shaft elevator for some simulated opal mining – and buy gems in the bargain. **Giulian's** has unset opals, including blacks from Lightning Ridge, whites from Coober Pedy, and boulder opals from Quilpie. The **Gemstone Boutique** sells an extensive range of opals, and also stocks coral, pearls, jade, and gold nugget jewelry.

JEWELRY

LONG-ESTABLISHED jewelers with 24-carat reputations include **Fairfax & Roberts**, **Hardy Brothers**, and **Percy Marks**. World-class pearls are found in the seas off the northwestern coast of Australia. Rare and beautiful examples can be found at **Paspaley Pearls**.

Victoria Spring Designs evokes costume jewelry's glory days, with filigree and glass beading worked into its sumptuous pendants, rings, earrings, and Gothic crosses. **Dinosaur Designs** made its name with colorful, chunky resin jewelry, while at **Love & Hatred**, jeweled wrist cuffs, rings, and crosses recall lush medieval treasures. **Glitz Bijouterie** has affordable hip silver and glitzy gold necklaces in up-to-the minute styles.

DIRECTORY

ONE-OF-A-KIND

Ausfurs
Queen Victoria Building.
Map 1 B5.
[9264 6072.

Hello Darling
Queen Victoria Building.
Map 1 B5.
[9264 8303.

The Looking Glass
Strand Arcade.
Map 1 B5.
[9221 5958.
Also: Queen Victoria
Building. **Map** 1 B5.
[9261 4997.

Mug Mania
Piccadilly. **Map** 1 B5.
[9264 5069.

Red Earth
Queen Victoria Building.
Map 1 B5.
[9264 2420.
One of several branches.

The Watch Gallery
142 King St. **Map** 1 B5.
[9221 2288.
Also: Skygarden.
Map 1 B5.
[9223 5328.

Wheels & Doll Baby
259 Crown St,
Darlinghurst. **Map** 5 A2.
[9361 3286.

AUSTRALIANA

Australian Craftworks
127 George St, The Rocks.
Map 1 B2.
[9247 7156.
One of two branches.

Australian Museum
6 College St. **Map** 4 F3.
[9320 6000.
One of two branches.

Done Art and Design
123 George St, The Rocks.
Map 1 B2.
[9251 6099.
One of several branches.

Makers Mark
Chifley Plaza. **Map** 1 B4.
[9231 6800.

Weiss Art
85 George St, The Rocks.
Map 1 B2.
[9241 3819.
Also: Harbourside Festival
Marketplace, Darling
Harbour. **Map** 3 C2.
[9281 4614.

BOOKS

Abbey's Bookshop
131 York St. **Map** 1 A5.
[9264 3111.

Angus & Robertson Bookworld
168 Pitt St, Imperial
Arcade. **Map** 1 B5.
[9235 1188.
One of many branches.

Ariel
42 Oxford St, Paddington.
Map 5 B3.
[9332 4581.

The Bookshop
207 Oxford St,
Darlinghurst. **Map** 5 A2.
[9331 4140.

Dymocks
424–430 George St.
Map 1 B5.
[9235 0155.
One of many branches.

Gleebooks
49 Glebe Point Rd, Glebe.
Map 3 B5.
[9660 2333.

New Edition Bookshop
328a Oxford St,
Paddington. **Map** 6 D4.
[9360 6913.

State Library of NSW
Macquarie St. **Map** 1 C4.
[9230 1611.

MUSIC

Birdland
3 Barrack St, Wynyard.
Map 1 A4.
[9299 8527.

Central Station Records and Tapes
46 Oxford St,
Darlinghurst. **Map** 4 F4.
[9361 5159.

Folkways
282 Oxford St,
Paddington. **Map** 5 C3.
[9361 3980.

Michael's Music Room
19 Town Hall Arcade.
Map 4 E3.
[9267 1351.

Red Eye Records
Tank Stream Arcade,
Cnr King and George Sts.
Map 1 B4.
[9233 8177.

Timewarp Records
289 Clarence St.
Map 1 A5.
[9283 1555.

Utopia Records
52 Clarence St. **Map** 1 A4.
[9283 2423.

Waterfront Records
89 York St. **Map** 1 A5.
[9262 4120.

ABORIGINAL ART

Aboriginal and Tribal Art Centre
117 George St, The Rocks.
Map 1 B2. [9241 5998.

Coo-ee Aboriginal Art Gallery
98 Oxford St, Paddington.
Map 5 B3. [9332 1544.

Hogarth Galleries Aboriginal Art
7 Walker Lane, off Brown
St, Paddington. **Map** 5 C3.
[9360 6839.
One of two branches.

New Guinea Primitive Arts
Dymocks Building,
428 George St. **Map** 1 B5.
[9232 4737.
One of two branches.

OPALS

Flame Opals
119 George Street,
The Rocks. **Map** 1 B2.
[9247 3446.

Gemstone Boutique
388 George St.
Map 1 B5.
[9223 2140.

Giulian's
2 Bridge St. **Map** 1 B3.
[9247 5119.

Opal Fields
155 George St, The Rocks.
Map 1 B2.
[9247 6800.
One of two branches.

Rocks Opal Mine
Clocktower Square,
35 Harrington St,
The Rocks. **Map** 1 B2.
[9247 4974.

JEWELRY

Dinosaur Designs
Strand Arcade.
Map 1 B5.
[9223 2953.
One of three branches.

Fairfax & Roberts
44 Martin Place.
Map 1 B4.
[9232 8511.
One of two branches.

Glitz Bijouterie
Imperial Arcade.
Map 1 B5.
[9231 1383.

Hardy Brothers
77 Castlereagh St.
Map 1 B5.
[9232 2422.
One of two branches.

Love & Hatred
Strand Arcade.
Map 1 B5.
[9233 3441.

Paspaley Pearls
42 King St. **Map** 1 A4.
[9232 7633.

Percy Marks
60–70 Elizabeth St.
Map 1 B4.
[9233 1355.

Victoria Spring Designs
37 William St, Paddington.
Map 6 D3.
[9331 7862.
One of two branches.

ENTERTAINMENT IN SYDNEY

SYDNEY HAS THE STANDARD of entertainment and nightlife you would expect from a cosmopolitan city. Everything from opera and ballet at Sydney Opera House to Shakespeare by the sea at the Balmoral Beach amphitheater is available. Venues such as the Capitol, Her Majesty's Theatre and the Theatre Royal play host to the latest musicals, while Sydney's many smaller theaters are home to interesting fringe theater,

A Wharf production poster

modern dance, and rock and pop concerts. Pub rock thrives in the inner city and beyond, and there are many nightspots for jazz, dance, and alternative music. Movie buffs are well supplied with film festivals, art-house films, and foreign titles, as well as the latest Hollywood blockbusters. One of the features of harborside living is the free outdoor entertainment so, for children, a Sydney visit can be especially memorable.

Signs outside the Dendy repertory cinema in Martin Place (see p210)

INFORMATION

FOR DETAILS of events in the city, you should check the daily newspapers first. They carry film, and often arts and theater, advertisements daily. The most comprehensive listings appear in the *Sydney Morning Herald*'s "Metro" guide every Friday. The *Daily Telegraph* has an events guide on Thursdays, with opportunities to win free tickets to special events. The *Australian*'s main arts pages appear on Fridays, and all the papers review new films in weekend editions.

The **NSW Travel Centre**'s tourist information kiosks and most of the major hotels have invaluable free guides such as *What's on in Sydney,* which is published quarterly, and the weekly *Where Magazine.*

Music fans are well served by the free weekly guides *On the Street, Drum Media,* and *3D World,* with youth culture information, interviews, and tour guides. They are found at video and music shops, pubs, and clubs. *3D World* has the best dance club information.

Many places have leaflets about forthcoming attractions, while the major centers have information telephone lines.

BUYING TICKETS

SOME OF THE popular operas, shows, plays, and ballets in Sydney are sold out months in advance. While it is better to book ahead, many theaters do set aside tickets to be sold at the door on the night.

You can buy tickets from the box office or by telephone. Some orchestral performances do not admit children under seven, so check with the box office before buying. If you make a phone booking using a credit card, the tickets can be mailed to you. Alternatively, tickets can be collected from the box office half an hour before the show. The major agencies will take overseas bookings.

If you are desperate to see a sold-out rock concert, there may be scalpers selling tickets

A street musician at Circular Quay

outside but often at hugely inflated prices. If all else fails, hotel concierges have a reputation for being able to find hard-to-get tickets.

BOOKING AGENCIES

SYDNEY HAS two main ticket agencies: **Ticketek** and **Firstcall**. Between them, they represent all the major entertainment and sports events.

Ticketek has more than 50 outlets throughout the state, open from 9am to 5pm weekdays, and Saturdays from noon to 4pm. Bookings by phone can be made from 8:30am–9pm, Monday to Saturday, and 10am–7pm Sundays. Overseas bookings can be faxed. The main Firstcall office is open Monday to Friday, from 9am–6pm. Other offices are open 10am–9pm and can be found at all the Greater Union

The annual Gay and Lesbian Mardi Gras Festival's Dog Show (see p49)

movie houses, the State Theatre, Theatre Royal, Capitol Theatre, and Footbridge Theatre *(see pp210–11)*. Firstcall has a 24-hour telephone service.

Agencies accept traveler's checks, bank checks, cash, Visa, MasterCard (Access), and American Express. However, some agencies do not accept Diners Club. A booking fee applies, with a postage and handling charge also added if tickets are mailed out. There are generally no refunds (unless a show is cancelled) or exchanges available.

If one agency has sold out its allocation for a show, it is worth checking to see if the other agency still has tickets.

Halftix booth selling cut-price tickets in Martin Place

DISCOUNT TICKETS

WHEN A SHOW isn't sold out, **Halftix** offers half-price tickets (plus a small booking fee) for the theater, concerts, opera, and ballet from noon on the day of the performance only (except for matinees and Sunday performances, tickets to which can be bought the day before). Bus tour, theater restaurant, harbor cruise, art gallery, and film tickets are also available at half price. Payment is by cash and credit card, and there is no limit on the number of tickets you can buy.

You can ring Halftix from 11am for recorded information on which shows are offering discounts. Be there early to beat the lines during the Sydney Festival *(see p49)*. Half-tix is also a Ticketek agency for regular advance sales.

Tuesday is budget-price day at most movies. Some independent theaters have special prices throughout the week. The **Sydney Symphony Orchestra** *(see p212)* offers a special Student Rush price to full-time students when tickets

The Spanish firedancers Els Comediants at the Sydney Festival *(p49)*

are available. These can only be bought on the day of the performance from the box office at the relevant spot. A student card must be shown.

CHOOSING SEATS

IF BOOKING IN person at either the venue or the agency, you will be able to look at a seating plan. Be aware that in the State Theatre's stalls, row A is the back row. In Sydney, there is not as much difference in price between stalls and dress circle as in other cities.

If booking by phone with Ticketek, you will only be able to get a rough idea of where your seats are. The computer will select the "best" tickets.

DISABLED VISITORS

MANY OLDER venues were not designed with the disabled visitor in mind, but this has been remedied in most newer buildings. It is best to phone the box office before-hand to request special seating

The highly respected Australian Chamber Orchestra *(see p212)*

and other requirements. Ask about the best street entrance. The Sydney Town Hall has wheelchair access at its Druitt Street entrance. The **Sydney Opera House** has disabled parking, wheelchair access, and a loop system in the Concert Hall for the hearing impaired. A brochure, *Services for the Disabled*, is also available.

DIRECTORY

USEFUL NUMBERS

Darling Harbour Information Line
📳 *1902 260568.*

NSW Travel Centre
📞 *132077.*

People with Disabilities NSW
📞 *9319 6622.*

Sydney Opera House
Information Desk
📞 *9250 7209.*
Disabled Information
📞 *9250 7189.*

Sydney Symphony Orchestra
📞 *9333 1600.*

TICKET AGENCIES

Firstcall
66 Hunter St. **Map** 1 B4.
📞 *9320 9000.*

Halftix
Martin Place (near Elizabeth St).
Map 1 B4. 📳 *0055 26655.*
🕐 *noon–5:30pm Mon–Fri, noon–5pm Sat.*

Ticketek
📞 *9266 4800.* FAX *9267 4460.*

Theater and Film

SYDNEY'S THEATRICAL VENUES are notable for both their atmosphere and their quality. There is a stimulating mix of productions, from musicals, classic plays, and Shakespeare-by-the-sea (and in the park) to contemporary, fringe, and experimental theater. Comedy is also finding a strong niche as a mainstream performance art. Prominent playwrights include David Williamson, Steve J Spears, Stephen Sewell, and Louis Nowra.

Australian filmmaking has earned an international reputation in recent years, and there is a rich variety of both local and international films to see, plus annual film festivals showcasing the best local and overseas offerings.

THEATER

THE LARGER, mainstream musicals, such as those of Andrew Lloyd Webber, are staged at the **Theatre Royal**, the opulent **State Theatre** (*see p82*), **Her Majesty's**, or the **Capitol Theatre** (*p99*).

The smaller venues offer a range of interesting plays and performances. These include the **Seymour Theatre Centre**, which has three theaters; the **Belvoir Street Theatre**, which has two; the **Ensemble**, a theater-in-the-round by the water; and the **Footbridge Theatre**. The **Stables Theatre** specializes in works by new Australian playwrights.

The well-respected **Sydney Theatre Company** (STC) is the city's premier theater company. Most STC productions are at **The Wharf** at Walsh Bay or in the Drama Theatre of the **Sydney Opera House**. The **Bell Shakespeare Company** gives the Bard an innovative slant without tampering with the original text. Its productions are an ideal initiation for young or wary theatergoers. While venues

vary, there are two Sydney seasons – one in autumn, one in summer. Shakespeare can also be seen at the **New Theatre** in Newtown.

Street performance and open air theater are popular during summer, especially the **Shakespeare by the Sea** production at Balmoral Beach (*see p55*) and *A Midsummer Night's Dream under the Stars*. The latter is staged in the Royal Botanic Gardens by **Elston, Hocking, and Woods** on most nights through summer until the end of April (*see pp104–5*).

For the more adventurous theater-goer, **Sydney Fringe Festival** is a celebration of original Australian theater, film, dance, music, and visual arts. Contrary to its "fringe" tag, the festival is accessible in its approach, and all works staged are usually of good quality. It is held over the second half of January at the Bondi Pavilion (*see p144*) and satellite venues including Bondi Beach.

CHILDREN'S THEATER

SYDNEY THRIVES on spectacles that delight children. You will often find jugglers, mime artists, and street musicians at Circular Quay. Nearby, **The Rocks Puppet Cottage** has free marionette performances every weekend and during school vacations for children under ten. Shows are at 11am, 12:30pm, 2pm, and 3:30pm.

Free entertainment can be found in Darling Harbour's Tumbalong Park on most days. Nearby, Harbourside Festival Marketplace often has street theater and magic shows. If you are lucky, you may be

able to see the athletic **Flying Fruit Fly Circus**. This troupe, age eight to eighteen, excels in aerial gymnastics and performs in Sydney every year.

FILM

THE CITY'S MAIN commercial movie center is in George Street, just one block south of Town Hall. **Hoyts**, **Village**, and **Greater Union** show all the latest blockbusters. Similar multiscreen complexes can be found in many suburbs. **The Pitt Centre** can be relied upon for its interesting mainstream and art-house selection.

Film buffs have plenty to choose from at the Paddington end of Oxford Street (the **Academy Twin** and the **Verona**, and the **Chauvel** in Paddington Town Hall).

The **Dendy** theaters show the latest art house films – the Martin Place Dendy has a bar and bistro, plus a shop filled with movie memorabilia: soundtracks, videos, books, posters, and magazines. Three other popular repertory venues are the **Walker Cinema**, the **Rialto**, and the **Valhalla**.

Most movie theaters offer half-price tickets on Tuesdays, although competition has seen bargain prices extend to other days of the week. The Valhalla sells cheap tickets from Mondays to Thursdays. Increasingly, adults are being admitted to G-rated films at children's prices.

The **Third Eye Cinema** has science fiction, art house and cult classics, movie marathons, and 3-D films. They strongly encourage local film makers to show their work. At the **Australia Cinema**, the latest Chinese movies, with English subtitles, are shown regularly.

Night owls will find late screenings of films at the major cinema complexes and some of the independent cinemas.

FILM FESTIVALS

ONE OF THE BEST events in Sydney's calendar is the **Sydney Film Festival** (*see p51*). The main venue is the State Theatre, with satellite

---

FILM CENSORSHIP RATINGS

G For general exhibition
PG Parental guidance recommended for those under 15 years
M 15+ Recommended for mature audiences age 15 and over
MA 15+ Restricted to people 15 years and over
R 18+ Restricted to adults 18 years and over

screenings at other venues. Dozens of new features, shorts, and documentaries from all over the globe are presented, and there are often tribute sessions and retrospectives.

Held under the stars at the Bondi Pavilion Amphitheatre at Bondi Beach, **Flickerfest International Short Film Festival** is run over ten days in January. The Short Poppies Festival is staged in tandem with Flickerfest and is a feast of student films and videos.

Sydney's Festival of Jewish Cinema, held at the **Academy Twin** in Paddington, begins in mid-November and lasts for ten days. Highly acclaimed international films with a Jewish theme are screened.

The Gay and Lesbian Film Festival runs over two weeks, starting mid-February. Films are shown at various inner-city venues as part of the **Gay and Lesbian Mardi Gras** *(p49)*.

COMEDY

SYDNEY'S MOST established comedy venue, the **Comedy Store**, is only minutes away by train from Central Railway Station. There are stand-up comics, sketches, or revues every night except Monday. Thursday is the night new comedians try out their stand-up skills.

Monday night is Comics in the Park at the **Harold Park Hotel**. Other comedy shows are held there throughout the week, as well as readings by popular local authors and poets. Monday is also the night for laughs at the Fringe Bar in the **Unicorn Hotel**. On Tuesdays, comedians perform at the **Hopetoun Hotel**, while Thursday night is stand-up comedy night at the **Bat and Ball Hotel**.

DIRECTORY

THEATER

Bell Shakespeare Company
C *9241 2722.*

Belvoir Street Theatre
25 Belvoir St, Surry Hills.
C *9699 3444.*

Capitol Theatre
13–17 Campbell St, Haymarket. **Map** 4 E4.
C *9320 5000.*

Elston, Hocking and Woods
C *(03) 9419 3411.*

Ensemble Theatre
78 McDougall St, Milsons Point. C *9929 0644.*

Footbridge Theatre
University of Sydney, Parramatta Rd, Camperdown. **Map** 3 A5.
C *9692 9955.*

Her Majesty's Theatre
107 Quay St (near Railway Square). **Map** 4 D5.
C *9212 3411.*

New Theatre
542 King St, Newtown.
C *9519 3403.*

NIDA Theatre
215 Anzac Parade, Kensington.
C *9697 7613.*

Seymour Theatre Centre
Cnr Cleveland St & City Rd, Chippendale.
C *9364 9400.*

Shakespeare by the Sea
C *9557 3065.*

Stables Theatre
10 Nimrod St, Darlinghurst.
Map 5 B1. C *9361 3817.*

State Theatre
49 Market St. **Map** 1 B5.
C *9373 6655.*

Sydney Fringe Festival
C *9365 0112.*

Sydney Opera House
Bennelong Point.
Map 1 C2. C *9250 7777.*

Theatre Royal
MLC Centre, King St.
Map 1 B5. C *9231 6111.*

The Wharf
Pier 4, Hickson Rd, Millers Point. **Map** 1 A1.
C *9250 1777.*

CHILDREN'S THEATER

Flying Fruit Fly Circus
C *(060) 217 0444.*

The Rocks Puppet Cottage
Kendall Lane. **Map** 1 B2.
C *9241 2902.*

FILM

Academy Twin
3a Oxford St, Paddington.
Map 5 B3. C *9361 4453.*

Australia Cinema
59 Goulburn St.
Map 4 E4. C *9281 2883.*

Chauvel Cinema
249 Oxford St, Paddington.
Map 5 C3. C *9361 5398.*

Dendy Cinema
Martin Place
MLC Centre, Martin Place.
Map 1 B4. C *9233 8166.*
George Street
624 George St. **Map** 4 E3.
C *9264 1577.*
Newtown
261–263 King St,
Newtown. C *9550 5699.*

Greater Union
525 George St. **Map** 4 E3.
C *9267 8666.*

Hoyts
505 George St. **Map** 4 E3.
C *11680.*

Rialto Cinema
150 Elizabeth St. **Map** 4 E3.
C *9267 1788.*

Third Eye Cinema
64 Devonshire St, Surry Hills. C *9380 5162.*

Valhalla
166 Glebe Point Rd, Glebe.
Map 3 A4. C *9660 8050.*
C *0055 20106.*

Verona Cinema
17 Oxford St, Paddington.
Map 5 B3. C *9360 6099.*

Village
545 George St.
Map 4 E3.
C *9264 6701.*

Walker Cinema
121 Walker St,
North Sydney.
C *9959 4222.*

FILM FESTIVALS

Flickerfest
C *190 224 2004.*

Gay and Lesbian Mardi Gras
C *9557 4332.*

Sydney Film Festival
C *9660 3844.*

COMEDY

Bat and Ball Hotel
495 Cleveland St,
Surry Hills. **Map** 5 A5.
C *9699 3782.*

Comedy Store
450 Parramatta Rd,
Petersham. C *9564 3900.*

Harold Park Hotel
115 Wigram Rd, Glebe.
C *9552 2999.*

Hopetoun Hotel
416 Bourke St,
Surry Hills. **Map** 5 A3.
C *9361 5257.*

Unicorn Hotel
106 Oxford St,
Paddington. **Map** 5 B3.
C *9360 3554.*

Opera, Classical Music, and Dance

MUSIC BUFFS CANNOT POSSIBLY visit Sydney without seeing an opera or hearing the city's premier orchestra perform in the Sydney Opera House. And that is just the start. Since the 1970s, music played in Sydney has considerably broadened its base, opening the door to all manner of influences from Asia, Europe, and the Pacific, not to mention local compositions. For the visitor, there is a wealth of orchestral, choral, chamber, and contemporary music from which to choose.

OPERA

AUSTRALIA has produced a number of world-class opera singers, including Joan Sutherland, and eminent conductors such as Sir Charles Mackerras, Simone Young, and Stuart Challender. The first recorded performance of an opera in Sydney was in 1834. For the next 120 years, most opera seen by Sydneysiders was imported from overseas.

In 1956, the Australian Opera (AO) was formed and it presented four Mozart operas in its first year. But it was the opening of the **Sydney Opera House** (see pp74–7) in 1973 that heralded a new interest in opera. The AO's summer season is held from early January to early March; the winter season from June to the end of October. Performances are held in the Opera Theatre of the Sydney Opera House. Crowd pleasers over the years have included *Turandot* and *La Bohème*. Every year at the hugely popular Opera in the Park (see p49), members of the Australian Opera perform excerpts from classical operas.

ORCHESTRAL MUSIC

SYDNEY's main provider of orchestral music and recitals is the **Sydney Symphony Orchestra** (SSO). Numerous concerts are given each year, mostly in the Sydney Opera House Concert Hall or the **Sydney Town Hall** (see p87). This season is complemented by the Meet the Music series – twilight concerts aimed at adventurous younger classical fans. These feature a new Australian work introduced by the composer, a masterpiece, and a concerto. There's a Tea and Symphony series mid-year, held on Friday mornings at the Sydney Opera House. For one week in November, the Babies' Proms are held in the **Eugene Goossens Hall** for children under five years of age.

The **Conservatorium of Music** (see p106), with its picturesque location in the Royal Botanic Gardens and castle-like architecture, provides an atmospheric concert setting. There are inexpensive concert evenings throughout the year at which you can listen to the Conservatorium's symphony,

wind, or chamber orchestras, or jazz big bands. The **Sydney Youth Orchestra** was formed in 1973 and is highly praised for its talent, enthusiasm, and impressive young soloists. It performs each year at Carols in The Domain (see p49) and once every couple of months at the Sydney Opera House or Sydney Town Hall.

CONTEMPORARY MUSIC

THE VERY FIRST concert held by **Musica Viva** was in December 1945, at the New South Wales Conservatorium of Music. What began with just a string chamber ensemble today promotes concerts of all kinds. Chamber music was Musica Viva's first love, but it now presents string quartets, jazz, piano groups, percussionists, soloists, and international avant-garde artists as well. Concerts are held at the Sydney Opera House, the **Seymour Theatre Centre**, and, on rare occasions, Sydney Town Hall.

Synergy is one of Sydney's best contemporary music groups and one of Australia's foremost percussion quartets. The group commissions works from all over the world and gives its own concert series at Eugene Goossens Hall every year. Synergy also collaborates with dance and theater groups.

CHAMBER MUSIC

UNDER DIRECTOR Richard Tognetti, the **Australian Chamber Orchestra** has considerably raised the profile of large chamber orchestras. This internationally acclaimed orchestra is noted for its creativity and interesting choice of venues, including museums, churches, and even wineries. Its main concerts are held at the Sydney Opera House, with dates throughout the year. There is also a smaller concert series at the Sydney Town Hall, plus a Church Series held over the Easter period.

The **Australia Ensemble** is the resident chamber music group at the University of New South Wales. It performs six times a year at the **Sir John**

FREE CONCERTS

Lunchtime concerts are very much part of Sydney life. There are free performances every weekday in the Martin Place amphitheater (see p84). Solo graduate students and small ensembles from the Conservatorium of Music give a free recital in Martin Place every Wednesday. The half-hour organ recital in St. Andrew's Cathedral (see p87), at 1:15pm on Thursdays, is a long-standing tradition. You will find street musicians, jazz bands, string ensembles, guitarists, or dancers most weekends and during school vacations at Circular Quay, The Rocks, and Darling Harbour. If the weather is fine, the Sydney Opera House provides free entertainment from noon on Sundays and holidays on the Forecourt or Northern Boardwalk. During the Sydney Festival (see p49), there are free concerts aplenty, the most popular being Opera in the Park, Symphony under the Stars, and the Australia Day Concert, all held in The Domain.

Clancy Auditorium and also appears for Musica Viva. Many choral groups and ensembles, such as the **Macquarie Trio** of violin, piano, and cello, like to book **St. James' Church** because of its atmosphere and acoustics (which, it must be said, are kinder than the seats). The trio also performs at the **Macquarie Theatre**.

CHORAL MUSIC

COMPRISING THE 200-strong Sydney Philharmonia Symphonic Choir and the 40-member Sydney Philharmonia Motet Choir, the **Sydney Philharmonia Choirs** are the city's finest. They perform at the Sydney Opera House every two months or so and, in December, are the focal point of the Sydney Symphony *Messiah* concerts and Carols in The Domain *(see p49).*

The **Australian Youth Choir** is booked for many private functions, but if lucky, you may catch one of their two major annual performances at the Sydney Town Hall in June and December. One of the city's most impressive vocal

groups is the **Café at the Gate of Salvation**, described as "a feral Aussie blend of *a cappella* gospel." Check the weekly listings *(see p208)* for performance dates.

DANCE

THERE IS AN eclectic variety of dance to be seen in Sydney. The Australian Ballet has two seven-week seasons at the Sydney Opera House: one in March/April, the other in November/December. The company's repertoire spans traditional through to modern, although it is perhaps most noted for classical ballets such as *Swan Lake* and *Giselle*.

Sydney Dance Company is the city's leading modern dance group, often combining its vigorous productions with innovative musical scores. It has performed in Italy, New York, London, and China. Productions are mostly staged at the Sydney Opera House, but are, on occasion, held at their studio at **The Wharf**.

The **Performance Space** is very popular for experimental

dance and movement theater. Artists with backgrounds in everything from dance, mime, and circus work to Butoh and performance art are likely to appear here. It is also where the challenging modernist troupe **Dance Exchange** performs its work each year.

Bangarra Dance Theatre uses traditional Aboriginal and Torres Strait Islander dance and music as its inspiration, infused with contemporary elements. The troupe makes international, outback, and interstate tours, but is based in Sydney. The **Aboriginal Islander Dance Theatre** is also contemporary with a traditional flavor. Its Sydney performances are usually at the Seymour Theatre Centre.

The smaller experimental companies rely on year-to-year funding or community-based work. These include Kinetic Energy Theatre Co., at the **Edge Theatre**; the collaborative **One Extra Company**; and **Darc Swan**. **ACE**, established by *Strictly Ballroom* star Paul Mercurio, draws on a range of movement from contemporary ballet to street dance.

DIRECTORY

ORCHESTRAS AND CHOIRS

Australian Chamber Orchestra
9357 4111.

Australia Ensemble
9385 4874.

Australian Youth Choir
9808 5561.

Café at the Gate of Salvation
9660 6850.

Macquarie Trio
9850 9447.

Musica Viva
9698 1711.

Sydney Philharmonia Choirs
9251 2024.

Sydney Symphony Orchestra
9264 9466.

Sydney Youth Orchestra
9281 1666.

DANCE COMPANIES

Aboriginal Islander Dance Theatre
9252 0199.

ACE
9314 3222.

Bangarra Dance Theatre
9569 4555.

Dance Exchange
9357 3576.

Darc Swan
9818 3039.

One Extra Company
9212 6411.

Sydney Dance Company
9221 4811.

CONCERT AND DANCE VENUES

Conservatorium of Music
Macquarie St. **Map** 1 C3.
9230 1222.

Edge Theatre
642 King St, Newtown South. 9516 1954.

Eugene Goossens Hall
Australian Broadcasting Commission, 700 Harris St, Ultimo. **Map** 4 D5.
9333 1500.

Macquarie Theatre
Macquarie University, Cnr Epping and Balaclava Rds,

North Ryde.
9850 7111.

Performance Space
199 Cleveland St, Redfern.
9319 5091.

St. James' Church
173 King St. **Map** 1 B5.
9232 3022.

Seymour Theatre Centre
See p211.

Sir John Clancy Auditorium
University of NSW, Anzac Pde, Kensington.
9385 1000.

Sydney Opera House
See p211.

Sydney Town Hall
Cnr George and Druitt Sts.
Map 4 E2. 9265 9007.

The Wharf
See p211.

Music Venues and Nightclubs

SYDNEY DRAWS the biggest names in contemporary music all year round. Venues range from the cavernous Sydney Entertainment Centre to small and noisy back rooms in pubs. Most of the venues cater to a variety of music tastes – rock one night, jazz, blues, or folk the next. The many weekly entertainment guides *(see p208)* will tell you what to see and when to see it.

GETTING IN

FOR THE MAJOR shows and outdoor concerts you can buy tickets through booking agencies such as Ticketek and Firstcall *(see p208)*. There can be a large price variation, depending on the act. You may pay from A$10 to A$35 for something at the Metro, but nearly A$100 for the best seats at a Rolling Stones concert.

At smaller places, you pay at the door. The price often depends on the band's popularity, and the takings are usually the band's total earnings for the night.

Dance clubs often have a cover charge, but some spots will admit you free before a certain time in the evening.

ALL-DAY CONCERTS

THE BIG DAY OUT, held at Royal Agricultural Society Showground on Australia Day, is a feast of local and international bands. There are a number of stages throughout the showground where bands perform their sets *(see p49)*.

The Australia Day Concert *(see p49)* brings the best of Australia's rock acts together for a concert in The Domain.

ROCK MUSIC

THE ROCK WORLD'S biggest names usually perform at the Sydney Entertainment Centre, the Sydney Cricket Ground, and Eastern Creek Raceway. There are also more intimate places for esteemed local and international rock acts. Many are old theaters, including the State Theatre, the Enmore Theatre, and the musically adventurous Metro, near the city's movie district.

Pub rock is a constantly changing scene in Sydney. Weekly listings have the latest news on when and where to see bands *(p208)*. Venues such as the Sandringham Hotel, Annandale Hotel, Bridge Hotel, and Selina's at Coogee Bay Hotel draw big crowds to their everchanging list of bands and performers.

The Hotel Britannia has a mixed bag of music, including rock, country, and bluegrass. You can drop into Round Midnight most nights for a dose of funk, soul, or blues.

JAZZ

FOR CONSISTENTLY excellent contemporary jazz, the Strawberry Hills Hotel, Café de Lane, and The Basement, almost an institution among Sydney jazz fans, are the pick of the crop. The Basement has both local and international artists, and the music played here includes blues and, at times, even respectable pop.

Other options are Soup Plus, Harbourside Brasserie, and the Orient Hotel on weekends. A jazz cruise, the Rocks Rhythmboat, leaves Pier 1 at noon every Sunday.

BLUES

THE BEST SPOTS to hear blues in Sydney are the Bridge Hotel, the Rose, Shamrock & Thistle (commonly referred to as the "Three Weeds"), the Cat & Fiddle, The Basement, and the Harbourside Brasserie. The Rose of Australia has a a big blues jam on the last Sunday of every month.

NIGHTCLUBS

DANCE CLUBS may come and go in Sydney, but there are still several constants on the scene. Nightspots playing a broad range of dance, soul, funk, disco, and rock include the Cauldron, Juliana's in the Sydney Hilton, Riva Night Club, and Kinselas. Clubs into dance music, house, and hip hop include the Bentley Bar, Sugareef, Mister Goodbar, Tunnel, and Q. Hard-core dance music starts on Saturday night at Blackmarket and continues all day Sunday with the Dayclub. Thursday night is the renowned Hellfire Club for the S&M crowd. DCM has a large dance floor and good music. Axis plays black beats, soul funk, and all the latest grooves, while Power Cuts is the place for reggae.

GAY AND LESBIAN VENUES

SUNDAY NIGHT is the big night out for many of Sydney's gay community, although there is plenty of action all through the week. Popular hotspots include the Beresford, Beauchamp, Flinders, and Oxford hotels, and the Midnight Shift. The Phoenix Bar at the Exchange draws big crowds on Thursday and Sunday nights. The Albury Hotel has entertainment all week, including drag shows.

For cocktails to kick off a night out, there's the Lizard Lounge at the Exchange, a favorite spot with lesbians, and the Oxford Cocktail Bar at the Oxford Hotel. One of the best lesbian nights out is On the Other Side upstairs at Kinselas on Sundays.

In Newtown, the Imperial and the Newtown hotels are popular gay and lesbian venues. The Imperial Hotel was featured in the movie *Priscilla, Queen of the Desert*.

CABARETS

THERE'S ENTERTAINMENT most nights at the Harbourside Brasserie, ranging from dinner shows to jazz, rock and late-night dance bands. The Tilbury Hotel – a cosy and atmospheric cabaret spot – also has dinner shows most nights of the week. At the Sydney Hilton, international acts of Al Jarreau and Pointer Sisters caliber are booked for its dinner and supper shows.

DIRECTORY

ROCK MUSIC

Annandale Hotel
17 Parramatta Rd,
Annandale.
📞 9550 1078.

Bridge Hotel
135 Victoria Rd, Rozelle.
📞 9810 1260.

Coogee Bay Hotel
Cnr Coogee Bay Rd and
Arden St, Coogee.
📞 9665 0000.

**Eastern Creek
Raceway**
Horsley Rd, Eastern Creek.
📞 9672 1000.

Enmore Theatre
130 Enmore Rd,
Newtown. 📞 9550 3666.

Hotel Britannia
103 Cleveland St,
Chippendale.
📞 9699 1169.

Metro
624 George St.
Map 4 E3.
📞 9264 2666.

Round Midnight
2 Roslyn St, Potts Point.
Map 5 C1.
📞 9356 4045.

**Royal
Agricultural
Society
Showground**
Driver Ave, Moore Park.
Map 5 C5.
📞 9331 9111.

**Sandringham
Hotel**
387 King St, Newtown.
📞 9557 1254.

State Theatre
49 Market St. **Map** 1 B5.
📞 9373 6655.

**Sydney Cricket
Ground**
Driver Ave, Moore Park.
Map 5 C5.
📞 9360 6601.

**Sydney
Entertainment
Centre**
Harbour St, Haymarket.
Map 4 D4.
📞 9320 4200.

JAZZ

The Basement
29 Reiby Place. **Map** 1 B3.
📞 9251 2797.

Café de Lane
15 Brisbane St, Surry Hills.
Map 4 F4.
📞 9264 5175.

**Harbourside
Brasserie**
Pier 1, Hickson Rd,
Millers Point. **Map** 1 B1.
📞 9252 3000.

Orient Hotel
89 George St, The Rocks.
Map 1 B2. 📞 9251 1255.

Rocks Rhythmboat
Departs Pier 1, Hickson Rd,
Millers Point. **Map** 1 B1.
📞 9247 2979.

Soup Plus
383 George St.
Map 1 B5.
📞 9299 7728.

**Strawberry Hills
Hotel**
453 Elizabeth St, Surry Hills.
📞 9698 2997.

BLUES

The Basement
See Jazz.

Bridge Hotel
See Rock Venues.

Cat & Fiddle Hotel
456 Darling St, Balmain.
📞 9810 7931.

**Harbourside
Brasserie**
See Jazz.

Rose of Australia
1 Swanson St, Erskineville.
📞 9565 1441.

**Rose, Shamrock &
Thistle Hotel**
193 Evans St, Rozelle.
📞 9555 7755.

NIGHTCLUBS

Axis
195 Oxford St, Bondi
Junction. 📞 9386 1006.

Bentley Bar
320 Crown St, Surry Hills.
Map 5 A2.
📞 9331 1186.

Blackmarket
111 Regent St,
Chippendale.
📞 9698 8863.

Cauldron
207 Darlinghurst Rd,
Darlinghurst. **Map** 5 B1.
📞 9331 1523.

DCM
33 Oxford St,
Darlinghurst. **Map** 4 F4.
📞 9267 7380.

Kinselas
383 Bourke St,
Darlinghurst. **Map** 5 A2.
📞 9331 3299.

Mister Goodbar
11a Oxford St, Paddington.
Map 5 B3.
📞 9360 6759.

Power Cuts
150 Elizabeth St.
Map 4 F4.
📞 9264 5380.

Q
44 Oxford St,
Darlinghurst. **Map** 4 F4.
📞 9360 1375.

Riva Night Club
Sheraton on the Park,
Castlereagh St.
Map 1 B5.
📞 9286 6666.

Sugareef
20 Bayswater Rd,
Potts Point. **Map** 5 B1.
📞 9357 7250.

Sydney Hilton
259 Pitt St. **Map** 1 B5.
📞 9266 0610.

Tunnel
1 Earl Place, Potts Point.
Map 5 B1. 📞 9357 3331.

GAY AND LESBIAN
VENUES

Albury Hotel
2–8 Oxford St,
Paddington. **Map** 5 B3.
📞 9361 6555.

Beauchamp Hotel
267 Oxford St,
Darlinghurst. **Map** 5 A2.
📞 9331 2575.

Beresford Hotel
354 Bourke St,
Darlinghurst. **Map** 5 A3.
📞 9331 1045.

Exchange Hotel
34 Oxford St,
Darlinghurst. **Map** 4 F4.
📞 9331 1936.

Flinders Hotel
63 Flinders St, Darlinghurst.
Map 5 A3. 📞 9360 4929.

Imperial Hotel
35 Erskineville Rd,
Erskineville.
📞 9519 9899.

Kinselas
See Nightclubs.

Midnight Shift
85 Oxford St, Darlinghurst.
Map 5 A2. 📞 9360 4319.

Newtown Hotel
174 King St, Newtown.
📞 9557 1329.

Oxford Hotel
134 Oxford St, Darlinghurst.
Map 5 A2. 📞 9331 3467.

CABARETS

**Harbourside
Brasserie**
See Jazz.

Sydney Hilton
See Nightclubs.

Tilbury Hotel
22 Forbes St,
Woolloomooloo.
Map 2 D5. 📞 9358 1295.

SURVIVAL
GUIDE

PRACTICAL INFORMATION 218-227
TRAVEL INFORMATION 228-237

PRACTICAL INFORMATION

Although Sydney has only fairly recently become a major destination for international tourists, facilities are now well established and most services are of a very high standard. Hotels in the city center are generally expensive, but clean, comfortable, cheaper accommodations are available (see pp168–77). There are cafés and restaurants in all price brackets that offer a wide range of international cuisines (see pp178–97). Public transit is reliable and inexpensive, especially

Lifesavers at Coogee Surf Carnival

if you take advantage of the numerous composite travelcards that offer combined bus, ferry, and train travel (see p230). Bureaux de change and cash machines are conveniently located throughout the city, and major credit cards are accepted by most hotels, restaurants and shops. Visitors will find Sydney a safe, clean, and welcoming city. They should encounter few practical problems as long as they follow a few common sense guidelines about personal security (see pp222–3).

Visitor information kiosk inside Central Railroad Station

TOURIST INFORMATION

Sydney's principal tourist information and booking center for accommodations, tours and travel is the state-run **NSW Travel Centre**. Tourist information booths can also be found at Sydney's major tourist attractions and beaches, and at several central Sydney locations. As well as providing information and advice, these booths have maps, brochures, and entertainment listings (see p208) available for free.

For visitors arriving by air, there is another branch of the NSW Travel Centre at Sydney's Kingsford Smith Airport. It is open from 5am to midnight, or while flights are operating.

If you would like to find out about Sydney and the rest of Australia before you travel, the **Australian Tourist Commission** can provide useful information and brochures.

MUSEUMS AND GALLERIES

Most of Sydney's major museums and galleries are close to the city center and readily accessible by public transportation (see pp230–35).

Although opening hours and admission charges vary, the majority of museums and galleries are open 10am–5pm daily (smaller galleries are usually closed on Mondays). Admission is often free, or else only a moderate fee is charged. There are discounts available for senior citizens, students and children.

Museums and galleries are often at their busiest on weekends, particularly when special exhibitions are being staged.

Art Gallery of New South Wales

SMOKING

Smoking is strictly forbidden in stores and many workplaces; also on public transit and outside designated areas in restaurants, theaters, and entertainment and sports venues. It is best to ask about smoking policies when making reservations in hotels and restaurants.

AUSTRALIAN TOURIST COMMISSION OFFICES

UK
Gemini House, 10–18 Putney Hill Rd, London SW15 6AA.
☎ 0181 780 2227.
🖷 0181 780 1496.

US and Canada
The Aussie Helpline,
1000 E Business Centre Drive,
Mt. Prospect, IL 60056.
☎ (708) 635-3612.
🖷 (708) 635-3718.

TOURIST INFORMATION

NSW Travel Centre
City Center
11–31 York St. **Map** 1 A4.
☎ 132077. ⏰ 9am–5pm
Mon–Fri; 9am–12pm Sat (for telephone bookings only).
Kingsford Smith Airport
International Arrivals Hall.
☎ 9667 6050.

The Rocks Visitor Centre
104 George St, The Rocks.
Map 1 B2. ☎ 9255 1788.
⏰ Feb–Nov: 9am–5pm daily;
Dec–Jan: 9am–7pm.

Darling Harbour
Palm Grove Carousel,
Darling Harbour. **Map** 3 D3.
☎ 9286 0111.
⏰ 9am–5pm daily.

Central Railroad Station
Sydney Terminal. **Map** 4 E5.
⏰ 6am–10pm daily.

Casual dress at a beachside café

ETIQUETTE AND TIPPING

WHILE SYDNEY customs are generally casual, there are a few rules to follow. Eating and drinking is frowned at on public transit, and also when traveling in taxis.

Dress code is generally neat casual, but is more relaxed in summer – although people do like to go all out for formal occasions. Topless bathing is accepted on most beaches, but not at public swimming pools.

People do not depend on tips for their livelihood so this is generally optional. However, it is the custom to leave a little extra for good service in cafés and restaurants (see p179), to tip hotel porters (see p169), and to leave any small change for bartenders and taxi drivers.

GUIDED TOURS AND EXCURSIONS

TOURS AND EXCURSIONS offer the visitor many different ways of exploring the city and its surroundings – from bus tours of the city's night spots, jaunts on the back of a Harley Davidson, guided nature walks, harbor cruises, and river runs, to aerial adventures by hot air balloon, seaplane, or helicopter.

As well as being an easy way to take in the sights, a guided tour can help you to get a feel for your new surroundings.

Perhaps the most economical and flexible introductions to Sydney's attractions are the unregimented tours provided by the State Transit Explorer Buses (see p231). The **State Transit Tourist Ferries** also run special sightseeing routes. In addition, commuter ferries (see pp234–5) provide a less costly alternative to all-out commercial harbor cruises.

Topsail schooner *Solway Lass*

STUDENT TRAVELERS

STUDENT TRAVELERS carrying the International Student Identity card are eligible for discounts in museums, theaters and cinemas, as well as a 40 percent reduction on internal air fares and 15 percent off interstate bus travel.

Overseas visitors who are full time students in Australia can purchase an International Student Identity card (with a guidebook included) for A$10 from Sydney branches of the **Student Travel Association**.

Seaplane moored at Rose Bay, available for scenic flight charter

DISABLED TRAVELERS

SYDNEY HAS RECENTLY made much-needed advances in catering to the disabled. State Transit is phasing in specially designed buses with doors at pavement level and ramps that allow people in wheelchairs to use the bus service. There is also priority seating for those with a disability, and bus handrails and steps are marked with bright yellow paint to assist visually impaired passengers.

The Circular Quay railroad station is completely accessible to wheelchair users. Several other stations have wide entrance gates, and most have ramps installed. The Public Transport Infoline *(see p230)* can give details on disabled access at each station.

Museums, newer hotels, and some major sights cater to the less mobile, including those in wheelchairs, as well as people with other disabilities. You are strongly advised to phone all sights in advance to check on facilities, allowing the most effective forward planning.

For detailed information on accessible services and venues, ACROD's *Accessing Sydney (see p170)* is available from all major bookstores. A map and directory for people who have limited mobility can be obtained from the **Sydney City Council One-Stop Shop**.

Sydney City Council One-Stop Shop

Town Hall House, Sydney Square, George St. **Map** 4 E3. **C** 9265 9333.

SYDNEY TIME

Sydney is in the Australian Eastern Standard Time zone (AEST). Daylight savings in New South Wales starts on the last Sunday in October and finishes on the last Sunday in March. The Northern Territory, Queensland and Western Australia do not observe daylight savings, so check time differences when you are there.

Australian Time Zones

City and Country	Hours + or − AEST
Adelaide (Australia)	−½
Brisbane (Australia)	same
Canberra (Australia)	same
Darwin (Australia)	−½
Melbourne (Australia)	same
Perth (Australia)	−2
London (UK)	−9
Los Angeles (US)	−17
Singapore	−2
New York (US)	−14
Toronto (Canada)	−14

IMMIGRATION AND CUSTOMS

ALL VISITORS TO Australia, with the exception of New Zealand passport holders, are required to hold a valid passport and visa, as well as a return ticket and proof that they have sufficient funds for the duration of their visit.

The customs allowance per person over 18 years of age entering Australia is gifts up to value of A$400, 1.125 liters (about 20 ounces) of alcohol and a carton of 250 cigarettes.

Quarantine regulations in Australia are very strict because of the debilitating effect that introduced pests and diseases would have, not only on the agricultural industry, but also on the country's unique flora and fauna. The importation of

Overseas cruise ship in port at Circular Quay passenger terminal

fresh or packaged food, fruit, vegetables, seeds, live plants, and plant products is prohibited. It is also illegal to bring in any items or products made from endangered species.

On all international flights to Sydney, the aircraft cabin is sprayed with insecticide just before landing. The customs declaration forms issued on the plane must be filled out and given to customs officers as you enter the country. The penalties for importing illegal drugs of any sort are severe.

DEPARTURE TAX

AS IN MANY other countries, Australia has a departure tax. All passengers age 12 or over are required to fill out a form and pay a A$27 departure tax when leaving the country. This tax is usually included in the cost of your airline ticket.

If you have not already paid departure tax, airport check-in staff will refer you to a post office *(see p227)*. Departure tax can be paid for in advance at most Australia Post offices.

Entrance gates with wheelchair access at Circular Quay railroad station

MEDIA

SYDNEY'S CHIEF daily morning newspaper is the *Sydney Morning Herald.* It includes a comprehensive listing of local entertainment on Fridays and Saturdays. The other Sydney daily is the *Daily Telegraph.*

The *Australian* is a daily national paper with the most comprehensive coverage of overseas news, and the weekly *Bulletin* is Australia's leading international news magazine. Foreign newspapers and magazines are widely available for sale at many newsstands.

Sydney is well served with AM and FM radio stations. The state-run ABC (Australian Broadcasting Corporation) stations cater to various tastes, from rock to classical, as well as providing current affairs and magazine-style programs. The commercial stations offer popular music, news, and talk shows. There are also radio stations with programs in community languages.

Sydney has two state-run television stations, the ABC's Channel 2 and the multicultural Special Broadcasting Service (SBS). Channels 7, 9, and 10 are commercially operated and offer the usual soap operas, news, sports, and gameshows.

A selection of daily newspapers

PUBLIC TOILETS

FREE PUBLIC TOILETS are to be found in Sydney's public places, galleries, and museums, department stores and all bus and railroad stations. They are generally well serviced and clean. Baby changing facilities

Drinking fountain in the city

are also quite common, particularly in department stores and major museums and galleries.

Clean drinking fountains can be found throughout the city. Spring or distilled water is also often freely available from dispensers in waiting areas of drugstores, travel agents, and offices.

Standard Australian three-pin plug

ELECTRICAL APPLIANCES

AUSTRALIA'S ELECTRICAL current is 240–250 volts AC. Electrical plugs can have two or three pins. Most hotels will provide 110-volt shaver sockets and hair dryers, but a two- or three-pin adaptor will be needed for other appliances. These can be bought from electrical stores.

CONVERSION CHART

US Standard to metric
1 inch = 2.54 centimeters
1 foot = 30 centimeters
1 mile = 1.6 kilometers
1 ounce = 28 grams
1 pound = 454 grams
1 US quart = 0.947 liter
1 US gallon = 3.6 liters

Metric to US Standard
1 millimeter = 0.04 inch
1 centimeter = 0.4 inch
1 meter = 3 feet 3 inches
1 kilometer = 0.6 mile
1 gram = 0.04 ounce
1 kilogram = 2.2 pounds
1 liter = 1.1 US quarts

Personal Security and Health

S TREET CRIME IN SYDNEY IS LESS prevalent than in many
other large cities, but it does exist. You can minimize
your risk of becoming a victim of crime by exercising
reasonable caution. Members of Sydney's police patrol
the city's streets and public transit system in pairs.
Mobile police stations, set up at crowded tourist areas
and at public events, have proved particularly successful
and are popular with the public. Farther afield, the surf
beaches and natural bushland can present a few dangers
of their own, and the following information offers some
practical advice for coping with environmental hazards.

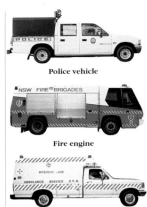

Police vehicle

Fire engine

Emergency ambulance

LOOKING AFTER YOUR PROPERTY

L EAVE VALUABLES and important
documents in your hotel
safe, and don't carry large sums
of cash with you. Traveler's
checks are generally regarded
as the safest way to carry large
sums of money. It is also worth
photocopying vital douments
in case of loss or theft.

Be on guard against purse
snatchers and pickpockets in
places where big crowds
gather. Prime areas for
petty theft are popu-
lar tourist attractions,
beaches, markets,
sports venues,
and on rush-hour
public transit.

Ambulance paramedic

Never carry your
wallet in an outside pocket
where it is an easy target for a
thief, and wear shoulder bags
and cameras with the strap
across your body and the bag
or camera in front with the

clasp fastened. If you have a
car, always try to park in well-
lit, reasonably busy streets.
Remember to lock the vehicle
securely. It is also important
not to leave any valuables or
property visible inside the car
that might attract a thief.

PERSONAL SAFETY

S YDNEY HAS NO definite off-
limit areas during the day,
but it is probably wise to
avoid the more unsavory
side streets and
lanes of areas such
as Kings Cross. If
you take reason-
able care, you can
go into most areas
at night, although
visitors are advised
to stay clear of deserted, poorly
lit streets and toilets in parks.

When traveling by train at
night, stay close to security
cameras on platforms, and use
those parts of the train in the

marked "Nightsafe" area of
the platform. Although more
expensive, taxis are probably
the safest, most efficient means
of travel at night, especially
for shorter journeys.

MEDICAL TREATMENT AND INSURANCE

S YDNEY HAS excellent medical
services, with highly trained
doctors and modern hospitals.
However, overseas visitors are
not covered by Australia's
government health plan, and
medical, dental, and ambulance costs are quite high.
Before leaving your own
country, be sure to buy
adequate insurance for any
medical, hospital, or dental
costs you may incur during
your stay. British passport
holders receive free basic
emergency medical and
hospital treatment.

If you are in need of emergency medical attention, dial
000 for an ambulance or go
to the emergency department
of the nearest main public
hospital. For less urgent treatment, look under "Medical
Centres" in the Yellow Pages
of the telephone directory.

The **Traveller's Clinic** offers
medical treatment for travel-
related illnesses as well as a
vaccination service. For non-
emergency dental treatment,
look under "Dentists" in the
Yellow Pages of the telephone
directory. The **Emergency
Dental Service** has a round-
the-clock phone line for
emergency cases.

Policewoman   **Policeman**   **Fire officer**

PHARMACIES

Pharmacies are generally known as "chemist shops" in Sydney and are liberally scattered throughout the city and suburbs. They sell a wide range of unrestricted drugs and other medical supplies over the counter. Pharmacists can be a source of advice on simple ailments such as colds and upset stomachs. You can ring **After-Hours Pharmacy** information if you need to find one that is open outside normal business hours.

Doctor's prescriptions from your own country cannot be filled by an Australian pharmacist unless they are first endorsed by a medical practitioner practicing locally.

Pharmacy in The Rocks

ENVIRONMENTAL HAZARDS

Take care when going out in the sun – the ultraviolet rays are very intense, even on cloudy days. You should wear SPF 15+ sun block at all times and reapply it regularly.

A hat and sunglasses are also recommended, as is staying out of the sun between 10am and 2pm (11am and 3pm during daylight saving). When swimming at an ocean beach, always check that there are lifeguards on patrol and swim within the "flagged" areas.

In their red and yellow caps, surf lifeguards keep an eye out for changing surf conditions, people in difficulty, and any surfers coming too close to areas set aside for swimmers only *(see p54)*. If signs on the beach indicate that the surf is dangerous, do not go in under any circumstances. Popular beaches have loudspeakers to warn people of hazards that may suddenly arise. If you plan to bushwalk, do not hike alone. Always tell someone where you are going and when you will be back. It is wise to take a map and a basic first aid kit, as well as food and fresh water, and additional warm, waterproof clothing.

Lifesaving flag

When walking through the bush, be aware that you are passing through the habitat of native animals, including some poisonous snakes and spiders. It is very unlikely that you will encounter any, but you should wear substantial footwear, keep a close eye on where you step, and check around logs and rocks before sitting on them.

Snake bite victims should be kept calm and, most important, remain still while emergency medical help is sought. Try to identify the snake by size and color so that the correct anti-venom can be administered.

The funnel-web *(see p89)* and the redback spider are both poisonous species found around Sydney. Anyone bitten by either of these should seek immediate medical attention.

Surf lifesaving sign indicating a dangerous undertow or "rip"

DIRECTORY

EMERGENCY SERVICES

Emergency Dental Service
9692 0598. *24-hour service including Sundays and public holidays.*

Police, Fire, and Ambulance
000 *from any phone. Calls are free (24-hour phoneline).*

GENERAL HELP

After Hours Pharmacy Information
9235 0333.

AIDS Information Line
9332 4000.

Alcoholics Anonymous
9799 1199.

Lost Property
State Rail
9211 4535 *(including all CityRail trains).*
Sydney Buses
9958 9221.
Sydney Ferries
9256 4656.

NRMA (National Roads and Motorists Association)
131111.

Poisons Information Center
131126.

Translating and Interpreting Service
9221 1111.

Travelers' Clinic
Suite 1, 13 Springfield Ave, Potts Point. **Map** 2 E5.
9358 3066.

Victims of Crime Counseling
9217 1000.

HOSPITAL EMERGENCY ROOMS

St. Vincent's Hospital
Victoria St (cnr Burton St), Darlinghurst. **Map** 5 B2.
9361 2520.

Sydney Hospital
Macquarie St (near Martin Place).
Map 1 C4. 9228 2111.

Banking and Local Currency

SYDNEY IS AUSTRALIA'S financial capital. In the central business district are the imposing headquarters of several of the country's leading banks, as well as the Australian head offices of major foreign banks. Visitors will find local, state, and national bank branches dotted at convenient intervals throughout the city and suburbs.

There is no limit to the amount of personal funds that visitors can bring into Australia. Most currencies can be exchanged on arrival at the airport (beyond immigration and customs). Although banks generally offer the best exchange rates, money can also be changed at bureaux de change, larger department stores, and major hotels.

Main street bank logos

BANKING

BANKING HOURS are generally from 9:30am to 4pm Monday to Thursday, and 9:30am to 5pm on Fridays. Some are also open to mid-day on Saturdays. Major city banks open 8:30am to 5pm on weekdays.

A valid passport or another form of photographic ID is usually needed if you are cashing traveler's checks. The current exchange rates, which can vary considerably from day to day, are displayed in the windows or foyers of many banks.

AUTOMATIC CASH DISPENSERS

AUTOMATIC CASH dispensers can be found in most bank lobbies or on an external wall near the bank's entrance. Ask your own bank which Sydney banks and cash dispensers will accept your card and what the transaction charges will be.

Australian currency (in $20 and $50 denominations) can be withdrawn from your bank

Automatic cash dispenser

or credit account. Most cash dispensers will accept various Australian bank cards, Visa and MasterCard (Access), as well as certain others. They are not only convenient, but may also provide a better exchange rate than cash transactions.

CREDIT CARDS

ALL WELL-KNOWN international credit cards are widely accepted in Australia. Major credit cards such as American Express, MasterCard (Access), Visa, and Diners Club can be used to book and pay for hotel rooms, airline tickets, rental cars, tours, and concert and theater tickets. Credit cards are accepted in most restaurants and shops, where the logos of most cards are shown on doors and counter tops. You can also use credit cards in automatic cash dispensers at most banks to withdraw cash.

Credit cards are a convenient way to make bookings and avoid carrying large sums of cash. They can be especially useful in emergencies or if you need to fly home on short notice.

CASHING TRAVELER'S CHECKS

AUSTRALIAN DOLLAR traveler's checks issued by major names like Thomas Cook and American Express are usually accepted (with a passport) in larger shops in Sydney. You may have problems, however,

in smaller outlets. Foreign currency checks can be cashed at banks, bureaux de change, and established hotels.

Banks are generally the best places to go as their fees are lower. Westpac Bank will cash traveler's checks in Australian dollars without charge. Other banks have varying transaction charges, so shop around.

BUREAUX DE CHANGE

SYDNEY HAS MANY bureaux de change in the popular shopping districts. Most are open Monday to Saturday from 9am to 5:30pm. Some branches also operate on Sunday.

While their extended hours can make bureaux de change a convenient alternative to a bank, their commissions and fees are generally higher than those charged by major banks.

DIRECTORY

FOREIGN CURRENCY EXCHANGE

American Express
92 Pitt St. **Map** 1 B4.
📞 9239 0666.
One of several branches.

Thomas Cook
175 Pitt St. **Map** 1 B4.
📞 9229 6611.
One of several branches.

AFTER-HOURS BUREAUX DE CHANGE

Thomas Cook
Shop 64, Queen Victoria Building,
22 George St. **Map** 1 B5.
📞 9264 1133. 🕐 9am–6pm
Mon–Wed, Fri & Sat; 9am–9pm
Thu; 11am–5pm Sun.

Travelex
37–49 Pitt St. **Map** 1 B3.
📞 9241 5722.
🕐 8am–8pm daily.
Also: 48a Darlinghurst Rd, Potts
Point. **Map** 5 B1. 📞 9357 3604.
🕐 8:30am–8pm daily.

Interforex
Wharf 6, Circular Quay. **Map** 1 B2.
📞 9247 2082. 🕐 8am–9:30pm
daily. ● 25 Dec.

LOCAL CURRENCY

THE AUSTRALIAN currency is the Australian dollar ($ or A$), which breaks down into 100 cents (c). The decimal currency system now in place has been in operation since 1966.

Single cents may still be used for some prices, but as the Australian 1c and 2c coins are no longer being circulated, the total amount to be paid will be rounded up or down to the nearest five cent amount.

It can be difficult to get $50 and $100 bills changed, so avoid using them in smaller shops and cafés and, more particularly, when paying for taxi fares. If you do not have change, it is always wise to tell the taxi driver before you start your journey to avoid any misunderstandings. Otherwise, when you arrive at your destination, you may have to find change at the nearest shop or automatic cash dispenser.

To improve security, as well as increase their circulation life, all Australian bank notes have now been plasticized.

Bank Notes
Australian bank notes are produced in denominations of $5, $10, $20, $50, and $100. There are two types of bank notes in circulation: the older paper bills, which are still legal tender, and plasticized bills in similar colors.

$100 bill

$50 bill

$20 bill

$10 bill

$5 bill

5 cents (5c) 10 cents (10c)

20 cents (20c) 50 cents (50c)

1 dollar ($1) 2 dollars ($2)

Coins
Coins currently in use are 5c, 10c, 20c, 50c, $1, and $2 (shown here at actual sizes). There are several 50c coins in circulation; all are the same shape, but have different commemorative images on the face. The 10c and 20c coins are useful for local telephone calls (see p226).

Using Sydney's Telephones

SYDNEY'S PUBLIC PHONES are generally maintained in good working order. Their prevalence on streets throughout the city and suburbs – as well as in hotels, cafés, shops, and public buildings – means that users seldom have to line up to make calls. To save money, avoid making calls from hotel rooms. Hotels set their own rates and a call from your room will invariably cost more than one made from a public phone in the hotel lobby.

Using a mobile phone at Bondi

Telstra Corporation logo

PUBLIC TELEPHONES

MOST PUBLIC PHONES accept both coins and phone-cards, although some operate solely on phonecards and major credit cards.

Phonecards can be bought from selected newsstands, as well as from other outlets displaying the blue and orange Telstra sign.

Although slightly varied in shape and color, all public telephones have a hand receiver and 12-button key pad, as well as clear instructions and a list of useful phone numbers. The **Telstra Phone Centre** has ten phones and is open 24 hours a day.

Telstra payphones

PAYPHONE CHARGES

LOCAL CALLS (those with the 02 area code) are untimed and cost A40 cents. Charges for long-distance calls can be obtained at no cost by calling 012 (for within Australia) and 0102 (for international). Phonecard and credit card phones debit 40-cent units in the same way as other telephones; however, all credit card calls have a A$1.20 minimum fee, making them uneconomical for local calls. Long-distance calls are less expensive if you dial without the help of an operator. Most international calls can be dialed direct, and there is little need for operator assistance except for collect calls. Savings can be made on both national and international calls by phoning during off-peak periods. Peak and discount calling times fall into three ascending price brackets: economy, 6pm Sat–8am Mon, or 10pm–8am daily; night rate, 6pm–10pm Mon–Fri; day rate, 8am–6pm Mon–Sat. Special rates and times may apply to calls to certain countries.

CELLULAR PHONES

MOBILE TELEPHONES are used extensively in Australia. They are available for short-term rental from the NSW Travel Centre's branch at the international airport *(see p218)*. Rates are approximately A$23 per day or A$125 per week.

Other rental companies are listed in the Yellow Pages of the telephone directory under "Mobile Telephones." Ask your service provider about whether your own digital cell phone will work in Australia.

FAX SERVICES

MOST SYDNEY post offices offer a fax service. There are also many copy shops that will send or receive faxes on your behalf. Look under the heading "Facsimile &/or Telex Communication Services" in the Yellow Pages for an agency near you.

Post offices charge per-page fees to send a fax to another fax machine within Australia. The cost per page is reduced after the first page. A fax can be sent to a postal address for the same charge, in which case the fax is sent to the local post office and delivered with the mail, usually the following day. A same-day fax to a postal

USING A COIN/PHONECARD OPERATED PHONE

1 Lift the receiver and wait for the dial tone.

2 Insert the coins required or insert a Telstra phonecard in the direction of the arrows shown on the card.

3 Dial the number and wait to be connected.

5 Replace the receiver at the end of the call and withdraw your card or collect any unused coins. Pay phones do not give change.

4 The display shows you how much value is left on your phonecard or coins. When your coins or phonecard runs out you will hear a warning beep. To continue, insert more coins if using coins. If using a phonecard, remove the old card and insert a new one.

6 When you finish your call, the phonecard is returned to you with a hole punched in it showing the approximate remaining value.

Phonecards

Telstra phonecards are available in A$2, $5, $10, $20, and $50 denominations.

address must be sent by 1pm, and there is a delivery fee. Delivery within 2 hours is available for a higher charge.

Overseas faxes can be sent to another fax machine or to a postal address. The cost is on a per-page rate, as with faxes to local numbers.

USEFUL INFORMATION

Telstra Phone Centre
100 King St. **Map** 1 B5.

Time
[C] 1194.

REACHING THE RIGHT NUMBER

• To call Sydney from the UK, dial 0061 2, then the local number.
• To call Sydney from the US and Canada, dial 011 61 2, then the local number.
• For long-distance direct-dial calls outside your local area code, but within Australia (STD calls), dial the appropriate area code, then the number.
• For international direct-dial calls (IDD calls): dial **0011**, followed by the country code (US and Canada: 1; UK: 44; New Zealand: 64), then the city or area code (omit initial 0) and then the local number.
• International directory assistance: dial **0103**.
• Local directory assistance: dial **013**.
• STD directory assistance: dial **0175**.
• International operator assistance: dial **0107** (public phone) or **0101** (private phone).
• Local operator assistance: dial **0176** (public phone) or **011** (private phone).
• Collect calls within Australia: dial **0176**.
• International collect calls: dial **0107**.
• Numbers beginning with **1800** are toll free numbers.
• Numbers with the prefix **014**, **015**, **018**, **019** or **041** are cell or car phones.
• *See also* Emergency Numbers, *p223*.

Postal Services

Australia Post logo

POST OFFICES ARE open 9am–5pm week days. Almost all post offices offer a wide range of services, including general delivery, fax, money orders, electronic mail, express delivery, parcel post, and telegrams, as well as stamps, envelopes, packaging, stationery, and postcards. Stamps can also be bought from hotels and shops where postcards are sold, and from some newsstands.

Australia Post postman

POSTAL SERVICES

ALL DOMESTIC MAIL is first class and usually arrives within one to five days, depending on distance. Be sure to include postcodes on mailing addresses to avoid delays in delivery.

Express Post, for which you need to buy one of the special yellow and white envelopes sold in post offices, guarantees next-day delivery in designated areas of Australia. International air mail takes from five to ten days to reach most countries.

Labels used for overseas mail

Typical stamps used for local mail

Stamp from a scenic series issue

There are two types of international express mail. EMS International Courier is the fastest service and will reach nearly all overseas destinations within two to three days. Alternatively, Express Post International will reach most destinations throughout the world in four to five days.

Standard and express postboxes

MAILBOXES

SYDNEY HAS BOTH red and yellow mailboxes. The red boxes are for normal postal service; yellow boxes are used exclusively for Express Post within Australia. Both types of mailbox can be found on most busy street corners as well as outside post offices.

GENERAL DELIVERY

POSTE RESTANTE letters can be sent to the General Post Office. Address mail to Poste Restante, GPO Sydney, NSW 2000. You will need to show your passport or other proof of identity before collecting mail sent to you poste restante.

USEFUL INFORMATION

General Post Office (GPO)
159 Pitt St (near Martin Place).
Map 1 B4. [C] 131317.
[○] 8:30am–5:30pm Mon–Fri, 8:30am–noon Sat.
Poste restante [C] 9230 7236.

TRAVEL INFORMATION

TRAVELING TO SYDNEY can involve a long and tiring flight. Visitors from Europe can take advantage of stopovers in Asia; those from the United States could break their journey in Hawaii or one of the other Pacific Islands. A break can mean the difference between arriving in Sydney jet-lagged or stepping off the plane refreshed and ready to take in the sights. Sydney is linked to Australia's other

Countrylink and Indian Pacific train logos

state capitals by efficient air, rail, and bus connections. Long-distance bus travel is comfortable and relatively inexpensive; interstate trains are more expensive, but they are generally a great deal faster. People traveling by bus should consider taking one of the scenic routes with stopovers offered by some bus companies. Car travelers can also plan their journey to Sydney to pass through scenic areas.

ARRIVING BY AIR

INTERNATIONAL FLIGHTS to Sydney can be expensive. They are also often heavily booked, especially from the months of December to February. December is peak season and therefore the most expensive time to fly. Midseason, from January 1 to April 12, is slightly less costly.

APEX fares are often the cheapest. Some stipulate set arrival and departure dates, or carry penalties if you cancel your flight. Round-the-world fares are a good value and an increasingly popular option.

Qantas Airways and **Ansett Australia**, Australia's international and major domestic carriers, link Sydney with other state capitals and major tourist destinations. Other domestic airlines service shorter routes. Flights within Australia are not cheap, but you can save by booking in advance.

Overseas visitors with international tickets are eligible for discounts on domestic flights.

ARRIVING AT SYDNEY AIRPORT

THE MAIN GATEWAY to Australia is Sydney (Kingsford Smith) Airport. As a result of this, congestion, especially at peak periods, can sometimes cause irritating delays. A duty free shop for arriving passengers can be found on the incoming side of the baggage collection and customs area. Just beyond this is the NSW Travel Centre's information desk *(see p218)*, as well as gift shops, a bureau de change, telephones, and car rental desks.

Flight arrivals and departures are displayed on TV monitors, and the location of toilets and other facilities are indicated using internationally recognized symbols.

Airport Express bus into the city center

Lining up for taxis at the Sydney Airport domestic terminal

GETTING INTO THE CITY

SYDNEY AIRPORT is about 9 km (5½ miles) from the center of the city, about a 30-minute express bus ride. Bus and taxi ranks are located directly outside the international and domestic terminals.

State Transit has four airport buses: Airport Express 300 to Circular Quay, Airport Express 350 to Kings Cross, Metro route 400 from Burwood to Bondi Junction via the airport, and Metro route 100 to Dee Why.

Kingsford Smith Bus Service leaves for various city hotels every 30 minutes 6am–5pm, then as needed until 12:40am. The Airporter Clipper goes to all city and Kings Cross hotels and hostels 4:30am–11pm.

Taxis are usually plentiful, but lines may form at peak times. The fare to the center of Sydney is around A$20.

ARRIVING BY SEA

THE MOST delightful way to arrive in Sydney is by ship. Passenger ships berth at the overseas passenger terminals at Circular Quay and Darling

International flight arriving at Sydney Airport

The *QEII* passenger ship berthed at Circular Quay

Harbour. At either terminal, you will find the city on the doorstep. Information booths, tour booking centers, buses, trains, ferries, taxis, and water taxis are all close at hand.

ARRIVING BY COACH

MOST LONG-DISTANCE bus or coach services arrive at the **Long-Distance Coach Terminal** at Central Railroad Station. The terminal has luggage lockers, and shower facilities and food outlets are found in the station above.

Competition between the bus companies is fierce, so it is worth shopping around to get the best price.

ARRIVING BY CAR

THE FOUR MAJOR routes into Sydney are the Pacific Highway from the north; the Great Western Highway from the west; the Princes Highway, which follows the coast from Melbourne; and the Hume Highway, which runs inland from Melbourne.

As they approach Sydney, these routes feed into freeways or motorways, which in turn lead to priority routes known as "Metroads" (marked by blue and white hexagonal signs). When you reach the city outskirts, look for the Metroad signs and stay in the lanes as marked for the city center.

ARRIVING BY TRAIN

ALL INTERSTATE and regional trains arrive at Central Railway Station. Australia's nationwide rail network is known by a different name in each state, but it still operates cohesively. The **Countrylink** reservations line will answer inquiries and take bookings (6:30am–10pm daily) for train services throughout Australia.

CityRail also has slower, but cheaper, services from nearby centers on which seats cannot be booked. Information about CityRail's country services can be obtained from the Public Transport Infoline *(see p230)*.

Country service passenger train waiting at Central Railroad Station

DIRECTORY	**British Airways**	**Singapore Airlines**	**Greyhound Pioneer Australia**

SYDNEY AIRPORT

Airport Information
℡ *9667 9111.*

AIRLINE INFORMATION

Air New Zealand
Reservations ℡ *132476.*
Arrivals and departures
℡ *9937 5299.*

Ansett Australia
Domestic reservations
℡ *131300.*
International reservations
℡ *131767.*
Domestic arrivals and departures ℡ *131300.*
International arrivals and departures ℡ *9693 8405.*

British Airways
Reservations
℡ *9258 3300.*
Arrivals ℡ *11601.*
Departures ℡ *9258 3334.*

Canadian Airlines
Reservations
℡ *9299 7843.*
Arrivals and departures
℡ *9317 2472.*

Japan Airlines
Reservations and flight information
℡ *9283 1111.*

Qantas Airways
Domestic reservations
℡ *131313.*
International reservations
℡ *9957 0111.*
Domestic arrivals and departures ℡ *131223.*
International arrivals and departures ℡ *11601.*

Singapore Airlines
Reservations
℡ *9667 3603.*
Arrivals ℡ *11601.*

United Airlines
Reservations ℡ *131777.*
Arrivals and departures
℡ *9317 8933.*

AIRPORT HOTELS

Sydney Airport Hilton
℡ *9597 0122.*

Sydney Airport Sheraton
℡ *9317 2200.*

LONG-DISTANCE BUS SERVICES

Long-Distance Coach Terminal
Eddy Ave. **Map** 4 E5.
℡ *9281 9366.*

Greyhound Pioneer Australia
℡ *132030.*

Kirklands Coach Service
℡ *9281 2233.*

McCafferty's Coach Service
℡ *9361 5125.*

TRAIN INFORMATION

Central Railway Station
General inquiries
℡ *9219 8888.*
Lost property
℡ *9211 4535.*

Countrylink
Reservations ℡ *132232.*
Arrivals ℡ *11678.*

Getting Around in Sydney

SydneyPass ticket

I N GENERAL, THE BEST WAY to see Sydney's many sights and attractions is on foot, coupled with use of the public transit system. Buses and trains will take visitors to within easy walking distance of anywhere within the inner city. They also serve the suburbs and outlying areas. Passenger ferries provide a fast and scenic means of travel between the city and harborside suburbs. Of the many composite and multiride tickets available, most visitors will find it best to invest in one that includes all three modes of public transportation.

People crossing at pedestrian lights in the center of the city

WALKING

T AKE CARE when walking around the city. Vehicles are driven on the left and often move quickly. It is wise to use pedestrian crossings. There are two types. Push-button crossings are found at traffic lights. Wait for the green man signal and do not cross at lights if the red warning sign is on or flashing. Pedestrian crossings are marked by yellow and black signs. Make sure vehicles are stopping before you cross.

COMPOSITE TICKETS

T RAVELING ON Sydney's trains, buses, and harbor ferries is not expensive, especially if you use one of the composite tickets or TravelPasses that are readily available.

These can be bought from **State Transit Information and Ticket Kiosks**, railroad stations, newsagents, and newsstands where the yellow and black "bus tickets sold here" sign is on display. For some visitors, TravelTen or FerryTen *(see p234)* tickets, which can be used on buses and ferries respectively, may prove useful.

TRAVELTEN TICKETS

T RAVELTEN TICKETS entitle you to make ten bus trips on public transit. Bus routes are divided into parts, or "sections." Tickets are color-coded according to the number of sections for which they can be used on each trip.

These tickets are useful if you need to travel the same route a number of times. Most visitors will need either a Blue TravelTen, valid for 1–2 sections, or a Red TravelTen, valid for 3–9 sections.

TravelTen tickets can be transferred from one user to another and can be shared by more than one passenger on the same trip.

A Blue Weekly TravelPass, Red TravelTen, and Blue TravelTen

TRAVELPASSES

T HE MOST ECONOMICAL of the composite tickets are the TravelPasses. These allow you unlimited seven-day travel on Sydney's public buses, trains, and ferries as long as you travel within stipulated zones.

They are sold in "bus only" or "bus–ferry" and "bus–ferry–train" combinations. The Red TravelPass, a combined bus–ferry–train ticket, covers all zones included in the usual tourist jaunts. The slightly more expensive Green TravelPass allows for bus, train, and ferry travel over a wider area.

SydneyPass

The SydneyPass allows either three or five days' use in any seven-day period, or seven consecutive days of unlimited bus and ferry travel, including trips on the Manly Jetcat, three Sydney Harbour cruises *(see p234)*, the Sydney Explorer and the Bondi & Bay Explorer buses, and the Airport Express services *(see p228)*.

You can buy a SydneyPass direct from the driver on any Airport Express or Explorer bus, travel agents where you see the SydneyPass sign on display, Circular Quay ferry wharf, and State Transit Information and Ticket Kiosks.

All-Day Tickets

If you only have one day for sightseeing, a BusTripper or DayPass ticket may be useful. These allow unlimited travel for one day on as many regular services as you like. BusTripper tickets can be used only on buses, while DayPasses can be used on buses and ferries.

USEFUL INFORMATION

State Transit Information and Ticket Kiosks
Sydney Airport
Outside arrivals halls at international, Ansett domestic, and Qantas domestic terminals. 📞 *9669 1118.*
Circular Quay
Cnr Loftus and Alfred Sts. **Map** 1 B3.
📞 *9219 4316.*
Queen Victoria Building
York St. **Map** 1 A5. 📞 *9264 5482.*
Wynyard Park
Carrington St. **Map** 1A4.
📞 *9299 8521.*

Sydney Ferries Information Office
Opposite Wharf No. 4,
Circular Quay. **Map** 1 B3.
📞 *9256 4670.*

Public Transport Infoline
📞 *131500.*

Traveling by Bus

STATE TRANSIT'S SYDNEY BUSES provides a punctual service that links up conveniently with the city's rail and ferry systems. As well as covering city and suburban areas, there are two Airport Express services *(see p228)* and two excellent sightseeing buses – the Sydney Explorer and the Bondi & Bay Explorer. The **Public Transport Infoline** can advise you on routes, fares, and journey times for all Sydney Buses. Armed with the map on the inside back cover of this book and a composite ticket, you can avoid the difficulties and expense of city parking.

Automatic stamping machine for validating composite bus tickets

USING SYDNEY BUSES

ROUTE NUMBERS and journey destinations are displayed on the front, back, and left side of all State Transit buses. An "X" in front of the number means that it is an express bus. Only single-trip tickets can be purchased on board regular buses. Single fares are bought from the driver. Try to have coins ready as drivers are not always able to change large bills. You will be given a ticket valid for that trip only – if you change buses you will have to pay again.

If using a TravelTen ticket or TravelPass, you must insert it in the automatic stamping machine as you board. Be sure the arrow is facing you and pointing downward. If sharing a TravelTen, insert it into the machine once for each person.

Front seats must be given up to elderly or disabled people. Eating, drinking, smoking, or playing music is prohibited on buses. To signal that you wish to get off, press one of the red buttons – they are mounted on the vertical handrails on each seat – well before the bus reaches your stop. The doors are operated by the drivers.

BUS STOPS

BUS STOPS are indicated by yellow and black signs displaying a profile of a bus and a boarding passenger. Below this symbol, the numbers of all buses traveling along the route are clearly listed.

Timetables are usually found on the bus stop sign or nearby shelter. The Sunday timetable also applies to public holidays, except when they fall on a Saturday. In this case, Saturday timetables apply after 6pm. While bus stop timetables are usually kept as up-to-date as possible, it is best to carry a current bus timetable with you. They are available from State Transit Authority Information and Ticket Kiosks in the city, as well as at Bondi Junction and the Manly ferry wharf.

Express bus

SIGHTSEEING BY BUS

TWO SYDNEY BUS services, the distinctive red Sydney Explorer and the blue Bondi & Bay Explorer, offer flexible sightseeing with informative commentaries. The Sydney Explorer bus covers a 26-km (16-mile) circuit and stops at 22 of the city's most popular sights and attractions. The Bondi & Bay Explorer travels through a number of Sydney's eastern suburbs, taking in much of the area's coastal and bayside scenery along the way.

These buses operate daily at intervals of 15–25 minutes. The great advantage of these services is that passengers can explore at will, getting on and off the buses as often as they wish in the course of a day. The best way to make the most of your journey is to choose the sights you most want to see and plan a basic itinerary. Make sure you take account of the opening times of museums, art galleries, and shops; the bus drivers can advise you about these. Explorer bus stops are clearly marked by the colors of the bus (red or blue).

Tickets can be bought on board the buses or from State Transit Authority Information and Ticket Kiosks.

A typical Sydney Bus used for standard services

The Bondi & Bay Explorer bus

The Sydney Explorer bus

Traveling by Train and Monorail

CityRail logo

As well as providing the key transit link between the city and suburbs, Sydney's railroad network also serves a large part of the central business district. CityRail's double-decker trains operate on seven major lines. The City Circle loop, which runs mostly underground, is the main line running through the city center. It stops at Central, Town Hall, Wynyard, Circular Quay, St. James and Museum. All suburban lines connect with the City Circle at Central and Town Hall stations.

An air-conditioned CityRail train

FINDING YOUR WAY AROUND CITYRAIL

Part of state rail, Sydney's CityRail system is mainly used by commuters. Although some visitors may not need to use the train at all, it is often the most efficient way to travel to and from outlying suburbs such as Parramatta, Cronulla,

and Cabramatta. Fortunately, the system is small enough not to be confusing, and visitors should have little problem in finding their way. CityRail staff are usually happy to help.

Trains run from 4:30am to around midnight. You will need to be more careful when using trains at night as there are not as many people about.

Some railroad stations, such as Cabramatta and Kings Cross, attract crime and petty theft. Stand in the "Nightsafe" areas, which are marked clearly on platforms, and only travel in cars near the conductor, marked by a blue light.

SIGHTSEEING BY MONORAIL

More novel than practical, Sydney's Monorail runs along a scenic loop through central Sydney, Chinatown, and Darling Harbour. Although it covers only a short distance, it can be a convenient way to travel between the city center and Darling Harbour if you do not feel like walking.

There are seven stops on the Monorail route: City Center, Darling Park, Harbourside, Convention, Haymarket, World Square, and Park Plaza. It runs from 7am–midnight, Monday to Saturday, and 8am–9pm on

Pedestrian concourse outside Central Railway Station

USING THE CITYRAIL ROUTE MAP

The five CityRail lines are color-coded, and route maps are displayed at all CityRail stations and inside the cars. All five lines travel through Central and Town Hall railroad stations. Distances shown on the map are not to scale, and the routes that lines are seen to take should not be counted on for true directions of the compass.

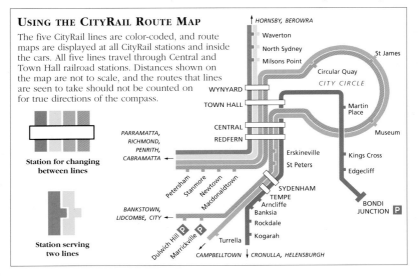

Station for changing between lines

Station serving two lines

Sunday. Trains run every 5 minutes, and the full circuit takes about 12 minutes. Token vending machines are found at each station. These accept most bills and coins and give change. Tokens are then used to pass through the turnstiles.

A Monorail Day Pass allows unlimited rides all day. It can be bought at any of the monorail station information booths.

Monorail leaving the city center, with Sydney Tower in background

COUNTRY AND INTERURBAN TRAINS

STATE RAIL has **Countrylink Travel Centres** throughout the city and suburbs that provide information about its country rail and bus services and also take reservations. The NSW Discovery Pass, valid for one month, allows unlimited economy travel by rail and bus in New South Wales.

Interurban trains run to the Blue Mountains to the west of Sydney, Wollongong in the south, and Gosford and Newcastle to the north *(see p229)*.

USEFUL INFORMATION

CityRail Information
Central Railway Station
Map 4 E5. 9219 4054.
Circular Quay Railway Station
Map 1 B3. 9224 3553.

Countrylink Travel Centres
Central Railway Station
Sydney Terminal. Map 4 E5.
9379 1808.
Circular Quay Railway Station
Map 1 B3. 9241 3887.
Town Hall Railway Station
Map 4 E3. 9267 1521.

MAKING A TRIP BY CITYRAIL

1 Study the CityRail route map. Route lines are distinguished by color, so simply trace the line from where you are to your destination, noting where you need to change and make connections.

2 Tickets can be bought from newsagents, ticket dispensing machines or ticket booths at stations. To obtain your ticket from a dispensing machine, press the button to indicate destination, then the button that shows the ticket type required (one-way, round trip, adult, child etc). Insert money into the slot and then collect your ticket and any change.

3 To pass through the ticket barrier, insert your ticket (arrow side up) into the slot at the front of barrier machines (indicated by green arrows). Take your ticket as it comes out of the machine and the barrier gates or turnstile will open.

4 To find the right platform, follow the signs with the same color code as the line you need and the name of the line's final station.

5 On the platform, display signs show all the stations the line travels through. Stations at which the next train will stop are lit up and are announced as the train arrives at the station.

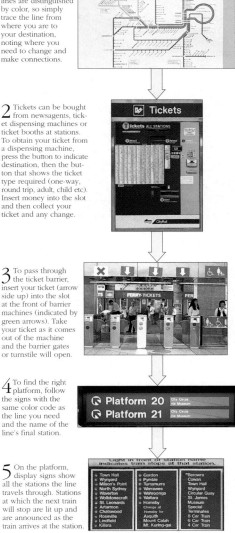

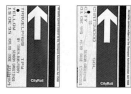

Tickets
Keep your ticket – you will need it at the end of your trip and possibly to show a ticket inspector on the train. A TravelPass (left) and a one-way ticket (right) are shown.

Traveling by Ferry and Water Taxi

For more than a century, harbor ferries have been a picturesque, as well as a practical, feature of the Sydney scene. Today, they are as popular as ever. Traveling by ferry is both a pleasure and an efficient way to travel between Sydney's harbor suburbs. Sightseeing cruises are operated by various private companies as well as by State Transit *(see p219)*. Water taxis can be a convenient, but pricey, alternative to the ferry.

DARLING STREET · BALMAIN

Sign for Darling Street Wharf

Harbor ferries coming and going at Circular Quay Ferry Terminal

USING SYDNEY'S FERRIES

There is a constant procession of State Transit Sydney Ferries crossing the harbor between 6am and 10pm daily. They service most of Sydney Harbour and several stops along the Parramatta River.

Frequent services run to and from Darling Harbour, Manly, Balmain, Parramatta, Hunters Hill, Taronga Zoo, Neutral Bay, Mosman, and Rose Bay, with numerous stops en route. State Transit's Sydney Buses *(see p231)* provide convenient connections at most wharves.

The staff at the Sydney Ferries Information Office *(see p230)*, open 7am–7pm daily, will answer passenger questions and provide timetables. You can also phone the Public Transport Infoline *(see p230)* for advice about connections, destinations, and fares, between 6am and 10pm daily.

MAKING A TRIP BY FERRY

All ferry trips start at the Circular Quay Ferry Terminal. Electronic destination boards at the entrance to each dock indicate the dock from which your ferry will leave, and also give departure times and all stops made en route.

Tickets and TravelPasses can be bought from the Sydney Ferries Information Office *(see p230)*. You can also buy your ticket from the machines on each dock. Only at Manly and Circular Quay are tickets checked through a turnstile. When boarding a ferry at any other point, you are usually able to purchase a ticket from a ticket seller on board, or from the machines when you arrive at Circular Quay.

Manly's large ferry terminal is serviced both by ferries and speedy Jetcats. Tickets and information can be obtained from the ticket windows located in the center of the

A State Transit harbor ferry

A State Transit JetCat ferry

A State Transit RiverCat ferry

HOW TO USE FERRY TICKET MACHINES

A coin-only ticket machine on each Circular Quay wharf sells the range of tickets from TravelTens and weekly TravelPasses *(p230)* to single-trip. Change machines dispense coins.

1 Press the button indicating the type of ticket – composite, one-way or round trip

2 The fare will be displayed. Insert your coins in the slot found at the top of the ticket machine.

3 Your ticket and change will be dispensed. Use your ticket to go through any of the ticket barriers indicated with a green arrow.

HOW TO BUY A TICKET

Press TICKET type.
FARE will be displayed.
Insert COINS.
Collect TICKET & CHANGE

TICKETS & CHANGE

COINS ONLY

Automatic Ticket Barriers
Insert the ticket in the barrier in the direction indicated by the arrows. Remove and pass through.

SYDNEY FERRIES

Electronic destination board for all ferries leaving Circular Quay

terminal. To pass through to the embarkation area you must feed your ticket into the turnstiles. No food or drink is permitted on JetCat ferries, but the larger and slower ferries have snack bars on board.

SIGHTSEEING BY FERRY

State transit has a variety of well-priced harbor cruises that take in the history and colorful sights of Sydney Harbour. They are a refreshingly cheap alternative to the commercial harbor cruises. There are morning, afternoon, and evening tours, all with a commentary throughout. Food and drinks are available on board, but passengers can, if they wish, bring their own.

Morning River Cruise
This 2½-hour cruise travels close to Sydney Opera House and several islands before turning westward. It then goes

under the Harbour Bridge and along Parramatta River, passing picturesque bays and coves.
Departures Wharf 4, Circular Quay. 10am daily.

Afternoon Harbor Cruise
The cruise to Watsons Bay and Middle Harbour takes 2½ hours.
Departures Wharf 4, Circular Quay. 1pm Mon–Fri, 1:30pm Sat, Sun & pub hols.

Evening Harbor Lights
Spectacular nighttime views of the city are features of this 1½-hour cruise.
Departures Wharf 5, Circular Quay. 8pm Mon–Sat.

Other Cruises
There is also an abundance of commercial sightseeing cruises. The **Quayside Booking Centre** has information about all river and harbor cruises from Circular Quay and Darling Harbour each day. They do not charge a booking fee.

WATER TAXIS

Small, fast taxi boats carry passengers around the harbor. You can flag them down like normal cabs if you spot one cruising for a fare. Circular Quay near the Overseas Passenger Terminal is the place to look. You can also telephone for a water taxi. They will pick up and drop off at any navigable pier. Rates begin at around A$35.00 for the first person and $5.00 for each additional passenger.

A water taxi on Sydney Harbour

USEFUL INFORMATION

Quayside Booking Centre
Wharves 2 & 6, Circular Quay.
Map 1 B3. ☎ 9247 5151.

Sydney Ferries Lost Property
Wharf 5, Circular Quay. **Map** 1 B3.
☎ 9256 4656.

Water Taxi Companies
Harbour Taxis ☎ 9552 2266.
Taxis Afloat ☎ 9922 4252.
Water Taxis ☎ 9955 3222.

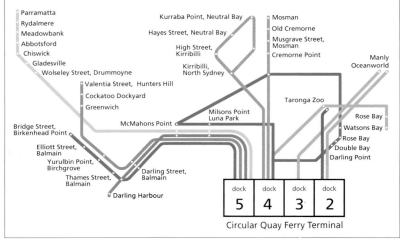

STATE TRANSIT FERRY ROUTES AROUND SYDNEY HARBOUR

Parramatta
Rydalmere
Meadowbank
Abbotsford
Chiswick
Gladesville
Wolseley Street, Drummoyne
Valentia Street, Hunters Hill
Cockatoo Dockyard
Greenwich
Bridge Street, Birkenhead Point
Elliott Street, Balmain
Yurulbin Point, Birchgrove
Thames Street, Balmain
Darling Street, Balmain
Darling Harbour

Kurraba Point, Neutral Bay
Hayes Street, Neutral Bay
High Street, Kirribilli
Kirribilli, North Sydney
McMahons Point
Milsons Point
Luna Park

Mosman
Old Cremorne
Musgrave Street, Mosman
Cremorne Point
Taronga Zoo

Manly Oceanworld
Rose Bay
Watsons Bay
Rose Bay
Double Bay
Darling Point

| dock 5 | dock 4 | dock 3 | dock 2 |

Circular Quay Ferry Terminal

Traveling by Car and Bicycle

D RIVING IS NOT THE IDEAL WAY to get around central
Sydney, although cars can be very convenient for
journeys into the suburbs and farther afield. The city
road network is confusing, traffic is congested, and
parking can be expensive. If arriving in Sydney by car,
make sure that your hotel provides parking. Cycling in
the city can also be difficult and dangerous for those
unfamiliar with Sydney's traffic and road conditions.

**Full service gas station in Balmain
(see p131)**

DRIVING IN SYDNEY

I F YOU ARE PLANNING to use a
car to drive around greater
Sydney, you will need a good
street directory. It is best to
avoid the rush-hour traffic
periods (about 7:30–9:30am
and 5–7:30pm). Regular traffic
update reports are broadcast
on many radio stations.

On a positive note, gas is
relatively cheap, being a little
more expensive than in North
America, but about half the
price of petrol in Europe. Dispensed by the liter, it comes
in super, regular unleaded,
premium unleaded, and diesel
grades. Most gas stations are
self-service and many of them
accept major credit cards.

Traffic Signs
*Always pay strict attention to
Sydney's parking and traffic
signs since fines for violations
can be very expensive.*

DRIVING REGULATIONS

O VERSEAS VISITORS can use
their own licenses to
drive in New South Wales, but
must have proof that they are
simply visiting. You must have
the license or an International
Driver's Permit with you
whenever you are driving.

Australians drive on the left-
hand side of the road and
pass on the right. Speed limits
and distances are indicated in
metric measurements. The
speed limit is 60 km/h (35
mph) in the city and
most suburban areas,
and 100–110 km/h
(60–65 mph) on
freeways and high-
ways, unless other-
wise indicated. The
wearing of seat
belts is compulsory
for drivers and
passengers.

Drivers must yield
to all police vehicles,
fire engines, and
ambulances. At
some intersections,
which are clearly signposted,
drivers are allowed to make a
left-hand turn at a red light
after stopping, but must give
way to pedestrians.

The 0.05 percent maximum
blood alcohol level for drivers
is enforced by random breath
checks. Drivers who are found
to be over the legal limit will
incur heavy fines, suspension,
or loss of license, and even
prison sentences. Should you
be involved in an accident
while over the limit (whether
or not you are at fault), your
insurance may be invalidated.

The NRMA *(see p223)* has a
free 24-hour roadside service
for members. Non-members
are charged a service fee and
enrollment fee. Most car rental
companies provide a free
roadside emergency service.

**Beware of
kangaroos crossing**

Traffic on the Harbour Bridge

PARKING

P ARKING IN SYDNEY is strictly
regulated with fines for any
infringements. In certain areas,
particularly along no-parking
thoroughfares, vehicles are
towed away if parked
illegally. Contact the
**Sydney Traffic
Control Centre**
to find out where
your vehicle has been
impounded if this
happens. There are
many parking lots
scattered around the
city area. They vary
widely, both in how
much they charge and
their opening hours.
Most close after mid-
night, but many close
earlier than this – so check
carefully before parking your
car for the evening.

Look out for the blue and
white "P" signs or look for one
of the metered parking zones
Almost all metered parking
zones are free after 6:30pm on
weekdays, on Saturday after-
noons, and all day on Sunday.

CAR RENTAL

M ETROPOLITAN RATES offered
by the major agencies
(**Avis**, **Budget**, **Hertz**, and
Thrifty) range from about
A$75 a day for a small car to
A$100 a day for a large car.
These rates usually include
comprehensive insurance.
However, many of the other
agencies listed in the Yellow
Pages offer highly competitive

prices, and rentals can be obtained for as little as A$35–$40 a day. Be sure to read the small print on rental agreements as deals may not be as attractive as they first seem – and be aware of the costs you could incur in the event of an accident if you opt for less than full insurance coverage.

Generally, rates are lower if you rent for more than three days, or if you take a limited, low-mileage deal. Extra charges may apply if you drive over 100 km (60 miles) a day, travel over rough rural roads, or return your vehicle late.

You must be at least 21 years old to rent a car. If you don't have a recognized credit card, you will need to leave a sizeable deposit. Rental company fuel refills are usually at prices comparable to gas stations.

TAXIS

Taxis are plentiful in Sydney, and you should have little difficulty in hailing one in the city and inner suburbs. There are taxi stands at many city locations, and taxis are often found outside large city hotels. The four main taxi companies provide a reliable telephone service, but you should call for your taxi at least 15 minutes before you need it.

Meters indicate the fare plus any extras, such as booking fees and waiting time. Fares, as well as extra charges, are regulated and are the same for any time of the day or night. Tips are not normally expected, but it is customary to round the fare up to the next dollar.

Sydney has a new fleet of taxis designed to accommodate disabled passengers, including

Cycling in Centennial Park

those in wheelchairs. These taxis can be booked through any of the major companies. Smoking in taxis is forbidden by law in New South Wales.

SYDNEY BY BICYCLE

While cycling is permitted on all city and suburban roads, visitors would be well advised to restrict their cycling to designated cycling tracks, or to areas where motor traffic is likely to be light. Helmets are compulsory by law.

Eager cyclists who wish to take advantage of Sydney's undulating terrain and pleasant weather can seek advice from **Bicycle New South Wales**. It publishes a handbook, *Cycling Around Sydney*, which has a map of good cycling routes.

Centennial Park is one of the most popular spots; on weekends and every evening groups of riders can be seen cycling through the park. You can take your bicycle on CityRail trains *(see p232)*, but you will have to pay an extra adult fare.

Cabcharge is a charge card for account customers only, but the majority of taxis also accept credit cards.

DIRECTORY

CAR RENTAL COMPANIES

Avis
(9353 9000.

Budget
(132727.

Hertz
(133039.

Thrifty
(008 652 008.

TAXI COMPANIES

Legion Cabs
(9289 9000.

Premier Cabs
(9897 4000.

RSL Taxis
(9581 1111.

Taxis Combined
(9332 8888.

BICYCLE RENTAL AND INFORMATION

The Australian Cycle Company
28 Clovelly Road, Randwick. (Near Centennial Park)
(9399 3475.

Bicycle New South Wales
209 Castlereagh St. **Map** 4 E3.
(9283 5200.

Centennial Park Cycles
50 Clovelly Road, Randwick. (Near Centennial Park)
(9398 5207.

Woolys Cycles
82 Oxford St, Paddington.
Map 5 B3. (9331 2671.

USEFUL NUMBERS

Parking Violations Bureau
130 George St, Parramatta.
(9841 8000.

Sydney Traffic Control Centre
(9211 3000. *24-hour service.*

Taxi Complaints
Department of Transport,
209 Castlereagh St. **Map** 4 E3.
(9916 5244.

The orange light, when lit, shows the taxi is available.

Taxi licence number

The taxi company name and phone number are displayed on front driver and passenger doors.

The taxi driver's photo licence must be on clear display inside the taxi.

SYDNEY STREET FINDER

THE PAGE GRID superimposed on the *Area by Area* map below shows which parts of Sydney are covered in this *Street Finder.* Map references given for all sights, hotels, restaurants, shopping, and entertainment venues described in this guide refer to the maps in this section. All the major sights are clearly marked so they are easy to locate. A complete index of the street names and places of interest follows on pages 246–9. The key, set out below, indicates the scale of the maps and shows what other features are marked on them, including railroad stations, bus terminals, ferry boarding points, emergency services, post offices, and tourist information centers.

Sydney Harbour Bridge
(see pp 70–71) viewed from
North Sydney Olympic Pool

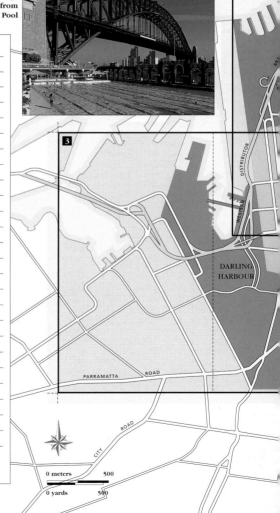

KEY TO STREET FINDER

- Major sight
- Place of interest
- Other building
- CityRail station
- Monorail station
- Bus terminal
- Coach station
- Ferry boarding point
- RiverCat/JetCat boarding point
- Taxi rank
- P Parking
- Tourist information
- Hospital with emergency room
- Police station
- Church
- Synagogue
- Mosque
- Post office
- Golf course
- Freeway
- Main road
- Secondary road
- Ferry route
- One-way street
- Pedestrianized street

0 meters   250

0 yards   250

0 meters   500

0 yards   500

DARLING
HARBOUR

PARRAMATTA   ROAD

CITY

ROAD

WESTERN   DISTRIBUTOR

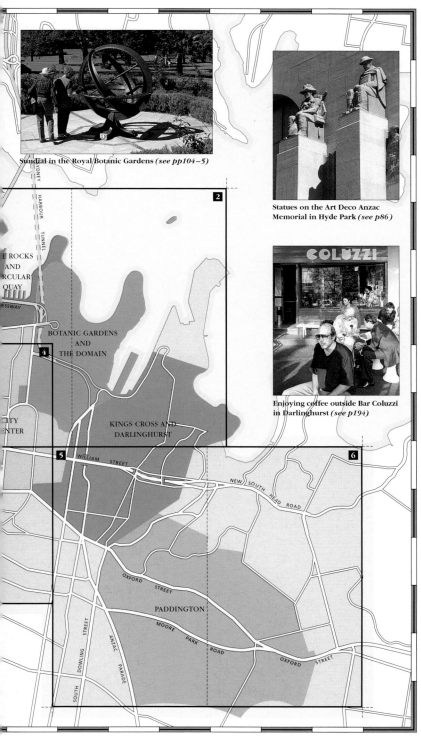

Sundial in the Royal Botanic Gardens *(see pp104–5)*

Statues on the Art Deco Anzac
Memorial in Hyde Park *(see p86)*

Enjoying coffee outside Bar Coluzzi
in Darlinghurst *(see p194)*

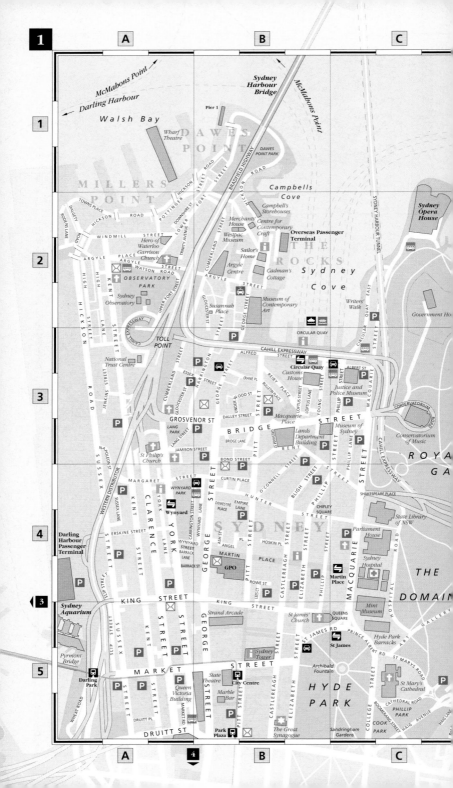

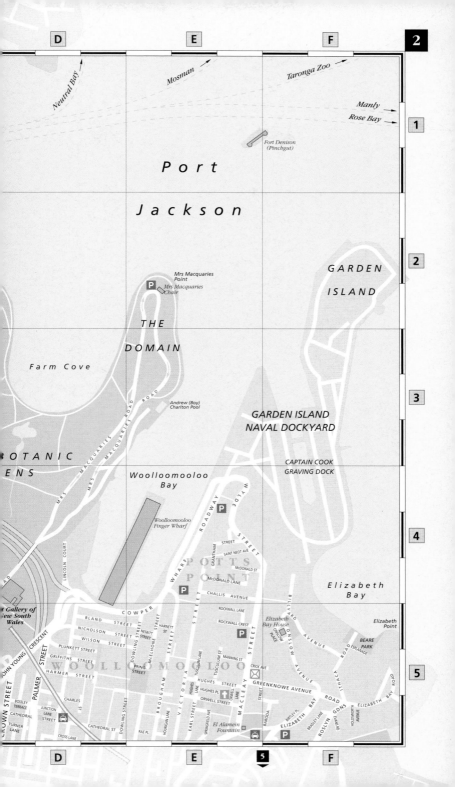

Neutral Bay

Mosman

Taronga Zoo

Manly

Rose Bay

1

*Fort Denison
(Pinchgut)*

P o r t

J a c k s o n

2

GARDEN

ISLAND

*Mrs Macquaries
Point*

P

*Mrs Macquaries
Chair*

THE

DOMAIN

Farm Cove

3

*Andrew (Boy)
Charlton Pool*

**GARDEN ISLAND
NAVAL DOCKYARD**

BOTANIC

ENS

CAPTAIN COOK
GRAVING DOCK

*Woolloomooloo
Bay*

WIDE

ROADWAY

P

4

*Woolloomooloo
Finger Wharf*

STREET

POTTS

GRANTHAM STREET

SAINT NEOT AVE

McDonald St

POINT

McDONALD LANE

P

WHARF ROAD

CHALLIS AVENUE

*Elizabeth
Bay*

Gallery of
New South
Wales

COWPER

STREET

ROCKWALL LANE

*Elizabeth
Point*

BLAND   STREET

NESBITT STREET

HARNETT ST

DOWLING STREET

MELEHONE STREET

ROCKWALL CREST

Elizabeth
Bay House

ONSLOW AVENUE

BEARE
PARK

ITHACA

ESPLANADE

5

NICHOLSON   STREET

WILSON   STREET

VICTORIA

STREET

TUSCULUM LANE

TUGGULUM LANE

MANNING ST

ONSLOW
PLACE

PLUNKETT STREET

GRIFFITHS   STREET

SPRING
STREET

HUGHES   STREET

CRICK AVE

ROAD

HARMER   STREET

W O O L L O O M O O L O O

BROUGHAM STREET

EARL STREET

HUGHES

CAHILL

LANE

GREENKNOWE AVENUE

MACLEAY

STREET

ELIZABETH

BAY

GDNS

BAYSWATER ROAD

ELIZABETH BAY ROAD

CROWN STREET

JOHN YOUNG CRESCENT

PALMER   STREET

CHARLES

JUNCTION
LANE
STREET

BOSSLEY
TERRACE

CATHEDRAL

TURNER
LANE

ROAD

DOWLING STREET

RAE PL

CATHEDRAL ST

CROSS LANE

SPRINGFIELD AVE

ORWELL LANE

ORWELL ST

BARONCOURT

*El Alamein
Fountain*

P

BARTLEY PL

BARODA

ROSLYN ROAD

ELIZABETH BAY

BRADLEY PL

ELAMANG AV

HOLDSWORTH AVENUE

5

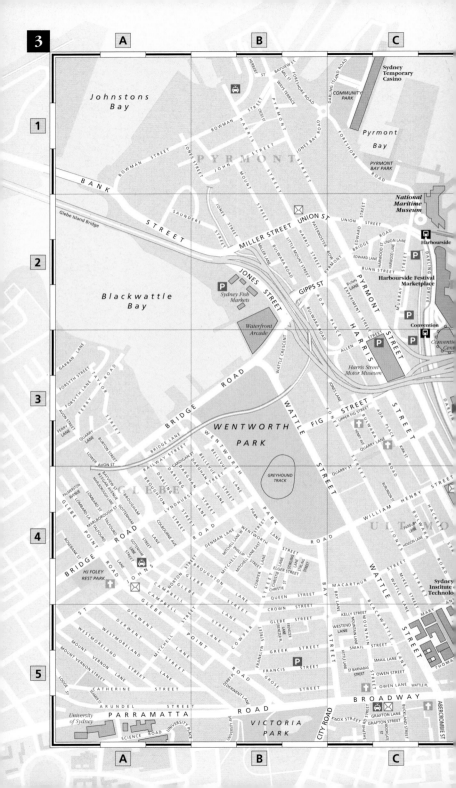

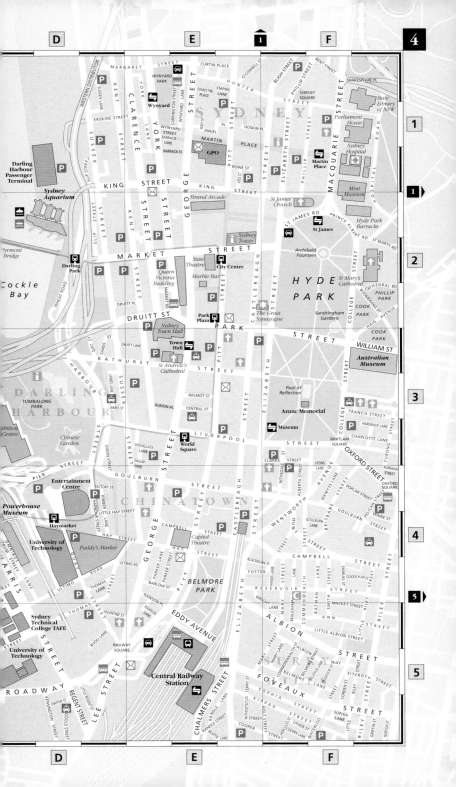

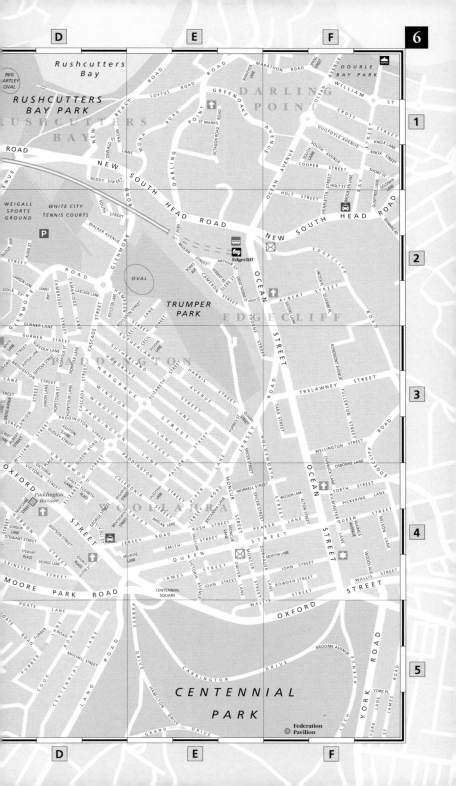

Street Finder Index

A

Abercrombie Street	3 C5
Ada Place	3 B2
Albert Square	6 D3
Albert Street	
(Edgecliff)	6 F2
Albert Street	
(Paddington)	6 D3
Albert Street	
(Sydney)	1 C3
Alberta Street	4 F4
Albion Avenue	5 A3
Albion Place	4 E3
Albion Street	4 F5
continues	5 A3
Albion Way	4 F5
Alexander Street	
(Paddington)	5 C4
Alexander Street	
(Surry Hills)	5 A4
Alexandra Lane	5 A5
Alfred Street	1 B3
Allen Street	3 C3
Alma Street	6 D2
Alton Street	6 F4
Amos Lane	5 C1
Angel Place	1 B4
continues	4 E1
Ann Street	4 F5
Anzac Parade	5 B4
Argyle Centre	1 B2
Argyle Place	1 A2
Argyle Street	1 A2
Arnold Place	5 A2
Art Gallery of New	
South Wales	2 D5
Art Gallery Road	1 C5
Arthur Lane	5 A4
Arthur Street	
(Edgecliff)	6 E2
Arthur Street	
(Surry Hills)	5 A4
Arundel Street	3 A5
Ash Street	1 B4
continues	4 E1
Ashton Lane	6 D3
Australian Museum	4 F3
Avon Street	3 A3

B

Bank Street	3 A1
Barcom Avenue	5 B2
Barlow Street	4 E4
Barncleuth Lane	5 C1
Barncleuth	
Square	5 C1
Barnett Lane	5 A1
Baroda Street	2 F5
Barrack Lane	1 A4
continues	4 E1
Barrack Street	1 A4
continues	4 E1
Bartlett Lane	5 B3
Bates Avenue	5 C3
Bathurst Street	4 D3
Batman Lane	4 F5
Bay Lane	3 C4
Bay Street	
(Double Bay)	6 F2
Bay Street (Glebe)	3 B4
Bayswater Road	5 B1
Bayview Street	
(Glebe)	3 A4

Bayview Street	
(Pyrmont)	3 B1
Beare Park	2 F5
Beattie Lane	4 E5
Beauchamp Lane	4 F5
Begg Lane	5 C3
Bellevue Lane	
(Glebe)	3 B3
Bellevue Lane	
(Surry Hills)	4 F5
Bellevue Street	
(Glebe)	3 B3
Bellevue Street	
(Surry Hills)	4 F5
Belmore Lane	4 F5
Belmore Park	4 E4
Belmore Place	5 C3
Belmore Street	4 F5
Bennett Place	5 A4
Bennett Street	5 A4
Bennetts Grove	
Avenue	6 D3
Bent Street	
(Paddington)	6 D4
Bent Street (Sydney)	1 B3
continues	4 F1
Berwick Lane	5 A1
Bethel Lane	5 B3
Bijou Lane	4 D5
Billyard Avenue	2 F4
Birtley Place	2 F5
Blackburn Street	4 E4
Blackwattle Lane	3 C4
Bland Street	2 D5
Bligh Street	1 B4
continues	4 F1
Bond Street	1 B3
Boomerang Street	1 C5
continues	4 F2
Bossley Terrace	2 D5
Boundary Lane	5 B2
	& 5 C2
Boundary Street	5 B2
Bourke Street	5 A5
Bowden Street	6 F4
Bowes Avenue	6 E2
Bowman Street	3 A1
Bradfield Highway	1 B1
Bradley Lane	2 F5
Bridge Lane (Glebe)	3 A3
Bridge Lane	
(Sydney)	1 B3
Bridge Road (Glebe)	3 A4
Bridge Street	1 B3
Brisbane Street	4 F4
Britannia Lane	6 E4
Broadway	3 C5
Brodie Street	5 C3
Brooklyn Lane	6 F2
Broome Avenue	6 F5
Brougham Lane	
(Glebe)	3 A4
Brougham Lane	
(Potts Point)	5 B1
Brougham Street	2 E5
continues	5 B1
Broughton Lane	3 B4
Broughton Street	
(Glebe)	3 A4
Broughton Street	
(Paddington)	6 D3
Brown Lane	5 C2
Brown Street	5 C3
Browns Place	5 C2
Buckland Street	3 C5

Bulletin Place	1 B3
Bulwara Road	3 B2
Bunn Lane	3 C2
Bunn Street	3 C2
Burdekin Lane	5 A4
Burlinson Street	3 C4
Burnell Place	5 A1
Burrahore Lane	5 A1
Burton Street	
(Darlinghurst)	5 A2
Burton Street (Glebe)	3 A3
Busby Lane	5 A1

C

Cadman's Cottage	1 B2
Cahill Expressway	1 B3
Caldwell Street	5 B1
Caledonia Lane	6 E4
Caledonia Street	6 D4
Cambridge Lane	6 D2
Cambridge Street	6 D2
Cameron Street	6 E2
Campbell Avenue	5 B2
Campbell Lane	3 A4
Campbell Street	
(Glebe)	3 A4
Campbell Street	
(Haymarket)	4 E4
Campbell Street	
(Surry Hills)	5 A2
Campbell's	
Storehouses	1 B2
Capitol Theatre	4 E4
Cardigan Street	3 A4
Carrington Drive	6 E5
Carrington Street	1 A4
continues	4 E1
Cascade Lane	6 D2
Cascade Street	6 D3
Castlereagh Street	1 B5
continues	4 E5
Cathedral Road	1 C5
continues	4 F2
Cathedral Street	2 D5
Catherine Street	3 A5
Cecil Lane	6 E3
Cecil Street	6 E3
Centennial Lane	6 D5
Centennial Park	6 E5
Centennial Square	6 E4
Central Railway	
Station	4 E5
Central Street	4 E3
Centre for Contem-	
porary Craft	1 B2
Challis Avenue	2 E4
Chalmers Street	4 E5
Chapel Street	5 A1
Chaplin Street	5 B2
Chapman Lane	5 A4
Chapman Street	5 A4
Charles Street	
(Surry Hills)	5 A5
Charles Street	
(Woolloomooloo)	2 D5
Charlotte Lane	4 F3
Chelsea Street	5 A5
Chifley Square	1 B4
continues	4 F1
Chinatown	4 D4
Chinese Garden	4 D3
Chisholm Street	5 A3
Chiswick Lane	6 F3
Christie Lane	3 B4

Christie Street	3 B4
Church Place	6 D4
Church Street	5 A3
Circular Quay East	1 C3
City Road	3 B5
Clapton Place	5 B1
Clare Street	5 A3
Clarence Street	1 A4
continues	4 E1
Clarke Street	4 F3
Clement Street	5 C1
Cleveland Street	5 A5
Clifton Reserve	5 A3
Colbourne Avenue	3 A4
College Street	1 C5
continues	4 F3
Collins Lane	5 A4
Collins Street	5 A4
Comber Street	5 B3
Commonwealth	
Street	4 F5
Community Park	3 C1
Conservatorium of	
Music	1 C3
Conservatorium	
Road	1 C3
Convention and	
Exhibition Centre	3 C3
Cook Park	1 C5
continues	4 F2
Cook Road	6 D5
Cooper Lane	4 F5
Cooper Street	
(Double Bay)	6 F1
Cooper Street	
(Paddington)	5 C2
Cooper Street	
(Surry Hills)	4 E5
Corben Street	4 F5
Corfu Street	5 A1
Coulton Lane	5 A4
Cow Lane	5 B2
Cowper Lane	3 B4
Cowper Street	3 B5
Cowper Wharf	
Roadway	2 D5
Craigend Street	5 B1
Crane Place	1 B3
Crick Avenue	2 E5
Cross Lane	2 D5
Cross Street	
(Pyrmont)	3 B1
Cross Street	
(Double Bay)	6 F1
Crown Lane	5 A1
Crown Street	
(Glebe)	3 B5
Crown Street	
(Woolloomooloo)	2 D5
continues (Surry	
Hills)	5 A3
Cumberland Street	1 A3
Curtin Place	1 B4
continues	4 E1
Customs House	1 B3

D

Dalgety Road	1 A2
Dalley Street	1 B3
Darghan Lane	3 B3
Darghan Street	3 A3
Darley Place	5 B2
Darley Street	5 B2
Darling Drive	3 C2

Darling Harbour
  Passenger
  Terminal   **1 A4 & 4D1**
Darling Island Road   **3 C1**
Darling Lane   **3 A4**
Darling Point Road   **6 E1**
Darling Street   **3 A4**
Darlinghurst Court
  House   **5 A2**
Darlinghurst Road   **5 A2**
Davies Street   **5 A4**
Davoren Lane   **5 A4**
Dawes Point Park   **1 B1**
Day Street   **4 D3**
Demestre Place   **1 B4**
  continues   **4 E1**
Denham Street   **5 A3**
Denman Lane   **3 B4**
Derby Place   **3 B5**
Derwent Lane   **3 A5**
Derwent Street   **3 A5**
Devonshire Street   **5 A4**
Dillon Lane   **5 C2**
Dillon Street   **5 C2**
Dixon Street   **4 D3**
Domain, The   **1 C4**
Dorhauer Lane   **6 E4**
Double Bay Park   **6 F1**
Douglass Lane   **4 E3**
Dowling Street   **2 D5**
  continues   **5 B1**
Downshire Street   **1 A2**
Driver Avenue   **5 B4**
Druitt Lane   **4 D3**
Druitt Place   **1 A5**
  continues   **4 D2**
Druitt Street   **1 A5**
  continues   **5 E2**
Dudley Street   **6 D3**
Duxford Street   **6 D3**
Dwyer Lane   **6 E4**
Dwyer Street   **4 D5**

E

Eagar Lane   **4 E3**
Earl Place   **5 B1**
Earl Street   **2 E5**
  continues   **5 B1**
Ebenezer Lane   **3 B5**
Ebenezer Place   **3 B5**
Eddy Avenue   **4 E5**
Edgecliff Road   **6 F2**
Edgely Street   **5 A5**
Edward Lane   **3 C2**
Edward Street   **3 C2**
Egan Place   **5 A1**
El Alamein Fountain   **2 E5**
Elfred Street   **5 C3**
Elger Street   **3 B4**
Elizabeth Bay House   **2 F5**
Elizabeth Bay Road   **2 F5**
Elizabeth Place   **6 D4**
Elizabeth Street
  (Paddington)   **6 D4**
Elizabeth Street
  (Sydney)   **1 B5**
  continues   **4 E5**
Empire Lane   **1 B4**
  continues   **4 E1**
Entertainment Centre   **4 D4**
Erskine Street   **1 A4**
  continues   **4 D1**
Esplanade   **2 F5**
Essex Street   **1 A3**
Esther Street   **5 A4**
Evans Road   **2 F5**
Experiment Street   **3 C2**

F

Factory Street   **4 D4**
Fanny Place   **5 A4**
Farrell Avenue   **5 B1**
Faucett Lane   **5 A1**
Ferry Lane   **3 A3**
Ferry Road   **3 A3**
Fig Street   **3 B3**
Fitzroy Place   **5 A3**
Fitzroy Street   **4 F5**
  continues   **5 A3**
Five Ways   **5 C3**
Flemings Lane   **5 A3**
Flinders Street   **5 A3**
Floods Lane   **5 A3**
Foley Street   **5 A2**
Forbes Street
  (Darlinghurst)   **5 A2**
Forbes Street
  (Paddington)   **6 E3**
Foreshore Road   **3 B1**
Forsyth Lane   **3 A3**
Forsyth Street   **3 A3**
Fort Denison   **2 E1**
Forth Street   **6 F4**
Foster Street   **4 E4**
Foveaux Street   **4 E5**
  continues   **5 A3**
Francis Lane   **5 A1**
Francis Street
  (Darlinghurst)   **4 F3**
Francis Street
  (Glebe)   **3 B5**
  continues   **5 A1**
Franklyn Street   **3 B5**
Fullerton Street   **6 F3**
Furber Lane   **6 D5**
Furber Road   **6 D5**

G

Garran Lane   **3 A3**
Garrison Church   **1 A2**
George Lane   **6 D4**
George Street
  (Paddington)   **6 D4**
George Street
  (Sydney)   **1 B5**
  continues   **4 E4**
Gipps Street
  (Paddington)   **5 B3**
Gipps Street
  (Pyrmont)   **3 B2**
Glebe Island Bridge   **3 A2**
Glebe Lane   **3 A4**
Glebe Point Road   **3 A4**
Glebe Street
  (Edgecliff)   **6 E2**
Glebe Street (Glebe)   **3 A4**
Glen Street   **5 C2**
Glenmore Road   **5 B3**
Glenview Lane   **5 C2**
Glenview Street   **5 C2**
Gloucester Street   **1 B2**
Goderich Lane   **5 B1**
Goldman Lane   **6 F1**
Goodchap Street   **4 F4**
Goold Street   **4 D5**
Gordon Lane   **6 D4**
Gordon Street   **6 D4**
Gosbell Lane   **5 C2**
Gosbell Street   **5 C2**
Gottenham Lane   **3 A4**
Gottenham Street   **3 A4**
Goulburn Lane   **4 F4**
Goulburn Street   **4 D4**
  continues   **5 A2**

Government House   **1 C2**
G.P.O. (General Post
  Office)   **1 B4**
Grafton Lane   **3 C5**
Grafton Street   **3 C5**
Grand Drive   **6 E5**
Grantham Street   **2 E4**
Great Synagogue   **1 B5**
Great Thorne Street   **6 E2**
Greek Street   **3 B5**
Green Park   **5 B2**
Greenknowe Avenue   **2 E5**
Greenoaks Avenue   **6 E1**
Greens Road   **5 B3**
Gregory Avenue   **5 B5**
Gresham Street   **1 B3**
Griffin Street   **4 F5**
Griffiths Street   **2 D5**
Grose Street   **3 B5**
Grosvenor Street   **1 A3**
Guilfoyle Avenue   **6 F1**
Gumtree Lane   **6 F2**
Gurner Lane   **6 D2**
Gurner Street   **6 D3**

H

Hackett Street   **3 C4**
Haig Avenue   **1 C5**
  continues   **4 F2**
Haig Lane   **1 C5**
Halls Lane   **6 E4**
Hamilton Drive   **6 E5**
Hampden Street   **6 D2**
Hands Lane   **4 F4**
Hannam Street   **5 A3**
Harbour Street   **4 D3**
Harbourside Festival
  Marketplace   **1 C2**
Hardie Street   **5 B2**
Hargrave Lane
  (Darlinghurst)   **4 F3**
Hargrave Lane
  (Paddington)   **6 D3**
Hargrave Street   **6 D3**
Harmer Street   **2 D5**
Harnett Street   **2 E5**
Harrington Street   **1 B3**
Harris Street
  (Paddington)   **6 E3**
Harris Street
  (Pyrmont)   **3 B1**
Harris Street Motor
  Museum   **3 C3**
Harwood Lane   **3 C2**
Harwood Street   **3 C2**
Hay Street   **4 D4**
Hayden Lane   **5 B2**
Hayden Place   **5 B2**
Heeley Lane   **5 C3**
Heeley Street   **5 C3**
Henrietta Street   **6 F2**
Henry Avenue   **3 C3**
Henson Lane   **3 C4**
Herbert Road   **6 E2**
Herbert Street   **3 B1**
Hercules Street   **4 F5**
Hero of Waterloo   **1 A2**
Hickson Road   **1 A2**
High Lane   **1 A2**
High Street
  (Edgecliff)   **6 E2**
High Street
  (Millers Point)   **1 A2**
Hill Street   **5 A3**
H.J. Foley Rest Park   **3 A4**
Hoddle Street   **6 D2**
Holdsworth Avenue   **2 F5**

Holdsworth Street   **6 E3**
Holt Street
  (Double Bay)   **6 F2**
Holt Street
  (Surry Hills)   **4 F5**
Hopetoun Lane   **6 D3**
Hopetoun Street   **6 D3**
Hopewell Lane   **5 B3**
Hopewell Street   **5 B3**
Hoskin Place   **1 B4**
  continues   **4 E1**
Hospital Road   **1 C5**
  continues   **4 F2**
Hourigan Lane   **2 E5**
Hughes Lane   **2 E5**
Hughes Place   **2 E5**
Hughes Street   **2 E5**
Hunt Street   **4 F4**
Hunter Street   **1 B4**
  continues   **4 E1**
Hutchinson Lane   **5 A3**
Hutchinson Street   **5 A3**
Hyde Park   **4 F2**
Hyde Park Barracks   **1 C5**

I

Ice Street   **5 B2**
Iris Street   **5 B4**
Ithaca Road   **2 F5**

J

James Lane
  (Darling Harbour)   **4 D3**
James Lane
  (Paddington)   **6 D2**
James Street
  (Darling Harbour)   **4 D3**
James Street
  (Woollahra)   **6 E4**
Jamison Street   **1 A3**
Jenkins Street   **1 A3**
Jersey Road   **6 D4**
Jesmond Street   **5 A3**
John Street
  (Pyrmont)   **3 B1**
John Street
  (Woollahra)   **6 E4**
Jones Bay Road   **3 B1**
Jones Lane   **3 C3**
Jones Street   **3 A1**
Josephson Street   **5 B4**
Judge Lane   **5 B1**
Judge Street   **5 B1**
Junction Lane   **2 D5**
Juniper Hall   **5 C3**
Justice and Police
  Museum   **1 C3**

K

Keegan Avenue   **3 A4**
Kellett Street   **5 B1**
Kells Lane   **5 A2**
Kelly Street   **3 C5**
Kendall Lane   **5 A4**
Kendall Street   **5 A4**
Kennedy Street   **5 A1**
Kensington Street   **4 D5**
Kent Street   **1 A2**
  continues   **4 D1**
Kettle Lane   **3 C5**
Kidman Lane   **5 B3**
Kilminster Lane   **6 F4**
Kimber Lane   **3 A4**
King Street   **1 A4**
  continues   **4 D1**

Kings Cross Road	5 B1	McGarvie Street	6 D4	Nesbitt Street	2 E5	Parramatta Road	3 A5
Kings Lane	5 A2	McKee Street	3 C4	New Beach Road	6 D1	Paternoster Row	3 B2
Kippax Street	4 E5	Mackey Street	4 F5	New McLean Street	6 E2	Peaker Lane	6 E4
Kirk Street	3 C3	McLachlan Avenue	5 C2	New South Head		Pelican Street	4 F4
Kirketon Road	5 B1	McLaughlan Place	5 C3	Road	6 D1	Pennys Lane	5 B1
Knox Lane	6 F1	Macleay Street	2 E5	Newcombe Street	6 D4	Perry Lane	5 C3
Knox Street		Macquarie Place	1 B3	Nichols Street	5 A3	Phelps Street	5 A4
(Chippendale)	3 C5	Macquarie Street	1 C4	Nicholson Street	2 D5	Phillip Lane	1 C4
Knox Street		*continues*	4 F1	Nickson Lane	5 A5	Phillip Park	1 C5
(Double Bay)	6 F1	Maiden Lane	5 A3	Nickson Street	5 A5	*continues*	4 F2
		Manning Road	6 F2	Nimrod Street	5 B1	Phillip Street (Glebe)	3 B4
		Manning Street	2 E5	Nithsdale Street	4 F4	Phillip Street	
L		Mansion Lane	5 C1	Nobbs Lane	5 A4	(Sydney)	1 B4
Lacrozia Lane	5 B2	Marathon Lane	6 E1	Nobbs Street	5 A4	*continues*	4 F1
Lands Department		Marathon Road	6 E1	Norfolk Lane	6 D3	Pickering Lane	6 F1
Building	1 B3	Marble Bar	1 B5	Norfolk Street	6 D3	Pier Street	4 D4
Lang Park	1 A3	Margaret Street	1 A4	Norman Street	4 F4	Pitt Street	1 B5
Lang Road	6 D5	*continues*	4 D1	Norton Street		*continues*	4 E4
Lang Street	1 A3	Market Road	1 A5	(Glebe)	3 A4	Plunkett Street	2 D5
Lawson Lane	6 D2	*continues*	4 E2	Norton Street		Poate Lane	6 D5
Lawson Street	5 C2	Market Street	1 A5	(Surry Hills)	4 F5	Poate Road	6 D5
Lee Street	4 D5	*continues*	4 D2			Point Piper Lane	6 E4
Lees Court	1 B4	Marlborough Lane	3 A4			Poplar Street	4 F4
continues	4 E1	Marlborough Street	3 A4	**O**		Pottinger Street	1 A2
Leichhardt Street	5 B2	Marshall Street	5 A4	O'Briens Lane	5 A1	Powerhouse	
Leinster Street	5 C4	Martin Place	1 B4	O'Connell Street	1 B4	Museum	4 D4
Lincoln Court	2 D4	*continues*	4 E1	*continues*	4 E1	Premier Lane	5 B1
Lincoln Place	6 F2	Martin Street	5 C4	O'Loughlin Street	4 E5	Prince Albert Road	1 C5
Lindsay Lane	5 C2	Mary Ann Street	3 C5	O'Sheas Lane	5 A3	*continues*	4 F2
Little Albion Street	4 F5	Mary Lane	4 F5	Oatley Road	5 C4	Pring Street	2 E5
Little Bloomfield		Mary Place	5 B3	Observatory Park	1 A2	Prospect Street	
Street	5 A2	Mary Street	4 E5	Ocean Avenue	6 F2	(Paddington)	5 B3
Little Bourke Street	5 A2	Melrose Lane	6 D4	Ocean Street	6 E2	Prospect Street	
Little Cleveland		Merchants' House	1 B2	Octagon Road	6 E1	(Surry Hills)	5 A4
Street	5 A5	Mill Street	3 B1	Olive Street	5 C3	Pyrmont Bay Park	3 C1
Little Comber Street	5 B3	Miller Lane	3 B2	Olivia Lane	5 A4	Pyrmont Bridge	1 A5
Little Dowling Street	5 A3	Miller Street	3 B2	Omnibus Lane	4 D4	*continues*	4 D2
Little Hay Street	4 D4	Mitchell Lane East	3 B4	Old Gaol,		Pyrmont Bridge	
Little Mount Street	3 B2	Mitchell Lane West	3 B4	Darlinghurst	5 A2	Road	3 B2
Little Oxford Street	5 A2	Mitchell Street		Onslow Avenue	2 F5	Pyrmont Street	3 B1
Little Regent Street	4 D5	(Centennial Park)	6 D5	Onslow Place	2 F5		
Little Riley Street	4 F5	Mitchell Street		Ormond Street	5 C3		
Little Stewart Street	5 C4	(Glebe)	3 A5	Orwell Lane	2 E5	**Q**	
Little Surrey Street	5 B2	Mona Lane	6 D1	Orwell Street	2 E5	Quambi Place	6 F2
Liverpool Lane	5 A1	Mona Road	6 E1	Osborne Lane	6 F4	Quarry Lane (Glebe)	3 A3
Liverpool Street	4 E3	Moncur Lane	6 E4	Oswald Street	6 D1	Quarry Lane	
continues		Moncur Street	6 E4	Overseas Passenger		(Ultimo)	3 C3
(Darlinghurst)	5 A1	Moore Park	5 A4	Terminal	1 B2	Quarry Street	
Liverpool Street		Moore Park Road	5 B4	Owen Lane	3 C5	(Paddington)	6 E3
(Paddington)	5 C3	Moorgate Street	3 C5	Owen Street	3 C5	Quarry Street	
Loch Avenue	6 F5	Morrell Street	6 E4	Oxford Square	4 F4	(Ultimo)	3 C4
Lodge Street	3 A5	Mort Lane	5 A5	Oxford Street	4 F3	Quay Street	4 D4
Loftus Lane	1 B3	Mort Street	5 A5	*continues*	5 A2	Queen Road	6 D4
Loftus Road	6 E1	Morton Lane	6 F4			Queen Street	
Loftus Street	1 B3	Mount Street	3 B1			(Glebe)	3 B4
Lombard Lane	3 A4	Mount Vernon Lane	3 A5	**P**		Queen Street	
Lombard Street	3 A4	Mount Vernon Street	3 A5			(Woollahra)	6 E4
Lower Avon Street	3 A3	Mountain Lane	3 C5	Paddington Bazaar	3 C5	Queen Victoria	
Lower Fort Street	1 A2	Mountain Street	3 C5	Paddington Lane	6 D3	Building	1 B5
Lyndhurst Street	3 A4	Mrs Macquaries		Paddington Street	6 D3	Queens Avenue	5 C1
Lyons Lane	4 F3	Chair	2 E2	Paddington Town		Queens Square	1 C5
		Mrs Macquaries		Hall	5 C3		
		Road	2 D4	Paddington Village	5 C3		
M		Murray Street	3 C2	Paddy's Market	4 D4	**R**	
Macarthur Avenue	5 B5	Museum of		Palmer Lane	5 A1	Rae Place	2 E5
Macarthur Street	3 C4	Contemporary Art	1 B2	Palmer Street	2 D5	Railway Square	4 D5
Macdonald Lane		Museum of Sydney	1 B3	*continues*	5 A2	Railway Street	3 A4
(Paddington)	5 C2			Palmerston Avenue	3 A4	Rainford Street	5 A4
McDonald Lane				Parbury Lane	3 C4	Randle Lane	4 E5
(Potts Point)	2 E4	**N**		Park Lane	3 B4	Randle Street	4 E5
Macdonald Street		Napier Street	5 B3	Park Street	4 E2	Raper Street	5 A4
(Paddington)	5 B2	Napoleon Street	1 A3	Parker Lane	4 E4	Rawson Lane	4 E5
McDonald Street		National Maritime		Parker Street	4 E4	Rawson Place	4 E4
(Potts Point)	2 E4	Museum	3 C2	Parkes Drive	6 E5	Reddy Street	6 D1
McElhone Place	5 A4	National Trust		Parkham Lane	5 A4	Regent Street	
McElhone Street	2 E5	Centre	1 A3	Parkham Place	5 A5	(Chippendale)	4 D5
continues	5 B1	Neild Avenue	5 C2	Parkham Street	5 A5	Regent Street	
		Nelson Lane	6 F4	Parliament House	1 C4	(Paddington)	5 C4

Reiby Place | 1 B3
Renny Lane | 5 C4
Renny Street | 5 C4
Reservoir Street | 4 E4
Richards Avenue | 5 A4
Richards Lane | 5 A4
Ridge Lane | 5 A5
Ridge Place | 5 A5
Ridge Street | 5 A5
Riley Street | 1 C5
  continues | 5 A2
Rockwall Crescent | 2 E5
Rockwall Lane | 2 E5
Rodens Lane | 1 A2
Rosebank Street | 3 A4
Rosella Lane | 5 A1
Rosemont Avenue | 6 F3
Roslyn Gardens | 2 F5
  continues | 5 C1
Roslyn Lane | 5 C1
Roslyn Street | 5 C1
Rowe Lane | 5 C3
Rowe Street | 1 B4
  continues | 4 E1
Royal Agricultural
  Society (R.A.S.)
  Showground | 5 C5
Royal Botanic
  Gardens | 1 C3
Roylston Lane | 6 D2
Rush Street | 6 E4
Rushcutters Bay Park | 6 D1
Ryder Street | 5 A2

S

Sailors' Home | 1 B2
St. Andrew's
  Cathedral | 4 E3
St. Barnabas Street | 3 C5
St. James' Church | 1 B5
St. James Road | 1 B5
  continues | 4 F2
St. James Road | 6 F5
St. Johns Road | 3 A5
St. Marks Road | 6 E1
St. Mary's Cathedral | 1 C5
St. Marys Road | 1 C5
  continues | 4 F2
St. Neot Avenue | 2 E4
St. Peters Lane | 5 A1
St. Peters Street | 5 A1
St. Philip's Church | 1 A3
Samuel Street | 4 F4
Sandringham
  Gardens | 1 C5
  continues | 4 F2
Sands Street | 4 D3
Saunders Street | 3 A2
Science Road | 3 A5
Seale Street | 5 A1
Seamer Street | 3 A5
Selwyn Street | 5 B3
Seymour Place | 5 A3
Shadforth Street | 5 C3
Shakespeare Place | 1 C4
  continues | 4 F1
Shepherd Street | 3 C5
Sherbrooke Street | 5 A2
Short Street
  (Darling Point) | 6 F1
Short Street
  (Paddington) | 5 A3
Shorter Lane | 5 A1
Sims Street | 5 A3
Sir John Young
  Crescent | 2 D5
Sisters Lane | 6 F2

Slip Street | 1 A5
  continues | 4 D2
Smail Lane | 3 C5
Smail Street | 3 C5
Smith Street
  (Surry Hills) | 4 F5
Smith Street
  (Woollahra) | 6 E4
Sophia Lane | 4 F5
Sophia Street | 4 E5
Soudan Lane | 6 E3
South Avenue | 6 F1
South Dowling Street | 5 A5
South Lane | 6 F1
South Street | 6 D2
Spence Lane | 5 A1
Spicer Street | 6 E3
Spring Street
  (Double Bay) | 6 F1
Spring Street
  (Paddington) | 5 B3
Springfield Avenue | 2 E5
Stafford Lane | 5 C3
Stafford Street | 5 C3
Stanley Lane | 5 A1
Stanley Street
  (Darlinghurst) | 5 A1
Stanley Street
  (Redfern) | 5 A5
State Library of NSW | 1 C4
State Theatre | 1 B5
Stephen Lane | 5 C2
Stephen Street | 5 C2
Stewart Place | 6 D4
Stewart Street | 5 C4
Stirling Lane | 3 B4
Stirling Street | 3 B4
Strand Arcade | 1 B5
Stream Street | 5 A1
Sturt Street | 5 A2
Suffolk Street | 6 D3
Surrey Lane | 5 B1
Surrey Street | 5 B1
Susannah Place | 1 B2
Sussex Lane | 1 A4
  continues | 4 D1
Sussex Street | 1 A3
  continues | 4 D1
Sutherland Avenue | 6 D3
Sutherland Street | 6 D3
Suttor Street | 5 A1
Sydney Aquarium | 1 A5
  | & 4 D1
Sydney Cricket
  Ground | 5 C5
Sydney Fish Market | 3 B2
Sydney Football
  Stadium | 5 C4
Sydney Harbour
  Bridge | 1 B1
Sydney Harbour
  Tunnel | 1 C2
Sydney Hospital | 1 C4
Sydney Jewish
  Museum | 5 B2
Sydney Mint
  Museum | 1 C4
Sydney Observatory | 1 A2
Sydney Opera House | 1 C2
Sydney Tower | 1 B5
Sydney Town Hall | 4 E2
Systrum Street | 4 D4

T

Talbot Place | 5 A1
Talfourd Lane | 3 A4
Talfourd Street | 3 A4

Tara Street | 6 F3
Taylor Square | 5 A2
Taylor Street (Glebe) | 3 A3
Taylor Street
  (Paddington) | 6 E4
Taylor Street
  (Surry Hills) | 5 A3
Terry Street | 4 E5
Tewkesbury Avenue | 5 B1
Thomas Lane | 4 D4
Thomas Street | 3 C5
Thomson Lane | 6 F1
Thomson Street | 5 A2
Thorne Street | 6 E2
Thurlow Lane | 5 A5
Tivoli Street | 6 D4
Towns Place | 1 A2
Trelawney Street | 6 F3
Trinity Avenue | 1 A2
Trumper Park | 6 E2
Tumbalong Park | 4 D3
Turner Lane | 2 D5
Tusculum Lane | 2 E5
Tusculum Street | 2 E5

U

Ulster Street | 6 D4
Ultimo Road | 4 D4
Underwood Street
  (Paddington) | 5 C3
Underwood Street
  (Sydney) | 1 B3
Union Lane
  (Paddington) | 6 D3
Union Lane
  (Pyrmont) | 3 C2
Union Street
  (Paddington) | 6 D3
Union Street
  (Pyrmont) | 3 B2
University Avenue | 3 B5
University Place | 3 A5
University of Sydney | 3 A5
Upper Fig Street | 3 C5
Upper Fort Street | 1 A2
Uther Street | 4 F5

V

Valentine Street | 4 D5
Vaughan Place | 5 A5
Verona Street | 5 B3
Vialoux Avenue | 6 D2
Vials Lane | 6 D4
Victoria Avenue | 6 E4
Victoria Barracks | 5 B4
Victoria Park | 3 B5
Victoria Place | 6 D4
Victoria Street
  (Paddington) | 6 D4
Victoria Street
  (Potts Point) | 2 E5
  continues | 5 B2

W

Waimea Avenue | 6 F4
Waine Street | 4 F4
Walker Avenue | 6 D2
Walker Lane | 5 C3
Walker Street | 5 C3
Wallis Street | 6 E5
Walter Street | 5 C4
Waratah Street | 5 C1
Ward Avenue | 5 C1
Waterloo Street | 4 F5
Watson Road | 1 A2
Watson Street | 6 D4

Wattle Crescent | 3 B3
Wattle Lane | 3 C4
Wattle Place | 3 C5
Wattle Street | 3 B3
Ways Terrace | 3 B1
Weedon Avenue | 5 C3
Weldon Lane | 6 F4
Wellington Street | 6 F3
Wemyss Lane | 4 F4
Wentworth Avenue | 4 F4
Wentworth Park | 3 B3
Wentworth Park
  Road | 3 B3
Wentworth Street
  (Glebe) | 3 B4
Wentworth Street
  (Paddington) | 6 D4
West Avenue | 5 B2
West Lane | 5 B2
West Street | 5 B3
Westend Lane | 3 C5
Western Distributor | 1 A4
  continues | 4 D1
Westmoreland Lane | 3 A5
Westmoreland Street | 3 A5
Westpac Museum | 1 B2
Wharf Theatre | 1 A1
Wheat Road | 1 A5
  continues | 4 D2
Whelan Lane | 6 E4
White Lane | 6 D3
Whitlam Square | 4 F3
William Henry Street | 3 C4
William Lane | 5 A1
William Street
  (Darlinghurst) | 4 F3
  continues | 5 A1
William Street
  (Double Bay) | 6 F1
William Street
  (Paddington) | 6 D3
Wilmot Street | 4 E3
Wilson Street | 2 D5
Windmill Street | 1 A2
Windsor Lane | 6 D3
Windsor Street | 6 D3
Wisdom Lane | 5 A1
Womerah Avenue | 5 B2
Womerah Lane | 5 C2
Woods Avenue | 6 F4
Woods Lane | 5 A1
Woolloomooloo
  Finger Wharf | 2 D4
Wright Lane | 4 E4
Writers' Walk | 1 C2
Wylde Street | 2 E4
Wynyard Lane | 1 B4
  continues | 4 E1
Wynyard Park | 1 A4
  continues | 4 E1
Wynyard Street | 1 A4
  continues | 4 E1

Y

York Lane | 1 A4
  continues | 4 E1
York Lane
  (Bondi Junction) | 6 F5
York Place | 6 F5
York Road | 6 F5
York Street | 1 A4
  continues | 4 E1
Young Street | 1 B3
Young Street
  (Paddington) | 5 C3
Yurong Lane | 5 A1
Yurong Street | 4 F3

General Index

Page numbers in **bold** type refer to main entries.

A

Abbey's Bookshop 206, 207
Aboriginal Islander Dance Theatre 213
Aboriginal and Tribal Art Centre 206, 207
Aboriginal peoples
  art 154, 206, 207
  community 41, 42
  culture 34
  land rights 29
  rock art 18–19, 154
Academy Twin 210, 211
ACE 213
ACROD NSW 169, 170
Across the black soil plains (Lambert) 110
Admiralty House 132
AGLTA (Australian Gay and Lesbian Travel Association) 170
Air New Zealand 229
Air travel 228–9
Airport information 229
Albury Hotel 214, 215
Alishan Guesthouse 170
All Seasons Menzies 172, **174**
Allan, Percy 98
Aloha Surf 54
American (US) Consulate General 221
American Express 224
AMP Building 63
ANA Hotel Sydney 172, **174**
Andrew (Boy) Charlton Pool 57, 105
Anglican Church 221
Angus and Robertson's Bookworld 206, 207
Annandale Hotel 214, 215
Ansett Australia 228, 229
Anzac Day 50, 84
Anzac Memorial **86**
  history 27
  Sydney's Best 36, 39
Apartment agencies 170
Archibald Fountain 79, 86
Archibald Prize 26
Archibald, Wynne, Sulman, and Dobell Exhibitions 50
Architecture **36–9**
  Elizabeth Bay House 22–3
  Sydney Opera House 75
Argyle Centre 38, **68**
Argyle Cut 64
Ariel (bookshop) 206, 207
Arizona Bar and Restaurant 196, 197

Armstrong's Manly 187, **189**
The Arrest of Bligh 21
Art Gallery of New South Wales 15, **108–111**
  area map 103
  Asian art 111
  Australian art 110
  contemporary art 111
  European art 110
  photography 110
  prints and drawings 111
  Sydney's Best 33, 34
  Yiribana Gallery 111
Art Gallery Restaurant 194, 195
Aurora Blessing of the Fleet 48
Aurora New World Festival 48
Ausfurs 206, 207
Aussie Boys (shop) 204, 205
Australia Cinema 210, 211
Australia Day 51
Australia Day Concert 49, 214, 215
Australia Ensemble 212, 213
Australia Square 39
Australian Antique Dealers Fair 50
Australian Ballet, The 213
Australian Beach Pattern (Meere) 33
Australian Book Fair 51
Australian Chamber Orchestra 212, 213
Australian Craftworks 206, 207
Australian Cycle Company, The 237
Australian Museum **88–9**
  shop 206, 207
  Sydney's Best 33, 34–5
Australian Opera 212
Austalian Pacific Tours 219
Australian rules football 52
Australian Sailing School and Club 54
Australian Tourist Commission Offices 218
Australian Women's Weekly 27
Australian Youth Choir 213
Australiana 206, 207
Automatic cash dispensers 224
Autumn Racing Carnival 50
Autumn in Sydney 50
Avalon 55
Avis 236, 237
AWA Radiolette 27
Axis (nightclub) 214, 215

B

Baby changing facilities 221
Bacon, Francis
  Study for Self Portrait 110
The Balcony (2) (Whiteley) 110

Bally 205
Balmain **131**
  market 131, **203**
  Birchgrove 143
  court house 143
  Darling Street 142–3
  East Balmain 142
  fire station 143
  guided walk 142–3
  post office 143
  town hall 143
Balmoral 54, 55
Balmoral Sailboard School 54
Bandemonium 51
Bangarra Dance Theatre 42, 213
Bank of New South Wales 22
Bank notes 225
Banking 224
Banks, Sir Joseph 17, 138
Baptist church 221
Bar Coluzzi 194, 195
  Sydney's Best 185
Bar Paradiso 194, 195
Barfly 194, 195
Barnaby's Riverside 187, **188**
Barnet, James 72
  Australian Museum 88
  Lands Department Building 84
Barney, Lieutenant Colonel George 127
Barrier Free Travel 169, 170
Barrington 20
Barton, Edmond 26
Bars *see* Pubs and bars
Basement, The 214, 215
The Basin 55, 155
Basketball 52
Bass, George 21
Bat and Ball Hotel 211
Bathers Pavilion (restaurant) 187, **188**
Bayswater Brasserie 186, **189**
  Sydney's Best 185
Beaches 54–5
  map 55
  Sydney's Top 30 Beaches 55
Beauchamp Hotel 214, 215
Beare Park **120**, 121
Beccafumi, Domenico
  Madonna and Child with Infant St. John the Baptist 108
Beckmann, Max
  Old Woman in Ermine 110
Bed and Breakfast Sydneyside 170
Bell Shakespeare Company, The 210, 211
Bellevue Hotel 196, 197
Belvoir Street Theatre 210, 211
Bennelong 20
Bennelong Restaurant 186, **189**
  Sydney's Best 184

Bentley Bar 214, 215
Beppi's 186, **192**
Beyond Sydney 151–65
  area map 152–3
  Blue Mountains 160–61
  Hawkesbury 156–7
  Hunter Valley 158–9
  Pittwater and Ku-ring-gai
    Chase 154–5
  Royal National Park 164–5
  Southern Highlands 162–3
Bibb, John 66
Bicentenary 28
Bicentennial Park 44
Bicycles 53, **237**
Biennale of Sydney 51
Big Day Out 49, 214, 215
Bilgola 55, 155
Bill's (café) 194, 195
Birchgrove
  Balmain Walk 143
  park 143
Birdland (shop) 206–7
Birtley Towers 119
Bistro Moncur 187, **193**
Black Vanity 204, 205
Blacket, Edmund 87
  Garrison Church 69
  Justice and Police Museum 72
  St. Philip's Church 73
  University of Sydney 130
Bligh, Governor William 20
Bligh House 38
Blue Mountains National Park
  160–61
  camping 170, 171
  Cathedral of Ferns 161
  Govett's Leap 160
  Grose River 160
  history 18
  Jamison Valley 161
  Jenolan Caves 160
  King's Tableland 161
  Leura 161
  map 160–61
  Mount Tomah Botanic
    Gardens 161
  Mount Wilson 161
  The Three Sisters 160
  Wentworth Falls 161
  Yester Grange 161
  Zig Zag Railroad 160
Blue Mountains Adventure
  Company 53
Boats
  The Borrowdale 20
  The Bounty 219
  Carpentaria 92, 95
  Dunbar 24, 136, 148
  Endeavour (replica), 95
  ferries **234–5**
  ferry sightseeing cruises 235

Boats (cont)
  harbor and river cruises 219
  HMB *Endeavour* 32
  HMS *Beagle* 23
  HMS *Sirius* 72
  Lady Juliana 20
  Matilda Cruises *(Solway Lass)*
    219
  National Maritime Museum 93,
    94–5
  Orcades 94
  Pittwater and Ku-ring-gai
    Chase **154–5**
  Royal National Park **164–5**
  sailing 54, 56
  Spirit of Australia 95
  Vampire 93, 95
  water taxis 235
  The Waverly 25
Boer War 24
Bondi Baths
  Bondi Beach to Clovelly Walk
    144
Bondi Beach **137**
  Aboriginal art 19
  baths 144
  beaches 54–5
  Campbell Parade 144
  guided walk 144–5
  Hotel Bondi 144
  map 129
  market **203**
  Pavilion 144
  Surf Bathers' Life Saving Club
    137, 144
Bondi Beach Coke Classic 49
Bondi Beach Serviced
  Apartments 170
Bondi Boards and Blades 53
Bondi North 144
Bondi Pavilion
  Bondi Beach to Clovelly Walk
    144
Bondi Surf Bathers' Life Saving
  Club 137, 144
Bondi Surf Co. 54
Bookshop, The 206, 207
Bookshops 206, 207
Boomerangs 19
Botanic Gardens and The
  Domain **102–15**
  area map 103
  hotels 172, **176**
  restaurants 186
  Street-by-Street map 104–5
Botanic Gardens Restaurant 186,
  188
  Sydney's Best 185
The Bounty 219
Bourbon and Beefsteak 196,
  197
Boy in Township (Nolan) 110

Boyd, Arthur 110
Box, The (café) 194, 195
Bracewell 204, 205
Bradfield, Dr John 71
Bradleys Head 45
Bradman, Donald 27
Breakfast Tours 170
Brett Whiteley Studio 34, **130**
Bridge to Bridge Power Boat
  Race 50
The Bridge in Curve
  (Cossington-Smith) 71
Bridge Hotel 214, 215
British Airways 229
British community 42
Bronte
  beaches 54–5
  Bronte Gully 145
  Bronte House 145
  Bronte Park 145
  Bondi Beach to Clovelly Walk
    144–5
Bruno Magli (shop) 205
Bubonic plague 59
Bungaree 23
Budget (car rental) 236, 237
The Bulletin 25
Bunny, Rupert
  A Summer Morning 110
  Summer Time 110
Bureaux de change 224
Burke (Nolan) 110
Buses **231**
  sightseeing by bus 231
  tickets 230–1
Busby's Bore 87
Busby, John 87

C

Cabaret venues 214, 215
Cabramatta 18, 40, 43
Cadman, John 68
  Street-by-Street map 65
Cadman, Elizabeth
  Street-by-Street map 65
Cadman's Cottage 68
  museums and galleries 35
  Street-by-Street map 65
  Sydney's Best 36, 38
Café at the Gate of Salvation 213
Café de Lane 214, 215
Cafés **178–85**, **194–5**
  coffee and tea 194, 195
  galleries and garden 194, 195
  snacks and light meals 194,
    195
  takeout food 195
Camp Cove
  beaches 54–5
  Watsons Bay and Vaucluse
    Walk 148

Campbell Parade
  Bondi Beach to Clovelly Walk
  144
Campbell, Robert 66, 139
Campbell's Storehouses **66**
Camping 170, 171
Canadian Airlines 229
Canadian Consulate General
  221
Capitol Theatre **99**
Captain Cook Cruises 219
Captain Cook's Landing Place
  138
Car rental companies 237
Carla Zampatti 204, 205
Carols in the Domain 49
Cars **236–7**
  car rental 236, 237
  driving in Sydney 236–7
  driving to Sydney 229
  driving regulations 236
  Infringement Processing
    Bureau 237
  parking 236
  Sydney Traffic Control Centre
    237
Castlereagh Inn 172, **174**
Castlereagh Street
  Sydney's Best 201
Cat and Fiddle 214, 215
Catholic church 221
Cauldron (nightclub) 214, 215
Cenotaph 84
  Street-by-Street map 81
Centennial Park 15, **127**
  cycling 53
  horseback riding 53
  Sydney's Best 45
Centennial Park Cycles 53, 237
Centennial Park Horse Hire and
  Riding School 53
Central Railway Station 218, 229
Central Station Records and
  Tapes 206, 207
Centrepoint 199
Centre for Contemporary Craft
  66
Centre for Leisure and Tourism
  Studies 169, 170
Chamber music 212
Charlies 196, 197
Charlton, Andrew "Boy" 27, 57
*Chaucer at the Court of Edward
  III* (Madox Brown) 110
Chauvel (cinema) 210, 211
Chifley Plaza 199
Children's theater 210, 211
Chinatown **99**
  Sydney's Best 200
Chinese community 41, 42
Chinese Garden **98**
Chinese New Year 49

Chisholm, Caroline 23, 25
Christmas at Bondi Beach 49
Churches
  Anglican church 221
  Baptist church 221
  Catholic church 221
  Garrison Church **68–9**
  Presbyterian church 221
  St. Andrew's Cathedral **87**
  St. Andrew's Church 143
  St. James' Church 36, 38, **115**
  St. Mary's Cathedral 25, 38, **86**
  St. Philip's Church **73**
  Uniting Church 221
Cicada (restaurant) 187, **188**
Circular Quay, The Rocks and
  city shoreline 59
City Center **79–89**
  area map 79
  hotels 172, **174–5**
  restaurants 186–7
  Street-by-Street map 80–81
  Sydney's Best 201
City Circle Railroad 87
City Crag Climbing Centre 53
City Mutual Life Assurance
  Building 39
City shoreline
  Garden Island to Farm Cove
    56–7
  Sydney Cove to Walsh Bay
    58–9
City to Surf Race 51
CityRail 232–3
CityRail Information 233
Claude's (restaurant) 187, **193**
  Sydney's Best 185
Clifton Gardens 55
Climate 48–51
Clontarf
  Balmain Walk 142
Clothes and accessories **204–5**
Cloud Nine Balloon Flights 219
Clovelly
  beaches 55
  Bondi Beach to Clovelly Walk
    145
Coach services 229
Coburn, John
  Curtain of the Moon 75
Coca-Cola World Sevens
  Tournament 49
Cockatoo Island 106
Cockle Bay 91
  flagpole 93
  Street-by-Street map 92–3
Coins 225
Collins Beach 147
Colonial history 35
Collette Dinnigan (shop) 204,
  205
Comedy Store 211

Comedy venues 211
Commonwealth Savings Bank
  39
Conder, Charles
  *Departure of the Orient –
    Circular Quay* 110
Conservatorium of Music **106**
  concerts 212, 213
Convention and Exhibition
  Centre (Darling Harbour) **98**
  Street-by-Street map 92
Coo-ee Aboriginal Art Gallery
  206, 207
Coogee 19
  beaches 54–5
Coogee Bay Hotel 214, 215
Coogee Surf Carnival 49
Cook, Captain James
  history 17, 138
Cook's Obelisk 138
Cooper Park Tennis Courts 53
Cooper, Robert 126
The Corso 146
The Cortile 196, 197
Cossington-Smith, Grace
  The Bridge in Curve 71
  Interior with Wardrobe Mirror
    110
Countrylink travel centers 168,
  170, 233
Country Comfort Sydney Central
  (hotel) 172, **175**
Country Road 204, 205
Courtney's Brasserie 187, **189**
Cox, Philip 39
Credit cards 224
Crescent on Bayswater (hotel)
  172, **176**
Cricket 52
  Donald Bradman 27
  test matches 49
  World Series 29
Cultures
  Aboriginal Peoples 18–19
  Sydney's Many Cultures
    40–43
Culwalla Chambers 26
Curl Curl 55
Currency 225
The Currency Lass (Geoghegan)
  23
Curtain of the Moon (Coburn)
  75
Customs House **72**
Cycling *see* Bicycles

D
Dame Mary Gilmore (Dobell)
  29
Dance **213**
Dance Exchange 213

Dangerfield (shop) 204, 205
Darc Swan 213
Darley Street Thai 178, 187, **191**
  Sydney's Best 185
No. 10 Darling Street
  Balmain Walk 142
Darling Street Wharf
  Balmain Walk 142
  ferry routes map 235
Darlinghurst Court House **121**
  Sydney's Best 37, 38
Darlinghurst and Surry Hills
  Sydney's Best 201
Darling Harbour **91–101**
  area map 91
  hotels 172, **175–6**
  restaurants 186
  Street-by-Street map 93
  Sydney's Best 200
  tourist information 218
Darling Mills 187, **188**
Darwin, Charles 23
David Jones 198, 199
  history 23
  men's clothes 204
  shoes 205
  women's clothes 204
David Jones Spring Flower
  Show 48
Dawn (Louisa Lawson) 25
Dawson, Alexander 72
Dayes, Edward
  A View of Sydney Cove 20
DCM (nightclub) 214, 215
Dee Why 55
Delfin House 39
Deli on Market 195
Dellit, Bruce 36, 39
Del Rio 117, 119
Dendy (cinemas) 210, 211
Dendy Bar 196, 197
Dentists 222, 223
Departure of the Orient –
  Circular Quay (Conder) 110
Departure tax 220
Desmond, a New South Wales
  Chief (Earle) 17
Destination Downunder 170
Dinosaur Designs 206, 207
Diprotodon 18, 33
Disabled travelers 220
  Barrier-Free Travel 169, 170
Discount agencies 170
Dive Centre Manly 54
Dixon Street 99
Dobell, William 110
  Dame Mary Gilmore 29
Dobell Memorial Sculpture
  (Flugelman) 84
The Domain 45, **107**, 212
  area map 103
Done Art and Design 206, 207

Dorchester Inn 172, **176**
Dorian Scott (shop) 204, 205
Dov (café) 194, 195
Doyle's Seafood Restaurant 136,
  148
Dragon Boat Race Festival 50
  Street-by-Street map 92
Drinking fountains 221
Driving regulations 236
Drysdale, Russell 110
  Sofala 108
Dugong Hunt
  (Wurrabadalumba) 34
Dunbar 24
  Watsons Bay 136, 148
Dupain, Max
  Sunbaker 108
Duxford Street
  Street-by-Street map 124
Dymocks 206, 207

E

Earle, Augustus
  Desmond, a New South Wales
  Chief 17
  View from the Summit 22
The Early Colony 20–21
Eastern Creek Raceway
  rock concerts 214, 215
Eastern Suburbs Railway 29
Eastcoast Motorcycle Tours 219
II Edna's Table 186, **188**
  Sydney's Best 184
The Edge (restaurant) 186, **189**
Edge Theatre 213
Edge of the Trees (Laurence and
  Foley) 85
Edward, Prince of Wales 26
El Alamein Fountain **120**
Electrical appliances 221
Elephant's Foot Hotel 196, 197
Elizabeth II, Queen 28
Elizabeth Bay 15, 119
Elizabeth Bay House **22–3**, **120**
  history 22–23
  Street-by-Street map 119
  Sydney's Best: Architecture 37,
  38
  Sydney's Best: Museums and
  Galleries 33, 35
Elizabeth Farm **138**
  colonial history 21, 35
Elston, Hocking and Woods 210,
  211
Embassies and consulates 221
  Canada 221
  New Zealand 221
  Republic of Ireland 221
  United Kingdom 221
  USA 221
Emden gun 87

Emergency services 223
Emporio Armani 204, 205
Endeavour, HMS 138
Enmore Theatre 214, 215
Ensemble Theatre 210, 211
Entertainment in Sydney
  208–15
  booking agencies 208
  buying tickets 208
  children's theatre
  comedy 211
  disabled visitors 209
  discount tickets 209
  gay and lesbian venues 214,
  215
  information 208, 209
  music venues and nightclubs
  214–15
  opera, orchestras and dance
  212–13
  theater and film 210–11
Environmental hazards 223
SH Ervin Gallery 73
Eternity, Mr. (Arthur Stace) 29
Etiquette 219
Eugene Goossens Hall 212, 213
Ewenton
  Balmain Walk 142
Exchange Hotel 214, 215
Experiment Farm Cottage **139**
  colonial history 21, 35

F

Fairfax and Roberts 206, 207
Fairy Bower 55, 146
Farm Cove 57
Fax services 226
Federation 26
Federation architecture 26
  Sydney's Best 38, 39
Female Factory 23
Ferries 230, **234–5**
  Bundeena 165
  Circular Quay Ferry Terminal
  234
  ferry tickets 234
  Hawkesbury River 153
  JetCat 234
  Portland 157
  RiverCat 234
  Sackville 156
  sightseeing by ferry 234
  Sydney Ferries Information
  Office 234
  Sydney Ferries Lost Property
  235
  Webbs Creek 157
  Wisemans 157
Ferrython 49
Festival of the Winds 48
Fez Café 186, **193**

Film 210, 211
Film censorship ratings 210
Film festivals 210–11
  Academy Twin 211
  Festival of Jewish Cinema 211
  Flickerfest International Short
    Film Festival 211
  Gay and Lesbian Film Festival
    211
  Sydney Film Festival 210
Firstcall 208, 209
The First Fleet 16, 20
First Fleet Ship (Holman) 20
Fishermans Beach 55
Fishface 186, **190**
Five Ways **126**
  Street-by-Street map 124
Flame Opals 206, 207
Flick's Café 194, 195
Flinders Hotel 214, 215
Flinders, Matthew 21, 22, 23
  cat statue (Trim) 112
Flugelman, Bert
  Dobell Memorial Sculpture 84
Flying Fruit Fly Circus 210, 211
Folkways 206, 207
Food and drink
  beers and spirits 179
  pubs and bars **196–7**
  what to drink 182–3
  what to eat 180–1
  see also Cafés; Restaurants
Footbridge Theatre 210, 211
Forbes Terrace 170
Foreign currency exchange 224
Fort Denison **107**
Forty One (restaurant) 186, **188**
The Founding of Australia
  (Talmage) 73
Foukes, Francis
  Sketch and Description of the
    Settlement of Sydney Cove 17
Franklin, Miles
  My Brilliant Career 26
Frattini 187, **192**
Freshwater 55
Fruit Bats (Onus) 111
Funnel-web spider 46, 223
  Australian Museum 89

G

Gallipoli 26
The Gap
  Watsons Bay 136
  Watsons Bay and Vaucluse
    Walk 148, 149
Garden Island 56
Garie Beach 153
Garigal National Park 44
Garrison Church **68–9**
  Street-by-Street map 64

Gastronomia Chianti 187, **192**
Gay and lesbian
  accommodations 170
  Film Festival 211
  Mardi Gras Festival 28, 49
  Mardi Gras Festival Dog
    Show 208
Gemstone Boutique 206, 207
General Pants Co. 204, 205
General Post Office (GPO) 38,
  84
Geoghegan, Edward
  The Currency Lass 23
The Georgian Era 22–3
Gibbs, May 35, 132
  Snugglepot and Cuddlepie 67,
    132
Ginger Meggs 67
Ginn, Henry 69
Giulian's 206, 207
Glasser, Neil 82
Glebe **131**
  market 131, **203**
Gleebooks 206, 207
Glenbrook Crossing 18
Glitz Bijouterie 206, 207
Glover, John
  Natives on the Ouse River, Van
    Diemen's Land 110
Golden Century (restaurant)
  186, **190**
The Golden Fleece – Shearing at
  Newstead (Roberts) 109, 110
Golden Gate (hotel) 172, **175**
Golden Harbour (restaurant)
  186, **190**
Gold rush 24
Golf 52
Gordons Bay 54, 55
Gotham Bar and Brasserie 187,
  189
Government House 58, **106**
Governor Phillip Tower 36, 39,
  85
Gowing Bros 199, 204–5
Grace Bros 198, 199
  shoes 204
  women's clothes 204
Grand National (hotel) 173, **176**
Grand Taverna 186, **193**
Great Australian Jumper
  Company 204, 205
Great Sydney Showground
  Antiques Fair 51
Great Synagogue 38, **86**
Greater Union (movie theater)
  210, 211
Greek community 41, 42
Green Bans 29, 120
Green Park Hotel 196, 197
Greenway, Francis **114**
  Conservatorium of Music 106

Greenway, Francis (cont)
  Hyde Park Barracks 114
  Macquarie Lighthouse 22, 137
  Macquarie Place obelisk 72
  St. James' Church 36
Greyhound Pioneer Australia
  229
de Groot, Francis 70
Grotto Point 45
Guide to Sydney for Travellers
  with Disabilities 169
Guided tours and excursions
  219
  air tours 219
  bus and motorcycle tours 219
  ferry sightseeing cruises 235
  harbor and river cruises 219
  walking tours 219
Gumbooya Reserve 19

H

Halftix 209
Hampton Villa
  Balmain Walk 142
Harbor cruises 58
  Captain Cook Cruises 219
  Quayside Booking Centre 235
Harbourside Apartments 173,
  177
Harbourside Brasserie 214,
  215
Harbourside Festival
  Marketplace 199
  Street-by-Street map 92
Hardy Brothers 206, 207
Harold Park Hotel 197
Hambledon Cottage 35, **139**
Hard Rock Café 194, 195
Harold Park Hotel 211
Harris Street Motor Museum 34,
  98
Harry's Café de Wheels 57, 195
Hawkesbury **156–7**
  Australiana Pioneer Village
    152, 156
Hawkesbury River ferry 153
Haymarket 99
Hello Darling 206, 207
Helplines 223
Her Majesty's (theater) 210, 211
Hereford Lodge YHA 170
Hero of Waterloo **69**, 197
  Street-by-Street map 64
Hertz 236, 237
Highfield House 170
History **16–29**
  Early Colony 20–21
  Georgian Era 22–3
  Postwar Sydney 28–9
  Sydney Between the Wars
    26–7

History (cont)
  Sydney's Original Inhabitants
    18–19
  timeline 18–29
  Victorian Sydney 24–5
HMB *Endeavour* 32
HMS *Beagle* 23
HMS *Sirius* 72
Hoff, Raynor 36
Hogarth Galleries Aboriginal Art
    206, 207
Holey dollar 22
Holman, Francis
  First Fleet Ship 20
Homestay agencies 170
Home Computer Show 51
Hoopla Circus and Street
    Theatre Festival 50
Hopetoun Hotel 197, 211
Horderns Stairs
  Street-by-Street map 118
Horizons Bar 196, 197
Hornby Lighthouse
  Watsons Bay and Vaucluse
    Walk 149
Horseback riding 53
Hospital emergency rooms
    223
Hostels 170
Hot Gossip Coffee Lounge 194,
    195
Hot Tuna 204, 205
Hotel Bondi
  Bondi Beach to Clovelly Walk
    144
Hotel Brittania 214, 215
Hotel Inter-Continental Sydney
    172, **176**
Hotel Lawson 173, 177
Hotel Nikko Darling Harbour
    169, 172, **176**
Hotels 168–77
  airport hotels 229
  booking addresses 170
  Botanic Gardens and The
    Domain **176**
  budget accommodations 170
  children 169
  chooser chart 216–17
  City Center **174–5**
  Darling Harbour **175**
  disabled assistance 170
  disabled travelers 169
  discount rates 169
  farther afield **177**
  gay and lesbian
    accommodations 171
  halls of residence 171
  hidden extras 169
  how to book 168
  Kings Cross and Darlinghurst
    176

Hotels (cont)
  Paddington **176–7**
  private homes 170
  rental apartments 169
  The Rocks and Circular Quay
    174
  where to look 168
Hoyts (movie theaters) 210, 211
Hughenden (hotel) 173, **177**
Hume and Hovell 22
Hunter Valley **158–9**
  Convent at Pepper Tree 159
  Golden Grape Estate 158
  Lake's Folly 159
  Lindemans 158
  Rothbury Estate 152, 159
  Wyndham Estate 159
Hyde Park 44, 86
Hyde Park Barracks **114**
  Sydney's Best: Architecture 37,
    38
  Sydney's Best: Museums and
    Galleries 33, 35
Hyde Park Barracks Café 194,
    195
Hyde Park Plaza (hotel) 172,
    174

I

Il Porcellino 113
Immigration and customs 220
Imperial Hotel 214, 215
Implement blue (Preston) 110
Infrigement Processing Bureau
    237
Inline Action 53
Inline skating 53
Insurance
  cars 236–7
  medical 222
Interdenominational church 221
Interforex 224
Interior with Wardrobe Mirror
    (Cossington-Smith) 110
International Student Identity
    Card 219
Interpreting services 40
Irish community 41, 43
Islamic
  community 40
  religious services 221
Islay 82
Italian community 41, 43

J

Jacob's Ladder
  Watsons Bay and Vaucluse
    Walk 148, 149
Japan Airlines 229
JetCat ferry 234

Jewelry 206, 207
Jewish
  community 41
  Great Synagogue **86–7**
  religious services 221
  Sydney Jewish Museum 35,
    121
  synagogue 221
Johnson, Richard 131
Jordon's Seafood Restaurant
    186, **190**
Joseph's Mens Store 204, 205
Joseph's Shoe Store 205
Juniper Hall **126**
Justice and Police Museum 35,
    72

K

Kame Kngwarreye, Emily 111
Kamogawa 186, **192**
Kampung 186, **191**
Keba
  Balmain Walk 143
Kings Cross
  Bed Race 50
  Carnival 48
Kings Cross and Darlinghurst
    110–21
  area map 117
  hotels 172, **176**
  restaurants 186–7
  Street-by-Street map 118–19
Kingsford Smith (Sydney)
  Airport 228, 229
Kingsford Smith, Charles 27
Kinselas 214, 215
Kirchner, Ernst
  Three Balloons 110
Kirklands Coach Service 229
Kirribilli House 132
Kirribilli Point 132
Ku-ring-gai Chase National Park
    154–5
  Aboriginal carvings 19
  camping 170, 171

L

Lady Bay Beach
  Watsons Bay and Vaucluse
    Walk 148
Lady Juliana 20
Lake Mungo, New South Wales
  history 18
Lambert, George
  Across the black soil plains 110
Lamrock Hostel 170
Lands Department Building 38,
    84
Lamrock Hotel 119
Land Titles Office 115

Lane Cove National Park 44
La Passion du Fruit 194, 195
Laurence, Janet and Foley,
  Fiona
  Edge of the Trees 32, 85
Lawson, Henry 24
Lawson, Louisa
  Dawn 25
Lebanese community 43
Legion Cabs 237
Le Kiosk 187, **188**
Le Petit Crème 194, 195
Leura Garden Festival 48
Lewin, John
  Waratah 21
Lewis, Mortimer 88, 121
Lindsay, Norman
  The Magic Pudding 67
Lime and Lemongrass 186, **191**
Lisa Ho (shop) 204, 205
Little Shark (Nolan) 76
Li Shan
  The Rouge Series No. 21 32
London Hotel
  Balmain Walk 143
London Tavern 196, 197
  Street-by-Street map 124
Long Reef 54, 55
Long-Distance Coach Terminal
  229
The Looking Glass 206, 207
Lord Nelson Brewery Hotel 172,
  174
  historic pub 14, 197
Lost property
  State Rail 223
  Sydney Buses 223
  Sydney Ferries 223, 235
L'otel 172, **176**
  cocktail bar 197
Love and Hatred 206, 207
Lower Fort Street 38
Lucio's 187, **192**
Luna Park 27, **132**

M

Macarthur, John and Elizabeth
  138
McCafferty's Coach Service 229
McElhone Stairs
  Street-by-Street map 118
Mackennal, Bertram 84, 86
Mackenzies Point
  Bondi Beach to Clovelly Walk
  144, 145
McLaren (hotel) 173, **177**
Macleay, Alexander 22
Macleay Street Bistro 186, **189**
Macquarie, Governor Lachlan
  22, 72
  Elizabeth 22, 106

Macquarie Chair, The 22
Macquarie Lighthouse **137**
  history 22
  Watson Bay and Vaucluse
  Walk 148
Macquarie Place **72**
Macquarie Street 112–15
Macquarie Theatre 213
Macquarie Trio 213
McRae, George 82
Madison's (hotel) 172, **176**
Madonna and Child with Infant
  St. John the Baptist
  (Beccafumi) 108
Madox Brown, Ford
  Chaucer at the Court of
  Edward III 110
The Magic Pudding (Lindsay) 67
Maitland House
  Balmain Walk 142
Maker's Mark 206, 207
Malaya (restaurant) 186, **191**
Mambo Friendship Store 204,
  205
Manly **133**
  Collins Beach 46, 147
  The Corso 133, 146
  Fairy Bower 146
  food and wine festival 51
  guided walk 146–7
  Jazz Festival 48
  Little Manly Cove 147
  Manly Beach 54, 55, 146
  Manly Wharf 146
  New Brighton Hotel 146
  North Head 133, 147
  Oceanworld 133
  Parkhill Sandstone Arch 147
  St. Patrick's Seminary 38, 146
  Shelly Beach 54, 55, 146
  viewing platforms 146
Manly Pacific Parkroyal 173,
  177
Man O'War Steps 58
Maps
  Australia 10–11
  beaches 55
  Blue Mountains 160–61
  Botanic Gardens and The
  Domain 103
  Central Sydney 14–15
  Central Sydney and suburbs
  12–13, 129
  City Center 79, 80–81
  CityRail route map 323
  city shoreline 56–9
  Darling Harbour 91, 92–3
  Early Colony 20
  Exploring Beyond Sydney
  152–3
  ferry routes 235
  Georgian Era 22

Maps (cont)
  Greater Sydney and Environs
  11
  guided walks 141
  Hawkesbury River 156–7
  Hunter Valley 158–9
  Kings Cross and Darlinghurst
  117
  19th-century Sydney 17
  Paddington 123, 124–5
  Pittwater and Ku-ring-gai
  Chase 154–5
  Postwar Sydney 28
  Potts Point 118–19
  The Rocks 64–5
  The Rocks and Circular Quay
  63
  Royal Botanic Gardens 104–5
  Royal National Park 164–5
  Southeast Asia and Pacific Rim
  10
  Southern Highlands 162–3
  Street Finder 238–7
  Sydney Between the Wars 26
  Sydney's Original Inhabitants
  18–19
  Taronga Zoo 134–5
  Victorian Sydney 24
  Walk Around Balmain 142–3
  Walk Around Manly 146–7
  Walk from Bondi Beach to
  Clovelly 144–5
  Walk in Watsons Bay and
  Vaucluse 148–9
Marble Bar **82**, 197
  Street-by-Street map 80
Marc's 204, 205
Marigold (restaurant) 186, **191**
Mario Bravo 205
Markets **203**
  Paddington Bazaar 201, **126**,
  203
  Paddy's Market **99**, 203
  The Rocks Market 65, 203
  Sydney Fish Market **131**, 200,
  202, 203
Maroubra 19, 54, 55
Marsden, Samuel 115, 139
Martin Place **84**
  Street-by-Street map 81
Matilda Cruises *(Solway Lass)*
  219
Maureen Fry Sydney Guided
  Tours 219
Maya Indian Sweets Centre 195
MCA Café 194, 195
Media 221
Medical treatment 222
Medina Executive Apartments
  173, **177**
Medina on Crown 170
Meera's Dosa House 187, **191**

Meere, Charles
  Australian Beach Pattern 33
Megalong Valley Heritage Farm
  53
Melbourne Cup Day 48
Merchants' House **66**
  Street-by-Street map 65
  Sydney's Best 32, 35
Merrony's 186, **188**
Metro (music venue) 214, 215
Metro Serviced Apartments City
  170
Mezzaluna 187, **192**
Michael's Music Room 206, 207
Mid City Centre 199
Middle Head and Obelisk Bay
  45
Midnight Shift 214, 215
*A Midsummer Night's Dream
  under the Stars* 210
Miro Tapas Bar 196, 197
Mitchell, Dr. James 69
Mitchell Library 112
Mitchell, Sir Thomas 22
MLC Centre 39, 199
Mobile phones 226
Monorail 29, 232–3
Moonlight, Captain 25
Moore, Henry
  Reclining Figure: Angles 110
Moore Park 45, 52
  golf club 53
  tennis courts 53
Morrissey Edmiston 204, 205
Mort Bay Reserve
  Balmain Walk 142
Mowarljarlai, David
  Rock Painting 88
Mr. Goodbar 214, 215
Mrs. Macquaries Chair 105, **106**
  city shoreline 56
  Victorian Sydney 24
Mohr Fish 187, **190**
Moreton Bay fig *(Ficus
  macrophylla)* 47
Mug Mania 206, 207
Mundey, Jack 67
Museum of Contemporary Art
  73
  Street-by-Street map 64
  Sydney's Best 32, 34
Museums and galleries (general)
  Sydney's Best 32–5
  tourist information 218
Museums and galleries
  (individual)
  Art Gallery of New South
    Wales 33, 34, **108–11**
  Australian Museum 33, 34,
    88–9
  Brett Whiteley Studio 34, **130**
  Cadman's Cottage 21, 35, **68**

Museums and galleries
  (individual) (cont)
  Elizabeth Bay House 22–3,
    33, 35, 119, **120**
  Elizabeth Farm 21, 35, **138–9**
  Experiment Farm Cottage 21,
    35, **139**
  Hambledon Cottage 35, **139**
  Harris Street Motor Museum
    34, **98**
  Hyde Park Barracks 33, 35,
    114–15
  Justice and Police Museum 35,
    72
  Macleay Museum, University
    of Sydney 130
  Merchants' House 32, 35, 65,
    66–7
  Museum of Contemporary Art
    32, 34, 64, **73**
  Museum of Sydney 32, 35, **85**
  National Maritime Museum 32,
    34–5, 93, **94–5**
  Nicholson Museum, University
    of Sydney 130
  Nutcote 35, **132–3**
  Old Government House 23,
    35, **139**
  Powerhouse Museum 32, 34,
    100–101
  Sailors' Home 35, **67**
  SH Ervin Gallery, National
    Trust Centre 35, 73
  Sherman Gallery 125
  Sotheby's Gallery 125
  Susannah Place 25, 35, **67**
  Sydney Jewish Museum 35,
    121
  Sydney Mint Museum 33, 35,
    114
  Vaucluse House 35, **136**
  Victoria Barracks **127**
  War Memorial Art Gallery,
    University of Sydney 130
  Westpac Museum 35, **68**
Music 212–15
  all-day concerts 214
  blues 214, 215
  cabaret venues 214, 215
  chamber **212**
  choral **213**
  free concerts **212**
  jazz **214**, 215
  music venues 214
  opera, orchestras, and dance
    212–13
  rock music 214, 215
Musica Viva 212, 213
Music shops 206, 207
Myall Creek massacre 23
My Brilliant Career (Franklin)
  26

N

Nag's Head (hotel) 197
Narrabeen 54, 55
National Herbarium of New
  South Wales 105
National Maritime Museum
  94–5
  Street-by-Street map 93
  Sydney's Best: Architecture 36,
    39
  Sydney's Best: Museums and
    Galleries 32, 34–5
National Mutual Building 38
National parks
  Blue Mountains National Park
    160–61
  camping 170, 171
  Garigal National Park 44
  Ku-ring-gai Chase National
    Park **154–5**
  Lane Cove National Park 44
  Royal National Park **164–5**
National Trust Centre **73**
National Trust Heritage Week 50
*Natives on the Ouse River, Van
  Diemen's Land* (Glover) 110
Naval Memorial Chapel
  Watsons Bay and Vaucluse
    Walk 148
Needlework, Craft and Art Fair
  51
Nepean River
  history 18
New Edition Bookshop 206, 207
New Edition Tea Rooms 194,
  195
New Guinea Primitive Arts 206,
  207
New South Wales Corps (Rum
  Corps) 20
New South Wales National
  Parks and Wildlife Service 68
New Theatre 210, 211
New Year's Eve 49
New Zealand Consulate General
  221
Newport 54, 55
Newspapers 221
Newtown Hotel 214, 215
Nielsen, Juanita 120
Nielsen Park 45, **136**
  Greycliffe House 136
Nightclubs 214, 215
Nolan, Sydney
  Boy in Township 110
  Burke 110
  Little Shark 76
No Names (restaurant) 186, **192**
North Arm Walk 44
North Head **133**
  preserve 147

North Head (cont)
　Quarantine Station 133
　Sydney's Best 45, 46
Novotel Sydney on Darling
　Harbour 172, **175**
Nowra, Louis 210
NRMA (National Roads and
　Motorists Association) 168,
　170
NSW Travel Centre 218
　entertainment information
　208, 209
　hotel bookings 168, 170
NSW YHA 170
Nude in a Rocking Chair
　(Picasso) 109, 110
Nutcote 35, **132**

O

Obelisk 87
Obelisk Bay 55
Observatory (hotel) 168, 172,
　174
Oh! Calcutta! 186, **191**
O'Keefe, Johnny 28
Old Gaol, Darlinghurst **121**
Old Government House
　(Parramatta) 23, 35, **139**
Old Sydney Parkroyal 172, **174**
Old Woman in Ermine
　(Beckmann) 110
Olsen, John
　Salute to Five Bells 76
Olympic Games 29
One Extra Company 213
Onkaparinga
　Balmain Walk 142
Onus, Lin
　Fruit Bats 111
Opals 206, 207.
Opal Fields (shop) 206, 207
Opera **212**
Opera in the Park 49
Orchestral music **212**
Orient Hotel 197, 214, 215
Overseas Passenger Terminal
　Street-by-Street map 65
Oxford Hotel 214, 215
Oz magazine 29

P

Paddington 37, **123–7**
　area map 123
　hotels 173, 176–7
　restaurants 187
　Street-by-Street map 124–5
　Sydney's Best 201
Paddington Bazaar **126**, 203
　Sydney's Best 201
Paddington Inn 196, 197

Paddington Street 38, **126**
　Street-by-Street map 124–5
Paddington Town Hall 123, **127**
Paddington Village **127**
Paddington and Woollahra 201
Paddy's Market **99**, 203
Palace Hotel 196, 197
Palm Beach 54, 55, 155
Paradiso Lunch Bar 194, 195
Paramount 187, **189**
Park Hyatt Sydney 172, **174**
Park, Ruth
　Poor Man's Orange 130
　The Harp in the South 130
Parkes, Henry 24
Parking 236
Parkroyal at Darling Harbour
　172, **175**
Parks and preserves (individual)
　Beare Park **120**
　Bicentennial Park 44, 47
　Birchgrove Park 143
　Blue Mountains National Park
　53, **160–61**, 170, 171
　Bradleys Head 45, 46
　Bronte Park 145
　Captain Cook's Landing Place
　138
　Centennial Park 45, 47, 53,
　127
　Chinese Garden **98–9**
　The Domain 45, 47, **107**
　Fitzroy Falls 162
　Garigal National Park 44, 46
　Grotto Point 45, 46
　Gumbooya Reserve 19
　Hyde Park 44, 47, **86–7**
　Ku-ring-gai Chase National
　Park 19, 53, **154–5**, 170, 171
　Lane Cove National Park 44,
　46–7
　Macquarie Place **72**
　Middle Head 45, 46
　Moore Park 45, 52
　Mort Bay Reserve 142
　Mount Tomah Botanic
　Gardens 161
　North Arm 44, 46
　Nielsen Park 45, **136**, 149
　North Head 45, 46, **132**, 147
　Obelisk Bay 45, 55
　Royal Botanic Gardens **104–5**
　Royal National Park 19,
　164–5, 170, 171
　Seven Mile Beach 163
　South Head 45, 46, 148–9
　Sydney's Best 44–7
　Taronga Zoo **134–5**
　Yurulbin Point Reserve 143
Parks and preserves
　(geographic)
　city parks 47

Parks and preserves
　(geographic) (cont)
　coastal hinterland 46
　open eucalypt forest 46
　rain forest and moist forest 46
　wetlands 47
Parliament House **112**
Parramatta 18, 35
　Experiment Farm Cottage 35,
　139
　Hambledon Cottage 35, **139**
　Elizabeth Farm 35, **138**
　James Ruse 139
　Old Government House 23,
　35, **139**
　restaurants 187
　St. John's Cemetery **139**
　Samuel Marsden 139
Parsley Bay
　beaches 55
　Watsons Bay and Vaucluse
　Walk 149
Paspaley Pearls 206, 207
Pemulwy 21
Percy Marks (jewelers) 206, 207
Performance Space 213
Periwinkle Guest House 173,
　177
Personal security and health
　222–3
Perspecta 49
Pharmacies 223
　After-Hours Pharmacy
　Information 223
Phillip, Captain Arthur 17, 64,
　73
Phonecards 226
Picasso, Pablo
　Nude in a Rocking Chair 109,
　110
Piccadilly (arcade) 199
The Pier (restaurant) 187, **190**
Pilot boats
　Watsons Bay and Vaucluse
　Walk 149
Pinchgut (Fort Denison) 107
Pitt Centre (movie theater) 210,
　211
Pittwater and Ku-ring-gai Chase
　154–5
　Aboriginal rock art 154
　Akuna Bay 154
　Barrenjoey Lighthouse 154
　Bilgola Beach 55, 155
　camping 170, 171
　Coal and Candle Creek 154
　history 19
　horseback riding 53
　Palm Beach Wharf 155
　Pittwater 155
　Whale Beach 55, 155
Police 222, 223

Polo Ralph Lauren 204, 205
The Possum Dreaming
(Tjakamarra) 74
Poster for the Vienna Secession
(Schiele) 111
Postal services 227
Poste restante 227
Post Office, General (GPO) 227
Postwar Sydney 28–9
Potts Point
Street-by-Street map 118–19
Powercuts (nightclub) 214, 215
Powerhouse Museum **100–101**
Sydney's Best 32, 34
Victorian Sydney 25
Poyntes, Edward
*The Visit of the Queen of
Sheba to King Solomon* 110
Prasit's Northside 194, 195
Premier Cabs 237
Presbyterian church 221
Preston, Margaret
Implement blue 110
*Western Australian Gum
Blossom* 110
Prince Alfred Hospital 24
Pro Dive Coogee 54
Public holidays 51
Public telephones 226
Public Transport Info Line **230**,
231, 234
Pubs and bars **196–7**
blues 214, 215
cabaret venues 214, 215
entertainment 197
gay and lesbian venues 214,
215
historic pubs 197
jazz 214, 215
rock music 214, 215
rules and conventions 196
Pukumani Grave Posts 109, 111
Pyrmont Bridge **98**
Street-by-Street map 93

Q

Qantas Airways 228, 229
history 28
Quarantine regulations 220
Quayside Booking Centre 235
Queen Victoria Building (QVB)
14, **82**
arcades and malls 198, 199
Street-by-Street map 80
Sydney's Best: Architecture 36,
38
Sydney's Best: Shopping
Streets and Markets 200
Queen Victoria Statue
Street-by-Street map 80
Quintus Servinton 22

R

Radio 221
Rainfall 50
Ravesi's on Bondi Beach (hotel)
173, **177**
Ravesi's on Bondi Beach
(restaurant) 187, **190**
Raymond Castles 205
Reclining Figure: Angles
(Moore) 110
Red Earth 206, 207
Red Eye Records 206, 207
Regal (restaurant) 186, **190**
Regent Club Bar 196, 197
Regent Sydney (hotel) 172, **174**
Regents Court (hotel) 172, **176**
Religious services 221
Republic of Ireland Embassy 221
Restaurants **178–97**
Asian 191–2
bistros and brasseries 189–90
Botanic Gardens and The
Domain 186
Chinese 190–91
chooser chart 186–7
City Center 186
contemporary 188–9
Darling Harbour 186
dress codes 179
eating with children 179
farther afield 187
French 193
how much to pay 178
Italian 192–3
Kings Cross and Darlinghurst
186–7
licensing laws 179
Mediterranean and Middle
Eastern 193
opening times 178
Paddington 187
reservations 178–9
The Rocks and Circular Quay
186
seafood 190
Sydney's Best 184
tax and tipping 179
what to drink in Sydney
182–3
what to eat in Sydney 180–81
where to eat 178
Restaurant Manfredi 187, **192**
Sydney's Best 184
Restaurant Suntory 186, **192**
The Revenge 20
Rialto Cinema 210, 211
Riberries 187, **188**
Riley, Edward and Mary 67
Ritz Carlton 172, **176**
Ritz Carlton Double Bay 173,
177

Riva Night Club 214, 215
RiverCat ferry 234
RM Williams (shop) 204, 205
Roberts, Tom
*The Golden Fleece – Shearing
at Newstead* 109, 110
Rock Fish Café 186, **190**
Rock Painting (Mowarljarlai) 88
Rockpool (restaurant) 186, **190**
Sydney's Best 184
The Rocks and Circular Quay
63–73
area map 63
city shoreline 59
history 21
hotels 172, 174
market 203
restaurants 186
The Rocks Opal Mine 206,
207
The Rocks Puppet Cottage
210, 211
Rocks Rhythmboat 214, 215
Street-by-Street map 64–5
Sydney's Best 200
visitors' center 67, 218
walking tour 219
Rockwall 119
Roma Caffè Ristorante 194, 195
Rose of Australia 214, 215
Rose, Shamrock, and Thistle
197, 214, 215
Rowe, Thomas 86
The Rouge Series No. 21 (Li
Shan) 32
Royal Agricultural Society
Showground 214, 215
Big Day Out 49, 214
Royal Botanic Gardens 57,
104–5
Spring Festival 48
Royal Clock 82
Royal Easter Show 50
Royal Hotel 126, 196, 197
Sydney's Best 185
Royal National Park **164–5**
Aboriginal carving 19
Audley 164
Bundeena 165
camping 170, 171
Cronulla 165
Curracurrang 165
Deer Pool 165
Figure Eight Pool 165
Forest Path 164
Garie Beach 153, 164
Hacking River 164
Heathcote 164
Jibbon Head 165
Jibbon Head Lagoon 165
Lady Carrington Drive 164
Little Marley Beach 165

Royal National Park (cont)
Wattamolla Lagoon 165
Werrong 164
Round Midnight 214, 215
Roy's Famous 194, 195
RSL Taxis 237
Rugby league 52
grand final 48
Rugby union 52
grand final 48
Rum
Corps (New South Wales
Corps) 20, 21
Hospital 113, **114**
Rebellion 21, 138
Ruse, James 139
Russell (hotel) 172, **174**

S

Sailing 54, 56
Sailors' Home 35, **67**
Sailor's Thai 186, **191**
St. Andrew's Cathedral **87**
St. Andrew's Church
Balmain Walk 143
St. James' Church **115**
concerts 213
Sydney's Best 36, 38
St. John's Cemetery **139**
St. Mary's Cathedral 25, 38, **86**
St. Michael's Golf Club 53
St. Patrick's Day Parade 50
St. Patrick's Seminary 38, 146
St. Philip's Church **73**
Salute to Five Bells (Olsen) 76
Samarai Park Riding School
53
Sandringham Garden 86
Sandringham Hotel 214, 215
Savoy Double Bay 173, **177**
Savoy Serviced Apartments 172,
175
Schiele, Egon
*Poster for the Vienna
Secession* 111
Scuba diving 54
Sculpture
Art Gallery of New South
Wales 110
Sebel of Sydney 172, **176**
Seidler, Harry 39
Seven Shillings Beach 55
Sewell, Stephen 210
Seymour Theatre Centre
theatre 210, 211
music 212, 213
SH Ervin Gallery 34
Shakespeare by the Sea 210,
211
Shark Bay
beaches 54, 55

Shark Bay (cont)
Watsons Bay and Vaucluse
Walk 148
Sharp, Ronald 76
Shawarma Grill House 186, **193**
Shelly Beach
beaches 54, 55
Manly Walk 146
Sheraton on the Park 172, **175**
Sherman Gallery
Street-by-Street map 125
Ships *see* Boats
Shops and markets **198–207**
arcades and malls 198
department stores 199
farther afield 199
how to pay
markets 202–3
sales 198
shopping hours 198
Sydney's Best: Shopping
Streets and Markets 200–201
tax-free sales 198
Sicard, François 86
Signal Station
Watsons Bay and Vaucluse
Walk 148
Silver Spring (restaurant) 186,
191
Sydney's Best 184
Simpsons of Potts Point 169,
172, **176**
Singapore Airlines 229
Sino Jin Jiang 186, **191**
Sir John Clancy Auditorium 213
Sirsi Newport Marina 54
Sir Stamford Double Bay 173,
177
*Sketch and Description of the
Settlement of Sydney Cove*
(Fowkes) 17
Skin Deep 204, 205
Skygarden 198–9
Street-by-Street map 81
Sloane Rangers (café) 194, 195
Smith, Richard 25
Smoking 218
Snugglepot and Cuddlepie
(Gibbs) 132
Sodersten, Emil 39
Sofala (Drysdale) 108
Solander, Daniel 138
Sotheby's Gallery
Street-by-Street map 125
Soup Plus 214, 215
South Head 45, 148–9
Southern Highlands **162–3**
Berrima 162
Berrima Gaol
Berry 163
Bowral 162
Bundanoon 162

Southern Highlands (cont)
Fitzroy Falls 162
Kangaroo Valley 162
Kiama 152, 163
Seven Mile Beach 163
Spanish Deli 194, 195
Specialty shops and souvenirs
206–7
Spears, Steve J
Spencer, John 84
Spirit of Australia 34, 95
Sports in Sydney **52–5**
Sportsgirl 204, 205
Sports Bard (restaurant) 187,
189
Spring in Sydney 48
Spring Racing Carnival 48
Stables Theatre 210, 211
Stafford (hotel) 172, **174**
State Library of NSW **112**
Bookshop 206, 207
State Theatre **82**, 214, 215
rock music 214, 215
Street-by-Street map 80
theaters 210, 211
State Transit Information and
Ticket Kiosks 230
State Transit Tourist Ferries 219
Statues
Flinders, Matthew 112
Mort, Thomas 72
Prince Albert 115
Queen Victoria Statue 80, 82
Strand Arcade **84**
arcades and malls 198, 199
architecture 38
Street-by-Street map 81
Strand Hatters 205
The "Strasburg" Clock 25
Strawberry Hills Hotel 214, 215
Streeton, Arthur 25
Student Travel Association 219
Study for Self Portrait (Bacon)
110
Suez Canal (The Rocks) 64
Sugareef 214, 215
Sullivans (hotel) 173, **177**
Summer in Sydney 49
A Summer Morning (Bunny)
110
Summer Time (Bunny) 110
Sunbaker (Dupain) 108
Sunshine 49
Surfing 54
Surf Life Saving NSW 54
Surf Dive 'n Ski 204, 205
Surry Hills **130**
Susannah Place 35, 38, **67**
Swimming 54, 223
Swimming pools 55, 105, 144
Sydney
Between the Wars 26–7

Sydney (cont)
coat of arms 17
getting around Sydney 230–37
Sydney (Kingsford Smith)
airport 228
airport information 229
Sydney Airport Hilton 229
Sydney Airport Sheraton 229
Sydney Aquarium **96–7**
Street-by-Street map 93
Sydney Boat Show 51
Sydney City Council One-Stop-Shop **220**
Sydney Cove Oyster Bar 197
Sydney Cricket Ground 52
rock concerts 214, 215
Sydney Dance Company 213
Sydney Entertainment Centre 52, 214, 215
Sydney Ferries Information Office **230**, 234
Sydney Festival 209
Sydney Film Festival 51, 210, 211
Sydney Fish Market **131**, 202, 203
Sydney's Best 200
Sydney Football Stadium 39, 52
Sydney Fringe Festival 210, 211
Sydney Gazette 21
Sydney to the Gong Bicycle Ride 48
Sydney Harbour Bridge 31, **70–71**
city shoreline 58
history 26–7
Sydney Harbour Oceanarium 97
Sydney Harbour Seaplanes 219
Sydney Harbour Tunnel 29
Sydney Helicopter Service 219
Sydney Hilton 172, **175**
cabaret 214, 215
Sydney to Hobart Yacht Race 28, 49
Sydney Hospital **113**
Sydney Jewish Museum 35, **121**
Sydney Marriot 172, **175**
Sydney Mint Museum 33, 35, **114**
Sydney Morning Herald
Half Marathon 50
Sydney Observatory **69**
Street-by-Street map 64
Sydney Opera House **74–7**
Bennelong Restaurant 75, 184, **188**
city shoreline 58
Concert Hall 75, 76, 212
design 77
disabled visitors 209
Drama Theatre 76, 210
history 28

Sydney Opera House (cont)
Northern Foyers 74
opera, orchestras, and dance 212
Opera Theatre 74, 76
The Playhouse 75, 76
roofs 75
Sydney's Best 37, 39
Sydney Philharmonia Choirs 213
Sydney Renaissance (hotel) 172, **174**
Sydney Opera House Sydney Swans 52
Sydney Symphony Orchestra 209, 212, 213
Sydney Theatre Company 69, 210, 211
Sydney Tower **83**
Street-by-Street map 81
Sydney Town Hall **87**
concerts 212, 213
Sydney's Best 36, 38
Sydney Traffic Control Centre 237
Sydney Tropical Centre 104
Sydney Travellers Rest (hotel) 172, **175**
Sydney University 129, **130**, 170
Sydney Youth Orchestra 212, 213
Symphony Under the Stars 49

T

Takeout food 195
Talmage, Algernon
The Founding of Australia 73
Tamarama
beach 54, 55
Bondi Beach to Clovelly Walk 145
Tank Stream 59, 72
Taronga Zoo **134–5**
Tarpeian Market **203**
Tasman Map 112
Taxis 237
water taxis 235
Taxis Combined 237
Te Aroha Festival 43
Teddy Bears' Picnic 48
Telephones 226–7
Television 221
Telstra Phone Centre 226, 227
Temperature 51
Tennis 52
Thai community 40
Theaters 210, 211
Theatre Royal 210, 211
Street-by-Street map 81
Third Eye Cinema 210, 211
Thomas Cook 224
Three Bathers (Kirchner) 110

Three Mimis Dancing (Wagbara) 111
Thrifty 236, 237
Thunderbolt, Captain 106
Ticketek 52, 208, 209
Ticket-of-leave 20
Tickets
booking agencies 208–9
CityRail tickets 233
composite tickets 230
discount 209, 210
ferry ticket machines 234
monorail 232–3
public transport **230**, 231
Quayside Booking Centre 235
Tidal Cascades Fountain
Street-by-Street map 92
Tilbury Hotel 214, 215
Time zones 220
Timewarp Records 206, 207
Tipping 219
hotels 169
restaurants 179
Tivoli Theatre 25
Tjakamarra, Michael Nelson
The Possum Dreaming 74
Tjapaltjarri, Clifford Possum and
Tim Leura Tjapaltjarri
Warlugulong 111
Toilets 221
Tourist information 218
Central Railway Station 218
Darling Harbour 218
NSW Travel Centres 218
The Rocks Visitor Centre 218
Traffic signs 236
Train
arriving by train 229
CityRail 232–3
Country and interurban 233
Countrylink Travel Centres 229, 233
tickets 230, 233
train information 229
Travel information 228–37
air 228
bicycle **237**
bus 230, **231**
car 229, **236–7**
coach 229
departure tax 220
disabled travelers 220
ferry 230, **234–5**
getting around Sydney **230**
guided tours and excursions 219
immigration and customs 220
monorail **232–3**
public transport 230–35
Public Transport Infoline 220, 230–31
sea 228–9

Travel information (cont)
  State Transit Information and
    Ticket Kiosks 230
  student travel 219
  taxis 237
  trains 229, **232–3**
  water taxis **235**
Traveler's checks 224
Travelers' Clinic 222, 223
Travelers' Information Service
  169, 170
Travelex 224
Tropicana Coffee Lounge 194,
  195
Tunnel (nightclub) 214, 215
Turkish community 40
Tusculum Villa 38, 118

U

Ulm 27
Una's Coffee Lounge 194, 195
Unicorn Hotel 211
United Airlines 229
United Kingdom Consulate 221
Uniting Church 221
University of Sydney 129, **130**,
  170
Utopia Records 206, 207
Utzon, Jørn 37, 77

V

Valhalla (cinema) 210, 211
Vampire 93, 95
Vaucluse 148, 149
Vaucluse House 35, **136**
  history 23
  Tea Rooms 195
  Watsons Bay and Vaucluse
    Walk 149
Vegemite 26
Verge, John 37, 120
Vernon, WL 108
Verona (movie theater) 210, 211
Vic Cooper Hats 205
Victoria Barracks 37, 38, **127**
  CityRail tickets 233
Victoria Spring Designs 206, 207
Victoria Street (Potts Point) **120**
  Street-by-street map 118–19
Victorian Sydney 24–5
Victorian terrace houses 25
  Paddington Street 126
  Street-by-Street maps 118–19,
    124–5
  Sydney's Best 37

Vidette
  Balmain Walk 143
Vietnamese community 40, 43
Vietnam War 28
View from the Summit (Earle) 22
A View of Sydney Cove (Dayes)
  20
Viewing platforms
  Manly Walk 146
Village (cinemas) 210, 211
*The Visit of the Queen of Sheba
  to King Solomon* (Poynter) 110
Vivian Chan Shaw (shop) 205

W

Wagbara, Samuel
  Three Mimis Dancing 111
Waldorf Apartment Hotel 172,
  175
Walker Cinema 210, 211
Walks 141–9
  Balmain 142–3
  Bondi Beach to Clovelly
    144–5
  Manly 146–7
  Watsons Bay and Vaucluse
    148–9
Walking in Sydney **230**
Waratah (Lewin) 21
Wardell, William 86
Warlugulong (Tjapaltjarri) 111
Warringah Golf Club 53
Warwick
  Street-by-Street map 125
Watch Gallery, The 206, 207
Watch House, The
  Balmain Walk 143
Water taxis **235**
Waterfront 206, 207
Waterman's Cottage, The
  Balmain Walk 142
Watsons Bay **136**
  beaches 55
  guided walk 148–9
  pilot boats 149
Wattle House Hostel 170
Waverley Cemetery
  Bondi Beach to Clovelly Walk
    145
The Waverly 25
Weather 48–51
Weiss Art 206, 207
Wentworth (hotel) 172, **175**
Wentworth, D'Arcy 139
Wentworth, WC 136
Werrington 118

West End (hotel) 172, **175**
*Western Australian Gum
  Blossom* (Preston) 110
Westpac Museum 35, **68**
Whale Beach 55, 155
The Wharf Restaurant 186, **189**
The Wharf Theatre **69**
  city shoreline 59
  theaters 210, 211
Wheels and Dolly Baby 206,
  207
White, Patrick 28
Whiteley, Brett 29, 130
  The Balcony (2) 110
Whitlam, Gough 29
Williams, Fred 110
Williamson, David 210
Williamson, JC 120
William Street (Darlinghurst)
  116
Windsor Street (Paddington)
  Street-by-Street map 125
Windsurfing 54
Winter in Sydney 51
Wisemans Ferry 157
Wockpool 187, **192**
Woodward, Robert 92
Woolloomooloo Finger Wharf
  57, **107**
Woolloomooloo Waters 169,
  172, **176**
Wooly's Cycles 237
World Series Cricket 29
World War II 27
Wrights on Piccadilly 205
Writers' Walk 72
Wurrabadalumba, Jabarrgwa
  Dugong Hunt 34

X

Xocoalt (café) 194, 195

Y

Yiribana Gallery 34, 111
York Apartment Hotel 172, **175**
Yulefest 51
Yurulbin Point
  Balmain Walk 143
  ferry route map 235

Z

Zofrea, Salvatore 76
Zoo *see* Taronga Zoo
Zoom Bar 214, 215

Acknowledgments

DORLING KINDERSLEY would like to thank the following people whose help and assistance contributed to the preparation of this book.

MAIN CONTRIBUTORS
Ken Brass grew up on Sydney's Bondi Beach. He began his career in journalism with the *Sydney Morning Herald* and later worked as one of its London correspondents before becoming a staff writer on national daily newspapers in the United Kingdom. Returning home, he worked on the *Australian Women's Weekly, Weekend Australian* newspaper and *Australian Geographic* magazine. His photographs appear regularly in a range of Australian magazines.

Kirsty McKenzie grew up on a sheep station in outback Queensland. She entered journalism after completing an arts degree. After making Sydney her home in 1980, she worked on a number of lifestyle and travel publications. Since 1987, she has written regularly for food, interior design and travel magazines.

ADDITIONAL TEXT AND RESEARCH
Leith Hillard, Siobhán O'Connor.

ADDITIONAL PHOTOGRAPHY
Claire Edwards, Leanne Hogbin, Siobhán O'Connor.

ADDITIONAL ILLUSTRATIONS
Leslye Cole, Stephen Conlin, Jon Gittoes, Steve Graham, Ray Grinaway, Helen Halliday, David Kirshner, Alex Lavroff, Iain McKellar, Chris Orr, Oliver Rennert.

ADDITIONAL CARTOGRAPHY
Dorling Kindersley Cartography, Sydwiy.

EDITORIAL ASSISTANCE
Charis Atlas, Jenny Cattell, Helen Partington, Phoebe Todd-Naylor.

DESIGN ASSISTANCE
Joy Fitzsimmons, Clare Forte, Lisa Kosky, Jim Marks, Kylie Mulquin, Louise Parsons, Tracey Timpson.

INDEX
Jenny Cattell.

SPECIAL ASSISTANCE
Art Gallery of New South Wales, in particular Sherrie Joseph; Australian Museum, in particular Liz Wilson; Ann-Marie Bulat; the staff of Elizabeth Bay House; Historic Houses Trust; Lara Hookham; Info Direct, in particular Frank Tortora; Professor Max Kelly; Lou MacDonald; Adam Moore; Museum of Sydney, in particular Michelle Andringa; National Maritime Museum, in particular Jeffrey Mellefont and Bill Richards; National Trust of Australia (NSW), in particular Stewart Watters; Bridget O'Regan; Royal Botanic Gardens, in particular Anna Hallett and Ed Wilson; State Transit Authority; Sydney Opera House, in particular David Brown and Valerie Tring; Diane Wallis.

PHOTOGRAPHY PERMISSIONS
DORLING KINDERSLEY would like to thank all those who gave permission to photograph at various cathedrals, churches, museums, restaurants, hotels, shops, galleries, and other sights too numerous to thank individually.

PICTURE CREDITS
t = top; tl = top left; tlc = top left center; tc = top center; trc = top right center; tr = top right; cla = center left above; ca = center above; cra = center right above; cl = center left; c = center; cr = center right; clb = center left below; cb = center below; crb = center right below; bl = bottom left; b = bottom; bc = bottom center; bcl = bottom center left; br = bottom right; brb = bottom right below; d = detail.

Every effort has been made to trace the copyright holders. Dorling Kindersley apologizes for any unintentional omissions and would be pleased, in such cases, to add an acknowledgment in future editions.

Works of art have been reproduced with the permission of the following copyright holders: © MUSEUM OF SYDNEY 1996: *Edge of the Trees* Janet Laurence and Fiona Foley, on the site of First Government House: 32tr, 85b; © LIN ONUS 1996 – Lin Onus (1948–) *Fruit Bats* 1991, 95 fiberglass polychrome fruit bats, Hills Hoist, polychrome wooden disks, Art Gallery of New South Wales: 111cr.

The publisher would like to thank the following individuals, companies and picture libraries for their kind permission to reproduce their photographs:

ACP: 27cb, 28bc; ANTHONY CRICKMAY: 76cla; EMANUEL ANGELICAS: 42br; ART GALLERY OF NEW SOUTH WALES: 25cb; © Sir William Dobell Art Foundation 1996 *Dame Mary Gilmore* 1957 William Dobell (1899–1970), oil on hardboard 90.2 x 73.7 cm, gift of Dame Mary Gilmore 1960: 29ca; © Bundanon Trust 1996 *The Expulsion* 1947–48 Arthur Boyd (1920–), oil on hardboard 99.5 x 119.6 cm: 31c; © Ms. Stephenson-Meere 1996 *Australian Beach Pattern* 1940 Charles Meere (1890–1961) oil on canvas 91.5 x 122 cm:

33tl; 34b; © The Cazneaux family 1996 *Bridge Pattern* Harold Cazneaux (1890–1961), gelatin silver photograph 29.6 x 21.4 cm, gift of the Cazneaux family 1975: 58bc(d); © Lady Drysdale 1996 *Sofala* 1947 Russell Drysdale (1912–81), oil on canvas on hardboard 71.7 x 93.1 cm: 108tr; 108ca; 108clb; © Tiwi Design Executive 1996 *Pukumani Grave Posts, Melville Island* 1958 various artists, natural pigments on wood 165.1 x 29.2 cm, gift of Dr. Stuart Scougall 1959: 109tc; © DACS 1996 *Nude in a Rocking Chair* 1956 Pablo Picasso (1881–1973), oil on canvas 195 x 130 cm: 109ca; 109crb; 109bc; © Estate of Francis Bacon *Study for Self Portrait* 1976 Francis Bacon (1901–92), oil and pastel on canvas 198 x 147.5 cm: 110tr; 110cla; © Wendy and Arkie Whiteley 1996 *The Balcony 2* 1975 Brett Whiteley (1939–92), oil on canvas 203.5 x 364.5 cm: 110bl; *Warlugulong* 1976 Clifford Possum Tjapaltjarri (1932–) and Tim Leura Tjapaltjarri (1939–84), synthetic polymer paint on canvas 168.5 x 170.5 cm: 111tr; AUSCAPE INTERNATIONAL: Kevin Deacon 96br; AUSTRALIAN INFORMATION SERVICE: 29tl(d); AUSTRALIAN MUSEUM: C. Bento 18tl, 18clb, 18cb, 19tl, 19c, 19crb; AUSTRALIAN PICTURE LIBRARY: John Carnemolla 28clb, 52bl.

BANGARRA DANCE THEATRE: Greg Barrett 42cla; GREG BARRETT: 209bc; BARTEL PHOTO LIBRARY: 160bc; MERVYN G. BISHOP: 20crb; BRUCE COLEMAN: John Cancalosi 45bc; Francisco Futil 44tr.

CENTREPOINT MANAGEMENT: 83br; CIRCUS SOLARUS: 48cr; COO-EE HISTORICAL PICTURE LIBRARY: 9ca, 61ca, 151ca, 167ca, 217ca.

DAVID JONES (AUSTRALIA) P/L: 23crb(d); DIXSON GALLERIES, STATE LIBRARY OF NEW SOUTH WALES: 8–9, 18tr, 20blb(d), 24cla, 70tr, 138br; MAX DUPAIN: 77br.

FAIRFAX PHOTO LIBRARY: 26bl; 52ca; 71bra; 114cl(d); 77tc; ASCUI 51br; Dallen 29cra; Gerrit Fokkema 28br; Ken James 209tr; McNeil 120bl; White 41bl.

GOVERNMENT PRINTING OFFICE COLLECTION, STATE LIBRARY OF NEW SOUTH WALES: 24clb, 26clb, 76blb.

HAPPY MEDIUM PHOTOS: 41tc; C MOORE HARDY: 208br; HOOD COLLECTION, STATE LIBRARY OF NEW SOUTH WALES: 71bl, 137br(d).

THE IRISH-AUSTRALIAN: 43cla.
LAKE'S FOLLY VINEYARDS: 159cr; LUNA PARK TRUST: 128tc.

MAZZ IMAGES: 28–9; MITCHELL LIBRARY, STATE LIBRARY OF NEW SOUTH WALES: 19br, 19bcb, 20br(d), 20-21, 21tl, 21ca(d), 21cb, 22clb(d), 22cb(d), 22bl, 23tl, 23ca(d), 23bl(d), 24cr, 24bc, 24br, 25tl, 25br, 27ca(d), 27blb, 29cb, 44tl, 71cra, 112tl; DAVID MOORE: 28cla; MUSEUM OF CONTEMPORARY ART: Li Shan *The Rouge Series No. 21* 1992: 32clb.

NATIONAL GALLERY OF VICTORIA: © Ann M. Mills 1996 *The Bridge in Curve* Grace Cossington Smith 1930: 71tl; NATIONAL LIBRARY OF AUSTRALIA, CANBERRA: 22tl, 22cla, 23brb(d), 25bc; NATIONAL MARITIME MUSEUM: 20cl, 34tl, 42tl; NATURE FOCUS: Kevin Diletti 47br(d); John Fields 44bl; Pavel German 47tr.

PARLIAMENT HOUSE: The Hon. Max Willis, RFD, ED, LLB, MLC, President, Legislative Council, Parliament of New South Wales. The Hon. J. Murray, MP, Speaker, Legislative Assembly, Parliament of New South Wales. Artist's original sketch of the historical painting in oils by Algernon Talmage, RA, *The Founding of Australia*. Kindly loaned to the Parliament of New South Wales by Mr Arthur Chard of Adelaide: 73bl; PARRAMATTA CITY COUNCIL: S. Thomas 40tr, 43tr; POWERHOUSE MUSEUM: 20tl, 21br, 22bcb, 24tl, 26tl, 26cla, 26cb, 26bc, 27crb, 27bc, 32t, 32br, 33cr; Tyrrell Collection 106tc.

ROYAL BOTANIC GARDENS: Jaime Plaza 48bl.

STATE LIBRARY OF TASMANIA: 20clb; STOPMOTION: 160tr; SUZIE THOMAS PUBLISHING: Thomas O'Flynn 74bc, 76clb; SYDNEY FILM FESTIVAL: 51clb, SYDNEY FREELANCE: J. Boland 49cl; SYDNEY OPERA HOUSE TRUST: 74tr, 74cla, 75tc, 75br, 75blb, 76br, 77cla, 77ca, 77cra, 77c; Willi Ulmer Collection 77bc.

VINTAGE ESTATES: 158bc.

WESTPAC BANKING CORPORATION: 68br.

Jacket: All special photography except WORLD PICTURES: front t; TELEGRAPH COLOUR LIBRARY: Colorific/Phillip Hayson front tl.

Sydney Transit Map

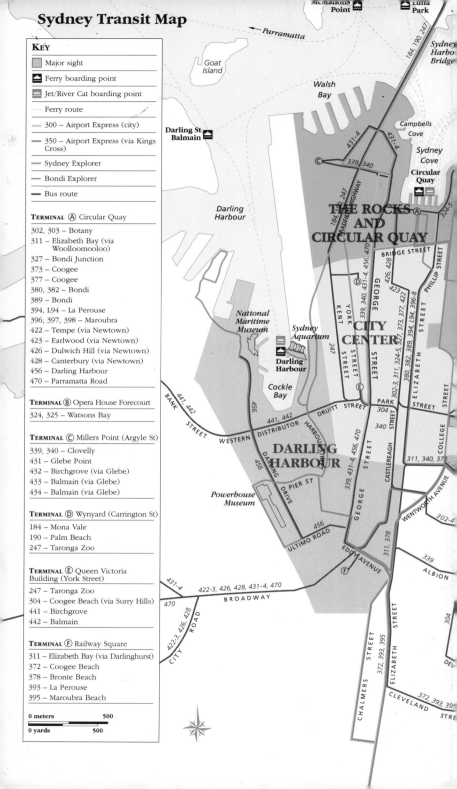

KEY

- ▓ Major sight
- ⛴ Ferry boarding point
- 🚤 Jet/River Cat boarding point
- ---- Ferry route
- — 300 – Airport Express (city)
- — 350 – Airport Express (via Kings Cross)
- — Sydney Explorer
- — Bondi Explorer
- — Bus route

TERMINAL Ⓐ Circular Quay

302, 303 – Botany
311 – Elizabeth Bay (via Woolloomooloo)
327 – Bondi Junction
373 – Coogee
377 – Coogee
380, 382 – Bondi
389 – Bondi
394, L94 – La Perouse
396, 397, 398 – Maroubra
422 – Tempe (via Newtown)
423 – Earlwood (via Newtown)
426 – Dulwich Hill (via Newtown)
428 – Canterbury (via Newtown)
456 – Darling Harbour
470 – Parramatta Road

TERMINAL Ⓑ Opera House Forecourt

324, 325 – Watsons Bay

TERMINAL Ⓒ Millers Point (Argyle St)

339, 340 – Clovelly
431 – Glebe Point
432 – Birchgrove (via Glebe)
433 – Balmain (via Glebe)
434 – Balmain (via Glebe)

TERMINAL Ⓓ Wynyard (Carrington St)

184 – Mona Vale
190 – Palm Beach
247 – Taronga Zoo

TERMINAL Ⓔ Queen Victoria Building (York Street)

247 – Taronga Zoo
304 – Coogee Beach (via Surry Hills)
441 – Birchgrove
442 – Balmain

TERMINAL Ⓕ Railway Square

311 – Elizabeth Bay (via Darlinghurst)
372 – Coogee Beach
378 – Bronte Beach
393 – La Perouse
395 – Maroubra Beach

0 meters   500
0 yards   500